Yvonne Carré-Valdor

Ice Cream, Cognac & "You"

novum pro

www.novum-publishing.co.uk

© 2022 novum publishing

ISBN 978-3-99107-906-4
Editing: Ashleigh Brassfield, DipEdit
Cover photos: Yvonne Carré, Anna Kuzmina | Dreamstime.com
Cover design, layout & typesetting: novum publishing
Internal illustrations: Yvonne Carré

The images provided by the author have been printed in the highest possible quality.

www.novum-publishing.co.uk

Acknowledgements

I would like to thank

Annelies Hophan-Widmer,
former director of Sony Music Switzerland

and

Tom Friedli.

Contents

Chapter 1 Beginning Of My Life 13

Chapter 2 Bye Bye, Bermuda – Hey Hey, U.K. 16

Chapter 3 Happy Childhood Memories 20

Chapter 4 My First Celebrity 24

Chapter 5 My Stage Debut 26

Chapter 6 First Lesson 28

Chapter 7 Animal Instinct 30

Chapter 8 My First Talent Competition 32

Chapter 9 Breadbaskets, Bananas and the Tarantula ... 34

Chapter 10 Walls Have Ears, Ye Gotta Have Bite! ... 36

Chapter 11 The Last Billet 39

Chapter 12 My Promise to Mum and
Food For Thought 42

Chapter 13 Holiday in Wales 45

Chapter 14 A Seven-Year-Old Rebel 49

Chapter 15 The London Palladium 52

Chapter 16 Love at First Sight – Switzerland 56

Chapter 17 Girl Power 60

Chapter 17a My First Date 62

Chapter 18 Plus ça change, plus ça reste
la même chose 64

Chapter 19 Second Lesson 67

Chapter 20 Surprise, Surprise 69

Chapter 21 Self-Opinion Decreasing 72

Chapter 22 At the Coconut Grove 73

Chapter 23 My First Marriage Proposal 77

Chapter 24 Summer Season 80

Chapter 25 The Big Spender 85

Chapter 26 The Ash Tray 88

Chapter 27 The Balloon Deflates 91
Chapter 28 Consolation 94
Chapter 29 Glasgow 96
Chapter 30 Greens Playhouse Sends Me an Angel 99
Chapter 31 "Keep It Under Your Hat" – Paris 102
Chapter 32 At the Albany Club 106
Chapter 33 At Selbey's 108
Chapter 34 TV Calls 110
Chapter 35 Who Wants To Feel Like A Virgin –
   Madonna? 112
Chapter 36 Prick Me Darlin' 115
Chapter 37 Dad and I Make a Deal 118
Chapter 38 Journey to Marseille 120
Chapter 39 The Fortune Teller 123
Chapter 40 I Meet My First Waterloo 126
Chapter 41 The Promised Land 130
Chapter 42 S.O.S. P.O. Box 134
Chapter 43 Highlights 138
Chapter 44 The Dutch Entrepreneur 140
Chapter 45 Harold Drops a Bomb 142
Chapter 46 The Waiting Game 145
Chapter 47 The Adventure Starts 147
Chapter 48 Arriving in the Promised Land 152
Chapter 49 Dov is a Real Pal 155
Chapter 50 Tiberias on Lake Genezareth 157
Chapter 51 My Very First Tragedy 161
Chapter 52 Rivka to the Rescue 165
Chapter 53 Birds of Prey 167
Chapter 54 Uncle Mick 170
Chapter 55 Forboding Instances 172
Chapter 56 The Gypsy Violinist 175
Chapter 57 Leaving Israel 177
Chapter 58 Famagusta – Cyprus 180
Chapter 59 Nicosia & Norma 185
Chapter 60 Let's Clap Hands 191
Chapter 61 Les Boutiques, Les Girls and Nick 195

Chapter 62 Istanbul 202

Chapter 63 The Hat Pin Story 204

Chapter 64 From Big Shows to Big Shock! 207

Chapter 65 Milano 213

Chapter 66 Sean Connery 216

Chapter 67 The Backfire 219

Chapter 68 The Perfect Lady 221

Chapter 69 Zürich 225

Chapter 70 Three Great Lifelong Swiss Friends 229

Chapter 71 A Legend: Heinz Hoffmeister 231

Chapter 72 A Paris Hat – A London Trapeze
            Help Clinch A Deal 234

Chapter 73 From Tipsy Nick to Literary Nietschke . . . 237

Chapter 74 Coca Cola Bottles 240

Chapter 75 The Lausanne Special 242

Chapter 76 At The Palace 245

Chapter 77 I Miss My Big Fish –
            My Second Marriage Proposal 248

Chapter 78 The Swedish Folkets Parks Tour 251

Chapter 79 Great News – Paris.
            Terrible News – London 253

Chapter 80 Tomorrow You Could Be Dead 255

Chapter 81 All That Glitters Is Not Gold 258

Chapter 82 Fun and Games in Showbiz 260

Chapter 82a The Wild Swinging 60s 262

Chapter 82b Moment 1 – A Sticky Situation 264

Chapter 82c Pushing Through 266

Chapter 82d The Most Unusual Lover 268

Chapter 83 Burgundy Shoes 269

Chapter 83a Helsingor, Denmark 276

Chapter 84 Mambo, Falsies and Ooh Love 279

Chapter 85 The Palais de Chaillot Triumph –
            Yet Another Marriage Proposal 282

Chapter 86 What Love Can Do! 285

Chapter 87 The Madeira Hat 288

Chapter 88 Frank Sinatra – Star Wars 291

Chapter 89 My Shotgun Marriage 294
Chapter 90 Morocco Oriental Dreams –
    Do As I Say, But Not As I Do 300
Chapter 91 Prisoners in Tito's Realm 303
Chapter 92 President Tito 309
Chapter 93 Journey to Dubrovnik 311
Chapter 94 A Clandestine Love Affair 314
Chapter 95 I See The Light 317
Chapter 96 Cocktails by Yvonne in Bremen 320
Chapter 96b Chérie Noire in Hamburg 323
Chapter 97 Pepito 329
Chapter 98 "Schwarze Perle" in Zürich 342
Chapter 99 The Beatles and Me 345
Chapter 100 Japan and Pepito 347
Chapter 101 Complications in Japan 350
Chapter 101a Kamakura – Japan 353
Chapter 102 Unforgettable Kyoto 358
Chapter 103 Wild Water Geisha Me! 360
Chapter 104 Sayonara Nippon – Goodbye Japan 364
Chapter 105 Frank's Cutting Edge – Walchwil 366
Chapter 105b My First Home Goes Red 372
Chapter 106 Goodbye Mum 374
Chapter 107 Australia – The Land of Oz 377
Chapter 108 South Africa 381
Chapter 109 Rhodesia – Zimbabwe 385
Chapter 110 Nairobi – Surprises 387
Chapter 111 A Little Wonder 393
Chapter 112 Mombasa – Why I Recorded
    "Malaika" 395
Chapter 113 Khartoum – in the Sahara Desert 397
Chapter 114 In Ethiopia – the Lawyer,
    the Emperor, & Italian Star – Me! 401
Chapter 115 My Private Life in Hamburg –
    The Girls! 405
Chapter 116 Roberto Blanco – The Black Bomber . . . 408

Chapter 117 **The Letter – Amir –**
the Total African Safari Vacation 414

Chapter 117b **Alone in Elephant Country and**
Tsavo Area 416

Chapter 117c **Ngorongoro Crater and**
the Kilimanjaro 418

Chapter 117d **"Hatari" – Danger –**
Hardy Krüger's Momella 420

Chapter 117e **The Statue in Kampala** 423

Chapter 118 **A Dream Home in Africa –**
Africa & Us. 425

Chapter No 119 **My Folk Album**
Goes Around the World and So Do I 427

Chapter 120 **My First Far East Tour** 437

Chapter 121 **Seeing Stars** 446

Chapter 122 **Hot Spot Beirut** 450

Chapter 123 **A Wild Dream Comes True** 455

Chapter 124 **Big Troubles – Mombasa –**
Helgoland and Hamburg too! 458

Chapter 125 **Dar es Salaam** 465

Chapter 126 **My Indian Bonus** 468

Chapter 127 **Vacation in East Africa** 475

Chapter 128 **Hong Kong Adventures** 479

Chapter 129 **The Price of Fame – The Chancellor,**
the President, and the Rapist! 486

Chapter 130 **"Good Lord!" – Lords Tour** 491

Chapter 131 **German TV / Sex Bomb – Me** 494

Chapter 132 **Amsterdam** 499

Chapter 133 **The Miami Kick, Manager Me, &**
the final Spanish Kick 503

Chapter 134 **Post Script India** 509

Chapter 135 **Ladies of Song** 513

Chapter 136 **Philippines** 516

Chapter 137 **The Intruders in Florida's Everglades** 522

Chapter 138 **The Night The War**
Broke Out (Masai Mara) 526

11

Chapter 139 **The Killer Waves** 528

Chapter 140 **Back Home in Switzerland** 534

Chapter 141 **Life Hits Back** 538

Chapter 145 **The Amazing Big Deal: Sometimes in Showbiz, The Most Amazing Situations Happen** . . . 548

CHAPTER 1

Beginning Of My Life

Has an embryo in the womb the power to think and sing? I imagine you, your family doctor, and most gynecologists in the world would answer adamantly "No way!" I'd have to go along with you, but if I could have sung at that stage – as I did a few years later – it surely would have been "Nothing's gonna stop me now!"

When I came into this world it was before the doctor could arrive – apparently, he got held up by the heavy sea mist often prevalent in Bermuda at that time of the year. It didn't bother me. I came in feet first and have had my two flat feet firmly planted on the ground ever since.

Mum, who had had a very bad birth on her third child, was told to stop producing if she wanted to live – but Dad was a temperamental Oriental, and Mum didn't have a clue...so, some years later, a fourth offspring arrived. However, with me it was years later, and Mum was already in her mid-forties and quite sure and slap happy that "All Her Trials," like the Bahaman folk song, "would soon be over." No more worries of using brand new bed sheets, or worst of all, bottles of hot cooked gin (known in those days as "Mother's Ruin" because it was believed it could give such a jolt to the entire system that it could bring on a period, and so ruin the chance of a further pregnancy. The Pill as we know it today only arrived in the 60s.)

I was more or less born on a beach, and when my father first set eyes on me in Mum's arms, he asked, "What is it, a boy or a girl?"

"A little girl," was the answer, whereupon Dad quipped, "Oh, it's covered with so much dark hair I thought it was a Pussycat!"

From then onward I got the nickname "Pussyface." I have no thick hair all over me now, but the name struck to me like glue. I do have a deep affinity for little furry felines with pretty faces – who to this day often have to fight for their rights to be completely independent.

Many years later, when Mum and I were sitting comfortably installed in the kitchen having a good cup of English tea, she confessed to me how hard she had tried to get rid of that fifth pregnancy. I asked casually, "Did you not know about the safe period?" Whereupon she answered:

"Oh yes, the middle of the month – but it still didn't help." No wonder!

I had to smile. "Oh heavens, Mum, be happy I was number five and not number fifteen – you certainly were naïve!"

In the 30s women were still often in the dark ages, and knew very little of birth control, births, or anything about sex, except trying to please their husbands, who were the bread winners. However, they still had dreams and very often, because they had no alternative, they said to themselves, "You've got to grin and bear it." We used to say "You've got to bear and grin it – innit?" just for fun. Anyway, the weather in Bermuda was much better than the weather in London.

The first thing I can remember at all is lots of eyes peering at me in my pink and white cradle. They all seemed to want to see the new baby and take photos. My Mother said proudly:

"Here she is, I think we'll call her Yvonne."

Cameras started to click, whereupon I was so nervous and disgusted at this intrusion into my privacy, I did a big business which seemed to stretch right up to my arm (I must have been tiny!). Mum was so shocked at my ruining her big moment of pride that she shouted to my nurse, "Bertha, Bertha, take her away immediately! … oh, the little stinker!"

Maybe that is why there are no baby pictures of me at all. Being born philosophic I am quite sure a little voice inside me said, "Not everything in life goes the way you want it to Mum, but don't worry, one day I will make you proud of me."

Even before I could walk Dad would take me on the beach and into the ocean saying, "Don't be afraid, the sea is your bed, just lay back and enjoy it."

I did, floating happily on my back with him holding my head up. I think I could swim before I could walk. I know I could think before I could talk. I stuttered as a small kid and was a slow talker. I think my husband Frank and my family and friends would agree I certainly made up for this later.

CHAPTER 2

Bye Bye, Bermuda – Hey Hey, U.K.

As Hitler started progressing across Europe, my father decided it was time to get back to the older members of our family (my older brothers and sisters) and get re-settled in the U.K. As I was only a two-year-old, the only recollections I have of Paget Beach are the rosy sands, that even when you fell over didn't hurt too much, then of course "my bed," as Dad had told me to call the sea, which I loved so much, and my mother's high soprano voice, when she would sing me a sweet spiritual lullaby at bed time. To be in her soft arms, pressed against her ample bosom was something like paradise. She called me "Piccaninny," the island name for a little black one – maybe I was? As far as I know, she had taken it from the black population in Bermuda. The Lullaby went like this:

> *Lula lula lula lula bye bye*
> *Does ye want the moon to play with?*
> *Or the stars to run away with?*
> *They'll come if you don't cry*
> *So lula lula lula lula bye bye*
> *Into Mami's arms acreepin'*
> *And soon you'll be asleepin'*
> *With a lula lula lula lula bye bye.*

It was also bye bye to the lovely nest life of Bermuda, of lazy hazy days and peaceful nights. It was Hey Hey U.K.: Wow!

London life, after sublime Bermuda, was like a bolt from the blue. No sun, no sand, no sea; everybody busy busy, and people everywhere. Many men walked along the streets whistling the latest tunes, and everyone seemed to be in a hurry.

For me the best thing about London was the men who rode about on tricycles selling Wall's Ice Cream. Their slogan was "Stop me & buy one!" You could stop him in the street and have an ice cream whenever you fancied one. If you did not have enough pennies to pay, he would take a vanilla "brick" and halve it. I discovered ice cream very early in life, and it has remained my favorite food ever since.

At age 4 it was decided I should join this busy throng of Londoners. Bertha, my nurse, who was white as snow with red hair – Dad had chosen her, as she was big and burly and he thought no one would notice the little, rather dark baby, as she almost enveloped me under her blue and white starched nurse's uniform – had come to London with us and had now found another job. Mum had gone to the Salvation Army, which her committee support-ed, and came back with a lovely jolly house maid called Maude. Soon she was joined by an older charwoman, Mrs. Dale, who came in three times a week to help out. There were five chil-dren of all ages – the three oldest were grown – but it was a big house on three floors. It was situated in a new, fine area, and from Mum's bay window one could watch world tennis tourna-ments. This was before the Oval and Wimbledon took tennis to the other side of the Thames.

Mum decided I should join my older sister Roxie and have pi-ano lessons with Mrs. Wand. Perhaps she thought with such a name she could do magic and turn us both into concert pianists. For little me, with my tiny hands that could never stretch an oc-tave (8 notes), it was a struggle; I loathed the left hand base notes and wished I could just concentrate on the happy right hand tre-ble clef. The nicest part of these Wednesday piano lessons was that I was allowed to go into the drawing room, with its grand Steinway piano and beautiful baroque furniture, with the dark mauve and gold cushions, and polished parquet flooring. This was barred to me til now. As I had to practice at least 30 minutes daily, apart from my Wednesday piano lesson with Mrs. Wand,

I could play and look at the beautiful painting from Monet in its heavy gold frame, and the delightful Dresden China ballet dancer figurines displayed on the mantle piece above the fireplace. These represented the much-adored London Ballerina with the Russian name – Anna Pavlova.

Both my parents loved music and they would very often walk about the house singing to themselves: Mum more classical and operettas, and Dad more the latest pop. Mum's best friend was related to Mischa Ellman the famous violinist; she also knew the violinist virtuoso Yasha Chaivitz and the Yehudi Menhuin family. Mrs. Chaivitz was once asked by a journalist, "How did you make a virtuoso of your son?"

She answered:

"Our children are like a beautiful brass plates, it is up to us elders to beat it til it is an outstanding piece."

If she had known then the word 'strategy' she probably would have used it!

Mum and Dad were mad about music. They often sang in duets, like Nelson Eddy and Jeanette MacDonald in those beautiful old movies. They liked to copy Anne Ziegler and Webster Booth, who were England's operetta duo of the day. All my parents' musicality was used for raising money at various charity concerts. Dad was always donating to this and that, and Mum belonged to various ladies' guilds who held teas etc. to raise money to help poor refugees thrown out of their countries by Hitler and his hordes, so I was raised on music and charities. We kids supported a nearby orphanage.

My eldest sister Frances was herself a ballerina and an excellent tap dancer – a real showbiz person – who worshipped Anna Pavlova, and later Margot Fonteyn. When she wasn't in a show she would help out in a dance studio, giving tap dance lessons to little ones. For my sister Rox and I she had arranged a special song and dance routine:

"You call me Sugar Plum, Sugar Plum means yum yum yum

It's yum yum yum, cos you're the one for me"

"I call you Lollipop, Lollipop means you're the top

And you're the top, cos you're the one for me"

All sweet, simple kids' stuff. Dad loved the trumpeter Harry James and his famous rendering of "The Flight of the Bumble Bee," top of the charts at that time. The fact that he was also married to the blonde pin up girl Betty Grable, the No. 1 Film Star, certainly helped matters. Mum was a fan of Bing Crosby and his top hit "Far Away Places"… "with the strange sounding names are calling me." This song haunted me and was to have an impact on my future goals for life.

CHAPTER 3

Happy Childhood Memories

In spite of Dad's dislike of babies – even with five offspring – he really enjoyed playing with us and teaching us to be competitive. On a rainy Sunday afternoon, he would get us altogether, and we were quite a bunch as we had always a sort of open house to all our friends, owing to Mum's terrific generosity and big heartedness. Dad would put on the gramophone and shout out in his special "teacher's voice":

"The first one to get right the name of the song and the soloist gets a sixpenny bit." This was a lot of money in those days! He'd put on a record and the first one to recognize the introduction and the vocalist got the silver sixpence. I loved this game, and even though I was the youngest, I beat a lot of the older kids because of my now famous sharp musical hearing and memory of songs. In time I got to sharing a red money box resembling a London public letter box with my sister Roxie…she agreed as she noticed how full it became once we joined forces.

If the weather was good on the weekend, Dad would shout out:

"Hurry up, all of you, we are going to the beach at West Cliff!" And here again who ever saw the sea first got a threepenny bit. In those days there were no safety belts or police making sure of law and order. Our car was invariably crammed with kids. I sat on Mum's lap up front, Roxie sat between Mum & Dad, and the other kids plus pals were all squashed in at the back. As I was up front and on high, I often saw the sea first, and did well til the others complained. I was duly put into the boot, which opened at the top. Although I felt like the cat's whiskers with that place to myself, and sharing it with all the goodies for the picnic, I never managed to see the sea first again.

We always had a picnic on the beach, and for me this meant FUN. Mum was a master at making succulent chicken sandwiches for us all, and Dad would buy a couple of bottles of Tizer, an orange-coloured fizzy drink with an indefinable taste and a terrible amount of fizz which invariably came down my nose – a kid's delight. Pepsi and Coke were still unheard of. We small ones were only allowed water, milk, or cocoa.

When the weather was only so-so, as it so often is in England, Dad would tell us,

"We are all going to Whitewebbs Park."

This was a sort of woods with lots of trees, bushes and ditches, and little overgrown paths, ideal for Hide and Seek. We generally played Cowboys and Indians. The boys were often the Cowboys and Dad and us girls Indians. Once hidden we had to give the famous Indian whooping call, and the Cowboys had to find us each separately. Dad would give them a certain amount of time and if they had not rounded up all of us, we would win. If they got us all, then the Cowboys were the winners. I generally made a mess up, as I would stand by a big tree and cover my face with my hands – so I could see nothing. I guess I believed no one could see me. I let the side down completely! The best part of these outings for me was that the moment we all got into the car, and it started moving, Dad would get us singing all the Olde Tyme Songs of his youth. His favorite seemed to be:

"My wife's gone to the country, hooray hooray!
She thought it best to take a rest, so she went away.
She's taken the kiddies with her, hooray hooray!
So girls don't miss a chance like this, my wife's gone away!"

Number two was something like this:

Looking back, I would say my infant days, after Bertha, who seemed to have a sadistic streak for hitting my bottom with the back of a big hard brush, had gone, were a very happy and funny time. My older brothers and sisters taught me to read, and as I was longing to be as good as they were, I learnt quickly. "Brrr Rabbit" was my favorite. Every week Maude, our maid, used to get "The Red Letter", a very spicy weekly about passion and having babies out of wedlock.

We were allowed Mickey Mouse, and my eldest brother Ray got the juiciest of all, with pictures of half naked women and terrible stories from the famous (at that time) James Hadley Chase, like "No Orchids for Miss Blandish" and worse still, "Lady Don't Turn Over". These paperbacks he would hide under a big brown cushion on an armchair and sit down innocently when anyone came into the lounge. No one else seemed to notice – but I did! And would secretly read all this illicit stuff, looking up words in the dictionary. Not quite the thing for little girls, though I am quite sure this particular episode happened a few years later, when I was on to regular visits to our local library and had turned into an avid reader. I would read just anything I could lay my hands on. The fact that war was just around the corner never entered my head. School came first, and after the tearful goodbye to Mummy, I went into the hall with our infants' class for role call and noticed some very nice-looking boys. One of them was taller than the rest and very good looking. Later I learnt his name was Michael Robbins. We little infants did not have desks but little chairs and tables. When we were told we could be seated he took my chair away and I fell on the floor at his feet. I knew all these boyish pranks from my brother Theo and his pals. I would have been angry, but as I picked myself up, he winked at me and gave me such an encouragingly nice smile that even then I knew that he fancied me, and to my little mind he was the pick of the bunch, so I began to like going to school even from day one.

CHAPTER 4

My First Celebrity

As still a very little girl, Rox and I were taken by Mum and Dad to Paris and to Daddy's favourite place, the Folies Bergères.

It was all terribly exciting, the audience elegant, and the aroma of garlic mixed with heavy real French perfumes was so alien to my nostrils that I remember that special smell to this day. However, the most memorable moment was being introduced to the world-famous star of the show, Miss Josephine Baker.

Dad, apart from his flourishing dried food warehouse, also owned a few cinemas and was regularly invited to "trade shows". Apart from knowing famous people like the then big film magnate J. Arthur Rank (whom Dad assured me some years later, made his fortune first with self-raising flour which all English housewives used), he was also well acquainted with the director of the Folies Bergères. So, Mum and Dad and us kids were taken backstage to meet the star of the spectacular show. In those days "The Folies" was The Place.

At first, I was stunned. This old lady with the lined face, who came towards us, looked so far removed from that slim young thing in the show that I found it almost unbelievable. Then, after being formally introduced to Mum and Dad, she turned, bent down, and held out her long-fingered hand to Rox and I. She gave us a dazzling smile and said in a warm contralto voice:

"And who are these 2 young ladies?"

Mum gave the answer as both Rox and I were dumbfounded – we were as if struck by lightning. Josephine Baker's personality was so warm and strong that suddenly, I for one found her to be the most beautiful woman I had ever seen.

It was the first time in my life I was confronted with a famous showbiz celebrity, who seemed able to do magic with her personality. That moment remains, for me, unforgettable.

CHAPTER 5

My Stage Debut

At Christmas our family and friends would put on a pantomime, an English specialty aimed at entertaining children over the holiday. Mostly pantomimes were based on a famous fairytale, but often, to make it more comical, the Hero would be also a girl but taller than the Heroine, and in Cinderella the two Ugly Stepsisters were invariably boys.

We all dressed up; it was great fun changing into our costumes for our dress rehearsal. The money raised went to give the orphans at the orphanage in our area a nice Christmas party. I was four years old and raring to go on the stage like the others, so I finally got the part of the little Page. I wore red satin shorts Mum had sewn for me and a white shirt and a silver high crowned cardboard peaked cap. I felt most important. My only lines were:

"To whom belongs this silver slipper, she will marry the prince."

In my hands I held a red velvet cushion on which was balanced the silver slipper Cinderella had lost, as she ran back to the carriage as the clock struck twelve – before it returned to being a pumpkin, and her beautiful ball dress turned back into tatters.

I spent hours practicing in front of a mirror – and had real problems with the word "slipper". I was told by my eldest brother, who was also the assistant producer, if worst came to worst I could say "shoe." At last the time came for my stage debut, and everyone smiled and clapped to encourage me. However "little Stinker" returned; I got nervous, and said out loud:

"Oh dear! I forgot my lines!"

The little hall rocked with laughter. I was so surprised, I laughed and laughed too, till the silver slipper fell on the floor. Bending down to pick it up I heard the souffleus (our maid Maude) saying my lines. I put the silver sandal back on the red velvet cushion, and with my head held high I piped:

"To whom belongs this silver shoe – oh! I mean slipper – she shall marry our Prince."

There was a big applause as I marched off the stage triumphantly, without falling over. Someone backstage pushed me out from behind the curtain to take another bow. I loved it all, and made up my mind there and then: I will be onstage, come what may! After all, it seemed to be a very pleasant way of making money.

Little did I know then that I had chosen the hardest profession in the world!

CHAPTER 6

First Lesson

Others – and I must say, as a small kid I belonged to that category – believe that luck will just come, and we spend our whole lives saying: "Ah well – when I get the numbers right in Lotto, or when I win the Pools." Some are old fashioned and just say: "When my ship comes in." It is nice to believe in luck – it gives us hope!

My first lesson in life, and my first move towards getting the things I cherished, came when I was five years of age. At that time, the neighbourhood of Stoke Newington, in the borough of North Hackney in London, boasted of a department store called "Stevens." It was so popular that even the bus stop was named Stevens, and the bus conductor would shout out "Next stop – Stevens!" and generally at least a dozen or so passengers would empty out there and go into the store. Of course, this (to my mind) huge store, with its wax models displaying various apparel, intrigued me. In those days there were not too many large stores, and even less with life-size display models, but what intrigued me most of all was a claw machine just outside the entrance. It was, I presumed, put there to attract small children such as me, because it consisted of a glass window, lit up and displaying a small crane which moved to pick up miniature toys – if you were lucky – or at least some very bright green candies – like M&M's or Smarties. These green sugared beans lay like a thick green carpet under and around the display of little toys. I watched other lucky kids putting the pennies that their parents had given them in the machine, and getting back toys, and I was determined that one day I would lure my dad to Stevens, and then persuade him to give me a penny and let me try my luck on that machine. My mother, for such things, was quite hopeless. Mum had a habit of saying: "Come away now dear, come away, we have no time for that rubbish," but Dad, I was sure, would let me have a try.

And, sure enough, that day came: one Sunday afternoon, when it was drizzling and we could not go to the woods for a picnic, he and I went window shopping, our favourite pastime for such grey Sundays, and Dad gave me a penny to try my luck. Throwing the penny in the slot, with a vengeance I watched fascinated as the little crane picked up a toy. I shouted out triumphantly, but to my horror it dropped the toy, and then it started rummaging in the bright green candies, picking up a fistful.

"Oh well," I said to my Dad, "I always wanted to see how they tasted." Then, as I watched with bated breath for the crane to throw the fistful of green beans into the drawer from which I could take them, the crane stopped in its tracks, opened its claws, and let the candies drop again on to the others. Then the machine turned itself off. The light in the display window went out and I had NOTHING!

If I knew the song then, I would surely have sung like Shirley Bassey "I – I who have nothing". As it was, I didn't know the song, and I was so disappointed I would have liked to cry – but before I could, Daddy turned to me, wagging his forefinger.

"There, my girl, is your first lesson of life – if you want something then go out and get it, work for it, don't rely on Lady Luck, because as you see, there is a pretty good chance she will let you down – 99% It Will Not Happen." So much for luck, or lucky stars…

Take my tip: if you really want something, then make a strategy, set your goals – get off your butt and go out and get it! At that time, as a kid, Dad was of course my "role model." That special "You", Cognac, and the name Pepito came years later – but Ice Cream – oh boy! – anytime!

CHAPTER 7

Animal Instinct

Apart from saying "put a little Bite into your life," one of my special virtues was my instinct, and it has helped me no end in various sticky situations. My eyes were so sharp that whenever anyone of our clan lost any watch, ring or ornament on the beach or in the woods – "Send the kid!" was the outcry, "Little Eagle Eye is sure to find it." – My instinct led me to the site of the happening, and the Eagle Eyes did the rest.

I also proved my worth in the kitchen, to my mother, who possessed a finely shaped nose, but could not smell. Whenever she was not sure of milk or any food stuff – one sniff from "Pussyface," and Pussy stayed true to her name. Mum, talking to her Ladies' Guild, once told them proudly of my virtue: "she can smell it a mile away if it's good or bad."

Because of these attributes I was used constantly – but the most unusual, almost animal instinct was that I could feel if anything living was in the room. We all went away for 6 weeks to Dad's beloved seaside, renting a bungalow. My eldest sister Frances, in spite of her outstanding good looks, had one drawback: She had a phobia of spiders.

I seemed to be born fearless, and with my now famous Eagle Eyes, I was always sent into each "new" room in our new beach home. It didn't matter if it was hiding in a corner – it was living, and oddly enough however an insect, bird, or animal pretended to "play dead," I knew by instinct it was alive. My big brother would be called in and little Eagle Eyes would point to the crevice or hiding place where the demon spider was, and he would get rid of it. I never waited to find out how. Today we'd use a vacuum cleaner, but as far as I know this modern device was not yet in every household.

Because of this well-developed instinct and the fact that I could climb up a tree or down a jagged cliffface with the agility of a monkey, never contemplating the consequences, Dad and the neighbours called me "Tomboy." Dad regarded me more as a son than a daughter (he was Oriental). He also called me "little wild animal." He assured me if I prayed to God every night – next morning I'd wake up as a boy! No such luck! I, as a naïve little fool, even believed him.

CHAPTER 8

My First Talent Competition

Although I was big for my age, I was only a tiny tot. However, Frances saw an advert for a kid's talent competition in Margate. As Dad had rented a bungalow for the summer holidays, only a few miles away from this famous seaside resort, she put our names down as entrants in the competition. We wore big yellow bows in our hair and the same big bows on our tap shoes, but otherwise just our simple summer frocks. Roxie and I did our usual routine – "You call me sugar plum, I call you lollipop".

There were lots of kids in the competition, one or two surprisingly professional, while Roxie and I were sadly amateurish, I thought. Also, some had very stagy costumes and seemed so confident. I must admit I was nervous among all those strangers. I felt as if I had two left feet, being sensitive, and Roxie was too; I could not keep her singing in tune. Our act was cancelled out almost immediately, along with numerous others.

The little girl who won the competition was, to my mind, different from all the other acts and super professional. In 2010 she could have easily done the popular "Nothing Sweet About Me". Instead of singing, she almost shouted out her number, and the dance she did was not the usual kiddie's tap dance or toe dance. It was a real London cockney folkdance – a "Pearly Queens Knock'em in the old Kent Road" dance or "Knees up Mother Brown" stamping dance. She even showed her bloomers! Frances was disgusted and said disdainfully: "Why, she's common as dirt!" The girl was very professional, wearing a perfect "Old Time" costume. Her bonnet, her buttons sewn on all over her costume, down to the black woolly stockings, knickerbockers and button up black boots were all perfect. The song she almost shouted at the audience was just as unusual: "I'd rather be an Old Man's Darling, than ever be a Young Man's Slave". These lines were then repeated, followed by the chorus!

"Gertcha Knock it
Never do a thing like that
Never do a thing like that again
Never do a thing like that!"

She then repeated this cockney chorus and animated all the audience to shout with her.

The jury and the audience of grown ups who till now were politely clapping at all the kiddies' sweet sameness of songs, and childish dance routines, got taken by surprise, by this little 11- or 12-year-old who went through her routine like a mature woman twice her age. It was electrifying! At the end they clapped and shouted "Bravo!" "Encore!" and stamped their feet. She had to return three times and do the chorus again in which everybody joined in. Like a prize boxer, she won hands down.

It was a clout in the eye for me, and even as Roxie took off her tap shoes with a deep sigh and said: "Ah well, we're no good! I think we should give it up and practice more on Daddy's typewriter instead. I'd rather work for him in the office and be among the family, than all these strangers who have no taste."

For my part, I had decided to go it alone. I knew with my flat feet I was a rotten tap dancer and a terrible ballet dancer, in spite of my eldest sister's great patience. I knew instinctively my voice, mimic and humour were my talents. For a change I said nothing, but I made up my mind – I am going to be different – that is how that girl won the competition. It was my first real stage lesson!

CHAPTER 9

Breadbaskets, Bananas and the Tarantula

When our enemy decided to drop "breadbaskets" – our nickname for the really huge bombs – one hit the Depot a few roads away during an air raid. I was 8 or 9 at the time and had learnt exactly how to act in panic situations and even how to put the breath of life back into people with shock and deal with hysteria. In war time children had to grow up quickly. I knew that my brother's best friend, Jacky Peters, lived quite close to the depot. As the all-clear siren went I made a dash for the road where his mum lived. The windows were all shattered, and the front door was ajar. I rushed in and there was Mum Peters having a terrible fit of hysterics brought on by the terrible shock. I steeled myself, inhaled a deep breath and did exactly what we had learnt at school. I held her frail body by the shoulder and slapped her face with all my strength, both sides and suddenly she stopped, as If coming back into our world again and said, quite calmly, "Thank you."

I was so amazed that it worked, I said, "Thank you too," and from then onwards, as I started to have my own money and loved dress designing, I went to Mrs. Peters as my first dressmaker.

One day the newspapers were agog. England had received a new consignment of bananas – but by some misdemeanour by the packers, the fruit had been imported with some huge dangerous spiders – tarantulas! It made front page news and we were told to be on our guard – although most of us had not the foggiest idea what this tropical spider looked like.

Coming home from school early, I went into the living room and Mrs. Barnet the cleaning lady had laid out all the bric-a-brac in the whole room and put all the different objects on the long table and was polishing the mantelpiece. I looked at all the bric-a-brac but one caught my eye – a huge spider with hairy long thick black legs plus eyes. I could swear it was living even though it stood like a statue at the end of the wooden table. I must be honest I was not sure, as you could buy all sorts of horrible things to put on our teacher's chair or table to shock her so we could giggle at the effect it had. They sold similar spiders at our school tuck shop. But although I had a good memory, I could not recall that object being in the room before and found it distasteful. I asked Mrs. Barnet if she remembered dusting it. Like me she couldn't remember ever having seen it before. I said, "It's living."

She said "No," and flicked her duster at it. In seconds it had sprint-ed across the entire table, but Mrs. Barnet was not sleeping, and rushed to the other end of the table whereupon the monster spider literally jumped on her pinafore. In a second, she had knocked it to the floor and put her heavy shoe on it – crushing it to death. To my mind, whatever I had been to Mrs. Peters – Mrs. Barnet was a real quick-thinking heroine, a great lady. Next day the lo-cal newspapers were full of our Mrs. Barnet's wonderful heroic deed. After all it had been my first sight of a live tarantula and in England the last – but Africa was yet to come.

CHAPTER 10

Walls Have Ears, Ye Gotta Have Bite!

It is not unusual for the baby of a family to be a rebel. Our dear jolly maid Maude called me "The Imp" and the older members, when talking intimately with their friends, would look around the room apprehensively and say: "Careful! You know sometimes walls have ears."

I could be in the next room or under the table – it didn't really matter; I invariably managed to overhear everything – an eavesdropper par excellence. Because of this talent they nicknamed me "Walls". As this happened to be the name of the famous vanilla ice cream, I didn't really mind – after all it was also the name of those men riding tricycles selling my favorite food.

About this time my teeth also became famous. My best friend sported all her life a scar on her back resembling teeth marks – they were mine! She was not alone. Even our kitchen linoleum covered floor, where it joined the red and white tiles of the scullery, had so many teeth marks, little lumps bitten out of it from my paddywacks I had gone into when I did not get my way, that Mum had to have it repaired with putty. I loved biting (I think I still do today) and sharpened my teeth on carrots and hard apples (preferably picked and nabbed from a neighbor's tree) and anyone's hand that got in the way! However sometimes bad things also have a good side.

At that time in our area, as kids in Hertfordshire, to where we were evacuated during the war, we lived in a solitary farm inhabited by the nicest farmers in the world. They would have done well in any story book or theater play. Farmer Johnson always wore beige corduroy plus fours and a red plaid shirt with rolled up sleeves. He had a full red face and a stocky body to match. His wife was a lovely woman who was very fond of Roxie and me, and soon we were given horses and started riding. Mine was an old grey mare named Bess. I felt so tall and important when sitting on her back. We learnt a lot about tractors and cows, and I was even allowed to drink some warm milk coming directly from Clarabelle's teat. This sojourn on the farm gave me a deep love of animals and a much better understanding, which my city family never ever developed. Mrs. Johnson was always in the dairy making fresh cheeses. She always wore a blue grey pinafore, which went well with her reddish hair worn in a bun, which never seemed to have enough hair pins in it, as long wisps of hair would hang down her back. A school bus brought us to school. Mum and Dad came down to visit us on weekends and get away from the "blitzkrieg" going on in London. All in all, I was happy and had no reason to bite anyone.

Then one late afternoon our school bus broke down, and as we had now no maid to pick us up from school and walk us back home, we had to go ourselves back to Johnson's farm. It was a longish walk, And the quicker way was to pass through the woods. I had heard vaguely of some madman who attacked children, from teachers gossiping at school, which I was not supposed to overhear; but I put it out of my mind. As Roxie was already twelve, we decided on the quicker way. Dusk was falling fast, and it was a little bit foggy, as it often is in the autumn. We walked as quickly as we could through the forest, singing songs we knew together to give us more courage. Suddenly a man appeared from out of a clump of bushes and he made an immediate grab at Roxie, saying:

"Got you my girl!"

He put his hand under her legs, trying to lift her up. In a second, I saw his hand with my "Eagle Eyes" and with my sharp teeth, I bit into it with all my might. He let out a yelp of surprise and dropped Roxie, and we ran like mad towards our farm. Fortunately, we were very near the Johnson's and could not wait to tell our foster parents what had happened. In no time two policemen came and we had to relate the horror story again to them.

A week later four men were put before us – as if in such a moment of terror we could recognise a face – but I did not look that high. I looked at the right hands of the four men. On one I saw my teeth marks. The man was taken into custody. It was an occasion I will never forget, but to this day, even when I bite my own tongue, I am grateful I am blessed with fine sharp teeth which saved us then, and have helped me a little in difficult situations throughout life. Sometimes you've gotta have BITE!

CHAPTER 11

The Last Billet

After the horrible attack on Roxie and my first experience of police and criminals, there seemed to be a lull in the "Blitzkrieg" – known to us as the "great fire of London" – and Mum and Dad came and took us home, which was really nice!

My eldest brother Ray was always punching with his boxing gloves on, a punch ball in the study, and decided to find a use for me, as everyone seemed to think – or at least say – that I was double-jointed, an expression for a kid who is unusually supple: In no time I could do backbends and acrobats, the Flying Angel from his broad shoulders being our "pièce de resistance." We did a few shows with others that brought in a little pocket money for me. I was quite determined to be independent, and I saved every penny I could get. I offered to clean all the shoes in the house. Maude, our dear, jolly live-in maid was happy I took this chore off her shoulders. I charged 2p a pair, and double if they were very dirty. But my big job was waking up Ray at midday on a Sunday afternoon. This was well remunerated, but also quite dangerous. My big brother, who was famous in our family for his girlfriends and night prowls (he was good-looking and an excellent ballroom dancer) paid me 4p every Sunday to creep into the boys' bedroom and throw cold water on his face – this without wetting the entire bed and pillow – no easy matter! If he got mad, I had to "scram" (beat it) as quickly as I possibly could before he caught me. Then I would be rewarded with double "wages." It was fun and suited me far more than Roxie, who loved babies and would walk prams quite serenely for her extra pocket money.

Then the sirens started wailing again as the Germans started sending "doodlebugs" (now called drones) – small bombers manned by robots. They had sort of red flashing tails and when you saw one coming you rushed like mad in the other direction.

As I rebelled about going down our air raid shelter, Roxie and I were sent again to our last billet. Our parents were assured it was a modern house with a bath. Til now, at the farm, it had been a tub put near the fire and filled up with kettles of hot water once every 10 days or so. As I was the smallest, I got mostly the dirty water left by the others – so I looked forward to this modern house with a bathroom.

Oh yeah – greater the disappointment. When I ran up the stairs to see the bathroom – it was not spic and span as I had hoped – no wonder: the bathtub was overflowing with black coal. Mrs. Grey explained to my mother and father, "They were stupid, they forgot to give us a coal shed – and you have got to put the coal somewhere." Ah well – back to "a cat's lick and a promise" – which was how Daddy summed up how I washed myself. Showers were still pretty well unheard of in England. Perhaps in Buckingham Palace – I had no idea…

The best part of this last billet was that Mrs. Grey had a tiny baby called Doreen and a husband, Fred, who worked at the nearby Air force Base. He was friendly with two young airmen and brought them back home to share a beer, some jokes and often fish and chips from the nearby fish and chip shop. These were generally wrapped in newspaper. It was wartime and there was a shortage of most things, but the Fishermen were brave lads and there was still plenty of fish in the nearby seas. As for chips – they are a mainstay of the Anglo-Saxon way of life, even though the "Yanks" (Americans) call them "French Fries". Mrs. Grey was happy to see the two young men, as cooking was not her forte. Every Sunday she roasted a leg of mutton with mint sauce and potatoes and cabbage or sprouts followed by "afters," which was rice pudding also baked in the oven with sugar and milk. This lasted through the week til Percy and Will came, and we all had Fish and Chips, and that put us all in a good mood.

My singing voice was noted and in no time, while Mrs. Grey took out her breast and fed baby Doreen in front of us all, I was put on a chair and the boys taught me all the dirty ditty songs they sang with the guys back at the base.

I learnt the words parrot fashion and would sing songs not half as refined as Leila Anderson's famous song for the forces "Lily Marlene", but more like "Lulu Lulu Working In A Knocking Shop". It went something like this:

> *"Some girls work in factories*
> *Some girls work in stores*
> *But Lulu worked in a "knockin' shop"*
> *with forty other whores*
> *Oh, bash away Lulu bash away Lulu*
> *Bash away good and strong*
> *Boys what we gonna do for a*
> *Good blow through*
> *When Lulu's dead and gone?"*

Later, much later, I heard the Les Humphries singers singing this song on the radio, but every time they got to a sticky word at the end of the verse, there was a tacit.

Thank heavens I only heard this once on the radio. After that it was surely banned.

I was just a little kid completely innocent, so I sang 2 or 3 similar ditties perfectly oblivious of their meaning – just happy at the laughter and applause. I enjoyed being a star. Roxie, earnestly like the good girl she was, carried on doing her homework, sometimes telling me to shut up!

CHAPTER 12

My Promise to Mum and Food For Thought

While other kids got measles, mumps, or chickenpox, I got them all; mumps twice and measles three times. I had no idea that, like Heinz tomato ketchup, there were about 57 different varieties. Once, after a very serious bout of gastric flu, the doctor took my mother aside and said he wished to talk to her seriously about me. They went into Mum's bedroom, and I crept down the stairs and listened at the door. At age 7 I was already almost a professional eavesdropper. The doctor knew Mum well and probably knew that she was worried about my future health, which she felt was to a great degree her own fault before I even arrived on the scene. He put on his most confidential manner.

"Now, don't worry so much about your little daughter. She is after all extremely highly strung, but I will personally make sure that she will get fresh oranges and we'll see to it she does not get scurvy."

This last word really threw me. I had to look it up in the encyclopaedia, where it said: "an illness often suffered by mariners caused by a lack of Vitamin C."

I was almost delighted that here I was, a kid, on the very verge of contracting some terrible disease which normally attacked only grown sailors.

"But," continued the doctor to Mum, "her defences are really down. Try carrots too, to build her up. However," he added, lowering his voice, "we must face the fact that physically she is not as strong as we should like her to be. She must lead a very quiet and peaceful life and not try to do too much – and all will be well."

Then there was a pause. I heard him clear his throat, and then he said, "I will see she gets oranges and lemons. Well, I must be getting along."

I made a beeline for the loo so that he could not see me.

After he had gone, I popped in to Mum after knocking on her bedroom door. I told her straight up I had heard what the doctor had said.

"Look Mum, don't worry, he is wrong. I may be physically not so hot, but my head will win. I am going to be an international singer. I am going to sing in all those "Far Away Places," Mum, Bing Crosby is always singing about, and I will show the world you must believe in yourself with the help of God. Mummy this is my first real decision. Believe in me Mum and I won't let you down, I promise."

Mummy looked at me with a strange far away look in her eyes. She took my two hands in hers and said, almost with a catch in her voice, "I'll stand by you little Tootsie."

It took me almost another seven years to find out why.

By the time I was 14, Mum and I had become close friends – that was when she confessed how she had tried to rid herself of my embryo.

"When I knew it was all too late – I was reading a book where the heroine was also pregnant, and she believed if you put your mind to it, you can in many ways will your child. I decided to try. I wanted a girl, a pretty happy and talented one, because I wanted that she should have the life I had dreamed of, but Fate had had other plans. I did not have the grit needed to realize my dreams. I wanted a strong gritty girl who could live the life I had wanted so badly – to travel the world, but not as a hippy – as a star singer giving the whole world a little joy."

I was so moved by this sudden confession. I took a deep gulp. "Mum, I promise you, I'll do my best to fulfil at least some of your dreams." And then, almost to myself, I said, "That's funny — I always wondered why I knew exactly what I wanted when other kids three times my age didn't even know what they wanted to do with their lives. Mum, you certainly made it simpler for me."

CHAPTER 13

Holiday in Wales

Our family at this stage generally consisted of Mum, Dad, and Roxie, my aunt Cissie (Dad's youngest sister), her husband Uncle Ralph, and their son, cousin Dennis. Everyone was getting tired of the war. Dad, dealing in food, was not doing too badly. Some of my uncles and my second brother were conscripted into the army and Mick Shaw, a pal of Theo's, was blown up while loading a bomber due for Hamburg. Frances was mainly with ENSA, entertaining the troops.

Dad suggested we all go to Wales, which he had heard was beautiful, and far away from battered London. He chose Llandudno – on the sea. It was like a pleasant dream. We went by train – me, Mum, Dad, and Roxie, and Aunty Cissie and Uncle Ralph and Cousin Dennis – and I think Frances joined us. The thing that intrigued me most of all as we got into Wales was the Welsh language! The names on the stations seemed all to be with about 26 letters, loads of consonants, and for us absolutely unpronounceable. The scenery was wild and picturesque, entirely different from orderly England.

Dennis, Roxie, and I were a famous happy trio. We were inevitably always trying to discover something new. Finally, we did. The fascinating object was a big new house, built on the other side of the beach. Inquisitive as we three were, we found a window which was not fastened, and although Roxie (who was older) had misgivings, Dennis and I in our childish innocence – always looking for something daring –opened the window and climbed in, and in no time we pulled Roxie with us. The house had no furniture and was obviously not yet lived in, but the water was turned on. We found this out, because Roxie, who had left Dennis and I to dance on the large ballroom floor, gave a shout.

"Come and have a look at this marvellous bathroom!"

I stopped singing and we both rushed to where Roxie's voice seemed to be coming from. The bathroom was large, and all the tiles and equipment were a bright primrose yellow, plus it had a separate shower with a glass door. We had never seen anything quite like it. The toilet was in the bathroom by the wall and next to it was something that intrigued Roxie. She had already re-moved her sandals and run the water and was sitting on the toi-let lid. She put her feet in the water of the "footbath" with a lit-tle spray in the middle. How odd to have a footbath like that, we thought, but Roxie was of the opinion that it was a great idea because it was so practical to sit on the toilet and wash your feet at the same time.

Later, Mum told me it was called a "bidet".

Til today my husband Frank sits on our toilet and uses our bidet as a footbath. OK, you can only put it one foot at a time, but he contends it's highly practical to kill two birds with one stone.

In no time our family had our regular place on the beach – the older ones installed on deckchairs, and us kids sitting and kneel-ing on the sands building castles with moats, and me with a pref-erence for modern houses with flat roofs.

Being true to my name, I was always curious as a cat about the other folk at our hotel and on the beach. One couple attracted me very much: They looked so happy. The girl always seemed to be wearing a different pretty sundress. I wondered if her Dad was in the "rag trade" textile business, because everything was rationed, particularly clothing, for which you had to have cou-pons. She was pretty and her young man was handsome, and they always seemed to be holding hands, sometimes giving a little kiss. They had much to talk about and laugh. All in all, they were thoroughly engrossed in each other's company.

Nearby were another regular beach couple. He was always enveloped in a large newspaper, and wore a white handkerchief on his head, knotted at the corners, to stop his head getting sunburnt. She sat pertly on her deckchair looking vaguely at the sea, and her magazine, which seemed to be of no interest. They hardly exchanged a word between them, but they didn't look really so much older than the lovebirds. I was really curious.

Finally, I approached Mum. Whispering quietly, I asked Mum to look at these two couples, and then I said, "Mummy why is it that the girl with the nice clothes and her friend look so very happy?"

"Well, dear," Mummy said quietly with a smile, "all those nice clothes are her trousseau, that is her new husband, they have just got married, and Mr. and Mrs. Summers are here on their honeymoon."

"Oh," I said, "but that other couple only a few deckchairs away don't look that old, but he only reads and reads the paper and they don't even talk to each other."

Mum laughed and said:

"Ah well, dear, anyone can see that they have been married quite a few years, and they have just come down for a respite from the "doodlebugs" and "breadbaskets." Their attitude is normal; you can't always be on a honeymoon, you know."

I had been squatting on the sand at Mum's feet. I now got up and said with fierce determination, "Mum, I never want to get married. Instead I'd rather have lots of honeymoons – and be really happy."

Mum gave a chuckle – she seemed to understand. Mum was a Gemini, and two quite different souls definitely slept within her tiny frame. As for me, I have never regretted that decision I made so many years ago. I believe in being a free spirit, and because of my desire for freedom, I am quite prepared to give freedom to my husband or my lovers – they do not belong to me, they belong to themselves, as I belong to myself. I do not believe in wedding rings or hypocrisy. If you want to come to me, then let it be true desire, sympathy and love – not, Heaven forbid, out of a sense of duty.

CHAPTER 14

A Seven-Year-Old Rebel

Seven is to most people around the world a lucky number. To me it was special. No longer an infant, I had headed the minuet and received much applause as our class won the first prize at the children's dance contest in our concert hall. I had won a lovely prize for "excellent work," and even Mrs. Wand, our piano teacher, was content with my version of the "Little Minstrel."

I rushed down the stairs to the hall and there was the big brass tray laden with birthday cards and presents. I opened the cards one by one and to my disgust, the personally penned messages were almost all identical.

"Hoping you will be a better girl in the future."

"What cheek!" I almost shouted "Fancy writing that on every birthday card!"

I could understand Mum & Frances writing that, because every time I got a smack I would hit back. I did not behave as they expected me to, which was to run away and cry. I was always being told "Little girls should be seen but not heard." After all, I was born a fighter from the moment my two tiny little flat feet hit "terra firma" on this planet. The reason Roxie would follow suit and write such a thing could only be my dislike of her "exciting midnight feasts." She read "The Girls Crystal" and apparently the schoolgirls were constantly having "Midnight Feasts." Roxie loved chocolate. I did not, I preferred spicy stuff and pickles. Just the same, she would get me to go with her on "chocolate binges." This meant pinching chocolates and chocolate biscuits and wafers from the grown ups when they were not looking. These were then hidden, and a couple of nights later when I was peacefully sleeping, she would wake me up, inviting me to her bed where all the chocolate spoils were laid out. This, she said, was our "exciting midnight feast." She would then gorge, and I would yawn and fall asleep while she would try to explain to me that this was the thing to do for real older schoolgirls. My behaviour on these nights made Roxie mad, and obviously she had joined forces with the family to wish I would be better in the future and even enjoy eating chocolates at midnight. All these thoughts went through my head while I opened the presents all wrapped up in coloured papers and tied with bows. There were games, a magic painting book, and a stencil set – these I really enjoyed – and then dolls and dolls. I already had 16 and preferred my 2 Teddy bears. At my tea party with my younger family, Mum and Dad, my special Aunty Sally and Uncle Jay, and some chosen friends, I stood up and made my first speech: I thanked everyone and then I said:

"You call me a rebel because I do not behave as most seven-year-old girls are expected to. Well, I think differently!"

Then I made it quite clear I wanted no more presents. I wanted instead for them to save their money (and this was particularly aimed at my parents), but when I reached puberty and my childish voice changed I could have singing lessons with a truly professional singing teacher. I had already read about this in a non-fiction book at our local library. You had to wait til after the first period (menstruation).

I added, "One nice present from you all would be fine – but my heart is set on being a singer."

I can't recall how the family and friends actually reacted to this statement at the time, but Frances, who was already established on the stage in many musicals and Christmas pantomimes, found me a well-known singing master when I was eleven and a half, so I could start singing lessons just before I was twelve.

My little speech had worked wonders. It was the end of lots of presents. I was growing up fast and I was happy. Now I had a goal. I knew what I wanted, and even then I knew it was going to be a hard fight and that I needed to have muscles.

CHAPTER 15

The London Palladium

Twelve seemed to me to be a very special age – my life started to take a definite direction. At seven I had made my first big decision – "No more presents for my birthday – but when I am eleven or twelve, let me have singing lessons with a first-class teacher." It had come to pass – but now I did not just have singing lessons: my teacher, Mr. Marcus, who was very taken with my youth and "lyrical soprano" (his description of my 3-octave voice) had arranged that I should sing for a really famous stage personality, who was also having his voice trained with Mr. Marcus. That was none other than the Austrian comedian, violinist and M.C. (Master of Ceremonies) Mr. Vic Oliver.

Vic Oliver had fairly recently been much in the limelight because of his marriage to the young film star Sarah Churchill. Sarah was the daughter of the world famous "Bulldog of Britain," ex-Prime Minister Sir Winston Churchill.

The marriage was a big surprise to most people and had given him much publicity. The public loved Vic Oliver, and his work for charities was renowned. Mr. Marcus had arranged for me to sing "The Merry Merry Pipes of Pan", with which I was not enamoured (I found it to be a bit like the songs we had to sing at school). The second choice was Ivor Novello's "Shine Through My Dreams", a strong ballad. I was nervous, but Mr. Oliver had that natural charm of an older man and made me feel at home immediately. He was very nice and did not call me "Fuzzy Wuzzy" because of my thick bush of frizzy hair and olive skin, as many other stars taking lessons with Mr. Marcus did. After he had listened carefully to my two songs, he asked me what I really enjoyed singing. I went immediately (with no music) into "Deed I Do" and "Honey Suckle Rose". He even clapped and seemed delighted. Then he turned to my teacher and said:

"Dudley, you can't put this little girl into the classics. She is a natural jazz singer."

But that was that; I never heard anything more from Mr. Oliver.

Some weeks later Dad asked me if I would like to sing at a big charity concert.

"We have managed to get Vic Oliver to be the Compère and do his act too. This show is going to be BIG TIME."

I asked, "At what hall?"

"We have booked the London Palladium, and you can do two songs, can't you?"

I couldn't believe my ears. Julie Andrews was singing as a "child wonder" in "Starlight Roof" (a big West End show) and setting London agog. Audrey, my cousin, who had been trained at the Italia School of Dancing, had a plum role as the little girl who gets murdered in the controversial drama "Tomorrow the World" at the Adelphi, and now I was to launch out on a singing career at the London Palladium. Oh my! I could feel all the butterflies flying around in my tummy and it was still weeks ahead. I was so surprised you could have knocked me down with a feather.

My teacher Mr. Marcus was, of course, delighted, and tried hard to make me believe this marvellous possibility of appearing onstage at the world-famous London Palladium all came to be because of the audition he had arranged for me with Vic Oliver. The fact that my Dad, who was paying for my singing tuition, was also on the Board of the Charity Organisation arranging the concert, he obviously pushed into the background.

He chose for me either Puccini's "One Fine Day" from Mme Butterfly, or, seeing I was not yet in my teens, Verdi's "Oh My Beloved Daddy." I chose Richard Tauber's "My Heart and I" – which I knew well and felt quite at home with. Richard Tauber, the great Viennese Tenor, had made a name with "Du Bist Mein Ganzes Herz" translated to "You Are My Heart's Delight" – not just in England, but the whole world, and now he had his own musical with his own composition "My Heart And I", a lovely song which had become very popular. I practised day and night, working with Marcus like mad til I knew the aria to perfection. The Tauber ballad was pushed into the background, because I could do this comfortably.

The night arrived. The House was packed. Vic Oliver gave me a wonderful announcement – apart from being highly intellectual, he was a kind man. My heart pounding like a hammer, in my little yellow rayon dress I thought much too childish and short, I went on stage and sailed through the operatic aria with no problems. I even dedicated it to my own Daddy. Now came "My Heart and I" and I felt I knew it back to front. It was easy – that's why it came to me as a shock that the top note of the climax of the song was just a little flat. Oh, "little stinker", why did you have to turn up again at such an important time?

After the show Dad was full of praises, particularly as I had said "Oh my Beloved Daddy" from Giuseppe Verdi was especially for him. He took my arm and said:

"Little Pussyface, you were a good girl."

I think he felt the same, as much of the audience, with no perfect pitch, seemed to think from their "Bravos" and endless applause. Then Vic Oliver brought me out a second time and whispered in my ear, "Your jazz would have got them all cooking."

I dropped into a curtsey in my too short frock, first to the applauding audience and then to him, just as Dudley Marcus had taught me. I ran off the stage and behind the curtain to where Mum and Dad were waiting. The relief was unimaginable.

Mum, who had "perfect pitch," gave me a disapproving look and said, "Tootsie, never be too sure of yourself. Singers are inclined to slip up on songs they think they know too well. Remember, *practice makes perfect.*"

CHAPTER 16

Love at First Sight – Switzerland

16

The war was over and won. Our class at school had all gone on a trip to Trafalgar Square, to celebrate with Nelson and thousands of others.

Dad was itching to go abroad. When he had participated with UNESCO he had been in Geneva. He had spent a day in the Tessin (Ticino) and was so impressed, he wanted to take Mummy, Roxie, and me there on a vacation. Apparently, he had colleagues in Lugano-Paradiso. Just the name brought wild wonderful dreams to my imagination.

We flew to Paris. Oh, what would 99% of the other girls at school say?! "Oh boy – what a superb experience." Thereafter we took the famous "Blue Train" to Bâle (Basel). We were only in transit in Paris, but the dirt and above all the "public conveniences" (toilets) I found disgusting. There were only 2 places for your feet and a hole – no seats, no nothing – under the guise that this was more hygienic. I could not use them – and oh, the stench to my sensitive nose! Then, you couldn't drink the water! On the train we used bottled water even to clean our teeth. All these discomforts we shared with a French lady who was in our 3rd bunk compartment. She was obviously quite used to all these inconveniences and regarded them as normal.

At Bâle we left this old romantic Blue Train and still had time for breakfast at the station and time to go to the toilet! I came back from the W.C. to the family at the breakfast table and announced:

"It was so clean and so comfortable you could have read a book in there and eaten a sandwich, too."

Then the "Schalen" (milk coffees) arrived in large round cups on large round saucers, with a basket full of the most delicious croissants. The fresh butter, the dark cherry jam – what wonderful things they did have in Switzerland – apart from the most outstanding scenery I had ever seen in my life on the train journey to Lugano-Paradiso. It was indeed a holiday to remember. Those beautiful clothes all made in Switzerland, and no coupons necessary! In the UK clothing was still rationed and the beautiful pure silk dirndl skirt and St. Gall lace off-the-shoulder blouse Daddy had bought me took my breath away completely. He and the older members seemed to be more interested in the Strawberry short cake and the thick fresh whipped cream in huge dollops on top. Born with a very sensitive digestion, I found out that even at 10 years of age, coffee and creamy cakes were not for me.

Roxie, who was already working for Dad as a shorthand typist/secretary, had her own money and purchased a wonderful outfit from a famous boutique and looked marvellous. She was already becoming a very smart lady. Perhaps that was one of the reasons that the young and good-looking night porter Luigi (Luc) at our luxury hotel "The Eden" fell in love with her and would stand at his desk and tell us all about Switzerland. What attracted me most was the direct democracy – everyone could vote over almost anything and everything he said. Back in London, sharing the bedroom with my two sisters, my bed was pushed against the wall by my parents' bedroom next door. Dad, being already rather deaf, spoke in a loud voice, and I had often heard through the wall how he complained bitterly about the way politics worked in the UK.

"Those damned ministers," he would say, "they promise us the world. You vote them in, and once there, they fill their own coffers and don't give a damn for us who voted for them and all their promises."

At 10 I didn't understand too much about our French speaking Luigi (Luc). It was directed mainly at Roxie anyway. As I felt tired, I said in my best French:

"Pardon, je sens fatiguée, j'irai accoucher."

He burst out laughing and explained to the bewildered Roxie and me that I had just said I was going to have a baby!

I guess we learnt all the wrong words at school. I had to use the verb "dormir" in the future and leave "coucher" to Lady Marmelade.

At our last "teatime" at that lovely open-air café under the pergolas, where they served these marvellous strawberries and whipped cream short cake, I stood up and said in a loud voice: "I have made a second decision."

Aunty Cissie, Uncle Ralph and Cousin Dennis, plus Mom and Dad, Roxie and the older ones (with the exception of Ray, who was already married to a platinum blonde model) all smiled condescendingly.

"One day when I have earned enough money singing, I am going to buy a house here. I love this beautiful clean country with their 'direct democracy.'"

When Luigi had explained how this worked, I had asked him to write down for me those two words. I had kept the paper and now I read the words "direct democracy" out to them with a flourish. At school, doing Shakespeare's "Julius Caesar", I had played the part of Marc Anthony, shouting "Friends Romans Countrymen – lend me your ears," etc., so I had no problem playing the Orator at this occasion.

But now I was not Marc Anthony, I was just little Tootsie, Pussyface, also known as "Little stinker" when I did wrong.

Now I was greeted with peals of laughter. That laughter remained in my memory, because I was already smitten with Switzerland, and marked it down as one of my goals. No matter, I said to myself – big successes often have very small beginnings.

CHAPTER 17

Girl Power

At twelve I thought I knew everything. I was big for my age (then, to my horror, stopped growing). I got lots of hand downs from my older sisters, giving me a sophisticated touch, and what with my enthusiastic self confidence I gave the appearance of being at least 5 years older. I was without a doubt terribly precocious. Frances had taken me to the most famous professional photographers for show biz people in London, Swarbricks Studios. The photographer got me to pose with only a sombrero for covering and had called me sultry and my mouth sensuous. I had to look both words up in the dictionary, as I didn't know what they meant. Of course, I was delighted, but rather surprised as the "sensuous mouth" came from pouting when I didn't get my way as a kiddy. Aha! I grinned, so I am SEXY.

As the boys we knew boasted about their power over us girls, I found it amusing and decided it was high time my 2 best friends should also know about their "girl power." I learnt a part from an excellent sex education at school, where our headmistress had super modern ideas, even though we girls thought her to be super strict. I decided she loved the power she wielded not just over us schoolgirls, but also over the teachers. The word "power" appealed to me, and I studied it, particularly "girl power" over the male sex. I found this out even before I was a teen. Let me explain:

When my two pals, Susan and Annis, both a year or so older than me, got their first bikinis, I got one too. In those days they were not the frivolous sexy bits of nothing, like today with "push-ups" etc. Mine was a royal blue knitted two-piece, but we were young and slim, 12–13 years, and very sure of our new body measurements. At that time, we three girls were at an open-air swimming pool near our homes. I decided then and there, after looking around, this was an ideal time to give my pals a short lecture and lesson on the word "power," from a female's point of view. There was a line of young men in their swimming trunks laying with their heads resting against the wall.

"Now we are going to go by, swinging our hips, and watch all their "little Willies" suddenly stand up."

It was fun! We slunk by the boys in our new high heels, bikini clad, getting a terrific kick out of seeing their swimming trunks suddenly shoot up. When we were well passed their stares, I turned to my pals and said:

"Now you know who has the power."

I was 12, and had started singing with an amateur band at our youth club dances, but apart from music and singing I had studied the word "power," and my name was not "Lolita"!

My First Date

I was just thirteen, a magical age – no longer just a kid, I was a teenager. Some teenagers at 18 or 19 were already married, and some were already mothers. I had now joined the brigade of girls who were almost grown up. At 16 one was counted as an adult almost everywhere, and that was only three years away.

At dancing at Freeman's school I had met a very nice boy who lived only two roads away from our house. His name was Bernard, and he had asked me for a date. Normally we girls were chaperoned by Theo, our big brother, when going away from our little area, and with him we were allowed to come home at 10 p.m. Mom knew Theo was a good boy and there would be no problems. Sometimes I went to the local youth club, but never alone, always with Sue, Jean and Anice. We went out as a little gang. No nonsense, lots of laughs and no danger. I asked Mom if, now being 13, I could be allowed to go out alone on my first real date. Mom agreed as she knew Bernard's family, but impressed on us both when he came to pick me up that I must be home by 9.30 p.m.

Besides bringing me a little posy of violets to pin on the lapel of my coat, he invited me for a light meal at a Lyons Corner House. I was in my element, and we chatted away like two old friends. As was the fashion he brought me home and thanked me for the delightful evening, and then in a trembling voice asked if he could kiss me goodnight before I went in – I had my door key on me. I said "OK," and he kissed me gently but forcefully and it really appealed to me – and so one kiss went to another. We both laughed and giggled and laughed at the pleasant effect, not noticing how the time was passing. My mother suddenly appeared at her bedroom window overlooking the porch where we were standing. She shouted:

"Stop that noise Yvonne, come in it's past your bedtime!"

This made us both laugh mischievously. Mom shouted again:

"Stop that row and come in!"

"Just another kiss," we said unanimously, and just as we were enjoying this new found pleasure a bucket of cold water came splashing down on our heads. We both realized Mom was not joking and meant business. Wet and still laughing, I ran quickly to our front door before another unwanted cold shower could take the wind out of my sails.

Silence once again reigned on the front porch and mother slept peacefully. I sat on the edge of my bed drying my hair with a towel as I wrote my diary of that very eventful evening and of that unpleasant but funny incident which certainly made my first date unforgettable.

CHAPTER 18

Plus ça change, plus ça reste la même chose

Mum, who was half French, used this expression often, so it was perhaps my first lesson in the French language.

Today we all get quite shocked when it comes to light in the media, that a famous personage like the nephew of ex President of France, Mr. François Mitterand, or world-famous film producer Roman Polanski had sex affaires with underage girls. We all seemed very sure of ourselves, "This must be rape." I for one am not so sure. After all, in Shakespeare's play "Romeo and Juliet", both were well underage. To my mind it does not depend on us, it depends on our hormones and our upbringing, and self discipline.

At 12 I was already going on a bus once weekly to the other side of London quite alone for my singing lesson with the much-admired classical singing teacher Dudley Marcus. I had learnt how to control my vibrato after having learnt how to breathe and sustain a long note. However, I was 6 months into puberty and already madly in love with a 15-year-old technology college student. When the public bus came to our bus stop, us schoolgirls who had become interested in the opposite sex all made a rush for the stairs, because we knew the boys from the Technical College would be with their satchels upstairs, too. Then we would have about 20 minutes of flirting – pure fun! I had finally plucked up enough courage to invite, for me, the handsomest J.D. to my next party. He had broad shoulders, proper muscles, a nice height, and a very devil-may-care grin.

He was a big success with all the girls at my party. We played the usual games, but when we played "Postman's knock", he managed to call my number and once the door to the party room was

closed and we were alone in the hall, he gave me such a passionate kiss, I fell in love with him immediately. Some weeks later
we sat on a park bench in the twilight. Some more mature people passed by, whispering, "Oh they must be lovers." I was elated that people regarded me not as a kid – but an adult lover! The
elation was short lived however when Joe told me his hand was
cold and could he warm it near my heart under my blouse. In no
time he had undone the buttons on my shirt with the dexterity of
an experienced male. Then came the "Oh..." I had no bras and
nothing to fill a bra with, and worse I felt no thrill – no nothing!

In spite of the disappointment on both sides, he still managed to
pluck up enough courage to ask me to have sex with him. I was
shocked and froze like a freezer that had just been re-iced. That
was the end of my first love affair!

To my utter disgust, not more than a week later I heard, as one
invariably hears, as word gets round so quickly through the grape-
vine in girl's high schools, that he had reached his goal with Tilly
Foreman. Tilly was 13 and therefore in a higher class than me.
She was known for her pretty face and very provocative young
figure. She made up for a lack of brains in the classroom by being a big success with all the boys. I was devastated and walked
around the house singing "What is this thing called love?" That
was the end of my first big "fantasy" love affair but the beginning of my determination to concentrate on my goal of singing
around the world and being so good that, if there should be any
hearts broken, it would be the other guy's heart and not mine! I
decided there and then – I will be a success and a heart breaker!

About that time, I shared a desk at school with an exceptionally
lovely girl from Scotland. She had black hair worn in a "pageboy"
as was the fashion, brown eyes, and white skin – trademarks of
my own mother – plus a quiet way with her. She was not pushy,
like so many others, but was reticent and I liked her very much.
One day she was absent. After three days of no Diana, I asked

our teacher if she knew if perhaps Diana was not well or possibly on holiday with her parents. I realized then because of her closed character, I really knew very little about her. To my horror the teacher lowered her voice and said:

"She has unfortunately passed away!"

"What?" I ejaculated incredulously.

"Yes, it was blood poisoning. Do not say a word to anyone but stay after the class."

I was in a state of shock. It was my first occasion to be confronted with death from someone so close to me. My grandmother had passed away and soon after my grandfather – but they were old. Mick Shaw got blown up loading bombs in a Bomber plane, and passed on, but he was Theo's friend, not mine, and I had only seen him once or twice, and he was definitely well in his 20s. To my mind this was "fairly old," but Diana was, at the most, just turned 13. How could she die?

Later when I was alone with our teacher "Barty" – (Miss Bartlett), she told me:

"Unfortunately, Diana got talked into sex, became pregnant and tried without help of anyone she knew, to rid herself of this horrible situation. Unfortunately," she said, looking at me and lowering her voice at the same time, "this act of surrender on her part was her death knell."

Psychologically that tragedy had an affect on me for the rest of my life: a) to remain a virgin (which somewhat later I seemed to forget), b) to beware of sweet-talking boys, and c) to concentrate on my chosen path and not be led astray by temptation. It was definitely a shock treatment and those last words from my teacher ring in my ears to this day.

CHAPTER 19

Second Lesson

Felix Mendelssohn and his Hawaiian Serenaders were playing a week at our local theatre. Dressed in the only nice garb I possessed, my off-the-shoulder blouse with a silk skirt and a Marguerite in my long dark locks, I asked if I could sing one song for him, for very little money. I did "Moonlight and Shadows," a Dorothy Lamour song, which I knew he featured in his Hawaiian show. His regular girl singer had apparently gone down with laryngitis, a rather normal happening in the cold damp English winter climate. This was my lucky evening – I was accepted on the spot. Apart from a sarong with sewn in falsies, which he provided, and a Hawaiian lei, I was barefooted and sang the song 5 nights consecutively. There were palm trees and a moon in a dark sky scenery, and three girls with brown make up and long black wigs dancing a languid hula behind me. I needed no make up because of my natural dark colouring, and I thoroughly enjoyed the idea of going to work after school was through: I got up especially early in the mornings to get my homework done.

I really looked forward to my salary, but it never came, and the Hawaiian Serenaders left North London on their tour without paying me a penny. I told Dad and he was adamant:

"Why, his father lives only a few roads away – now this is your second Life Lesson my girl. You must go to Mr. Mendelssohn senior, tell him of your dilemma, and be really nice and ask him if he would be so kind and pay his son's debt, which probably he forgot."

I did just that what Daddy told me; "Don't be afraid to ask for what you deserve."

With Dad's voice ringing in my ears, I visited Mr. Mendelssohn senior. Actually, I was a bit nervous. He was very kind and seemed to be a little amused. He gave me the £2 10 shillings that his son had promised me for the 5 nights, and I went home walking on air. I was saving hard for some real professional stage dresses, and this big amount of money was a windfall against the pennies I earned mowing neighbours' lawns, cutting hedges, and returning bags of plums or tomatoes etc. because there were a few foul specimens in the bag and "the lady of the house" did not like to return the wares to the greengrocer herself.

Dad had had a hard life as a youngster and seemed intent to teach me a little of what he had learnt. I knew when Roxie and I had gone with him in the car on a rainy Sunday morning to his large warehouse with dozens of bales full of the pungent aromas of raisins and almonds, dessicated coconut, crystallised fruits, and the delicious smell of ginger; that there on a rude wooden pedestal was a wheelbarrow. Underneath was written in white painted letters:

"All things made to last have small beginnings."

Words he would tell us often, as if he was a preacher. We knew he had run with that very wheelbarrow to the docks, where he could pick up some sacks of flour or sugar that were no longer in a 100% perfect condition, but good enough to sell to the poorer bakers whose clientele was not so fussy.

Today when I saw the big trucks with his name on, the large warehouse, the offices, and the cinemas, I had a heart full of admiration for my innovative and terribly hardworking father. I decided there and then to remember his words and like little Oliver Twist in the book of the famous English author Charles Dickens – to never be ashamed to ask for more.

CHAPTER 20

Surprise, Surprise

Life is full of surprises; this I found out at quite an early age. At age 10 I had announced to the family, full of childish confidence, that I loved Switzerland and would one day purchase a house there. The confidence was spurred on from the fact I had passed the scholarship before I was 11 with honours, enabling me to go to the most famous "blue stocking public school for girls." In time this honour should help me to enter either the Oxford or Cambridge Universities with ease and so further my diplomas to be a successful female lawyer as my father wished. I was now "in Dad's good books" so to speak, as I was the only child to receive this honour.

Apart from this, while in Lugano I had made friends with a nice blond boy from a village in Differdange Luxembourg, who had initiated me into the delights of a "Cassata," an Italian Ice Cream speciality. We corresponded until I was completely engrossed in my singing. It was an ideal opportunity to improve my French and even get a photo of a "Continental Boyfriend" to show off to the girls at school. Life was good!

Our next family vacation was Cannes in the south of France. However stingy Dad was in our four walls at home, when it came to going away and being seen by outsiders, he always chose 5-star hotels — if not the very top, then the next one. This time we stayed at the Martinez, which was next to the top hotel on the Croissette, the Carlton. The Martinez was a lovely place, and I revelled in the gorgeous dresses worn by the younger "chic" set at dinner, which was served outside on the terrace, to the accompaniment of a pleasant five-piece band led by Jimmy Dee.

It was also there where I saw people ordering as an "hors d'oeuvre" something that, to my untrained eyes, resembled a Water Lily. I told the waiter with my usual precociousness, "Un comme ça, s'il vous plait" – "I'll have one of those please," pointing to the dishes served to a near by table. The family thought I was mad – fancy coming to the south of France to eat a Water Lily! No one at our table knew what it was. My love of adventure had come charging through again. The Artichoke was served with only olive oil and a touch of vinegar; it was horrible. I have no idea how I managed to finish it – so tasteless. Ugh! Surely it required an acquired taste and a special sauce to improve my "Water Lily", but that came some years later, when I decided to learn the art of making good sauces.

One evening the bandleader asked if anyone could sing – as a sort of small competition to get the clientele involved. There were only 2 or 3 others who ventured to go on stage, so full of confidence I went on stage too. The fact that I could sing in French won me special applause and the big American crowd just lapped up the Al Jolson numbers "April Showers" and, of course, "California Here I Come". I won easily and could give a small bottle of champagne to Dad – my prize.

Then the Manager came over to our table and told Daddy, if he wanted, he and Mum could stay on another few days gratis at the hotel, if he would allow me to sing just those 3 or 4 songs: The Lucienne Boyer number "J'attendrai" and Jean Sablon's "Clopin Clopon" and of course the Al Jolson numbers, as he awaited a large party of Americans who would "just love his little daughter."

Dad behaved like a real VIP and explained he could not possibly stay on another day or two away from his business – which could not run properly without him. Frances however stepped into the breach. Cannes and the south of France was just her cup of tea and she relished the idea of a few more days at the lovely hotel. So, it came to pass that we two stayed on for another 3 days. I even sang "You Made Me Love You" for the large, well monied American party and they loved it...I think they believed me.

I decided to take my fate into my own hands. I went into the writing room and typed a short letter to Edmundo Ros, the King of Tropical Music (his Wedding Samba had rocked the entire world and he was a favourite with the Royals). I also wrote to Cyril Stapleton – the biggest modern orchestra of that time on the radio.

"Do you want a girl singer with a great voice, great looks and great personality? I am appearing nightly now at the Hotel Martinez in Cannes, but expect to be back in London shortly. Please write me there, where and when I can audition for you. Sincerely, YC."

Surprise, surprise! Both gentlemen gave me auditions in London.

CHAPTER 21

Self-Opinion Decreasing

When a letter arrived from Cyril Stapleton inviting me to audition for him, I was so proud of myself for achieving this honour I wanted to frame it. However, I managed to keep everything secret.

The famous orchestra leader cut my audition song short. He had been eyeing me up and down.

"Does your mother know you have played truant from school to come here this afternoon?" he asked.

Mum did not know – I had rushed down every morning to the hall to quickly confiscate any letter that bore my name.

I felt crestfallen. "No," I answered in an embarrassed whisper. I could feel myself blushing all the way down the back of my neck.

"Come back in five years time", he said. "Maybe we can get together then", he added, smiling.

I only wanted to find the door as quickly as possible. Thank Heavens he did not ask how old I was, I said to myself.

All the pride and joy I had felt in Cannes, which had spurred me on to send those two confident letters as if I were thoroughly grown up, seemed to disintegrate. I felt empty and sad. This orchestra leader had seen I was still a schoolgirl. My self-opinion decreased violently!

CHAPTER 22

At the Coconut Grove

Edmundo Ros was a whole other kettle of fish – so to speak. He was a huge black guy from Trinidad with a terrific personality. He was called the King of Tropical Music, and this was no understatement. He auditioned me at the Coconut Grove, his famous nightclub, and the whole atmosphere intrigued me.

I didn't want to make the same mistakes I had made with Mr. Stapleton, so I asked one of my big brothers to take me one evening before my audition. I put on make up and my high wedges I had saved up to buy. I looked at least 21 years old, and Ray was pleased with my appearance.

The band started and the tropical music was like balm to my ears, and then suddenly Edmundo Ros arrived from the back of the stage, towering over all the musicians. He went straight to his big conga drums with such a resounding heavy beat that everybody in the Club stood up and started clapping. He then went immediately into "The Wedding Samba", the tune he had rocked the entire world with, and which had made him also a great favorite with the Royal family. No wonder! His voice as he spoke had that undeniable lilt of the Caribbean Islands. His swagger was that of a black man who had been not just accepted and admired by the community, but who had leaped over the wall and was admired by Royalty. Edmundo Ros was a BIG name!

I auditioned for him two days later, with a flower in my hair and hope in my heart. I chose "Ascercate y mas", "Come closer to me". I decided to avoid any long-held notes of the slower South American pops, in case I showed my nerves and my voice trembled. In "Come closer to me" I could flirt and forget it was an audition. When I had finished the three musicians who had accompanied me clapped, which fortified my courage.

Edmundo Ros said brusquely, "Well, you dooo look the part."

He gave me a pair of claves and put some music into my hands, they were all from Southern Music in Denmark Street in the West End.

"Go there and practice as often as you can. I know you are very young, but I want you for our second band run by Roberto Taylor, who will play on Sunday evenings at Churchill's Club – as a sort of Sunday club for the younger set."

I could not believe my ears.

"Get yourself a red taffeta ankle length skirt, wear that same Mexican Style blouse but off your shoulders plus a wide black belt, and don't forget a flower in your hair. Practice these four songs keeping in rhythm with the claves. You'll get the rest of the Info from my office."

Without any further ado he strode off through the back of the stage, leaving me slightly dazed with my mouth half open. Emundo Ros wanted me – I was flabbergasted!

The first song I had to sing with the band was "It's Easy When You Know How", and how right that song was. I went to Jackie's mum, Mrs. Perkins, who made up the bright red taffeta in the popular bell design with a cuff just above the ankles. The skirt was made with Mum's financial support as Dad was totally against the idea. My appearance won the Tropic Band at Churchill's full approval.

Keeping time with the claves nearly drove me crazy as, as the evening drew on, I became tired, and my beats became slower.

The musicians' smiles turned sour. I knew keeping the rhythm with a pair of claves was not for me. If I wanted to keep my job at Churchill's Club on a Sunday evening I just had to improve. I bought a small pair of maracas, made from real Coconut Shells, and hand painted them myself. With Mum's words at the Palladium firmly implanted in my mind, I practiced and practiced and practiced. My God, it looks so easy to sing a song and shake maracas gracefully all at the same time – but boy, is it difficult!

That first song Edmundo Ros had chosen for me, "It's Easy When You Know How," is a title I'll never forget – whoever wrote such clever words deserved a Grammy award.

They forgot to mention how much sweat and frustration we have to endure – til we do know how!

After four weeks the law came down and said: "NO MUSIC ON SUNDAYS." Probably feeling sorry, Edmundo booked me for a few private parties – but that was it. Still, I was getting stage experience in a night club atmosphere and my confidence was slowly returning.

Because of Edmuno Ros I was welcomed by Southern Music – really nice people, and so helpful. I also discovered Denmark Street was the equivalent of New York's Tin Pan Alley. Musicians met and gigs were 2 a penny if you were lucky.

Jack Moss, who had been playing the 4 new numbers I was to sing at Churchills, knew all the musicians, and it was he who pointed out a pleasant looking gentleman.

"That's George Scott Wood," he said. "He has the most famous Accordion Band in the World. I know he is looking for a girl vocalist to go with his band to Scotland. Go and introduce yourself and say Jack Moss sent you. It's for November, so you will be 14 and its all ok then legally." (For any regular work in the U.K. at that time you had to be at least 14).

George Scott Wood was a man of his word and a friend of Jack's.

"If Jack sent you then you're in. We board the train on 31st October at Liverpool Street Station. All the info you get from my office. See you have your "dots" and a few long dresses. Take a fur jacket, Glasgow can be very cold. OK?"

It's a very bumpy road in show business, and I was learning fast.

CHAPTER 23

My First Marriage Proposal

Roxie was going to ballroom dancing classes at Freeman's School of Dancing. In those days, if you were from a good middle-class family you had to be light on your feet and a good ballroom dancer. I went with her and even managed to get my Bronze Medal with her help. We learnt Waltz, Quick Step, Foxtrot and Tango, and I just loved them all.

Then came the New Year's Eve Ball. It was fun and we – Roxie, Sue (my neighbour friend) and I – all joined in the Valleeta, Hokey Pokey and the Paul Jones. In the latter the girls form a circle holding hands and the boys form a circle outside the girls. You go round in different directions, when the music stops, the guy opposite you is your next dance partner. To my surprise, mine was truly Mr. Tall Dark and Handsome, sporting a moustache. I was just 13, I was quite sure he had to be at least 21. Suddenly the music stopped, and Mr. Freeman counted 1, 2, 3, 4, 5 – Gong!

"Happy New Year Everybody, Kiss your partners!"

In a second, long strong arms encircled me and gave me such a long strong kiss – that all the others who had finished kissing, stood round us clapping or whistling.

His name was Jack Winehouse. He was 21 and a watch maker. He also smoked a pipe. He was, for me, a real man. I told him I was 17. In no time he became my new romance, to the envy, I think, of Roxie and Sue, and the disgust of my eldest brother Ray who complained bitterly, "The kid is going out with a man much taller than me."

Ray was 5 ft 8" and Jack probably just over 6 ft. Mum, thank Heavens, was on my side – explaining delicately I was now a teenager and was growing up. Then the worst happened, Jack wanted my hand in marriage. I was appalled when he told me "we both had good jobs" and he was going to visit my folks and ask them personally. I was so overwhelmed by his good heart, good looks, and good dancing ability, I was loathe to tell him that I was still a 13-year-old schoolgirl – so I took my parents into my strict confidence and told them the truth. I asked Dad to be nice, but in no way to mention I still go to school, but just to say 17 was too young for marriage and Jack should look for someone older and not his daughter who was bent on an international singing career and not a cooking wife with babies. It sounded good to me. I was very fond of Jack, and sang to him the song "I'll remember April," which month it was, and which words were perfect, when we first met and fell in love.

"This lovely day will lengthen into evening – we'll sigh Goodbye to all we've ever had."

I hoped he'd got the message, but he was determined to make me his wife and arrived at our house for dinner with a huge bouquet of Daffodils and Tulips and Mimosa for Mum. I introduced him to Dad and said:

"Daddy this is Jack Winehouse – you know we met at Freeman's School of Ballroom dancing."

Dad shook hands with my beau and wanting to make him feel at home, he said:

"Come on Gerald, pull up your chair to the table, we're going to have dinner – don't be shy Gerald. what would you like to drink, how about a whisky with me?"

I was shocked. "Dad," I said, "his name is Jack not Gerald."

Dad raised his hands with a bewildered smile.

"Gerald, Jack, Jack, Gerald, oh, my daughter has so many boyfriends – one on the phone, another at the door and now you at the table. I just can't keep up with them all."

Jack gave me a curious side ways look, as if he could hardly believe what he had just heard. I shrugged my shoulders and made a face like a distressed hen. I had a mad feeling of wanting to giggle, so I rushed out of the room muttering.

"I'll go to help Mum in the kitchen with the dinner."

I couldn't wait to tell Mum of the awful blemish on my flirty character Dad had delivered, and we both burst out laughing.

Needless to say, that was the end of my first proposal of marriage.

CHAPTER 24

Summer Season

Needless to say, at this period of my life I was mad about opera. I had sung "One Fine Day", the famous aria from "Madame Butterfly", and cried my eyes out over it when I had to sing "so a bit to hide and not to die at our first meeting." I found the crescendo with these terribly sad words heart-rending. I was just not able to sing of this hope in Butterfly's sadness, knowing full well her "Big Love" would arrive with his American wife by his side, to shatter all her dreams.

When I was finally classified as a mezzo soprano, I was at first horrified, but when my next teacher said I would make an ideal Carmen I was absolutely elated and threw myself into learning every note and every nuance. I learnt "La Habaniere" – in English, "Love the Vagrant" – and the nightclub of "Lilas Pastia" – "Près des ramparts de Seville chez mon amie Lilas Pastia" – in French, as Bizet would have wished.

All this hard work was not in vain, however. One day I scanned through the "Wanteds" in the Melody Maker and noted one advertisement:

"A young girl singer for our large summer orchestra in Ramsgate. Must be versatile and able to sing classical and pops. Month August, possibly last two weeks of July. Then a box number."

As now I had some good professional photos, I felt capable enough to apply for the job.

At that time, you could not leave school until you were 14 years of age, but those six weeks mentioned were exactly our school holidays. I decided to apply. Afterwards I was told 5000 vocalists had applied. After the second audition I got the job. I had saved to make a demo-record with my teacher of "La Habanera" and "Oh You Sweet One" – a very simple pop of the day – and the classic "Blue Moon", all in shortened versions, plus a very good, toothy smile photo from Swarbricks. It was impressive and I won! A new balloon full of hot air was now going up into the stratosphere of my ambitions.

My parents were on different footings regarding my future career: Mum pro, Dad con, but as it was school holiday time at a seaside resort not so far from London, and above all singing mainly classics, wearing proper normal attire, Daddy gave in. Anyway, I would be 14 in October, and that counts. The good thing was the concerts were all in the open air at the bandstand in the middle of the park, so it was always in daylight wearing normal summer dresses. We on the bandstand were under cover – the audience were on fold up chairs or standing in the open air. I must have done something good because it was an excellent summer. It was a wonderful experience for me to be able to sing every evening and on the weekends plus a matinee. The musicians were all nice men, and Frederic Hargreaves an excellent conductor and a fatherly man. There was a male singer, a nice blond young man of about 28, and we sang a few duets like "Oh You Sweet One". He was a pop singer with no formal tuition, and he did no classics.

The council had arranged for us "artistes" board and lodgings, and mine was with a plump widow who took one look at little me and said:

"Oh please don't call me Mrs. Belsey, call me Aunty."

So I did. She was a dear old lady who suffered from "hot flushes," as I blushed often myself. I could feel for her, how uncomfortable this can be. She was very kind and her "Welsh Rarebits", as she called "Welsh Rabbit", were quite delicious. I have never tasted better since. There was only one drawback: the bed. It was soft and got warm quickly so that I didn't need my hot water bottle, but I started to get big red bumps. I didn't know if they were bites or "heat bumps," and they itched like mad.

One day, sitting on the only chair and studying the words of the popular "Near You", a brown insect hopped on my crossed leg. I tried to swot at it, but after it had stung me it did not fly, but hopped on to my other bare foot, and I suddenly remembered a little ditty we sang at school about the "hopping flea." For such a small mite, the bites were huge. I told "Aunty". In her essentially English cool, comforting art she said:

"Oh – oh yes, that could be fleas. You are after all sleeping in the cat's bed, but Jasper died some months ago. I didn't know animal fleas bothered us human beings."

In no time I had bought DDT powder and dowsed the whole mattress with that famous "kill all" powder – so that battle was won! It was my first acquaintance with fleas – but after that wherever my voice took me, DDT came with me.

My favourite night was Wednesdays. They were "Olde Tyme" nights, and we did all the famous old songs and had special Old Tyme costumes. It was fun. Alan (my singing partner) and I rode on a tandem to "Daisy Daisy", and I had a little poke bonnet and a small cage with a stuffed bird in it for "My Ole Man Said Follow The Van". It was a riot. The crowd generally joined in the second chorus, and sometimes Fred Hargreaves would call out "Let's Do it Again" and the public would sing so loudly that I could take a well-earned rest. In those days we often sang 20 songs per night.

The afternoons with the classics were a rest. I only had to do the two Carmen arias and a duet with Alan. To add to this lovely month, I got some "fans" – the most special for me was a young student from Paris, over here to improve his English. He was accompanied by his sister Henriette. He was cute and played a very good game of tennis, which I learnt at school as it was on our curriculum on Wednesday afternoons. We had "netball" – now called basketball in the winter and tennis in the summer, and Friday mornings were always devoted to swimming. As we had a half hour of gym daily and I biked when I could with friends, we had no lacking of physical training.

My new friend's name was Jacques Duteuille. He was studying chemistry so that when his father retired he, as the only son, could take over his Dad's big successful Pharmacy on the Champs Elysées. I was delighted to be able to speak French again and I learnt such everyday expressions as "tant pis," "merde" and "zut alors!"

Leaving Aunty Belsey was a tearful departure and we both hugged each other and wept. I promised to write, and I did for the next few weeks.

I hadn't been home for even a week when something amazing happened. I received a letter from the Carla Rosa Opera Company, saying one of their talent scouts had seen me and asking if I would be interested to join the company. At that time the Carla Rosa Opera Co. was a touring opera company, but very famous and second only to the Covent Garden Opera Company. I felt honoured.

Well, well, I was going on 14 and the Carla Rosa Opera Co. was interested in engaging me. I wondered what Mum and Dad would say? Dad was proud that a representative of the Carla Rosa Opera Company had called on us, but was not at all contented with the salary offered for my services. Even when the man said that after the first month or so I would for sure get a small solo singing part, there again the salary offered was so negligible that Mum told me in plain language:

"Heavens, you have to live on bread and water if you want to be an Opera singer."

So, my schoolgirl dreams of playing Carmen, for which the Carla Rosa man said I would be ideal, in time "went for a Burton" – right down the drain! They were only pipe dreams.

Mum made a decision for me:

"Listen my child, I know your main dream is to sing in the entire world and get to know the people there. You are a born cosmopolitan. Remember what Vic Oliver told Mr. Marcus? Aim to be multilingual. Use your natural charm and personality. Get a good repertoire for a solo act entertainer, not just a singer in a band. Even if you don't have a record on a hit parade you will always have work and be able to fulfill your ambitions of being able to see the world on your own without belonging to a company or a group doing as you are told, which is not exactly your virtue."

Mum was right. I practiced with good pianists who either believed in me or fancied me. I went to see every good act I could possibly afford, mostly standing at the back, having managed to charm the manager. I went to see Frank Sinatra, Eddie Fischer, Dinah Kaye and Diana Washington.

Little did I know that my first engagement would be a week at the Albany Club arranged by Rudy Rome, and later the famous and well-loved dinner dance restaurant "Selbey's" would be on my list.

CHAPTER 25

The Big Spender

Somewhere about this time my father was becoming more than a little perturbed. His oldest daughter Frances was well into her twenties, but in spite of the fact that she was a beautiful young lady from a good middle-class family, she had not yet found a suitable husband. As already said, Dad was essentially Oriental in his deductions of life. A girl had to have a lovely face, if possible, a curvaceous but slim figure, and a good head of hair. In other words, she had to look good, whereas a man had to have a lovely pocketbook or bank account or, best of all, both, and if he owned some estate – all the better. The virtues that us girls looked for, like being handsome, charming, or good company, were to my father's mind irrelevant.

He considered this touchy situation very carefully. After all, what sort of a father would he be thought of in the community with a good-looking daughter going on 30 and not yet married. Oh dear!

The war of course had played havoc with all his good intentions. Most suitable men had been conscripted into the services. To add to this internal discomfort his eldest son, in spite of having been at one time Mr. North London, had fallen in love with a girl at Woolworths, and as he was over 21, had gone to a registry office and married her. Truthfully, she had taken on his religion (which he did not personally adhere to), and even my father had to agree she was outstandingly good looking with her platinum blonde hair, excellent long shapely legs, and a very pleasing outgoing personality.

My brother Ray, who was a favorite partner with many a show girl, including Audrey Hepburn, seemed always to know all the right people. In no time he had arranged that his new wife should become the main model for a special company of luxury furs. As she worked on salary and commissions her boss and my brother soon discovered she was also an excellent saleswoman. These facts all appealed to Dad, who had a weakness for blondes anyway, anytime, particularly if they made money.

He had great ambitions for his eldest daughter to attract some lord or millionaire. He had acquiesced to sending her to RADA (Royal Academy of Dramatic Art), where she had been in the coffee breaks group with Bobby Breen, the famous stage show man and film star Joan Collins – but Joan was the oldest daughter of Will Collins, the famous theatrical Agent of that time, and with her forceful personality had had it comparatively easy in showbiz.

Frances was, for some unknown reason, more self-conscious and did not seem to hit it off with the opposite sex as he had wished. Apart from that, he had to realize he was big among bakers and grocers but was not a showbiz magnet.

Recently, at a donations party, Dad had been introduced to a Mr. Carlo Zerreto – a big Italian industrialist. He was fairly tall and portly, with brown eyes, dark "Brillcreamed" hair, and a swarthy complexion. He was in no way good looking, but his pockets must have weighed him down, because he gave the heaviest donation of all at Dad's last charity ball. This carried great appeal with my father. The next charity party was arranged to be an informal tea dance.

As I was not yet 14, I was allowed to attend, but only in my turquoise afternoon party dress – as the description would have been in those days. Dad had arranged that Mr. Z would be seated by Frances, and it would be an excellent but simple way of getting them together. As they danced by, Dad turned to Mum saying, "Nice pair, aren't they?"

I did not hear Mum acquiesce to this remark. I thought he looked 20 years her senior, very important – rather ugly, but definitely everything about him – his custom tailored dark grey suit and his rings and gold bracelet – shouted of V.I.P. And, the scar down the side of his right cheek certainly did not help matters. I gave it no more thought til suddenly he stood by my chair and asked me to dance. For his bulk he was quite light on his feet, and he politely compared me with a feather. From then on, we danced almost every dance till donation time, when once again Carlo Zerreto became a Hero of the day, outbidding all with his donation. As the tea dance party ended, Mr. Zerreto asked me for a date and not my big sister. I had, to Dad's horror and quite unwittingly, upstaged my eldest sister!

CHAPTER 26

The Ash Tray

The chauffeur driven Rolls Royce limousine arrived, and as I was literally walking on air, Mr. Zerreto took my hand and asked me to call him Carlo. It seemed in no time the chauffeur and porter of the 'Mirabelle' Night Club were escorting me out of the car and into the club as if I was Princess Elizabeth herself. The Club was the most expensive at that time. We were escorted to our table, and I made a mental note not to order artichokes for hors d'ouvres. The menu was in French, and I was delighted with myself that I could read it all.

In any case, I need not have worried, as "C" was for Carlo but also for "Control," and turning to me he said, "We'll take 'melone a la porto. Tresoro n'est ce pas?" and before I could nod my head he added, "and 2 Steaks Turnedos Rossini. They are always good here" – "saignant" of course, or do you prefer medium rare?"

He actually acknowledged my presence! The thought of having to eat raw meat put me off completely, but before I could even murmur a word a waiter arrived at our table telling us my VIP was wanted on the phone. My escort stood up saying, "Not even at dinner do they leave me alone," and rushed off.

At least I had time to take in my surroundings. So, this was a "posh place," as our maid Maude would have said.

It was my first introduction to a super elegant Night Club. So, the décor had to be rather dark and mainly with dark red walls with gold chairs to sit on – a bit stiff, not like the laidback tropical atmosphere of the Coconut Grove, where the younger set came and I felt a lot more comfortable. My partner soon returned and the melon balls in Port wine were fine. I even enjoyed the wine ordered. It was Chateau Neuf du Pape, a name I decided to remember too.

From thence on the waiter, calling Carlo to the telephone for yet another and then another important phone call, had become our third party. I wondered vaguely how Carlo could manage to get through his Filet Steak before it was stone cold, but I had an instinctive feeling Carlo Berreto delighted in his own importance. Once he even turned to me half smiling, holding his hands up in true Italian style, and said to me half in French, "Dis donc c'est incroyable" – it is just deplorable – "it seems the whole world is wanting me."

I could not help but think to myself, if it is so deplorable, why in the hell did he give this Club telephone number to the "world" so he could be more away from the dining table than sitting comfortably there. We finally managed to have a dance or two, but by then I had made up my mind that this would be the last time such an evening would happen to me again. I will be the one who is wanted all over the world – but not my escort. My ambition reared its lively head. I thought about this for a moment and decided the industrialist was no gentleman, leaving me for the best part of the evening alone while he did business deals on the telephone.

To remind me for life of my first night club date, with a chauffeur driven "Rolls" (as we called these luxury limousines) the most elegant and expensive Club in the West End of London (Mayfair) and with a gentleman old enough to be my grandfather – an Italian millionaire industrialist – I needed a souvenir. I took the new ash tray our waiter had put down. The waiters were most attentive, and a new ash tray was put down. Immediately my chain-smoking escort left the table, and I took the opportunity of slipping a new one into my handbag. I was happy I still had no proper evening bag, which would have only held a tiny compact, a comb, and a dainty handkerchief. I sat for the best part of the evening alone and unobserved, and made a silent resolution: I may be only going on 14, but this night I will not forget. And the little ash tray will help me to remember.

After all, it must have been quite a shock for my father, who had quite different intentions. Perhaps also for my eldest sister who had, until this incident, regarded me as the flat-chested kid, and certainly not competition – sorry Dad and Frances, this won't happen again!

CHAPTER 27

The Balloon Deflates

The fact that I had been invited to the so-called "best place in town" for a dinner dance by an Italian millionaire added to the blowing up of my ego balloon. Although I did realize, turning the unusual evening over in my mind, that the clever entrepreneur realized that Frances did not really fancy him as a husband in spite of his wealth, and Roxie was busy dancing with a much younger suitor. Probably he decided not to upset Daddy but to do something harmless like inviting little me. No matter; I could show off at school about this conquest, and I was learning fast about the growing art of life.

Ros, Ray's wife, had become friends with a showgirl named Joan North who was appearing in the biggest hit musical in the West End. She was often in the luxury fur boutique where Ros worked and as Joan was the boss's newest acquisition – that is to say girlfriend – she had already done well having been present-ed with a beautiful wild mink coat (the most expensive of all). Now she had her eye on a chinchilla stole.

While looking at superb furs and conversing with my sister in-law, she mentioned her "good friend Val Parnell," who was at that time the biggest producer of musicals. Ros latched on and mentioned her kid sister in-law. In next to no time, a private au-dition was arranged for me.

I had already found out that public auditions were out. a) I was too small and to my disgust I seemed to have stopped growing. b) I was too dark. Frances had already had her fill and knew that anyone under 5'3 was considered unacceptable. Furthermore, it was a blonde era.

The exotic brunettes from Italy on celluloid had not yet arrived in the UK, like Anna Magnani, Gina Lollobrigida, and later Sophia Loren.

Of course, I was amazed and delighted at getting this private audition and regarded this almost 6-foot showgirl as a female magician. Frances came with me that afternoon. I had practiced non-stop the numbers I would sing for the great producer, so I was well prepared. I always remembered Mum's words at the Palladium and that was "practice makes perfect."

When I had performed my audition of three entirely different numbers, he turned to Frances, who came with Joan, and said:

"That little girl could really be great. I would like her father to send her for one year to the Buddy Bradley School of Dancing. It is the most modern and goes on the true American style. We would then coach her inside our fold for stardom. Let me show you a 15-year-old whom I think would be a role model for her."

"Lights, music," he shouted, and suddenly a young girl danced out from a wing of the stage and almost shouted a swing number that was very popular, "Mr. 5 by 5." Then three young fellows came on stage and did a very modern dance routine with her. It was great. We three clapped and then the girl was carried off and was touched up by the three male dancers almost everywhere. Frances was shocked – I think she was by nature rather prudish. I was surprised, but Joan apparently thought it quite normal and tried to explain that these were the usual backstage antics from the younger set. Val Parnell smiled, and told Joyce, the girl, that she was great. Then he shook hands both with Frances and me and said to Frances:

"Speak to your father, if he is willing to give her a one year intensive course of stage technique and dancing at Buddy Bradley's, and if he is, we are waiting to groom her in a year from now when she'll be 14 going on 15 which is just the right age to start."

I was speechless with joy and thanked Miss North at least three times, but Frances did not say a word apart from a curt, "Thank you, Joan – that really *was* an experience."

I did not realize then that she was no longer on my side, and I strutted about like a peacock. My god, what a marvelously interesting year this had been. I felt on top of the world. My ego ballooned to such a degree that I did not even notice that Frances seemed annoyed. She took Dad aside as soon as she could and told Dad this 15-year-old entertainer Joyce was a real "tart." She told Dad about the 3 boys and the touching which the 15-year-old seemed to enjoy – and to crown it all that Joan North had called it all "normal" for youngsters having fun. To add salt in the wound, she advised Dad strongly not to send me to the famous dancing school because a) I had feet flat as a pancake – she must know as a ballet dancer; b) because I was turning already into a prime little flirt and who knows how all this "so-called stage grooming" could end? This offer was definitely NOT for a young girl from a prestigious family.

It all went quickly. Dad was shocked. All along he had wanted me to be a lawyer and perhaps sing at the occasional charity concert and then preferably marry a rich man. He stopped my singing lessons, stopped my pocket money, and told me in no uncertain manner I was getting out of hand, showing off and not studying at school sufficiently.

So much poison was put against me that the whole family "sent me to Coventry" – an English expression at that time, a little like mobbing. No one spoke to me and if I spoke to them, they did not answer. Only my Mum and Roxie were on my side and played secretly immune. Anyway, I had my friends and I managed not to lose my smile. It was a terrible let down. My ego balloon had definitely deflated, and here I was again, right at the bottom where I had started. Why oh why did I have to be from such a pious, prudish family? Ten years later there would have been no problems.

CHAPTER 28

Consolation

My one consolation was that at the end of October I would be 14 and at that time, when England was still in an upheaval after the war years, I could leave school and in November take on the job Jack Moss at the Southern Music Publishing Co. had seemingly arranged for me with George Scott Wood and his Accordion Band. I had of course no official contract – I was in any case too young for such formalities, but crossed my fingers and prayed to God it might materialize. I had only the red taffeta skirt and white lacy off the shoulder blouse. How was I going to juggle this unpleasant and sticky situation?

Like most young girls, I read lots of teeny Magazines and decided that apart from cutting people's hedges, I could become a model. I started at the Regent Polytechnic and slowly to photographs, mainly for my hands, with my long fingers, filbert nails and dimples that certainly helped.

Also, my hair – I had the thickest head of hair in the whole school. I could almost sit on it, and it was full of luxurious waves, the fashion in the late 40s. Being any sort of model is hard work and extremely tedious and the money I made was nothing to write home about, but then something great happened: Frances fell in love and was to be married in early September to a good looking, charming young man – who had not much money but youth and optimism on his side. Dad decided to take him into the business as a rep, which kind of work he had previously done. He had been a traveller in ladies' underwear, which sounded most exciting. Roxie and I as bridesmaids had lovely long pink dresses, custom made with tiered skirts and sequined sweetheart necklines.

Now I had an extra stage dress — also the family was in a good mood and mobbing was long forgotten. I still got the occasional "gig" and, saving hard, I bought a black, boned velvet top and made with Mum's help a long tulle skirt. It's amazing what you can get away when you are young and determined.

CHAPTER 29

Glasgow

Kings Cross Station was, as usual, terribly crowded, but the instructions I had received from the George Scott Wood office were quite clear. Gripping the navy blue rexin case I had saved hard to buy, plus a utility bag Mum had kindly said I could use, I made my way to the correct platform for the Scotland bound train.

It seemed to me like a huge family gathering, as if every musician had not just his wife with him, but many with children or other members of their family. From a very early age I had learned to be independent. At school, after the first prize giving when I was about 7, Mum was far too busy with her fundraising parties and Dad had never set foot in any school where I was a pupil. There is a huge difference between an only or second child and number 5 or 6. The good side of a war and a stoic upbringing is you are made from an early age to be tough, in a tough world.

I was the only one of the whole band who was alone. Fortunately, the leader spotted me immediately and he was a real gentleman. He came over to me shook my hand warmly and said:

"Oh, good to see you, my dear. Now, I know you won't let us down, as you have been practicing diligently with my friend Jack Moss. I know this is your first time going away with an orchestra – so far from home. Now let me give you some good advice: As the only girl in the band, *keep your nose clean.*"

I hadn't the foggiest idea what he was getting at. I had had a terrible row with my father over accepting this engagement so far away in Glasgow, and only managed to be at the station at all with Mum's help. Mummy was wonderful and I realised, somehow or other, I was fulfilling her life's dream. I gave Dad a solid promise: if I was not a star or well on the way to stardom by the time I was 21, I would throw out the whole idea of being an international singer and I would study at university and become the lawyer he so wanted in his family.

Right now, I didn't know what the band leader meant and taking out my handkerchief. I mumbled, "Sorry, but I don't have a cold," touching up my nose.

Mr. Scott was visibly amused. "Listen, my child," he said in a fatherly tone, "while the men are away from home – you must grow up and take into account that they are *men*. Many are sure to find girlfriends or flirts while they are away. Many a Scotch lass may fall in love with one or the other members of our band. Do not put your nose into other people's affairs. You are to turn a blind eye on what you see and a deaf ear to what you hear from these men. Remember they are away from home and many of the younger ones want to have a good time. You keep your mind on your songs. When some wives talk to you, you be sweet but intelligent, and when we come back think of the three wise monkeys: *you saw no evil, you heard no evil, you will speak no evil.* Got me, my girl?"

I nodded and realized this was one of my first and best life lessons I may ever receive from a stranger. It all was not half as hard for me as perhaps it would have been if I had had no brothers and their friends constantly in our house at home, where I learned pretty quickly about the male mind and desires – having secretly read excerpts from James Hadley Chase's "No Orchids for Miss Blandish" and "Lady Don't Turn Over" – the latter dealing with the prevalent white slave traffic, which had shocked the world and became a bestseller.

Before we boarded one wife after another came over to me – all saying very much the same:

"Little girl – be so good and keep a close eye on my husband, won't you?"

I smiled innocently and said: "Yes, of course," – remembering exactly the words George Scott Wood had told me.

Fortunately, there were quite a few older men who were serious enough to be not looking for "a good time."

CHAPTER 30

Greens Playhouse Sends Me an Angel

Greens Playhouse was the largest and most famous dance hall in Scotland and a number 1 venue for only the most famous orchestras in the United Kingdom. This was a dance hall era. Glenn Miller was deceased, but his music and big bands lived on and were in demand.

All the younger set either went ballroom dancing or were themselves musicians playing in various bands. It was the "In Thing," and the Dance Halls were unimaginably huge and called Palais. Both Arthur Murray in the States and Victor Sylvester in the UK were literally raking it in with dance lessons and music for strict ballroom dancing.

Greens Playhouse was formidable, and when I saw it first, I suddenly felt very small and cold. Scotland is not famous for a warm climate and boy – on stage was that draughty!

As a normal vocalist, you had to come on stage with the rest of the musicians, sitting in the front row at the very end. I was not required to sing very many songs, and I was really happy I could wear my slacks under the long dresses. I had brought my maracas along and was happy for the beguines, boleros, and rumbas, when I could stand up and play them, which with a few dance steps kept me warm. The little rabbit fur jacket slung over my shoulders, which I had picked up at Berwick Street Market in London, became a good friend in keeping out those awful draughts.

The main star soloist was a smallish, wiry older man with light thinning hair and very bright, lively blue eyes. His name was

Norman, and from the start I felt he had taken an interest in me. He was a first-class musician and his finger dexterity on the accordion got my full admiration. In no time he asked me if I was free over the holidays, where he had a few solo engagements at some excellent hotels. If so, we could rehearse a good repertoire while in Glasgow. I was more than delighted. I lived in "digs" where porridge and haggis were mainstays. Glasgow was, after the war, a real coal pot – dark and dreary. We had tea dances from 4 to 6 pm on Wednesday afternoons and weekends, but Mondays, Tuesdays, Thursdays and Fridays we could rehearse.

Being a real old fox at the game, he saw in me a talent to mimic and in no time, I could parody Rose Murphy and her "Brr Brr Brr – Busy Line", which was a top hit at that time. Then there was Lena Horne, the coloured singer whose hot blooded version of "I Feel So Smoochy" was sweeping the Western World. I practiced on a broom stick all her smoochy gyrations – which I would do as she did with the microphone stand when the time came to do an act with Norman. When we returned to London all the wives came up to me asking if their husbands had been "good," I did not lie; I said "Yes – of course."

A few days later Norman came to our house and asked Mummy and Daddy formally if they would allow me to do some shows with him as a cabaret act at two excellent Hotels over the holidays in Bournemouth. Mrs. Marsters came with Norman. She was a lovely motherly plump lady, much on the style of Mum, and in no time they and Mum and Dad were like old friends, and, wonder of wonders, I could go, and Norman could come and practice with me on our Steinway grand.

The galas were so pleasant, with such lovely intimate audiences. Because of Norman we were treated grandly – wonderful accommodation and food. After the "digs" in Glasgow it was like a trip on a magic carpet. These were the wine and champagne audiences – where the appreciation was from both sides. Shame such "gigs" are few and far between. I never saw Norman or Mrs. Marsters again, but only heard much later on "the Street" from other musicians that, owing to poor health and the changes going on in the popular music world, he had left the country.

CHAPTER 31

"Keep It Under Your Hat" – Paris

Today, with Bank automats everywhere and credit/debit cards as a way of life, I think none of us can comprehend the hardships that faced most Europeans after the war years.

Here we were happily landed in Paris at Dad's favourite hotel, Hotel de Paris, sitting in the reception hall and it was Sunday – late afternoon. There were no "change kiosks" at that time. Money to travel – like clothing and some other commodities – was rationed, and even at the hotel the banking arrangements were closed, and Dad could not change his Travellers cheques absolutely anywhere.

We sat there like 3 frozen peas and Dad, who was by this time hard of hearing, complained loudly in no uncertain manner of his misfortune: "Here I am rushing you girls (meaning Mum and me) off to Paris to catch the "Folies Bergères" show on a Sunday when in London everywhere is dead, and now we can't go, because even this big Hotel cannot change my Travellers Cheques and give me some French Francs on a Sunday."

He was really down! With my latest, rather successful last few months of my singing career, Dad had initiated me once more to the fold. I was not quite sure if it was his love for me or of my "Child's under 16" portion of Travellers cheques, or my courage in going through the English customs with the things he was afraid to go through with himself.

His complaints were so loud that Mum had to say "Shush, shush."

Suddenly a middle-aged man with a ruddy complexion and round face rose from a nearby seat opposite us and smilingly came over to Dad

"How many Francs do you want?" Just like Billy Swan, he said "I can help."

Dad was dumbfounded and regarded the generous dapper little Londoner (because his accent to me was unmistakeable) as if he was an angel, who just came down from Heaven. When he came to words Dad stuttered a bit: "But, but you can't do that – you don't even know me." Dad still felt it was all too good to be true.

"Well," said the stranger, "one thing I do know is you are all from London – so am I. I live here now and if you can't help a neighbour then you are a bad man. How much do you want?" he asked, wasting no time, and drawing out a well filled leather wallet. "I overheard you have just flown in from London and you want to go to the Folies. Of course, you must name the amount and it's yours." Dad still felt at any moment he may awake from this beautiful dream. "My name is Harry Janes." Dad was a fan of the famous American trumpeter Harry James – so the name appealed to him almost as much as the money.

They fixed the amount Daddy thought to see us through till Monday at 10am when the change counter at the Hotel would open. Dad could hardly believe his good fortune as the money transferred from one pocket to the other.

Dad asked, "What can I give you in return?"

"Oh, that's alright," said the man, "all I want is to be able to take out your lovely daughter this evening."

Dad did not hesitate for a moment, and in true Oriental fashion he looked at me and said: "Pussyface, be a good girl and go with this nice gentleman."

I swear he would have sold me on the spot if he could have got enough money for me.

Fortunately, Mummy butted in and said, "We must arrange at what time and Café we will meet after the Folies and which show you have in mind to offer my daughter."

I said, "I'd like something French where the real French people go – to improve my lingo."

He suggested Luis Mariano in the Musical "Le Chanteur de Mexico." "The Theatre is not far from the Folies," he added

I felt a lot safer and bid farewell to my parents and started out on my first private adventure abroad – feeling slightly disturbed at Dad's quick readiness to "sell me," and at the same time extreme-ly adult with my middle-aged man of the world new companion. The show was a delight. Luis Mariano was excellent, and I un-derstood the French well. Just when I was settling down to en-joy the show without a care Harry took my hand in the dark – I thought amiably, but within seconds he put it on something warm and soft and held my hand there with his two hands.

It suddenly got harder, and I knew this was the "Girl Power" I had shown off about with my girl friends at the swimming pool when I was 13. As I could do nothing – I resigned myself to con-centrating on the show, making up my mind to quickly retrieve my hand when the interval must come, and the lights would go up all over the theatre – and they DID! Quick as a wink this "smart Alec" Harry slammed his Bowler hat on it and held my hand there in quite an iron grip.

"Hey ho!" I said to myself.

"Keep it under your hat" is a good English expression.

After the show all was – as if nothing had happened. We made a bee line for the Café where Mum and Dad were waiting, and I tried to stifle a deep deep sigh of relief when I saw them. So this Mr. Janes, whom my father now treated as a long lost soulmate, was actually a sort of wolf in sheep's clothing – but as I saw both my parents looking so happy and I had no idea at that time he would be offering a joint business proposition to my father, I decided to only praise Luis Mariano and to keep Harry Janes' actions as a secret "under my hat" – like the three wise monkeys.

CHAPTER 32

At the Albany Club

I now had a little money and before Christmas I took myself to our local Greggs School for an intensive course of shorthand typing and the rudiments of bookkeeping.

I chose Greggs, which was American, because it needed no lined note paper like Pitmans and I reckoned in an emergency – for sure – lined paper would not be available. Apart from that Roxie had taken Greggs Shorthand at School and could be if needed a help. Unfortunately, I signed on on the last day of November, and finding out I had a voice they got me to lead the Christmas carolling which I loved, and at the end of the course I could at the most only do 60 words a minute.

After the lovely Bournemouth engagements, I bought a second-hand typewriter, put an advert in our local paper, and did typing for various people, the most illustrious being the father of Leonard Salzedo, a new friend of my brother Theo. Leonard later became the conductor of the London Philharmonic. His father was a retired International Lawyer who only took on jobs he found satisfying. I learnt a lot about International Laws, but I noticed the old man wanted to learn more about my body, so I took on no more illustrious clients. I concentrated more on a good repertoire with the world-known Cyril Kaye, a famous popular "pianist," who had lost an arm in a car accident and was now giving lessons to Jazz singers to help his finances.

Rudy Rome was a tall, handsome man, who had all the best Sunday's gigs in town – a good businessman and in all the right circles. He had his band all week at the Albany Club, a smart nightspot where the cabaret changed weekly. I had done many functions with him on Sundays, and we got on very well together, as once again, apart from the pops, I was ideal for the dinners with my classical training. The audience loved the musicals like "Bless the Bride with the Greek/French Georges Guitary," and later, during dancing, the popular songs of the day.

One day out of the blue, Rudy Rome said, "Get a point number or two and you are in with your own act at our club. We'll fix the numbers together."

It was a terrific experience. Point numbers at that time meant risqué ditties with all the right movements. I went as often as I could to watch Dinah Kaye, a cousin of Cyril's, a famous nightclub act. She certainly knew how to "accentuate the positive," and how!

I chose "An Occasional Man" (which I seemed to have kept to ever since) and "There must be Something Better than Love," a Billie Holiday or Kate Smith number. I did my two Bournemouth parodies of Rose Murphy and Lena Horne, plus some pops of the day. I think I drove them wild with my rendering of "Granada." It was such an unusual repertoire that it shocked, and was 100% successful. I'm sure being so young was a great help too.

At that time the band and my self also did a big party for a certain lady. She was a sort of modern "La Traviata," a very high-class harlot. Rudy pointed to her and said, "That chick makes a fortune – you've got the looks, the talent and the sex appeal and youth on your side – play your cards right and that could be you in a year or two."

He started to get closer. I suddenly realized I was still a virgin, and somehow, I was afraid of sex, even though it seemed to be all around me. I thought of Mum and Dad, and then of George Scott Wood's advice and steered away. However, when I got home at night, I decided I must get rid of fear, which after all is born on the wings of the unknown. I do believe, going on 16 years of age, many of us feel the same.

CHAPTER 33

At Selbey's

Two things stand out in my memory of my successful weeks at Selbey's.

First the noise of musicians shooting, I thought at bottles, in the intervals – later I heard it was at the rats! Rats were very prevalent in London at that time, to such a degree that you could call the Rat Brigade, who would come down to your abode, garden, restaurant, hotel, etc. and rid you of the rodents in next to no time.

Incidentally about a year or so before that engagement, while playing the piano on a summer afternoon at home, with the French windows wide open, I had a feeling eyes were watching me. When I looked up, there were two black rats quietly standing on the white carpet listening to my music. I got up, and they ran out to their family, where about 5 more were playing on the lawn in the garden. I called the brigade and they got rid of the rats immediately. Incidentally I never saw these unprecedented visitors at my home thereafter, or at the most popular theatre restaurant in town at that time Selbeys.

Two: my last performance was on the Saturday night, and I had invited Mum and Dad, and they in their turn had invited many family members and friends. It was a huge success and the whole atmosphere was familiar and happy. I was the "floor show," as there was no stage but tables all around and mirrored pillars holding up the beautiful, decorated ceiling. As the crescendo came from the band to announce the end of my show, I stole a hurried glance at myself in one of the square mirrored pillars, and to my horror I saw my dress was no longer standing out proudly as a semi crinoline should. The petticoat, with a hoop that started just below my hips, was tied with a bow at my waist. It had somehow come undone and had dropped to the floor – fortunately still covered by the red satin skirt of my dress. For a moment my heart stood still – what should I do? Applause and then more applause, I reacted quickly to this "horror." I bent down as if to curtsy, picked up the hoop from the front, so it went up at the back, and backed my way from the still clapping crowd. I did not dare to turn for one moment. I quickly retied the bow behind the scenes in the kitchen, throwing the red satin skirt over it, and returned for an encore. Average audiences are wonderful; almost no one except Mum and Frances realized my dilemma. It's amazing what you can get away with if the crowd likes you.

Mr. Selbey was very happy and told me I could have a return engagement whenever I wished. But I was busy meeting new people and getting new offers, so I could not take advantage of his generous offer.

Jack Simpson, the famous xylophone player and best friend of the super famous from Television band leader Billy Cotton, had formed his own sextet and was offered really big money for a month's engagement at Greens Playhouse. His manager Bob offered me so much money to be the star vocalist I could not refuse. So, in no time, I was back in Glasgow, but not in the wintertime, thank Heavens.

CHAPTER 34

TV Calls

Billy Reid, who some years later composed the No. 1 Hit in the UK "There's a Tree in the Meadow," followed it up with the world hit "I'm Walking Behind You On Your Wedding Day," which had literally helped to make Dorothy Squires the most popular lady pop singer at that time in England. In her prime she married Roger Moore, a then-unknown handsome young actor. With the 007 films he became a household name too, after following Sean Connery. Billy introduced me to his manager brother George, who got me into the BBC TV shows, starting with "Opportunity Knocks." I did my own promotions in the biggest newspapers and magazines in London, stating I would be wearing a Jacques Fath model evening gown. The publicity worked great. Of course, I could not afford a real Fath model but our friend Netty made me a gorgeous sequined, beaded, tight-fitting affair – extremely sophisticated, and no one was any the wiser. I looked like a 20-year-old diva, which was just what I wanted to be. I had to pay up in instalments – but the effect is what counts.

Some years later I got "Starlight Time" and some other good spots in shows.

When you are 15 going on 16 and pretending to be 20, there are a lot of little life problems; one was smoking. This was "en vogue" – everyone who was anyone smoked. In films it was invariably the thing to do, to portray not just nervousness but that you were a real woman of the world – to be taken seriously. At a party for George and Billy some musician I recognised from Greens Playhouse came up to me offering a cigarette in a silver cigarette case with the words:

"Hey Yve – nice to see you here – cigarette – or are you still too young?"

That did it – I had to take one. He lit it up for me and I sat there alone trying to enjoy it and to look like I'd been smoking all my life. I was wrong – the damned smoke kept going in my eyes. Heaven knows why – and my mascara started to run. I tried to check it, then George came over and said, "My dear, what's happened? You look terrible – who gave you a black eye?"

I rushed to the ladies' room, took off all my make up and left by a side door as quickly as I could. From then on, I practised smoking in front of a mirror. Looking good and well composed is a "must" for show biz.

The second personal problem was I was not yet quite 16 and still a virgin – underage and not wanting to be – but no one wants to deflower a young girl from a good family. How much easier, I thought, for a poor little waif like Edith Piaf, who never had to hear constant remarks from agents, bosses and musicians like "Give it up – cabaret and stage life is not for a nice girl like you." But how does one not be a "nice girl?"

But I was sold – I wanted a "green nightclub tan," as that pale never seeing sunlight look was called. I wanted to be a woman of the world like Rita Hayworth and to sing like Dinah Shore or Doris Day. To put it plainly, I had ambition, and I wanted to conquer the world!

CHAPTER 35

Who Wants To Feel Like A Virgin – Madonna?

Both my sisters, considerably older than myself, were virgins when they were married. I think they both thought being married was some sort of achievement. They could finally leave the home nest and make their own decisions – sometimes – knowing full well they have a husband who would protect them, a sort of shelter in the hard world outside.

However, I had no desire whatsoever to marry, and I did not regard my singing engagements as a sort of fill in until I should marry some nice middle-class lad from a nice middle-class area and settle down to a nice middle-class life in a nice middle-class home.

As long as something is unknown, we are a little afraid. I wanted, like Marco Polo, to be a world traveler, taste everything that life has to offer in this world, and conquer every audience with my voice and charm, both of which I considered to be gifts from God. If God has been so gracious to give me these gifts, then I must polish them and give them to this wonderful and interesting world in return.

I had read about first nights and the breaking of the little membrane, the hymen. I knew about the red blood on sheets hung outside on balconies in Sicily, the proof that a virgin has been broken in, so to speak. I knew I had to lose that "darned thing" to not be afraid of the unknown. I had spent two nights at a youth camp in Bogner Regis with my new ice-skating boyfriend Basil. Although I had rubbed him until he ejaculated into a large white handkerchief (at that time all young men had large white handkerchiefs), he knew my family and he would not have even dreamed of going all the way with me.

I waited and decided the most sensible thing to do would be to take an older person from out of town. So, it came to pass that four fellows were at our younger set's dance hall. They were from Brighton, a famous seaside resort not terribly far from London. It seemed in next to no time three older girls attached themselves to these young men, leaving one smaller one over who asked me to dance. I couldn't say I had anything in common with the three other girls. They were very sophisticated and well dressed and obviously knew the ropes of a "dirty weekend." I pretended I did too and took the opportunity, as my parents were on holiday in Bournemouth.

Sidney my partner was a small man with dark hair and about 26 years old. He had a car and we drove down to the resort with another couple. I regarded the whole thing more as a "Voyeuse" than as a direct player. We were signed in as Mr. and Mrs. And we four couples had dinner together and then left for the bar and then our rooms.

I had a couple of cognacs after an ice-cream sundae to get my courage going. I did what was expected of me and then, because I was curious, after some kisses and foreplay I started to count how many strokes he needed to have an orgasm. I didn't anticipate anything happening to me, which was all for the best because I was not a bit as excited as I had been some years before when Jack Winehouse had kissed me. I felt a slight rubbing motion, which did not turn me on, and after I had counted 12 pushes, I lost interest. Seeing a newspaper on a chair laying open near the bed, and having excellent eyesight, almost without thinking I started to read the newspaper til he had finished. Immediately after I jumped out of the bed and started washing myself furiously and then I dressed in seconds. I left the room and hotel and ran round the block hoping the French letter (condom) had no perforation and that I would not get pregnant. Anyway, I did not bleed. Perhaps I did not have a hymen to break at all. I had felt almost nothing, and I was shocked that this sexual love was all "hot air," and to put it straight – a huge disappointment. Men must be mad, I thought, to pay for such a stupid waste of time.

Whether I lost my "virginity" horse riding, doing acrobats, or running on Sports Day, I had no idea. Some years later I broached the subject with Mum, and she told me with no sports at all she had never bled either – so that was the end of my fear of my virginity. I realized I needed the right "You" to feel any enjoyment. Best of all, I surmised, I should be in love. A good lover with good feelings would be a huge asset – but, who?

It's very hard to sing about something you don't believe in!

CHAPTER 36

Prick Me Darlin'

When George Ried told me of my salary at Greens Playhouse, I'll admit I was very surprised. It was more than double the salary I had received with George Scott Wood's Accordion Orchestra, but, lowering his voice, he warned me that Jack Simpson had a sextet because apart from being very "in" at that time (he was noted for his superb Xylophone playing) he was also noted as a "wolf" and even as a sex maniac.

I had only one goal in my life and that was to be free and thoroughly independent. Mum had impressed upon me that having your own money was the only way to be really happy. Being so much older than me, I felt it a great asset to have a real Mum with lots of experience, and not, like many other girls, a young "chick" for a mother, who would even flirt with any boyfriend they brought home.

I needed, for my goal, to have money, so I agreed and went with George to see the Simpson Sextet Band Manager "long Bob." Boy, was he tall! When we went out, I would wear my highest heels and thickest platforms and still he would walk in the road, while I remained on the pavement, so we could at least converse. The band was very pop and lively, and when I saw the vocalist, Joan, I heaved a sigh of relief. She wore spectacles, had short, rather straight, middle blonde hair, and gave the impression of being a country housewife: nothing sexy about her or her evening dress. She looked to me like the epitome of "Plain Jane and no nonsense."

After my experience in Paris with that "generous" businessman, Harry Janes, and later in a hotel room in Brighton, I thought hard of the money I would get and grinned at the idea of knocking his present singer "into a cocked hat."

Second time round in Glasgow, this time in the summer, I felt a lot more at ease and even had a few young fans who recognised me from my winter engagement last year. Rehearsals went well. I was a lot more used to working with small bands, and Jack Simpson seemed pleased with me and amiable.

Then the first night came and Jack came into my dressing room all wired up and said, "Prick me darlin' I can never go on stage till I've come."

Of course, at school we knew all the right words used at that time, so I knew what he meant by "prick me darling," but before I could think further he put it into my hand and asked me down right to "wank him off."

I had no option but to oblige and was amused when the big white handkerchief came out. He was so relieved he gave me a big kiss on my forehead and told me he knew it would be great with me. I had such beautiful artistic hands.

I said, "Don't tell me you said those same words to Joan, because she really looked more like a suburban housewife, and I particularly noticed her hands – they were more like *a farmer's wife – big.*"

"That's it," said Jack, laughing. "It was fun, her hands were big but strong, stronger than her voice." He laughed again. "Bring on the changes," he cackled. "Don't worry darling, you are exactly the opposite – you're gorgeous." He kissed both my hands, saying "you made me feel great," then he left me wondering what sort of twisted minds some men seem to have.

From then on, the words "prick me darlin'" became a ritual before every show. It seemed he was jovial, but very nervous always before going on stage. Thereafter thoroughly relaxed and a winner, he did not need to sing the Rolling Stones number "I get no satisfaction," he surely got his! The Rolling Stones were not even heard of in those days.

My songs were simple, popular bouncy stuff like "I'm looking over a 4 leafed clover," then Jack would always point to me and blow me a kiss – which seemed to appeal to the dancers. I found the whole deal fun. I felt I could stand up to my father's dominant character much better – knowing older men were easy bait. I wondered how I would fare with the younger ones.

In those days, anyone with red hair like film star Rita Hayworth (later the wife of the infamous Ali Khan), or brunette like Ava Gardner (she became a film star by marrying Mickey Rooney, the Number 1 box office attraction at that time – later she married Frank Sinatra) were considered vamps, while the blondes like June Allyson or Doris Day were invariably the good girls.

I wanted to be a vamp and not a goody goody. I wanted to be seductive, but I was not yet 16, and still had a lot to learn.

CHAPTER 37

Dad and I Make a Deal

My Dad was a born workaholic. He loved being busy working on some project. Only with such qualities could he have had a flourishing business, a few cinemas (which were good business in those days before television was big) and still worked for various charities, trying to help others whom he felt had not been as lucky in life as him.

In 1949, when Israel became a recognized state, he was invited for a trip to the new state by their government. The invitation was extended to his wife and a few others who had devoted so much time raising money to help younger folk escape the gas chambers in Germany, Austria, and Holland etc. and get them safely to Israel, far from persecution. It had been no easy matter. That year he received various honours, so many that he had to ask the new government, under Ben Gurion, if he could postpone his visit. It was arranged that Mum and Dad could go a year later, also, when necessary, with guides in a set program. The invitation was mainly to see the country and be present at the Independence Day celebrations in Tel Aviv. A meeting with the King of Jordan was also arranged. Many English musicians had played for him, so I knew he liked music. I was madly interested.

Dad was a generous man with charities he deemed suitable, but a real skinflint with the family. Roxie, who now worked for him, told me he would never give her a rise, not to mention a Christmas bonus. Oddly enough, when she got married, Dad gave her a huge wedding with 500 dinner guests, plus the younger set, who were invited for the evening celebration. Dad loved to be thought of as special. Money was no object when it came to impressing others. He also had that old Oriental habit of giving a dowry for his daughters. It was normally a 50% down payment on their new house, something that would have been appreciated by any future son-in-law. I of course knew this, and that Frances had received her share. Roxie, who was now engaged to a young handsome suitor from a very good nearby family, would also get her share, enabling her and her spouse to live in their own home, and not in a rented apartment.

I went to Dad and made a deal! My mother and father were going as invitees of the new Israeli government to Israel, and later for a couple of days to Jordan. The King of Jordan, Hussein at that time, was married to a young English woman, and Dad had been a mediator between the two countries. King Hussein was a really nice guy and loved jazz – he was most musical, and to my mind sympathetic.

The deal with Dad was to keep my dowry money, and use it to pay for my part of the holiday to Jerusalem, Nazareth, the Wailing Wall and biblical wonders, and Tel-Aviv.

I would then be able to see the King and Queen of Jordan, and the wonderful excavations of the ancient city of Petra. Dad was at first adamant, but I cajoled him by saying I would take an intensive course of modern Hebrew, and a smattering of Arabic to see us through the two days there. Therefore, I would also be a help. Dad finally surrendered. Now here was I embarking on a new adventure, to two entirely different countries, on my list of "must be seen." Life was definitely exciting.

CHAPTER 38

Journey to Marseille

We three, Mum, Dad and I, flew to Paris, where we were met at La Gare des Invalides by Harry Janes, who behaved now like an old friend to my parents and a sort of uncle to me. He had already booked rooms at the Hotel and we just had time to have a light meal together. We all took mushroom omelets, because nobody makes an omelet quite like the French. Then Dad and Harry discussed business, mostly what Harry had in mind, while Mum and I went for a short walk. Then we said goodnight, as we had to take the early morning train to Marseille.

Harry motioned to me to stay a moment and, dropping his visiting card in my hand, he whispered "Whenever you want to come to Paris, be my guest. I've a flat conveniently placed near the Champs Elysees. I promise I'll behave." I smiled to myself, remembering well that theater evening when he kept "it" under his hat – not a Bowler, but a Trilby.

"You're good at keeping secrets, aren't you?" I said, grinning knowingly.

He added, "Keep in touch," gave me a peck on the cheek and headed for the door.

I looked at the card with the plan of throwing it in the Foyer bin, then I thought better of it and said to myself, "In life you never know, better to keep it."

I couldn't help thinking that during my 15 years on this planet an awful lot of unusual things had already happened to me.

Til now I invariably got a thrill just being in a big railway station with all the different signs and platforms, and people with suitcases hustling and bustling everywhere. However, an airport was for me so exciting I could hardly sleep the night before flying to Paris.

Marseille was completely different. There were ships galore, the bracing sea air, the pungent smell of fish mixed with exotic fruits, and other unusual cargoes. I firmly believe I was travel crazy. All the men looked to me like Fernandel, the famous French film actor, with his big moustache, and they too had that rich Southern accent when they spoke.

Dad broke into my reverie and shouted, "There it is – that's our ship, the Zim Line's *Negbah.*"

It was small compared to the P&O Liners Mum and Dad took when they went off to Madeira for their winter vacation, and the great ship continued on to South Africa. No matter; it was going to be our home for the next few days. Much of Dad's charity work had helped this happen.

"There will only be a few passengers, as the ship is rigged out to carry as many refugees who managed to escape the holocaust as possible," he explained.

Dad, as usual, seemed to know everything.

I shared a cabin with a very tall, blonde Dutch girl called Grit who was, like me, traveling with her parents. I never asked, but I guessed she was probably two or three years older than me. We chummed up almost immediately.

In no time I found out the refugees were all down in the hold; loads of them, mostly from Eastern and Central Europe – but all sorts and mainly young. Eating was never my great talent, so

I would skid down the back staircase and bring at least my dinner to them. They had food, of course, but what I regularly put
aside for them was most welcome. Dad didn't seem to notice,
but Mummy often gave me a fair portion of her evening meals
too, to take down to the hold. She said, "It is such a good feeling to help the needy."

CHAPTER 39

The Fortune Teller

The Refugees were mainly Jews or with Jewish ancestry, but also quite a sprinkling of Romani, as Hitler had planned to eliminate them, too.

One evening, on the second deck, there was a largish group sitting cross legged – listening to a real gypsy woman who was reading hands and telling fortunes. Full of curiosity, Grit and I joined them. She, being a tall girl, put herself more at the back and being small, I pushed myself more in front to get a better view of this dark, heavy-complexioned older woman. She was sitting on a chair in front, with her black shawl and her long golden earrings to match her long black hair tinged with grey. Various people went to her, stood up and asked her to read their fortunes. It was, for me, quite new and most interesting.

Suddenly she pointed to me, and in a low, husky voice she said, "Come here little lady, I want to read *your* hand."

I felt a bit embarrassed that she should choose me, who was not superstitious and never asked to have my hand read.

"Don't be shy – I know that you're a special one."

Being curious as a cat, I got up and put out both my hands for her to read. She scanned my hands carefully, only for some moments speaking of some wealth, and then she said in a loud voice:

"You will always have three men who want you.

"The first one will not want to dine without seeing your lovely countenance across the table. He needs your company.

"The second one will always want to converse with you and take you to operas, ballets and shows – he needs your free spirit company.

"The third one cannot sleep without you – he wants to have your body and have you for his lover till eternity."

There were whistles and a loud murmur from the crowd which by now drew older folk standing at the back. Suddenly I heard a familiar voice which shouted, "Come away child, this nonsense is not for you."

Mum fairly pushed me out holding my hand firmly. I was too stunned to resist.

"Fancy saying all that, with a booming voice, in front of all those people. It's disgusting for such a young girl as you to hear such things." She was really shocked.

"Mum, don't worry, you surely don't believe for a minute I'll pay attention to such fortune telling, I want a career and to travel the world – men don't matter! I for one am not superstitious."

Mum looked worried. She was very superstitious. I remembered how once I had put a brand new pair of shoes on the kitchen table for her to admire, and she had almost yelled at me:

"Take them off the table this minute – shoes on the table bring bad luck!"

She would never walk under a ladder.

The gypsy woman then stood up. She was tall and gaunt. She pointed a dark forefinger at me: "She will always have three men who want to love her."

Her voice was loud and ominous; it sounded almost like a sooth-sayer from Shakespeare's Julius Caesar saying "Beware the Ides of March."

It was the sort of prediction that, try as I may, I could not quite forget.

CHAPTER 40

I Meet My First Waterloo

Being a small ship in comparison to the Cruise ships of today, the officers and the very congenial Captain would dine at their table but not far from ours.

Two nights before our arrival, one officer played records on an old gramophone. Some danced and some officers eyed Grit and me, and suddenly one, who told me his name was Elly, asked me to dance. As we danced, he told me he had heard what the gypsy woman had said and he wanted to be my number three – my lover! I wanted to laugh – he wasn't my cup of tea at all! He was too young and too gauche, with frizzy ginger hair. Then Grit joined us on the floor, dancing with a very handsome young officer. He caught my eye and suggested we go to the officers' mess, as most other passengers, including Grit's parents and Mum and Dad, were saying goodnight.

Grit and I followed the two officers, and Elly hissed in my ear, "Tonight you will be with me."

I said "No way!"

The handsome dark-haired guy, who Elly told me was the radio officer, plied us girls with drinks. Then he turned to Elly and said, "It seems we both want the same girl. Let's play a game of craps and whoever wins gets her."

The guy with the thick dark hair and blue eyes said his name was Gad Ben Ari (English translation – "son of a lion"). I thought "Hm, that name suits him."

Then there was a shout – he had won. As Grit went towards Elly, he suddenly turned and said to me, "I lost, but this will give you something to remember me by," and without a moment of hesitation he grabbed me and became a vampire as he kissed my neck and gave me such a resounding love bite of a kiss that it really hurt.

I cried, "Ouch. I'll be marked for life!"

I was really horrified at this display of Levantine passion.

I looked at Grit peevishly, but she just smiled and shook her head. Maybe, being older and more experienced, she had experienced such a vampire's kiss in Holland. Suddenly I remembered sitting on a park bench on our common when Jack Winehouse bit my earlobe so violently, I screamed and shot up, asking him if he'd gone mad. He answered:

"I love you, that was my passion."

Slowly I began to conceive the male animal is in many ways quite different to the female.

Gad ben Ari saved the situation; he turned to me and said, "Come on "Habibi," let's get out of here." He put his arm round my shoulder, and it felt pleasant. "Come with me, I'll show you my cabin."

I wondered vaguely what else he wanted to show me. His cabin had one bed, a cupboard, and a washbasin – not a lot different to ours. The shower and toilets were outside on the corridor, which was quite normal at that time. At home my own parents had put in a washbasin in their bedroom, and we kids and our maid had gone to look at it, full of wonder at this new luxury.

Then it happened – something like a volcano erupting – this gorgeous piece of masculinity took me into his arms and kissed me so passionately that the vampire was completely forgotten and the whole world rocked. I had no idea how old he was, perhaps 24 or 25, but his whole approach was that of a young man with experience who wanted me passionately and wanted to make me happy. He undressed himself and me too, in next to no time. I felt as if I had drunk a whole bottle of wine. and somehow, I was suddenly catapulted into paradise. His kisses were wonderful and his body gleaming in the moonlight through the porthole was just beautiful. In a sort of misty haze, I thought, this is real love. After every session we got up and washed. I went first, and then him. Just looking at his muscular shoulders and back turned me on again. Then after 3 wonderful sessions, I slipped out of bed while he slept, dressed quickly, and crept back to the cabin I shared with Grit. She was sound asleep and so was I within minutes, but not before I said to myself, "Heavens above, I've fallen in love."

Next morning, I looked in the mirror and there on the side of my neck was this damned "love bite," a big red scar. Grit saw it too.

"Oh, that crazy Elly," she said. "Put on that small headscarf you have like a cowboy and it will cover it completely and your folks will not be any the wiser."

I did as she said, and with the shirt blouse it even looked quite "cool."

Going to breakfast I passed Elly, who looked at me and sneered, "I told you, you'll never forget me."

I looked at him as if he was the lowest scum on earth and sneered back, "If you had been a gentleman, you could have at least bought me a scarf," and stalked off in the opposite direction.

Living with deriding brothers and their friends you learn early how to deal with such male rubbish.

The last night with Gad was again unforgettable, we seemed so perfect for each other. It was his complete "savoir faire" that so impressed me.

I had told Gad I was 19, which I hoped I looked, but I reckoned since Jack Winehouse thought I was 17 when I was only 13, surely at 15 I could get away with being nearly 20. I told him the name of our hotel and he said he had a couple of days off and would come by to see me and perhaps meet my folks.

As Dad had quite a heavy schedule we had to say "Le Hitraot" (Au Revoir). He had to work on the ship, so I gave him my address and he promised to write, and I promised that somehow, I hoped to return to his land. I was so in love I really meant every word that was spoken.

As neither Grit nor I were intimate old friends, we did not speak of our conquests. The ship arrived and we joined our respective parents with our well packed suitcases. I knew even then that this first real ship journey to a brand new country, plus that brand new feeling of falling in love, would remain in my memory for ever.

CHAPTER 41

The Promised Land

As we disembarked some of the older refugee immigrants rushed off to kiss the ground they hoped to live on, peacefully. A great big flag with the words "Shalom – May peace be with you" greeted us, with the guides and the Israeli flag, the Star of David. The whole thing was an amazing sight, and it was surprisingly well organised.

Our guide whisked us off to our hotel in no time. That evening we dined in the hotel, and I was delighted to see that they had a trio. There was a very good-looking violinist, who doubled on alto saxophone, called Andree, a pianist called "old man Mo," short for Moses, and a drummer who seemed to be called Dov. Later I found out, he was originally called Bernhard or Berny. This, to Israeli official's ears, sounded like Baerli. Bear in Ivrit is Dov. Andree went round the tables playing special requests and I took the opportunity of fixing with the pianist, Mo, and Dov on drums my keys of a few old classics like "All of Me" and "Blue Moon" and even "Slow Boat to China." The other guests loved those songs and the boys in the band were delighted. Dov said immediately, "You must come back. There are no Jazz Singers here, and the Yemenite Singers like Yaffa Yarkoni don't sing in English and we want to attract tourism, you'd be a hit!"

While Mum and Dad were busy visiting big wigs like President Ben Gurion, I got busy asking Dov if he was serious and did he know of any decent agents. Here again I gave him my address, but then on second thoughts I said, "No, I don't want my dad to know. I'll write you to this hotel and I will see if I can get a postbox or something."

I had no idea of anything in that line, but I thought at least it sounded good. After all, sooner or later I wanted to become a woman of the world. At that time my ideal, apart from Judy Garland, was definitely Rita Hayworth – I think in the 40s and 50s most girls dreamed of being a film star. My peers were Marco Polo and Samuel Pepys. I admired both for their wander lust. I wanted to discover the beautiful world God had given us. My desire to travel and try everything was insatiable.

A day later we were taken to the desert, Negev, to see how with careful watering, crops could be grown there. We saw trees and trees, that had been planted with the money raised by people in the States and UK to bring a better climate to this new little country deep in the heart of desert lands. We stayed at night on a Kibbutz where, some years after her reign as first woman president, Golda Meir lived. We saw how melons, avocados and even papayas were being planted. We visited ruins and dig ups, and the remains of Solomon's Temple and the Wailing Wall. The fact that even well before the birth of Christ people of that era could carry such huge hewn stones and mount them so high, proved to me immediately that this must have been a clever civilization. They lived and worked and were able to do all that without the help of Edison's electricity and our machine age. It was truly incredible.

We also visited an older couple Mum knew vaguely through a French cousin, and we brought a large parcel of food and cosmetics that were certainly not available in Israel at that time. They were retired and lived in a small modern flat in Tel Aviv with a balcony and a sitting bench and a small table overlooking many more similar apartments. Most of the condos were alike; whitewashed walls, modern, on concrete block pillars so there were no basements or ground floors, the latter used as car parks. There was no room for private garages. Mrs. Lazarus told Mum if I ever wanted to return, I was welcome to sleep on that bench.

Mum said, "Thanks, but no, no."

I thought of all the nice-looking young men around (I guess I was somewhat "boy crazy"), plus the possibility of being the first modern singer in this country. It sounded like fun. I wrote down in my diary the old couple's name and address and put it together with that of Harry Janes in Paris.

The only thorn in the eye for Dad was when he asked to see the land he had contributed to – it was just a pile of stony ground well outside of Tel Aviv. Dad was no visionary for the future, and was absolutely disgusted.

We went to the Dead Sea where, because of the high salt content, even Mummy floated, although she could not swim a stroke. Then we went over the border to Jordan. There, especially arranged for our delegation, we met the King Hussein and his English Queen. Everyone in England knew that the King loved popular music of the day as did his wife. I sang for them "Heaven Bless This Happy Go Lucky Day," which made everyone happy, and we were on our way to the rose-colored ancient city of Petra. I am not very interested in ruins and excavations, as we had been shown many in Israel, but the excavations there and the color of the soil was exceptionally spectacular – unbelievable and well worth seeing.

We returned to Israel the day before the National Holiday of Independence. I preferred Israel because it was modern and over-flowing with young men from all over the whole world who had come to fight for this little country's independence. When Dad would take a photo of me, guys would cluster around me like bees on a honey pot. They were easily 10 to 1. It certainly was a young girl's paradise.

One professional photographer took a portrait photo of me wearing an off the shoulder blouse, similar to the one that had impressed Edmundo Ros. The wind blowing in my hair made me look almost defiant. Later it was used on a placard trying to get girls to enlist in the "Haganah" – the Israeli army.

From all these admirers I chose a nice-looking young Moroccan. The fact that he was French speaking was his number one appeal. While Mum and Dad went to the celebrations, we heard it all between looking at the crowds from my hotel room window. We spent the best part of the day and evening making love. After being awakened by Gad to the joys of lovemaking, I decided this sport was so much better than just joining all the throngs in the heat of the day celebrations. I also wanted to break the chains that seemed to bind me to a "dream lover" I may never see again. Somehow, his white uniform and the gold braids remained like an indelible photograph in my mind.

When I flew back directly to London with Mom and Dad, I contemplated on the plane what wonderful experiences I had had. Far better than a 50% down payment on a house when I should marry, but why should I want to marry and settle down when life could be so full of great adventures? "Formidable," I said to myself in French before I dropped off to sleep.

CHAPTER 42

S.O.S. P.O. Box

Both my parents kept diaries, Dad's was mainly about the food served, any VIP he met, and if a restaurant or hotel had a pretty blonde waitress whom he referred to as a "nice chippy." Mum's diary was mainly about the places visited, and the people. My diary forgot the food but remembered the men. As it had been such an unusual trip we had just undertaken, and the delegate with whom Dad was part of had met the first President of Israel and the King and Queen of Jordan, and even seen the ancient excavations of the wonder of the world Petra, Mum had invited the whole family to dinner.

We were by now a crowd, as the older ones brought their spouses. Ray came with Ros, Frances with George, Tod had married a pretty blonde, and Rox brought her young, handsome fiancée, Herman. Ray also brought Jack Singer, whose three sisters were making a name for themselves as the Green sisters, the British reply to the popular Andrew sisters. One of them was a close friend to Frances. Both Jack and his sister Jeannette were almost considered part of our clan. As I had no partner, I was allowed to invite my neighbor friend Susan. We were 14 in all, and how Mum managed to serve a three-course meal to 14 of us and still look good, with no maid (Maude had now left us), was, to un-domesticated me, nothing short of amazing.

We all sat round the long dining table and Dad began his story of our travels. When he stopped to eat his melon (he was always served first being the head of the family), Ray suddenly stood up and waved an envelope in the air and said, "No sooner than they arrive back in good old England and have the whole family gathering here to dinner, than a letter arrives already from Israel."

All eyes were turned toward Ray who tore open the envelope and took out the handwritten letter inside, with a flourish. He then read it out aloud to all and sundry.

"This letter is addressed to *the hottest thing on earth*."

Everyone gasped, including me.

"Who is this atomic bomb here?" he joked.

Then the letter seemed to go into such details of those two romantic nights in the radio officer's cabin that everyone knew to whom this letter was intended. I could feel my whole face and neck getting hotter as I blushed to the roots of my hair and wished with all my might I could fall through the floor, as all eyes were now turned on me.

Thank God for Mum. She stood up and said in her loud voice, specially kept for exceptional occasions, "That envelope was not addressed to you Raymond. You do not even live here anymore. Give that very personal letter to the rightful owner! In this house we do not read other people's correspondence!"

Mum, in her wonderful, protecting way, had stepped into the breach, to try to save the terrible embarrassment of hot, sticky and horrified little me. Mom took the letter from Ray and gave it to me. Before I could leave the room Dad got up, his face almost black with wrath, pointing a forefinger directly at me, and said:

"Your indecent behavior on that ship makes you not worthy of being my daughter. All of you around this table shall know that that little "squirt" is disinherited. You will not get a penny from me, not now or ever."

He almost spat out the words in his rage. I was so mortified I rushed out of the room into the toilet upstairs. The only place

where I could be alone and re-read that incriminating love letter – my first!

If I had gone into the bedroom I shared with Roxie, I'm quite
sure that she, dear soul that she was, would have come to comfort me. Right now I needed to be alone and have time to think.
Even only going on 16 I knew that problems come to us from
God, to make us use our brains and find adequate solutions. I
was really upset. Dad and I had got along so nicely during our
visit to the near East, and I loved and admired him, but the picture of his angry face was so fresh in my memory, that I felt as if
I was on the "Titanic" and the ship was sinking underneath me.
I did not care about any inheritance. I had seen so much of death
in the war years, so I wished my wonderful Mum and Dad could
live forever. It had been such a warm nest feeling being alone
with them on holiday in the Orient. It was the first time I felt
we were like three friends – except for the generation gap. Dad
had seemed so proud of me singing and making King Hussein
happy. I closed my eyes and tried to think.

"Oh God help me," I said to myself – and God did.

Now I remembered the words I had said to Dov the drummer
at our hotel in Tel Aviv, when he dreamed of making me the
youngest Jazz singing star in his country.

"Don't worry," I had said "I'll get a postbox, and then I'll give
you my address."

When I had unthinkingly given Gad Ben Ari my address at home,
I hadn't dreamed for a minute he would write. I was far too in
love to think clearly.

Monday was an important day. Dad went to his solicitor and
disinherited me. I went to a different post office, far from ours,
and took out a key to a post office box No. 260 for a Mr. Dick

Carter. The news of this new acquisition was sent to Dov for any theatrical agent he deemed suitable to help me. As an after thought I sent it also to Harry Janes, perhaps a night or two in Paris by the Champs Elysée could be interesting. My spirit of adventure returned.

CHAPTER 43

Highlights

Once again, my flat feet came down to earth with a bang, and I had to stand on them firmly and pull myself together. Fortunately, I had taken that intensive course at Greggs Business School and, in spite of my poor levels in shorthand typing, my knowledge of the French language helped me to get a most congenial part time job (only 5 mornings in the week) in a small office in the city, where the kind boss was a French man from the Savoie.

I needed Monday afternoons free to go down to Denmark Street to my dear friend Jack Moss at Southern Music and see if I could get a gig or two for the following week. Then afternoons I would practice often with a lady pianist who somehow believed in me, to get more of an interesting and commercial repertoire. I had to have enough money also to be able to see all the greatest singing stars at the London Palladium in the West End, like Eddie Fisher, Nat King Cole, and of course Frank Sinatra. Sometimes a gig would end late, but I found it a new experience to hitchhike a lift back home, and then walk to our house as dawn broke and daylight slowly descended on the still peaceful London suburbs. It was somehow a marvelous feeling. In spite of the lack of sleep, I tried never to be late for work, which I also thoroughly enjoyed. There was only one other girl working full time in the office and she loved to hear my adventures as a singer, which I told "con molto gusto!" Our boss liked me also, because I would always be happy to stay late if necessary. I knew how important that was in a small business from my own father, as Roxie had often explained to me. Then there was the boss's wife, who was a blonde Swedish model and at least a foot taller than him. She would often join us in our coffee break and was quite amusing with her stories from her life as a mannequin. She was not just much taller, but also considerably younger than our boss, and I had a feeling she could easily twist him round her little finger, leaving him often quite perplexed, and wondering why his wallet seemed to be that much lighter.

About this time the famous impresario Harold Davidson popped into to see Jack Moss and, as luck would have it, Mr. Davidson lived fairly near our home and offered me a lift in his car. We became good platonic friends. Harold was deep in an affair with the famous blonde jazz singer Marion Ryan. Later he managed to steer Marion's son Barry Ryan to the top of most world hit lists with his rendering of "Aloise," now considered a classic. Mr. Davidson heard me sing and brought me to the world-famous trombonist and Big Band Leader Ted Heath, who found my 4 octave voice and timbre plus my jazz feeling interesting and engaged me for his big concert – then called "One Night Stands". It was a fantastic experience to be able to rehearse and work with such great musicians as Saxophonist Don Lusher and drummer Jack Parnell (the first musician in the UK to get an Academy Award) who also gave me the honour of work with him when he had a gig with his own band.

At first the great Ted Heath orchestra blasted my ears, and I had to concentrate like mad to count the bars to know when to come into the second half of my songs. After the next sixteen bars, often in another key, I had to sing again, but in my key and to finish the song perfectly. Today it is made easy, but in that era complicated arrangements of music scores were in. A singer did not have to dance or swing her hips, but have good ears and a fine point of musicality. I was in my element, but all the personality and entertainment part of me was completely unused; I was a band singer, and part of the orchestra, and not an entertainer at all.

CHAPTER 44

The Dutch Entrepreneur

Then a most unusual person came into the show business scene in London, from Holland. At that time all big restaurants had a band, many with dinner dancing, but none with a cabaret show. That was only for the smaller, expensive nightclubs like the Albany, which often finished after 2 am. The Dutch entrepreneur Gerard Van der Meer intended to be the first to change all that.

He made Harold Davidson his manager for the shows and music side of his business and sat through many auditions. Unfortunately, he was so dissatisfied with the English talent he had seen and heard, he brought in a popular singer entertainer from Holland called Bobbie de Luxe. She did the openings of the three large restaurants he had bought in the West End of London: a Vienna Café, very popular in that era; a Belgian style brasserie, quite new for the British public; and a French Gourmet restaurant.

The Dutch singer belonged to the Van Houton dynasty and her salary, like her name, was a hundred percent de luxe. I went to see her do her three shows with Harold. She was bouncy and definitely good, a Betty Hutton or Liselotte Pulver type – but not a ballad singer at all. Good slow romantic ballads were most popular in the 50s to make a really good show. The challenge was on, I was now 16 and wanted to do much better.

Later, when I found out what a salary Bobbie de Luxe received and what a pittance in comparison I received for doing 3 shows nightly in his three different restaurants, I began to realize why Mr. Van der Meer liked me so much and gave me such a long contract. The Vienna Café was true to its name. I did Continental style songs, wearing short, flared-skirted floral dresses. The Belgium Brasserie was huge, and I stood nightly on a large wooden box so that everyone could see me. My pink bridesmaids' dress from Frances' wedding was perfect for Friday and Saturday nights, and the red taffeta skirt and the long tulle skirt Mom had made for me, worn with various tops, was just fine for the shows during the week. My show was popular and bright and went down well with the audiences. Finally, pure elegance at the French Gourment Restaurant, where my red satin ballgown, made and paid for with the Albany Club week's engagement, fit perfectly. Here I could do a more sophisticated repertoire, mingled with the very popular French songs like "Domino," "Le printemps chante en moi Dominique." It was the French era and Mademoiselle de Paris and musette waltzes were "the thing."

Doing three entirely different shows in three entirely different restaurants required big costume changes, apart from the music, lighting, and other requisites necessary to make those shows successful. I had to change in the taxi to get through the traffic jams and be on time for each restaurant. Fortunately, London cabs are large, and I kept the same one for the three shows nightly, six times a week. I was happy that I had worked so hard beforehand on a good big repertoire, so that I could master all these different shows with ease. Even changing in the taxicab in the busy London traffic amused me. I had to give in my notice at the office with some regret, but such a long engagement in London's West End was, for an aspiring young singer, a dream come true!

CHAPTER 45

Harold Drops a Bomb

Gerard Van de Meer had a cheerful and hospitable nature. His three restaurants were doing well and in next to no time he became friends with other gourmet restauranteurs. Sometimes, if Harold was not too busy, he would invite him with me to some special lunch. Because of the three shows I could not contemplate dinner at that time.

One day Harold and I were invited to the swankiest Italian restaurant in London town, because the boss had received a small consignment of Prosciutto di Parma. Neither Harold nor I had even heard of this delicacy. Gerard was a real Continental gourmet, and attacked his plate with no problem, but both Harold and I started to eat the asparagus which we both liked and with which we were well acquainted. I found the Ham tasty, but I had to really put my sharp teeth to work to get through this raw meat. I stole a quick glance at Harold to see how he was faring. Only a little better than me, but he was much older, and I wondered if he had false teeth – as I knew Dad, who had false teeth, could never bite tough meat, and that was why Mum's cooking was 90 % fish. Harold gave me a quick look of despair and I had to really smother a giggle in my napkin, which also served as a marvelous disposal bag for the super tough ham, as neither of us wanted to disappoint our host.

Once alone in Harold's car we both blurted out to each other our great wish not to offend our host but, at the same time, being unable to swallow the raw ham served. It seemed we both had the same idea and deposited the best part of the half chewed meat into our large table napkins. Then we both laughed, and somehow that unusually funny situation, both choosing the same way out, had brought us closer together. Suddenly Harold stopped laughing and said quite seriously:

"Do you know, I think Gerard has fallen for you in a big way? He keeps inviting us to lunches because he is, in spite of his big business acumen a bit timid and afraid to be with you alone. Yvonne, be a good girl and give him a bit – the poor man's mad over you."

I was so surprised I just gasped. "Huh?" I queried. "He is really very nice and I like him a lot he is so interesting, but he is an older man, more likely my Dad, and I had never given it a thought." My thoughts strayed quickly to Carlo Baretto, the Italian industrialist. True, we had danced, but even in the big limousine he had not tried to kiss me – just a quick peck on the cheek as I said "Goodnight!"

My first real sexual experience had been with that handsome young radio officer Gad Ben Ari. At home I was still very much regarded as the little "squirt," a teenage "Pussycat," so it had never dawned on me that a man of Dad's age could fall in love with me. True, Mr. Salzedo and even Rudy Rome seemed to have "wandering hands" – but that this international tycoon should fall in love with little me?! I could hardly believe it.

I was surprised, but under these questionable circumstances I said I'd do my best, after all I was now 16 – an adult, and I thanked my lucky stars I was no longer a virgin, so I was not afraid.

Gerard and I got on very well. He had a terrific sense of humour and found me "bright as a button" and hard as the nuts he wished to crack – and almost as brown.

I felt terribly grown up and important as he, the boss, would steer me through the crowds in the brasserie, or to our reserved table at the gourmet french restaurant. There was always a table reserved for us after my show there. I wasn't in love – that feeling was reserved for Gad, but heaven knew if I'd ever see him again. I was still under the illusion that falling in love was for the young. However, that sense of being respected and treated like a real diva was something no young girl could resist. I felt so terribly important, walking by Anouk (his nearly 6ft daughter, who was the chief of the Brasserie) arm in arm with her father. After all, she and her brother Alain (who was the head of the French Restaurant) were much older than me. Dad's "Pussyface" felt like the Cat's whiskers. It was a very happy time of growing up.

There was only "one fly in the ointment" – in spite of being "mad over me" (as Harold had put it) my salary had not been augmented! I wondered if all good businessmen were careful with money like Dad and Gerard seemed to be, or was I not playing my cards right? How about being like Charles Dickens, Oliver Twist and asking for more!

CHAPTER 46

The Waiting Game

In spite of such a heavy schedule, I still found time to give both Dov, the drummer in the Trio at our hotel in Tel Aviv, and Harry Janes in Paris my new name and P.O. Box Number. The latter answered promptly that he and his wife would be glad to have me anytime for a couple of days or more, and should be delighted to show me around if time allowed. The fact that he had mentioned his wife put my qualms at rest and I decided to accept his invitation should the opportunity arise.

Quite a long lapse went by till I heard from Dov, but what he wrote was absolutely positive. Apparently, he had found a very good agent, originally from Berlin – so according to Dov that meant very orderly! The agent was very interested, and I should immediately send good photos, which he felt could enable him to close a deal quickly, which should be beneficial to both parties. It sounded very business like, and I immediately wrote to Mr. and Mrs. Lazarus and asked if their offer of a bench on the balcony still held. Winter in England was slowly drawing on, and the idea to get away for some time from the fog and the slush, as my parents did in Madeira, definitely appealed to me. At the same time I sent 4 excellent Swarbrick Star Photos to a Mr. Hans Wollenstein, who was the agent Dov had recommended.

In those days there was no "quick fix" with all the technology to hand today – and I had just to be patient and wait.

As I was kept so busy, 6 long nights weekly, it left me very little time to even notice how long the mail could take to such a new little country as Israel.

Finally, the long-awaited contract arrived for a night club in Tel Aviv, and Mr. Wollenstein wrote he would be happy to pick me up at Lydda Airport and bring me to the club to meet the two bosses who had engaged me for a trial month, with the possibility of prolongation. He was also pleased that I had a place to live with friends of my parents, as dwellings were difficult to find this winter season. I must not forget to get a visa. My one-way Air Ticket would be reimbursed after my opening night. I had only to do one show, at most 2, but always at the same club so no necessity of hurriedly changing in a taxi. The money offered, although in Israeli pounds, was also very good, especially when I did not have to pay for my "digs", which could work out to be expensive.

Full of excitement, I rushed to the new Israeli Embassy to get my visa. To my disappointment I was told I had to be 18 years of age. I asked to see the Ambassador (or chief of the Visa department). Fortunately, he was young and very sympathetic. He looked me up and down and spoke to me for a while. I told him how I had longed to be 16 and therefore regarded as a fully fledged adult. How I had worked diligently and saved to buy my air ticket, and now he was going to dash all my hopes to the ground. Suddenly he laughed and said:

"Do you know, I have a funny feeling as small as you are, you are like cork from a bottle of champagne – no matter how stormy the sea of life may be, just like a cork you will come up again and float on top. I believe you'll make it."

And with that and a big grin he wrote my age as 18 and I got my visa. My reaction was so full of surprise and joy all mingled in one, I just threw my arms round his neck and kissed him firmly on the cheek and left the embassy in a state of euphoria. I had my contract, my ticket and now my visa. I felt like a dish at a take-away restaurant – ready to go!

CHAPTER 47

The Adventure Starts

The only ones who had an inkling of what I was planning were Roxie (my second mum. We were thrown together so often in almost everything and Mummy had given Roxie to understand she had to be responsible for me. We were both staunch supporters of each other, so I could trust her implicitly) and Gerard Van der Meer himself. During the evenings we had spent together I found out how he had started and realized he too had been an adventurist and, in many ways, we were soulmates. He understood why Dad had disinherited me and I think he felt that I had fallen in love with that Naval Officer Gad Ben Ari. Although he knew he would miss me, his business acumen was such that he knew it was time for a change of entertainment in his three restaurants. He, like Roxie, had said: "You go ahead and take a chance."

Roxie and I saw Mom and Dad off on the P.O. Lines ship at Southampton, on their way to Madeira. Only a few days after, Gerard Van der Meer saw me off on the first lap of my adventure, the plane to Paris. Overflowing with excitement I left London two days earlier than I had anticipated, as I was told by the travel agent I had the opportunity of a stop over in Paris on my way to Tel Aviv. As Harry Janes now seemed to be doing business with Dad and had written me that he and his wife would be pleased to show me a little more of Paris, I felt perfectly at ease and put the unsavory happening of his trilby hat covering his "privates" plus my unwilling hand right out of my mind. It would be an added experience – another feather in my cap, I told myself.

As planned, Harry was waiting for me once again at the Gare des Invalides, but this time I was alone with no parents. We took a cab to the Champs Elysée and a small side street where a block of flats, old-style with a concierge, greeted us. Harry unlocked the door and there it was, a tiny old-fashioned apartment – a tiny kitchen, a normal sized bathroom with a pretty floral plastic curtain for the hand shower, a wash basin, and a bidet extra where you had to put the water in yourself, with a jug underneath, enabling you to do this easily. The bedroom had lace curtains with dark floral drapes and a brass bed in true French style. It all appealed to my romantic mind. The living room boasted of a small wrought iron balcony but no flowers. These were in a vase on a round table with a lace centre piece. There was a sofa with over size cushions, and I said to myself "I presume I shall be sleeping here, as there was no guest room or office."

"Where is your wife?" I asked.

"Oh, she's working now, let's go and meet her," he said.

In no time we were at the small intimate hotel Adelphi, at the bar where Didi, his wife, had poured out a Scotch whisky for Harry and a Cinzano for me. She was blonde and pretty to my way of thinking, a typical Parisienne with a sparkle in her blue eyes, perhaps 35 years of age. I noticed she wore a couple of rings, but no wedding ring, and the way she and Harry flirted and teased each other, I was quite sure – this was his mistress, but not his wife. We left soon after this deduction and, as it was unusually sunny and pleasant, Harry took me to Le Jardin des Tuillieres and after to buy perfume at Galleries La Fayette. During this time he mentioned Didi had seen me and liked me very much, and was quite excited over my young, pert little breasts. I, who had awaited a nice plump middle aged lady befitting to Harry Janes, who had told me today was his 50th birthday, expected a real wife in my idealistic world. I'll admit I had qualms about what lay ahead. I had read about "les ménages a trois," but as adventurous as I was, still I had no intention of being part of those three. We had a light lunch and then picked up Didi and drove to "a real Parisian restaurant" as Harry had said. It certainly was different, and I wondered what Mom and Dad would say about it. There were long tables with red check cloths and all laid and ready. As the wine came, so came plates with a large bread roll perfectly made in the shape of a penis, complete with its fireman's helmet and of course the balls in a bag. I had never seen anything like it in my life and never have done since! The walls of the restaurant were plain, but one side, where all eyes were focused, was lit up and had lots of green shutters and little flowerpots as if it was full of windows.

I asked Harry and Didi if it had a meaning. They looked at each other and grinned saying, "Wait and see."

I think the food served was very special, each course had a different sauce, but I had no idea of what I was eating as the red wine was really good. It was similar to Chateau Neuf du Pape. I did not sample my bread roll as I was determined to get some lacquer the following day so I could retain it as a souvenir of this most unusual restaurant in Paris.

Lots of jolly French people poured in and in no time, there was no empty chair. I'm sure I was the only foreigner there. Then lights went out and somebody shouted out "La voici le dessert." The shutters flew open and in each window was some sort of doll or puppet with one or both breasts hanging out and behind faces of old bearded men with big grins and bright eyes. This moment was obviously what most clients had been waiting for, and there were shouts of "ooohs" from the public. The lights went on, the shutters remained open, and people carried on drinking and eating as before.

By this time, I had seen so much and ate and drunk too much I was quite befuzzled.

All my good intentions of sleeping on the couch disappeared as Harry picked me up and laid me gently in the middle of the brass bed and Didi undressed me, almost like a mother, probably to put me at ease. I just giggled and suddenly we were 3 nude bodies. I can't remember anything clearly except Didi's body was so sweet and soft I could understand why men seemed to need the female body so much. She felt lovely as she kissed and licked me all over. This, I thought through the fog was the high school of French love making.

Then I heard Harry's voice as if from another planet. He said, "Now I am going to have my 50th birthday present."

And that was me – but I was so tipsy I only knew it was all ok and I fell asleep directly after.

The next morning my period arrived, probably from shock, but for the first time I was happy to get it and greeted it like an old friend. That night had been something special, but I felt a terrific sense of relief to be able to sleep alone on the couch the second night before leaving for Tel Aviv.

At breakfast we ate petit fours and drank strong French black coffee and laughed a lot. Harry bought me more perfume and lacquer for my special souvenir bread roll. Everything went so quickly, it seemed in no time I was on the plane bound for Israel. I had never felt so free in all my life. No parents to caution me, no brothers to cheer and jeer; somehow the feeling of liberty was marvelous. I had my visa and the contract tucked firmly in my handbag by the bread roll. The contract was for a very good salary, and I would be able to pay my return ticket after they had reimbursed my one-way ticket, which I had purchased myself; otherwise I had almost no money with me at all. After all, I was going to make money – not to spend it! I was oblivious to all. Liberty and Freedom were implanted in my mind.

Little did I know, sitting snugly in the P.O. Box 260 marked Dick Carter was a telegram, terse and to the point:

CLUB CLOSED. CONTRACT CANCELLED. DON'T COME.
Hans Wollenstein.

(wann Unwissenheit bringt Glückseligkeit wäre es Torheit wei-
se zu sein)

Sometimes the old English proverb "Where ignorance is bliss,
'tis folly to be wise" comes true!

Hans Wollenstein sat in his self-made cubicle sized office which
adjoined the living room, as it was originally planned to be part
of that area. He pondered, there had been no reaction to his telegram, and then he made a quick decision. He had a friend who
was on the ground staff at Lydda Airport. He decided to go to see
his old comrade and just hope that the little girl from the other
part of the world would not arrive. In any case she had friends in
Tel Aviv who had offered her a bench on their balcony, so that
that difficult part would be taken care of. He then decided to
alert Nickita Norovski and Rudi Kaufman that there was a possibility that the girl did not receive his cable and could – heaven
forbid! – arrive. No, he must act quickly and go to the airport.

CHAPTER 48

Arriving in the Promised Land

The plane started to touch down and the loudspeakers came on and announced that we would be landing. I awoke full of joy in anticipation of being a success and perhaps, with luck, meeting that big romance Radio Officer Gad Ben Ari again.

Hans Wollenstein was there, just as I had hoped – a slim middle-aged man, in his 40s perhaps, looking very trim in his white short sleeved shirt with two small breast pockets and small lapels on the shoulders. He wore khaki shorts and knee length white socks (something I had expected more in Africa) and brown sandals. It was February, but very warm. He looked as Dov had written, typically German and orderly, except he had dark hair. He filled me in on the contents of his cable quickly. Before he could finish his little speech, I butted in with my usual spontaneity:

"Well, I have no money because I am determined to work and be a success. Let me meet these two bickering partners."

Triumphantly, HW smiled: "That is just what I have arranged," he said. "Now, I will bring you to Mr. and Mrs. Lazarus the friends of your Mum & Dad, and I will pick you up tomorrow morning at 10.15 am and we will meet at least Mr. Norovski – he was the one who showed the most interest in you."

My heart, which had almost sunk in horror, now settled down to normality and Mr. and Mrs. Lazarus greeted me so warmly that I felt calm, and I started to breathe evenly and to enjoy Tel Aviv in a February "Chamsin," which is the Hebrew word for the hot spells of desert wind which generally made most people uncomfortable. After the cold damp winter weather in London and Paris, this desert wind felt good to me.

It was arranged we would meet the two partners the following day at Genati Yam – a large open-air restaurant on the main road by the sea. We walked there and, even at 10.15 in the morning, most tables were taken primarily by men drinking coffee and seemingly thoroughly engrossed in deep conversation, some jotting down notes on notepads. Mr. Wollenstein explained to me in Tel Aviv there was a terrible dearth of office space and housing generally, therefore many people, including ourselves, did their business there – decidedly better than in a bed-sitting room far away from the sea and the pleasant aroma of fresh coffee brewing.

Shortly after 10.30 am Mr. Norovski arrived. He was a man of middling height, perhaps 40 years old, with thinning blond hair and a slim build. He wore a very modern dark beige gabardine suit, which was all the rage in England at that time. His light blue shirt, open at the neck, matched almost perfectly with his somehow piercing deep blue eyes. When he saw me, his thin lips parted in one of the most engaging smiles I had ever seen. He was a Ukrainian and his voice was a deep rich baritone with that slightly Russian accent when speaking English – which I could not help but find very attractive. He greeted us with "Shalom," and then, "So this little lady should have been our star."

He took my hand, squeezed it and kissed it lightly, and then looked at me straight in my eyes as if he could see right through me and muttered "charming, charming" and sat down next to Mr. Wollenstein. However, although he immediately went into a deep discussion with Mr. HW in Hebrew he never seemed for a minute to take his eyes off my face.

Then a heavy dark gentlemen arrived, with a double chin, a thick moustache, and large belly to match. He was of heavy build and for me totally unsympathetic. HW introduced me formally to

both men, but as the fat gentleman Mr. Kaufmann had obviously been paid off from his part in the Tel Aviv night club, he said
with a very heavy accent he had nothing more to do with the
club and only wished to have a quick look at me to see if I was
as young and pretty as the photos they had received. Without
joining us for a coffee he left, and I never saw him ever again –
thank heavens!

Mr. Norovski was undoubtedly a ladies' man; his smile was absolutely disarming and his soft voice talking English was like a
caress. I was immediately on my guard and left the talking to my
manager. They spoke in Hebrew quickly and even though I could
read slowly I did not understand one word. Finally, Wollenstein
turned to me and said, "You are in Lucks way – Mr. Norovski
likes you and believes you could be a big success here, so he will
look for a suitable venue where you should be a star."

Mr. Norovski broke in, saying, "Mr. Wollenstein has explained
to me your situation. I will make a new luxury club for you – little princess," and he took both my hands and kissed them again
and bid us both farewell, but not before he took out some Israeli
pounds and said: "Just to tide you over."

HW turned to me after Norovski has gone and said, "Mr. Norovski
is apparently from some famous high-class family. He is said to be
a smart businessman – but all this super courteous charm makes
me just a little uneasy."

"Well, at least he seems to be on our side," I said, trying to speak
practically.

Truthfully, the boyish smile, the deep foreign voice and the very
up-to-date suit had impressed me immensely and at 16 one is
easily impressed by charm.

CHAPTER 49

Dov is a Real Pal

Of course, I was longing to meet Dov and perhaps being in the arms again with Gad. It didn't take long and suddenly Dov was standing there at our table. He joined us for another coffee and something I had never seen before; "falafel," a sort of pancake filled with little meat balls in a spicy oriental sauce. He seemed to have great faith in Mr. Norovski and his smart business acumen. Apparently, the same trio I had sung with at the Hotel Yarkon when there last year with Mum and Dad, had been playing at Norovski's luxury night club in Tel Aviv, which had gone well, but the two bosses were so different that it was doomed to bring trouble.

"Good that Kaufmann has gone," he said. "By the way, Norovski fell in love with your photo and every night he put a red rose by it on a table and said: "This little singing girl is for me like a Madonna. Look at her sweet innocent face." I am quite sure he will come up with something interesting – perhaps in Tiberias, it is in the Galilee on a large lake. Here it is the big tourist attraction."

I had visions of Bournemouth and crossed my fingers.

Dov was right Mr. Norovski wasted not one moment. He took over a bar and had it renovated into a luxury night club in next to no time and Dov's nice trio and myself had a contract there for the season.

Tiberias was new ground for me, but the fact that Dov was going to be there with his wife and the kind and handsome violinist André and the pianist old Moses made me feel comfortable. I also had to write to Mum and Dad to let them know that all was well and I was going to be a star at a super luxury club, earning a good salary at the best tourist place in Israel, Tiberias on the lake of Genezareth.

I wrote how nice Mr. and Mr. Lazarus have been to me. How wonderful it was to be able to fall asleep under the stars on their balcony, and how unusual it was to awaken to the fresh new mornings and to the sound of dozens of housewives beating their carpets and rugs. Obviously, vacuum cleaners seemed to be unheard of in this part of the world. Mum wrote back to me immediately that whatever I do, not to eat anything that flies had touched – typically Mum!

I replied: "I am sitting on a street café enjoying a coffee and a Danish almond paste bun. It is a fight between me and the flies who eats it quicker. Don't worry Mum, I always was a fighter – I'm winning!"

CHAPTER 50

Tiberias on Lake Genezareth

I arrived in Tiberias with Dov and his wife Rivka by "Cheroot" – this is a multiple Taxi. All people traveling in the same direction can get into the cab and the driver squeezes in as many as he can. During the drive he takes the fares, which can be passed from person to person until the taxi diver gets his share. Cheroots are a normal way of getting about not just in Israel, but in most countries in the Levante. When we arrived at our destination, I saw to my horror that the main road and all those surrounding were open roads – no asphalt, just stones. My London outfit, a turquoise wool suit with a tight-fitting skirt ending just below the knee, looked well in the city but felt extremely uncomfortable in the hot climate of this – to my mind – primitive resort. Worst of all, my grey suede ankle-strapped shoes had platforms and a super high heel (I had refused to wear flat heels ever since puberty when I stopped growing). I wanted to be a diva – a real woman, and a cigarette holder and high heels were in my opinion part of the deal. The joy of being youthful never once entered my head. Unfortunately, the roads (what there were of them) were certainly not made for stiletto heels. Just to get to my digs became a torture, and Dov seeing my problems said:

"Don't worry, tomorrow we will get you a pair of the Tiberian sandals."

We had to rehearse and do a show that night, so I had very little time to get stock of my surroundings – everything was rude and simple. The lady who lived where the room was allocated to me was fat and wore, to my mind, a terribly artificial looking wig. I had no idea why.

Apart from the good old classic jazz numbers, I didn't really know what the Israeli audiences expected of me. Fortunately, Israel had captured the romantic side of the broad public of our Western world. Many young men of all nations and creeds had felt the call to help the poor little country against the huge Arab hordes and the so-called justice of the U.K. It was a call to help David against Goliath and they had won.

Leo Fuld had captured the hit lists with his heart-rending ballad of the refugees, "Tell me where can I go?" I had learnt this especially, also some gypsy classics like the Russian "Black Eyes," a well worn favorite, and the Hungarian Hora (which the Israelis took over as their national dance) Hava Nagila, which was becoming very popular everywhere.

Mr. Norovski was there already when I finally made it, picking my way over the stony open roads. The house where I was to live was thankfully just two blocks away from the club. He immediately smiled when he saw me arrive with Dov. He proffered me a drink at the elegant bar. It looked like mentholated spirit — a deep lilac color.

"It is called "Parfait d'amour," he murmured with his deep soft voice, "a liqueur especially for you."

I sipped at it obligingly — it was sweet, a little perfumed, and quite pleasant. From then on, whenever I arrived, I was greeted with a big smile and a small "Parfait d'amour."

It was a Thursday and the public had only a smattering of English and American tourists. I opened the show with the jazz classic "On The Sunny Side Of The Street." When I got to the line "Just direct your feet to the sunny side of the street," I shouted out, together with the boys, "Tiberias!" By the second verse I made the audience shout out "Tiberias" too. It was a good idea and a rip-roaring success. From then on whatever I did was greeted with cheers and I thought happily – the Israelis know what's good, they liked me.

They were not the only ones who liked me – the mosquitoes at night going back to my room literally dive bombed me – they loved me!

The next day Dov, Rivka and I bought sandals and a cream which we were told held the mosquitoes at bay – but apparently those darned insects had never read this, as they seemed to enjoy attacking me anyway.

The second night a nice grey-haired man approached me and asked me to come to his table. He then gave me his card and introduced himself formally. He was the boss of the biggest (and I do believe the only) music publishing company in the country. He congratulated me on my lovely voice and brought out from a brown leather briefcase a sheet of music with my photo on the cover. It was entitled "Shuva Elai". He explained to me that Tangos were "in" in Israel, and the title meant "Return to me". I asked him how he managed to have my photo on the cover.

"Oh," he said, "Mr. Norovski gave this to me and asked me to choose a song befitting to the photo for your debut here."

I must admit, I was really surprised. It seemed to me the boss of this club was really on the ball.

My contract included the evening meal, which I had taken with the three musicians. On the Friday Mr. Norovski asked me to his table, which was situated overlooking the lake. It could have been quite romantic if there were not so many insects. Apart from mosquitoes there were huge flying cockroaches – I had never seen them in my life before – and just as the boss started to talk to me about my repertoire (he loved the classic jazz numbers, but for his public he needed more gypsy songs, some of which he was quite prepared to get for me), suddenly he stopped and bent over the table, flicking a large cockroach which had landed in my very bushy hair.

Going home he gave me a small torch, which was all for the best as my digs were in complete darkness; I had no idea why. I managed to open the front door with the key given me – it was Friday night and the boys had to play til 1 am or later. What I saw quite shocked me; laying on a large rug on the floor were five tiny kiddies, sleeping, and all around them were those large cockroaches. I rushed into my room, and one was on my bed, so I killed it with my Tiberias sandal. I decided there and then I must get out of this place. Feeling very tired and still half dressed I dropped off to sleep.

Early next day I told Dov of my plight and in no time Mr. Novroski was alerted and – true to his name "quick Nick," as I had heard some people call him – he managed to get me into a hotel room just a little further from the club.

CHAPTER 51

My Very First Tragedy

Suddenly there was an unexpected knock at the door of my tiny single bedroom at the small new hotel. My room could only be described as diminutive, but the big attraction was I had not seen one cockroach, let alone those huge ones that can fly. The good thing was it was in walking distance to the club and coming home at night, there were no problems.

I opened the door thinking perhaps it was a maid, and there standing on the threshold was the very reason why I had tried so hard to return to Israel – for my dream man – Gad ben Ari! I couldn't believe my very eyes, as after that amazing love letter addressed to "the hottest thing on earth," to which I had replied in no uncertain manner and sent it to the SS Negbah, I had had no answer. So much had happened in between, it seemed like in another era. He didn't look quite as glamorous as in his officer's uniform with the gold epaulets on the shoulders, and even gold braid on his short-sleeved officer's shirt. However, the simple white short-sleeved shirt, opened at the neck, could not mask the muscular arms, nor the navy shorts the muscular legs. Suddenly I saw once again the tanned broad shouldered slim back, as he had washed after our second session in his cabin on that fateful night. I felt myself falling in love again with a yearning to feel those tanned muscles close to me and his arms encircling me, but curiosity prevailed.

"Where have you been? Why did you not answer my letter to your ship? How did you know I was here?"

The questions gushed out from my mouth like a waterfall rushing down to the mountain side.

Before I got an answer, he took me into his arms with a resounding lover's kiss and then whispered, "I have been waiting for this moment so long."

I could feel myself flying to the moon, and in my fantasy I could see myself proudly introducing him (in his officer's uniform of course) to my Mum and Dad, saying, "This is Gad, my fiancé. We are engaged to be married."

We sat on my narrow single bed, because there was nowhere else to sit, and he told me how he had seen my picture in a newspaper and a very good review of my songs at the club. He couldn't believe his eyes and couldn't wait till he got a week's leave to make his way to hold me once again in his arms.

I was blissfully delighted and could hardly believe that this very moment was not a dream but was true. "But, but why – if you received my letter and knew what an awful predicament you had let me into – did you not reply?"

For a moment the carefree devilish smile left his lips, and his roguish tanned face became grave. His voice seemed to become an octave lower, and I felt him take a deep breath as he said, "Well, you know I am 27 years old, and most men at 27 are already married and I am no exception. But I have a week's leave and we can have a week together making love."

I was dazed. "But if you are on leave, surely you want to spend your time with your wife?" I questioned, noticing how my voice faltered, as my daydreams came crashing to the floor.

"Oh, that's no problem," answered Gad, having fully regained his composure. "I made sure I'd get my wife pregnant and now she is well on the way to being totally busy with the forthcoming baby, so we have plenty of time for us."

I was 16, from a good middle-class family, and Jack Simpson and Gerard van der Meer were both older men – much older, and also in show business. I had never given a thought to either if they had a wife or not. I had fantasized that this young man was from a similarly good middle-class family with ideas like my own. In our circle adultery and divorce were shocking, particularly if you were not in show business.

The fact that Gad had got his wife pregnant so he could carry on having a good time shocked me to the marrow – I was absolutely distraught. Taking a deep breath, I pulled myself up to my biggest height in an effort to regain my composure, and almost spat out my reply.

"Get out – how horrible can a man be to leave his wife at such a time? I never want to see you again." All my feelings had turned to stone.

Gad's face blanched, and without a word he stood up, turned on his heel and disappeared out of my life forever.

Had this tragic episode in my life happened a decade or so later, and I had seen the much talked about world famous film "Doctor Zhivago," where the hero, played by the handsome Egyptian film actor Omar Sharif, falls in love and has a passionate affair with a young librarian, alias Julie Christie, while his own wife is highly pregnant with his child I may have felt differently; but we were not in a civil war and I had not yet read Boris Pasternak's romance. I was still imbued with a lot of deep, almost religious principles and ideals.

I closed the door and walked over to the mirror on the wall, put there to make the little room look larger.

"What a fool you are," I said to myself. "You have come all this way planning and hoping – not just to see if you could be a star in another country, but to meet your dream man again again, and you did. He even came to you, but his character was as bad as that of the other devil-may-care smile in your life — when still at school — Joe Davidson! Why do girls fall in love with sort of guy? Because they are fools — fools rush in where wise girls never go — it is time to get wise."

Once again, I decided to throw myself into my work, and I tried hard to learn the new songs I had been given by Mr. Norovski — also known as "quick Nick."

CHAPTER 52

Rivka to the Rescue

My boss Nick Norovski was not always at the club, but when he was, he would invite me to sup with him, mainly on the excellent fish from Lake Genezareth.

Tonight was Wednesday, our quietest night normally. The tourists who had come for a long weekend had left yesterday and the new ones were due to arrive earliest on Thursday.

It was hot and damp, and in spite of the heat I could feel shivers running down my spine. I declined the Parfait d' Amour offered me and I had almost no appetite to eat, but when Mr. Norovski had time, I would enjoy listening to his stories of his childhood in Odessa in the Ukraine, the tales of the big house and his mother's soup kitchens in the great hall for the poor. I never really did find out how he came to Israel or Palestine, as it was called at that time. Somehow or other it seemed he was first in Romania, as the Russian civil war turned him and his family, who were wealthy, into fleeing refugees. I would listen to all these stories often spellbound. History lessons in the UK were so full of the British past, that I hardly had an idea where Odessa was, not to mention Bukarest in Romania; this is really a very sad truth.

I managed to get through my songs for my first show to a very thin audience. Then the boss came over to me and said, "Child, you look poorly, go home to bed – I think we'll close early tonight – it so quiet it's hardly worth staying open."

I started for my hotel room, but my ankle was so swollen from some super large mosquito bites, I could hardly walk on the rough road ahead. To add to this, in spite of the heat, I felt freezing and shivery, although I normally never perspire, I could feel my head and body breaking out in a cold sweat. I tried very hard to concentrate on my steps and not to faint. Suddenly I fell backward and my whole world turned black, but not before I heard Dov's voice shouting, seemingly miles away in the background:

"Look out she's falling – grab her André!"

I heard no more.

When I finally came to – I had no idea where I was till I saw Rivka, Dov's wife, with a cloth mopping my brow and face with cold water. She offered me some water to drink, and finally I returned into the world and heard her voice and realised I was on her couch, not in my hotel bed or in London or somewhere else. She explained to me in kind almost motherly tones – that Mr. Norovski was worried about my health and had left old Moses to carry on tinkling the piano, and asked Dov and André to try to follow me as I looked so ill – not at all my usual cheerful self. He had a feeling it could be malaria. They had just caught up with me when I suddenly swayed and fell backwards almost into Dov and André's arms. They had brought me to Dov's apartment, where his wife Rivka had cared for me, as it seemed I had a bad spell of malaria. The next morning the only known doctor had been called in to diagnose and give the only injection of quinine he had to counteract the disease. I had been more or less unconscious for two days, and there was no hospital in Tiberias at that time. Rivka had pulled me through, and I stayed in her good care until I was strong enough to resume my show at the club. Dov, and above all, Rivka, had come to my rescue.

CHAPTER 53

Birds of Prey

I was absolutely determined to do my best in spite of my weak disposition. I managed a few half-hearted shows but slowly regained my strength. Then one day, Mr. Norovski, who was very concerned over the well being of his "little star" who had been so good for business, particularly after her appearance on "Kol Israel" (The Voice of Israel – the BBC of this little land), turned to me and said, "Little star, I don't like it, you are turning completely yellow. We must get you to the only specialist I know who possesses some real medicine. We must get you completely better. The drive is over some very barren hills and desert, but he has a small clinic, and he is very clever. You can lay in the back of my car. Don't worry, I know the area well."

Once again, the specialist was of German or Austrian origin. With this doctor's clinic, medicine, and nurses, plus Nick Norovski's caring and ever interesting stories, I finally improved and was strong enough for the journey back to Tiberias. But then good news prevailed. In all this time I had been at the clinic, quick Nick had been busy. The season in Tiberias was coming to a close, and without me as the big attraction business had deteriorated – so he had decided in spite of the romantic setting and candlelight dinners beside the Lake – that business and I would be better in Tel Aviv. I breathed a sigh of relief, as the big town was for me like coming back into civilisation. He had taken over the right spot near the seashore. The Trio I now regarded as my dear friends were once again booked to accompany me. I was happy.

We started off in his car for the journey back to Tel Aviv over the rough roads – the sky was ever as it was in the 1950s, stark blue. This was well before the thousands of newly planted trees changed the climate, which I discovered when I finally returned to Israel some twenty years later to sing again. When we got to the hilly, mountainous part of our trip, it was dry, heat and desert. The car started making an odd noise and stopped. We were stuck in the middle of no man's land with no help. It was then that I was really amazed at this man – he lifted up the bonnet of the car and looked at the motor, which was hotter than we were, and ripped off his shirt and got down under the car. Staring into the distance at the mountains surrounding our desert track and feeling extremely forlorn, I noticed a dark cloud that seemed to be moving nearer and nearer in our direction. Suddenly I saw to my horror that it was a flock of large birds which had come from those highlands. Now they started circling above us; like dark devils they wheeled towards me and our broken-down vehicle with the legs of a man protruding from underneath. They were menacing, ugly vultures. As they circled around and around above us, my lips became parched, my mouth went dry. It was the most frightening moment of my life. I could feel myself starting to pray.

"Dear God, don't let me be so well cared for by Rivka, and the kind good hearted Mr. Norovski, only to die of thirst here in the desert and be eaten by vultures. Dear God, please help us."

It was a terrible pathetic moment. I had combated malaria and then jaundice with the help of this wonderful man, who was much older than Gad ben Ari, with no broad shoulders, far less hair, no visible big muscles – but somehow he could move mountains. I realised, like one who suddenly sees the light, God was with me and this was yet another hard lesson of life. Character is all supreme; good looks are as a veneer – fine, but the wood below must be of good quality, or everything is worthless – be it furniture or a person.

Just at that moment I heard a noise and Mr. Norovski stood up and grinned at me that special sort of smile, putting his head to one side; the motor was working. He looked at me and said, "Little star, we've done it, get in before the vultures swoop lower."

"Not before I kiss you with all my heart," I said, trying to hold back the tears which started to well up in my eyes. I threw my arms around his neck, and he drew me to him, and in this poignant moment in the middle of the desert with the flock of vultures above we kissed each other passionately.

Nick looked at me and said, "With all this sun you are becoming really black. I shall call you my sweet black pudding and you must call me Nick."

"Is it short for Nicholas or is it Nikolai?"

He did not answer, he just laughed and said, "Where did such a young girl as you learn to kiss like that?"

I am quite sure Nick had thought I was a virgin.

As we drove off, we watched the flock of vultures (the sanitary department of the desert) fly back to the mountains. With high hearts filled with triumph we arrived back to civilization and sanity in Tel Aviv, and I thanked God sincerely that those birds did not get their prey.

CHAPTER 54

Uncle Mick

Even though I was back to the bench on the balcony and Mr. and Mrs. Lazarus' home, the relief and happiness of being back in Tel Aviv was immense. I decided I would make no mention of my attack of malaria and jaundice because I did not want my parents to know, and I reckoned that if Mrs. Lazarus knew she would call my mother immediately.

I knew such news would upset Mum and she would say, "That's the price you have paid for being so head strong! Malaria does not leave you. It returns year after year to remind you of your complete inadequacies and ignorance of how to protect yourself against deadly diseases."

Unfortunately, this it did for the next ten years at least. In any case, I see no point in talking of something negative that happened in the past.

Nick engaged me of course for his new nightclub on the shore and Mr. Wallenstein, the agent, rebuked me quite harshly for accepting the same conditions I had had in Tiberias.

"That Norovski is a smart cad getting you to accept the same salary as you had before you were known here, why there are other clubs who want you and we could get decidedly more."

He even kept his word — as the new club (once again a rush job, like Tiberias) was not ready I did two weeks at another club, for my mind at an astronomical salary. I was riding high.

It was at that time, sleeping on the Lazarus' balcony bench, I, who rarely dreams, had an odd premonition concerning Mum's only brother, my Uncle Mick. He visited us at home rarely, as he lived with his family over the other side of London. He worked with my father as a representative and spent a good deal of his life driving and visiting would be customers. He was a large man with a red face and a gruff voice. He was not close to us, and I did not know him really well. Therefore, I found my dream all the more unusual.

Suddenly he appeared by my bench in Tel Aviv, looked down at me holding out his hand, and said simply, "Yvonne, goodbye." When I took the hand held out to me, it was the hand of a dead man. I awoke, as one does from a nightmare – in a state of shock.

Next morning at breakfast I could not wait to tell Mr. and Mrs. Lazarus of this horrid dream, and I was really relieved when Mrs. Lazarus suggested I should phone Mum and tell her. Also, as I had not written home for a far too long a period, it would stop my mother worrying about me. This I did, and told Mum of all my successes and of my shows for the Haganah, and of course of my regular airings on Kol Israel. Then I told Mum of the queer dream I had had last night.

I heard Mum take a loud breath, and then she said, "Huh, you were named after your great grandmother, who was supposed to be the wise woman in the village who also had premonitions. That is really odd. Uncle Mick died in his car this very morning; it must have been, with the time difference, just about the time he came to say goodbye to you – how very strange."

First Betty Hutton, now Uncle Mick – I prayed to God to stop giving me such sad premonitions. I decided I'd rather not to be so wise and just get the bad news with everyone else. Finally, they did stop!

CHAPTER 55

Forboding Instances

It was about this time in Tel Aviv that Nick's romance with me started to flower, and he took me to the most elegant boutique in Tel Aviv to have two smart dresses made; one white with red and green polka dot trimmings and one with straps at the shoulders and a little bolero. A very pretty outfit in the color lilac, which, as I got more sun, made me look even more like a black pudding. As Nick and I grew fond of each other, he rented for me a small studio in a modern block near the shore. One day also he introduced me to his wife, a simple, nondescript woman, perhaps in her forties. He had told me already he was only 39. He had compared my bust to two fried eggs – very edible, while he likened his wife's bosom to two washed out old socks. She was easily old enough to be my Mum, and I found this description of her female assets most unkind. I felt sorry for her, and would have told him so if his son in Army uniform had not suddenly walked into the Norovski home. He was easily 6ft and more, about 20 or 21, and very good-looking, but with the brown eyes of his mother. I fancied him immediately, and Nick, ever observant, noticed this and immediately mentioned to his son that his girlfriend Esther should be coming soon and we had to be going.

The next surprise was a small box with a beautiful blue aquamarine ring set in gold. The setting raised the lovely round diamond-cut stone, and underneath were two hearts entwined in gold.

Nick was smart; he knew most young girls including myself were romantic. Apart from this he was an experienced, terrific lover and showed me the difference between a quick fix of the younger set, who were capable of at least 3 sessions, and the long, slow.

real love session, making it really interesting with various positions, displaying the nature of a more senior man's capabilities. Once he even set the alarm at one hour. This man amazed me in many ways!

My getting so sick had not delighted my agent Hans Wollenstein, as no work meant no salary, and for him no commission. He therefore negotiated a contract with an older blonde chanson singer from Austria called Lilo Alexander, whom he immediately publicized as the "Toast of Vienna". Her songs were old fashioned and her age of about 40 could not be hidden with clever make-up, or with the very young population at that time in Tel Aviv. She was a flop, and would soon be on her way back to Europe. Before leaving she came to the club to catch my show and I imprudently showed her my ring, of which I was so proud. The blonde lady was not impressed; she turned up her nose and said, "My, an old man like Nick Norovski should give a young and upcoming star like you a diamond as big as that."

I was really surprised; Gerald van der Meer was an old man in my eyes, but he was intelligent and had a great sense of humor we talked and laughed a lot together. He was not a sexpot and had actually not bought me anything at all. He said I was bright as a button, and I knew somehow, he would be a friend for ages. Nick to my mind was not old at all. He was undoubtedly very charming, and a great lover, and I reveled in his advances and loved the ring he had given me. It was my first and made quite a change to the rings Mum often gave me from the legs of the fowls she bought to cook for her large family. These, I would flaunt on my engagement finger when I was a very little girl. No, I wanted to put Lilo's remark quite far out of my mind.

Then one evening, coming down the stairs on my way to sing at Nick's new club, I met our janitor. He took me aside and said, "You are a young girl and new here – beware of that man I have seen you with. He is from the underworld and not for you."

I was mad – I looked at him fiercely and said, "This man saved my life and I love him. Now, let me pass."

And with my head held high, I went on my way to the club res-olutely, but I could not put out of my mind the words of the Austrian singer nor those of the house janitor.

CHAPTER 56

The Gypsy Violinist

Nick Norovski seemed to know the whole world, and it seemed to me the whole world knew Nick. He greeted almost every guest as if they were old friends and to my mind, they greeted him back from Tiberias as if he were some prize ewe coming back to the fold.

Later in the evening he would sit at his table with a large bottle of Dimple Scotch Whisky in front of him and when I joined him, he invariably drawled, "Don't be vague, ask for Haig."

It was a very popular advertisement for this excellent brand of Scotch whisky. I invariably sat down grinning and would answer, "I don't like whisky, I prefer a good nip of quick Nick."

This made him laugh and he would kiss my hand quite openly. I think by this time of night he, a man who could really hold his drink, was becoming a bit tipsy. He swore it was not the alcohol, but the culprit was me – I was not so sure.

Then one night he told me I was to meet an old friend from the past when he was a young rogue in Bukarest. His name was Meier Lanski – it did not ring a bell for me (although it certainly would today) – and he would be bringing two companions with him, one of whom seemed to be a perfect bodyguard; young, big and muscular. The other was introduced to me as the most famous gypsy violinist from Romania. He uttered a name that sounded to my untrained ear like Abrasha Lupescu. Late at night Nick's voice often slurred. I wasn't quite sure. I was curious – the more so because André, our club violinist, was quite excited to see and hear this famous violinist personally.

The men arrived and another bottle of Scotch whisky was put on the table and the man they called Gypsy took a few shots and stood up, brought out his violin, put it under his chin and started to play just for our table. It was late and many guests had already left. The gypsy played staccato tones I had never heard in my life. He had a temperament that bound you and the three men stared at him as if mesmerised. I, who was alien to Romanian gypsy music, could only presume the tones and the way he played them with such pathos must have brought back memories of their youth.

Suddenly the tones hit a tragic minor key and to my horror the three men sitting at the table laid their heads on their arms and wept bitterly.

I was shocked. I had never ever seen a man cry. In the circle I moved in, in London, crying would have been considered highly unmanly. In my complete embarrassment I did the only thing I could do; I got up and left the table, put on my jacket and went home to bed.

Lying in bed I tossed and turned and thought things over. Somehow, I realized then that Slavs and half Latinos, or whatever Romanians considered themselves to be, did not possess the British discipline injected into us at high school. They were a hard-drinking but music-loving lot and their schooling was certainly not the "stiff upper lip" type so admired by the British.

Needless to say, Nick Norovski did not visit me that night. In fact, I didn't see him for a couple of days, and when I did neither he nor I ever broached the subject of the gypsy violinist again.

But the picture of those three older men sitting at that round table with a large bottle of whisky, sobbing their hearts out while a wild gypsy played peculiar half tones, haunted my memory for years.

CHAPTER 57

Leaving Israel

Although Dad told Mum a hundred times, "Annie don't worry – the kid can take care of herself," Mummy was not so sure this was possible at 16. She finally persuaded Dad to holiday again in the land of newly planted trees, and see his daughter's success for himself. I was overjoyed and so was Nick. He managed to obtain for Dad two large wooden boxes of the best Havana "Corona," and for Mum a beautiful, real suede and leather handbag in the latest style. Inside, instead of tissue paper, he filled it up with Israel's best perfume from Elite, two Yemenite embroidered hankies, a pretty little pink and blue pure silk head scarf, and a Parker pen. I gasped; these were things you just could not buy in Tel-Aviv. In this new land, where the first Hebrew word you learnt was "ain" – this meant "none" or "nothing." This was usually said with a shrug of the shoulders with the hands open wide, with the palms facing upwards. Israel had oranges from Jaffa, a load of sweet prickly Sobra fruit from cactus everywhere, aubergines cooked in every possible way imaginable, and eggs and yoghurt from the communal farms – called "Kibbutzim." All those specialties in the pretty black handbag meant for Mum were unseen, and often unknown. I couldn't help but wonder if those three weeping gentlemen were reminded of their youth, and how good and plentiful life had been to them then and how bare it must seem now.

Mum and Dad arrived, and Nick and I went to Lydda Airport to pick them up, but not before Nick had told the press of their forthcoming arrival. Cameras were flashing, making Dad feel like a real V.I.P.; particularly when next day there were headlines saying: Israel's youngest Jazz & Folk Singer Gives a Great Welcome to Her Ma & Pa flying in from London.

Nick introduced himself as the club owner, and me as "His Little Shining Star." He was a guide par excellence and put them up at the best hotel, with a room for me next door, so during their 10-day visit we could be together as much as possible. At breakfast Dad could hardly wait to show me a picture of Harry Janes in the News Chronicle, a serious newspaper and not just a sensation paper like The Daily Mirror. The words under the large picture read: *The Continent's Biggest Black Market Racketeer Finally Caught In His Own Net.* In England, the Continent meant all the countries over the Channel – in particular France, Germany, Austria, and the Benelux countries. Apparently, it had a lot to do with hams and all the other good stuff which found their way on to the Black Market at exorbitant prices. Dad was happy he had only started to do business with him, in a rather small way.

During their holiday, visiting places of interest they had had no time to see on their first visit and sometimes with Dad and I throwing ourselves into the warm Mediterranean for a swim, no one could ever dream that Nick and I were lovers, and I was loathe to mention a word to either Mum or Dad. Nick was an admirable actor, courteous and caring, he took us three out to all the best places available in Tel-Aviv. I only did a few shows in those 10 days. Mr. & Mrs. Lazarus came and lots of Dad's connections, and of course all of Nick's cronies, but neither Meier Lanski or his violin playing gipsy were among them. I was a rip-roaring success and even Mr. Wallenstein was beaming. In no time Nick and Dad became good friends. Over a glass of good Scotch whisky things seemed to run – at least to my mind – somehow or other much more smoothly.

Wallenstein found time to talk to me seriously. He told me stories of Famagusta and Nicosia in Cyprus – only a ferry boat away – who were longing to engage me, as they still had British garrison over there. The Greek agent had written him, "A little bit of London Pride would surely do wonders for the boys over there and therefore for the Night Club business without a doubt."

Even Istanbul, in Turkey, where an old agent pal of his worked, showed great interest in me. He booked acts to the largest hotels there and was of the opinion that their clientele would lap me up; a real Jazz Singer from the UK. But coming from Israel and able to sing some Modern Hebrew songs, it seemed I had no competition, and with gypsy songs from Romania which Nick had practiced with me diligently, slowly I built up a very varied and unusual repertoire.

I had now to face up to facts. I really loved Nick and I felt so comfortable with Dov, André and old Moses, but as Dad had taught me, "change is the law of life." My mad desire to ape Marco Polo and discover the world was stronger than all those comforting thoughts of remaining. Mum, who had strong instincts, felt I was too close to Nick, and he was far too old for me. Israel was, after all, only a small strip of land by the ocean, originally dedicated by the British Balfour Agreement to give homeless Jews a place of refuge. Soon people would say, "She's good, she's great, but we've seen her now about 10 times," and Dad would say, "Unless the Club belongs to the singer, like Don Ho in Hawaii or Wayne Newton who was year in year out in Las Vegas… You may be loved, you may bring in good business but sooner or later, like a good loaf of bread, you get stale and one needs a rest from the crowd & the crowd needs a rest from that particular artiste."

Finally, my spirit of adventure overwhelmed Nick and the boys and I could hear myself singing: "Famagusta Here I Come." I wanted to discover Cyprus and get to know the Greeks, and possibly the Turks too.

CHAPTER 58

Famagusta – Cyprus

Mr. Hegedush, a little grey-haired older gentleman wearing a tired looking grey suit, was there to meet me when the ferry arrived from Israel. He greeted me warmly. In the 50s, before the Turks decided to take over part of Cyprus for themselves and Famagusta was removed from the Greek side, it was still a part of Cyprus. When I arrived, it was still a British Protectorate and both Greeks and Turks lived together most amicably. After all, they were all Cypriots and proud of their lovely island. Driving to the club, which was called "The Copacabana," I noticed British "Tommies" in uniform almost everywhere; indeed, Famagusta was a British garrison town.

In no time I met the boss, Mr. Papadopolos – "Papa" for short, a tall middle-aged man in a dark, well-cut suit, wearing sunglasses. Later on, I noticed he wore them even when the sun was not shining, as very often he was bored with the company around him and took refuge behind those dark glasses to close his eyes and have a little snooze. Mrs. Papadopolos was a comely blonde from Macedonia, with a fancy for rather low decolletés on all her dresses, showing off a good part of her well endowed white bosom. Later on, I was told she had come to work at The Follies, as a dancer hostess, had won over the boss and now showed business acumen in making Mr. Papa's establishment the No. 1 place in Famagusta.

As I was engaged to bring in all the Tommies and Officers, my opening number and signature tune was to be "London Pride." It was neither Jazz nor Folk, but more a popular marching song, so I had to learn it in a hurry. Because I did not possess the sort of stage costumes Mrs Papadopolos thought fit for "London Pride" and, to my consternation, to end my show with "There'll Always Be An England" (both songs just had to be in my repertoire – so said the boss' wife), Mrs. P. whisked me off to her dressmaker where she chose a Norman Hartnell style evening dress for my show, similar to one worn by the Queen. It was white tulle dotted with silver sequins with a front panel in silver lamé. I was almost surprised that Mrs. Papadopolos did not say it had to be in red, white and blue (the colours of the Union Jack). However, she was adamant at having foam falsies sewn into the ball gown, which she assured me was far sexier and made my slim waist look even more regal – no hoop like the one that fell down at Selbys. At the first fitting my own bust (the 2 fried eggs, as Nick called them) was too flat to hold the falsies in place, so she and I opted for a one shoulder affair which was extremely new and trendy at that time and kept the desired false bust in place.

As the British Law was stricter by far than it was in Israel, I was not allowed to mix with the public, as I was underage, but allotted to the table where the bosses of ABB the biggest Corporation in Famagusta had a table reserved for them and their entourage. The band were boys from England, so the rehearsals went off fine. There was a trumpet fanfare as I walked on to the stage in my Norman Hartnell copy. There was an audible gasp from the audience – I really think some Ladies almost expected the Queen herself to arrive. Mr. Papadopolos, without his sunglasses, introduced me to the packed house thus:

"Ladies & Gentlemen, finally we persuaded her to come to our beautiful Island, and here she is, the Forces Own Little Sweetheart straight from London – Miss Yvonne Carr."

There was no question of an "e" with an accent; I was to be as English as Carr's Water Biscuits or Crème Crackers.

The ABB people were lovely, and the boss's wife took me under her wing, and they sent me a big bouquet of flowers. It was a large hall in comparison to the small clubs I had known in Israel, and the Tommies stamped their feet and banged their fists on the table and shouted again and again "Bravo" and "Encore". As arranged with Mrs. Papadopolos, I had to finish with "There'll Always Be an England" and all the officers stood up, including our ABB table. I was quite relieved as I had thought the whole idea a bit over the top. I felt very sorry for the Greek singer who had been initially the star of the show and now was put in the middle of the show. The big establishment had an acrobatic couple from Austria, a dancing couple from Hungary, and about a dozen other single dancers mainly dancing to their own folk music, wearing their traditional costumes and introduced to the audience by Mr. Papadopolos himself. There were also some pretty girls at the bar, which was immense, whom I found out later on were all the hostesses. As I always sat at the ABB table, I had very little time to fraternize with the military, let alone the Greek public.

One day a young soldier came over to our table and introduced himself as Private Bill Thompson, and looking at me he said, "I heard you are a young lady from Hendon, I am from there too."

Naturally he was asked to pull up a chair, and so quite often we would chat and exchange notes when we heard from our respective mothers, mainly about the weather in London, so different from the mild Mediterranean climate in Famagusta. One Saturday night, just after I put on my brand new pink tulle ball gown with the lovely spray of black velvet leaves stretching from the bodice to three quarters of the very wide long skirt, which Mrs. Papadopolos made quite sure I had made at her dressmaker, I looked at myself in the long mirror of the artists' dressing room and saw a tall, dark, slim figure behind me – it was the young Greek singer from Limasol, Melina Michaelides. She was smoking a cigarette, which was normally not allowed in any dressing rooms. She was obviously very nervous.

"Nice dress," she said with her heavy Greek accent.

"Oh, do you like it?" I asked, almost in surprise.

"Oh yes," she said, "but you will not like it when you see your two new stage dresses with holes burnt all over them, after you have worked so hard to pay for them, that dressmaker Mrs. Papa took you to knows how to charge – I know it."

With that remark and a cruel smile, she put her lit cigarette far too near to my nylon tulle ballgown. I jumped out of her way as quickly as I could, but she grabbed at my shoulder and fairly hissed, "Don't you dare speak one more word with my Bill Thompson – he is mine, and you, English girl, are not allowed to come between us or I will burn your dresses happily and even the whole damned place."

I had never til now been confronted with a Greek woman's wrath, especially one who seemed to be completely oblivious to the fact that I could not even fancy her boyfriend Bill Thompson – why, if he and I had been conversing in French we would have still been addressing each other in the unfamiliar polite form of "vous." I was shocked – how could anyone be that jealous to want to set the place on fire? Needless to say, I did my best to avoid Private Bill Thompson and I never said a word to him again.

I really had paid no attention to the staircase going upstairs, til one night there was a loud scream, just as the music stopped and the dancers were leaving the floor. One of the dancers came rushing down those stairs shouting, "He took out a knife at me – look, he slit my skirt."

Her leg was bleeding. In seconds, like a horde of sugar ants on a sweet piece of fruit, many stewards were at her side. The young woman was rushed away in a long dressing gown and taken to the room marked "Sanitary." I never even got a glimpse of the culprit to know if it was some drunk soldier or a Greek gone be-serk. It was all done so quickly, and the ABB family immediately drew my attention in another direction. I only had time to ask, "What's up there?"

"Oh, there are the separees," said Mrs. Brown casually, "it's your time to go home anyway, it's far too late for you."

We were all standing up, then one of the gentlemen offered me his arm and said, "Come, we're all going the same way home."

Later I looked up the word "separee" in my French dictionary, it said a small separate compartment.

I wondered if Mrs. "Pappa" had started the idea of separees. I was beginning to see the light and why the "Copa," as most people called it, was such a success. Then it was not only me! I was learning fast.

CHAPTER 59

Nicosia & Norma

Not for a moment did I dream that when I was away in Cyprus I would hear from Nick as often as I did. He wrote nice letters and always called me "My sweet Black Pudding." Most young teenagers are slim, and although I certainly was not skinny, apart from my round tummy, no part of me resembled a pudding. Finally, I found out why. Nick had heard from the British occupation of Palestine how much the men missed Christmas Pudding at that time of the year. They had explained to him it was black from all the brandy used in it, and that it was packed with dried fruit and nuts, and even silver coins. It had so much Brandy you could set it alight, and as it burned make a wish and that wish would come true. As I was a Brit, and slowly became the colour of good cognac under the hot Israeli sun and was also sweet as the brown sugar used in Christmas Pudding, he found that name really suitable. I was amused. He also added if I could find someone to give me a couple of bottles of Scotch whisky he would be happy to reimburse me. Then these were difficult to get in Israel, although he seemed to always have it.

Nicosia had a magical note for me. Many hostesses and dancers at "the Copa" were dressed very trendy and smart. We all ate together in the early evening before the club opened, and I could not help noticing their simply gorgeous accessories, namely fine leather shoes, handbags, and even gloves. When I asked where they got them from, the answer was invariably Nicosia. So, when Mr. Hegedush summoned me to his little office and told me of the very good offer he had for me at "the Coq d'Or" I was agog. Of course, I would love to go, but there was one fly in the ointment: he explained to me that all the ladies working there were expected to make commission. I must tell you, at that time I had no idea what that word meant. I knew that "Coq d'Or" meant Golden Cock, and probably all the cocks that walked in were expected to pay so much that, to the boss, they were gold. Mr. Hegedush explained that when I was invited to a table, then I must order the most expensive champagne, on which I would receive a commission. I was now 17-19 on my papers, so no problem. I immediately had a vision of myself arriving home in London dressed like a million-dollar movie star. I said I'd try – although I didn't care for champagne.

Mr. Hegedush laughed. "Oh, you don't have to drink the stuff," he said, visibly amused. "You just order it and see that the people who have invited you to their table, drink it – the waiters do the rest."

He also told me not to worry on that account, as the No. 1 hostess was a tall, redhaired beauty from Israel and she would teach me all the ropes. She was very clever, and as he said, "she had her head screwed on the right way." She was called Norma – I bet her name was Naomi in Israel, but Norma sounded better here. Inquisitive as a cat, I agreed to go.

I had spent a lot of my Famagusta salary on those two beautiful ballgowns, and now I needed a second large case to house them in for the trip to Nicosia. In the meantime, the British garrison had pulled out of Famagusta and were sent to Gibraltar. Both Mr. & Mrs. Papadopolos of the "Copacabana" and Mr. and Mrs. Brown of ABB bid me a warm farewell, and I was off to Nicosia, but not before Mr. Hegedush told me the lady I should meet would look after me. I had already studied "Yassu" Melina's big success, and one of the musicians had written a small arrangement of the song in my key. I could also greet the primarily Greek audience with "Kali Esperassus" – "Good Evening," and say "Effharisto poli" – "Thank you very much." It all went down well and the public – mainly men – were warm and friendly. After the show

I asked for Norma and was directed to a table where the tall red-head sat drinking champagne with 3 Greek gentlemen – all in dark suits with white shirts and ties. They got up when I arrived, and I noticed Norma was immediately friendly but businesslike.

"This is our star from London, the famous Yvonne Carr – Waiter," she turned to the steward hovering behind us, "bring a new bottle of your best champagne," then, pointing to their half full glasses, and the half full bottle in the cooler, "this, with all our talk has gone warm and flat."

Then she whispered something in the steward's ear and pointed to me. He nodded his assent, and before the three men could even think, the waiter swept away the four glasses and turned the half full bottle of champagne upside down in the cooler and marched off with his trolley triumphantly.

Norma adroitly changed the subject to me and my show and an ever-attentive waiter put down little dishes of almonds, pistachios, and potato chips on the little round table in front of us. Norma said, "You just cannot imagine how Miss Carr wowed the British forces in Famagusta, why, even the General went mad."

I had not even met a Captain, let alone a General. However, the men seemed very impressed and before I could answer a new bottle of champagne arrived on the trolley, a larger round table was put in front of us, as well as 5 new glasses. Then Norma whispered in my ear, "This is your commission."

I had discovered as a kid that, although as a 10-year-old in Lugano I quite liked Asti Spumante, I really found the so-called Moet Chandon too acidy and fizzy for my taste. I was definitely no drinker. The steward opened the new bottle with a flourish. The older man made a toast to me, and we all clinked glasses. The men drank thirstily. I sipped at my glass politely and before I could look around Norma's glass was empty, and she was asking the waiter to refill it. She then turned to the men and said, "Surely you are not going to let me drink alone! Waiter, fill the gentlemen's glasses up."

Then she looked at my full glass and said:

"I think our star is not so keen on the Moet Chandon, would you gentlemen not mind if we ordered her preference for Demi Sec?"

The men just had to acquiesce and so bottles were put to my account, and to the bill of the 3 men, 2 of which got up and asked Norma if they could be excused and went off to dance with two hostesses with extraordinary curves, super high heels and super low-necked dresses. The older man asked Norma if she cared to dance, but she declined, saying her ankle was in recuperation after a sprain. He then went to dance with another lady sitting at the bar and Norma and I were left alone. She then enlightened me as to how she worked. She really was one astute lady. While she spoke the waiter emptied the half full bottle of Moet Chandon champagne and my nearly full Demi Sec in the cooler and went off, taking with him a small, wilting palm in a pot that stood on a high stand placed next to the chair where Norma was sitting. In next to no time, he returned with a fresh new little palm in the same pot. Then Norma told me in a low voice her story. Israel was too small to really make money.

"I was young and beautiful and had nothing to sell except myself. There are quite a few prostitutes in Tel-Aviv, but I did not want to be one of them. Then I heard about this place and decided to try my luck here. The boss is a spry little bitty man and fell for me immediately and taught me all the tricks of the trade. To be a good hostess: A) you don't have to drink, you have to order and make sure the clients drink. The potted palm is there to drink for you. You can throw your drink superstitiously on the floor or accidentally knock your glass over on the table. This of course causes much distress to all around you, and under these circumstances, calls for another bottle of champagne. Most important – the champagne flows! B) You certainly don't have to have sex with any man you don't fancy … for that you can introduce them to one of the girls sitting at the bar. C) You do not wear sexy clothes, you dress elegantly but quietly. D) If you are with more than three men, ask a bar hostess over to your table and she will drink plenty for you, while you are casually feeding the potted palm."

These last words she said with a little giggle.

"My game is to sit alone at a table quietly dressed, looking nice but not over sexy at all. On the whole men who come here are mostly idiots when it comes to women, and they think I am a sad widow, or divorcée. Whatever I am, I make them feel intensely sorry for me. This, explained the boss to me, is very important, and could bring some extra money – "just to help me out a little" – into my purse."

This was said with a special smile while she took a deep breath and went on.

"The waiters are all in the game and when a man is entranced from a "come hither" smile from a bar girl, he will ask to be excused and the waiter will empty the old bottle quickly in the cooler, and a new one will be there to welcome the clever lady with that special smile. Most men, stupid as they are, feel too ashamed to have to say they did not order any more drink and feel obliged to accept the new bottle."

Then she let out a hollow laugh, "Ssh! The music stopped, they're coming back – watch this."

They all sat down a bit awkwardly. One had invited his bar dancer to join us. The steward stood there waiting to pour the new bottle of Demi-Sec – the three men tried it, I liked mine, but the bar hostess named Helena made a face and said she only drank Moet Chandon, and two of the men seemed to agree with her. Just as I was contemplating what would happen next, I felt a shower of cold fluid over my feet.

"Oh, how funny, whatever's that?" I cried spontaneously, then I saw Norma's face and realized she had tipped her drink on the floor. Helena drank her glass down as if it had been water…maybe it was! I drank a half a glass and felt my arms feeling peculiarly heavy. I knocked the newly refilled glass over the table. We all sprang up quickly. Two waiters came to our rescue. Norma gave me a knowing look of contentment and hurriedly ordered a new bottle of Moet Chandon and a Demi Sec for me and the older man who seemed to have my taste also. A couple of minutes later, Norma asked the men and lady hostess if they would excuse us, as I was the star of the show and had been invited by another group of admirers, and she had to act as chaperone, me being so terribly young and innocent.

Alone in the ladies' room she told me joyfully she had made 3 bottles before I had arrived, and now – so had I! It was an excellent start for a first day or night!

"Heavens!" I said, "I'm going home while I still can, I am dead tired and slightly tipsy."

I made my way to my room happily contemplating the super accessories I could buy with all this extra commission money. Norma, gee! What a smart teacher … wow … she really was something else!

CHAPTER 60

Let's Clap Hands

Cyprus was a lovely Island and I well understood when many Cypriots really believed the Greek myth that Aphrodite – the Goddess of Love – came from out of the Sea at Paphos, a scenic little place.

The shops at Ledra Street in Nicosia were a delight for me after the scarcity of luxury goods in Israel. The grapes in the autumn were huge, sweet, and luscious – so big you could bite into them and there was still a good half left; there were some pips, but the black skin melted away. During this time, I decided to be adventurous and take myself to a restaurant, so I hailed a taxi and was soon at a nice little place with whitewashed walls with blue borders. I immediately ordered a small bottle of mineral water and then, before I could ask for a menu, the waiter disappeared. I coughed and even sung out loud, but no one came, and I was quite alone in the restaurant. I could do nothing. Then the Greek singer at the Coq d'Or who came from Athens walked in; ignoring me completely, she sat down and clapped her hands with such a loud tone I jumped. In no time a waiter appeared with a menu. She told him her wishes and then once again, without even giving me a glance, he disappeared into the kitchen – as if I was not even there. Within a short time, the mature singer from the mainland received whatever she had ordered. As if I was invisible, the waiter returned to the kitchen. I did the only thing I could do, I summoned up all my courage and, feeling a complete idiot, I clapped my hands resolutely hard and to my utter joy the waiter appeared at my table with the menu as if he had been a Genie in Aladdin's lamp. Another lesson I learnt about Greek hospitality – clapping was important!

The taxi driver taking me back to the nightclub told me he was a Turk and said if I wanted to see more of the countryside, he would be glad to drive me around. He also mentioned apart from driving a taxi, he worked at the local Forces P.X. and he would be glad to get me any product that seemed unobtainable or too expensive in Nicosia. I decided to mention the fact that my father was part Turkish – that helped. I thought of Nick and the Scotch whisky and asked him for four large bottles of Johnny Walker, which he even delivered to my room the next day. The Turkish driver, called Ismuth, said he'd be happy to oblige, and in no time he became "my" taxi driver.

One Sunday, driving around the countryside, he asked me if I would like to drive. The road appeared to be quite clear. I had tried my hand at driving a car in London, when Dad bought an old Hillman Minx for Rox to practice on so she could get her driving license. She drove it, even in the rain with brown paper bags patching up the holes in the roof when the rain dripped through, and hooted at any young boys we both fancied as we drove by. It certainly reminded me of happy days trying my hand at driving Roxie's little old car.

I of course said "Yes," to Ismuth "I'd love to drive." Firmly seated in the driving seat with Ismuth beside me, we started to sing "Deep in the Heart of Texas." I became as I often did, completely engrossed in the song, and left the wheel to clap my hands. It went: "The Stars at night are big and bright." 1, 2, 3, 4 (when you had to clap your hands), "Deep in the heart of Texas." We both clapped, full of youthful joy. At the second verse "The sage in bloom is like perfume," 1, 2, 3, 4 (clap clap clap), "deep in the heart of Texas," the car swerved into the middle of the road, and I skidded into an oncoming truck I had not noticed. The truck driver got out. We got out, but after the first shouting contest, Ismuth explained I had no license, and then who I was, and Ismuth would be glad to pay for the repairs (mostly a paint job and one light) and to take the truck driver (who apparently also had no license) to the famous Coq d'Or to hear me sing. Naturally I told Ismuth I would repay him as long as it was not too expensive, whereupon he gave the bump on the van's wing a bash and it bounced back almost to normality. The truck driver did likewise to our taxi. Both the men seemed soon, over a glass of Greek wine at a nearby bistro, to behave like old pals. Cyprus was indeed a friendly island.

Nicosia could also boast of a big hotel called "The Ledra Palace." I had not been inside, but it looked most imposing. I decided there and then I would invite Mum and Dad for Christmas, and I booked a nice room with a balcony for them without further thought. I knew full well if I paid for the Hotel, Dad, as a hard-baked businessman, would fork out the air fares, and then tell the world his young singing daughter was inviting him and Mum to the biggest hotel in Cyprus. It was well before the tourist trade in the 60s and at that time it was considered by far the best on the Island.

Unfortunately, the weather did not play its part and just before the holidays the weather changed violently and became very cold, and to my utter consternation the Ledra Palace had no heating – only braziers which they put out on tables in the corridors to warm one's hands in passing. It didn't matter if your feet were freezing!

I searched and searched for an electric stove, to no avail, and finally bought an oil stove for their room – it smelt of oil but at least kept out the damp cold. In various places in the corridors the rain came through the roof. The only thing the staff could do was to put large flowering pots and plants underneath to catch the water.

The change in the weather unfortunately made the 8-day holiday a bit of a disaster, but at least Dad enjoyed the Greek "Messas," which we ordered often with the famous Greek Ouzo. Oddly enough, Mum and I thoroughly enjoyed that too. It all tasted so good and kept out the cold. The fish was good, but best of all,

Dad was in his element getting service. Instead of snapping his fingers and shouting "Oi," he followed my lead and clapped his hands as loud as he could, Mum invariably got embarrassed and said, "Ssh ssh ssh, not so loud Sid."

When they left, Dad looked at me and grinned, shaking his head from side to side, "You know what, I'm proud of you kid, thanks for making us come to Cyprus – the weather was not on our side, but in any case I had great fun clapping my hands for service."

CHAPTER 61

Les Boutiques, Les Girls and Nick

By the time I left Cyprus I was decidedly far richer, in spite of having to pay to get Ismuth's taxi "ship-shape" once more. The fact that Norma played the part of my chaperone was the greatest help of all. Even Dad fell for her beauty and captivating charm and immediately ordered a bottle of the best champagne – which Norma honestly and promptly put to my account. She treated me as if I was a novice when we were with others, giving them the impression of my complete innocence and virginity. The fact that I always managed to spill champagne over the table showed my lack of savoir faire, which added to this impression. My love of nature made it necessary to have a little potted palm between Norma and I wherever we sat. We worked together like mother and daughter. The results were positive in spite of the Ledra Palace hotel bill for my folks, and the fact that I had done a lot of shopping – mainly accessories in the color of cognac, which was by far the trendiest color at that time. Apart from the shoes, gloves, and handbags, all in the softest of leather, there was a hat to match, and my biggest thrill of all, a long umbrella with a cover in the identical color, plus black vertical stripes. I also bought black sandals with little yellow leather flowers at the side, and my "piece de resistance" was a brown crocodile handbag with matching shoes; even though they were a little bit too long at the back, the shoes did match perfectly, and I just had to buy them.

The regular sips of champagne here and there, and the dishes of nuts and potato chips to ward off the feeling that my head was too light and my legs too heavy left their mark, and the two dresses that Nick had had made for me were too tight and I had a feeling they would split at the seams any minute. I had to get a couple of costumes and dresses custom made. One was a warm black material for winter, for when I would be back in Europe. It had large buttons in black and white all the way down – the latest fashion, slimming and elegant. The other was a two-piece in fresh apple green which complemented my tanned colouring.

I was also far richer in experience of life. I heard stories from the dancers of kilos of gold they had lying in safe deposits at the banks from the money they made with fantasy-filled men. The girls were mostly from Hungary and Romania and assured me that they were in the game only for the money. The way they danced reminded me of this fact – but definitely! One from Hungary had had a bust operation to make her bosom larger and had heavy scars underneath. They were still pretty flat considering her mannequin height. I could not help but wonder how terribly flat chested she must have been beforehand. One girl, who was only a bar hostess, was far younger than any of the others. She had dark hair and a small, narrow face, already slightly lined. She told me she was sold by her father as a concubine to some rich, old, prestigious man in their village. She had managed to escape from the harem by climbing over a wall and pretending she was a boy. After giving me the lurid details, she said here in Nicosia she made money and above all she was free. I think she dreamed of meeting a Prince Charming who would take her away in his white Cadillac, and who would be kind to her and marry her and so give her some status. I think she was not alone in her dreaming. There was one act that was by far the best for me: a young belly dancer from Armenia. As she was only 15, she traveled with her mother, who appeared to be a nice, very intelligent woman. The girl's name was Nana. Later she became the most famous belly dancer in Europe and made constant headlines in the newspapers in Italy. She had something most oriental belly dancers do not have, apart from a nice firm young body; terrific vitality and sex appeal. She would go to various men at their tables, shaking her little silver bells around her hips at them and getting a real kick out of watching their little whatnots stand up, reminding me of the sojourn at the swimming pool with my two girlfriends when I was about 13. She would come back to her Mum quite excited in the dressing room and laugh her head off over their reactions. She had lots of long, dark, naturally curly hair like me, and we both liked each other. The fact was, the acrobatic act was excellent but stale, Nana and I were fresh.

My new, large case was absolutely jammed full, and I was ready to get on the ferry for Israel and see Nick again. Ismuth turned up trumps and procured for me an old strong straw carrier bag which many Greek housewives used to go to the market. It held the 4 large bottles of Scotch whisky perfectly. He told me to put a few dirty clothes on top and may be a half-eaten sandwich, which his experience obviously told him would help me get through the Israeli customs, whom he said were quite strict. To add to all these good things, at the local radio station I had been given a really melodious Greek song to learn and sing called "Thyobrassina Matia," which in Greek means "Green Eyes". The young man who told me to learn this much-loved ballad was called Pheathros, and he told me he was studying British law to enable him to become a judge in Cyprus, which was still a British Protectorate. Some years later he studied at London University and invited me to see him called to the Bar and receive his wig and gown, a fine experience for me as well. Later he became a much-revered judge in his own country. The song about the green eyes brought the house down at the Coq d'Or and I decided to keep it in my repertoire for the future.

Slowly I was able to joke with the audience about the differences in our two languages.

"The Greeks," I said, "say "Ne" a great deal, but it does not mean "No" it means "Yes" …so young girls like me have to beware. We have to say "Ochi," because "Ochi" means "no," but go and find a young English girl who can say "ch" …so men, you are in luck's way!"

I was in luck too. The ferry arrived and there were two or three Customs Officers – young military men who rushed to our boat. Porters came with trolleys to take large cases, and one Customs Officer asked if he could help me as I struggled with my handbag and the long umbrella that didn't fit into any of my luggage, plus the old market carrier, which was really heavy. I smiled demurely and asked him if he would be so kind and take the carrier from the ferry over the borderline for me. He said, "Certainly," and lifted it up with a swing as if it was a feather and put it down at the feet of Nick, who was waiting on the Israeli side nervously. When I told him what the contents were, he could not contain his joy.

"My word," he said, "you really are a clever girl – what a great idea."

I grinned, and deep inside me I thanked Ismuth.

Then he scrutinized my new clothes, my hat, my umbrella, and me.

"I'm fatter," I said, pouting with disgust.

"No matter," said Nick, "my sweet black pudding, there is only a little more to love. Here we don't expect you to drink and eat so much, so you'll lose that extra weight in no time."

He took me to the hotel and asked me how much he owed me for the whisky, and if I would be his guest at dinner at a new restaurant that had opened in Tel Aviv. I was dying to feel his arms around me and in no time I did. Then he asked me, "What can I do for you to really make you happy?"

Oh, I said to myself, this man loves to put me on the edge of a table and make love to me there. Bed was ordinary but comfortable and in the middle of the desert was in the past.

"How about making love to me outside the President Ben Gurion's house? I know there is a bench on the roadside there, now that would be fun. It's nice to know before you die, you have made love in every imaginable nook and cranny and in most countries of this planet. Then you can die with a big grin on your face and say I did it all!"

Nick burst out laughing — no matter if he was 39 as he said, or even 45 — he enjoyed doing the unspeakable for fun, and sometimes behaved like a youth in his teens.

"OK," he said, "tonight after our special dinner," and then as an afterthought, "hopefully there are not too many police on the prowl. Now, in spite of your shopping expeditions in Cyprus, there is a new ladies' boutique here. Let's go and get you absolutely something stunning."

"Well, it better have a full skirt if we make love on that bench on our way home." I said, thinking practically for a change!

Before he went he looked through my clothes in the wardrobe and chose the new pink tulle ball gown with the black velvet leaves.

"That is particularly pretty, Black Pudding, you must wear that for the special show I'm arranging for you at my club. It's one long show and three times your normal salary. I know Wollenstein has a lot of engagements for you up his sleeve and I want to get in before they start. By the way, how would you like to be guest star in a real Romanian revue with a famous Romanian woman comedian? It's a Kibbutz tour and will end in Beer Sheba, they want to build it up there so it's sure to be a successful tour as all the venues are full of Romanian emigrants. It's a short two-week tour in all, money is great and it would be a new experience for you being on tour. How does that dig you Baby?"

"Super," I said, "but after that I think I should hear what Mr. Wollenstein has to offer."

"Hopefully the engagements are not too soon and not too far away," said Nick ruefully, "I'd rather hold you here for myself."

I realised then that Nick, and possibly all men, could never understand this terrific urge in me to sing around the world and not want as so many women do, one man and total security. How could any man understand my love of adventure?

The dress (it was a belated birthday present) was black and white, the dinner was delicious, the wine good and a pleasant change to Peiper Heidesek Demi Sec champagne and the lovemaking on the bench on the roadside – a quick fix, but not everyone can say they've made love outside the President's house. I was just 17 and ecstatic!

My guest appearance at Nick's place filled the house, and by the time I left for the Romanian revue I was gaining confidence on stage rapidly.

The Romanians were a boisterous jolly lot, and the comedian – about 50 odd – funny and much loved by her community.

On the road in the bus, I picked up a lot of tricks they seemed to use regularly. One of the gang would chat to the would be victim, while a small kid crawled on the floor under the table and swiped a handbag or shopping bag, whatever was put on the floor. Then there was a pickpocketing trick that was for one person alone, who so mesmerised the victim that they could pick his wallet with light fingers without anyone noticing, and him least of all. Another trick was where in a crowd, robust but light fingers could do the same job. The victim could not notice this happening because he was being jostled on all sides by the crowd. They were an amazing lot!

My English-Yiddish Romanian gypsy songs like "My little Yaas" went down as expected – with great applause – but the younger set loved my jazz classics. I seemed to be riding on a real high down there in the Near East. I had no idea then how I would use those tricks of the trade later to become an entertainer as well as a singing star.

Nick was right, I lost weight on that tour, and when I got back to the hotel room Nick had reserved for me, among the few letters on my bed was one from Agent Wollenstein. It read:

"Dear Yvonne, I am delighted with your success in Cyprus and both establishments loved you. Nicosia would give you a return engagement anytime. I know you also had success here in that Romanian revue, but now I have a terrific offer for you for Istanbul."

He hoped I would be interested. You bet I was!

CHAPTER 62

Istanbul

An evening meal on the Bosphorus, eating fresh fish and gazing out at the famous bridge that links West and East, is an unforgettable experience.

The Hotel public in a primarily Muslim country was far more mixed than in the famous Nicosia Night Club. I did not have to order Piper Heideseck Champagne under the jurisdiction of the good-hearted Norma. There were no girls nor other acts, only the band, which played quietly for dinner and later on was louder and lively. What I thought was a great idea: the orange juice which I drank was the same price as a double whisky, cognac, or coupe de champagne.

Already on the first night I was invited to a mixed group of businessmen – all French speaking – some with wives, all Israelites. In no time I was invited here and there and felt thoroughly at home. Moreover, the bandleader, a pianist, was a Czech named Fritz Kerten, who not only wrote my first orchestration for a large orchestra, a marvelous Gershwin potpourri, but who had a lovely blonde wife who befriended me almost immediately. She took me everywhere and, to my utter joy, to the Grande Bazaar – this was before the big fire. The weighing of gold was all new to me, and she promised me when I was ready to leave for home – and I must admit after all those months away I was beginning to feel the pangs of homesickness – then she would see I should buy gold sovereigns and have them put on heavy gold chain bracelets so that the money I earned would be safe. Hard currency was no problem in Cyprus, which was still under British Protectorate, but Turkey was a Republic, and I was paid 80% in Turkish Lira, and so gold would be important when I wanted to leave for home.

The original Grande Bazaar was an incredible huge cave, as if hewn out of a "Thousand and One Nights", overflowing with men selling gold coins and gold jewellery; oddly enough, each vendor had a cat on his shoulder (cats seemed to be everywhere in Istanbul at that time). When I asked why, I was told that all these men there were dealing with an immense amount of gold and the cat on the shoulder was to bring them good fortune.

Turkish men are quite known for their hot blood and ingenious ideas of how to get a woman. Indeed, in a predominantly Muslim country you have to be ingenious to get yourself laid with a woman who is not a prostitute in a brothel. And so it came to pass when I was appearing at that famous Istanbul Hotel that many men tried their luck with me in various ways, but to no avail. Finally, one got the bright idea to not just stay over at the Hotel – after all, that was no big deal – but he paid the night porter a good strong "pourboire" to let him into my room, where he promptly hid in my closet.

I came up to my room after the show and got the shock of my life when I opened the closet to take out a hanger, to discover a man inside the wardrobe, who desired me – oh God – another!

I shouted the vilest insults I could think of that would have made any man's hard on go soft and shouted at him "get out." I ran to the door with a hanger in my hand, waking up all of the neighbors shouting at the fleeing intruder or would-be lover:

"Look at yourself in the mirror – I would be blind or stark raving mad to even contemplate going with anyone as ugly as you."

Such direct insults can hurt a man's ego far more than any whip can. Just to be sure, I threw the coat hanger at him, and it caught him on the ear as he was running down the stairs. He had a nice little bruise on his face for a short while. I wonder if his wife asked him how it got there.

CHAPTER 63

The Hat Pin Story

My mother was the oldest in her family of 5 sisters and one brother. She, as so many other girls at that time, had to get married to Daddy, as her father who had arranged the marriage pointed out that Dad had a good job at the bank and everyone predicted a great future for him. Apart from that, my grandfather said one less mouth to feed would be a great help.

Maidy, the second eldest, had worked too hard at her bank to help her Dad finance the other 4 and had been afflicted with an incurable illness and was an invalid for life, which was a great shame as from an old sepia photo I found in an old photo album – she was by far the prettiest of all the girls. She never got married, she was our maiden aunt and we all called her "Maidy."

When Maidy found out I would be going to sing in Istanbul, she sent me something which was indispensable. It was an oversized Hat Pin. She told me at the hospital she had to visit regularly for treatment, she had become very friendly with the nurses, two of which had worked as nurses in the Near East – namely Turkey. They told lurid stories about the men there. I think those stories prompted dear old Aunt Maidy to send me this hat pin. She wrote me:

"Maybe in Istanbul you will be very happy to be able to counteract all those sex-starved men with this hat pin – it's not their fault – it's their religion you know."

Beyoglu was the main street and I loved to walk down it, looking at all the shops. After all, Istanbul was a big city and a prosperous one. It was a town of men with wandering hands. Pinching a girl's firm bottom was a pastime they could not resist, particularly if she was alone. So, this mega sized hat pin worked overtime when I went walking down the main street. Without turning I would give a hard jab at what ever was behind me trying to pinch or feel my "derrière." I would just hear a gasp of surprise and pain and by the time I left Turkey I became a champion at hat pin jabbing at wandering hands.

Being the star singer at the best hotel certainly makes life a lot easier. Being 17 and only a half portion, I looked like a child and was promoted as "the lovely young star of the Levante." Coming directly from Israel was all something entirely new for Istanbul and the, at that time, fairly large rich Israelite congregation. They came in crowds and groups and loved "Bab el Wad, Song of the Negev, and Finjan" which everyone enjoyed as it was a clapping song, and even the Muslim Turks enjoyed this happy little folk song. Of course, most of the upper set in Istanbul spoke French. French was in any case absolutely "en vogue" in the 50s and I had quite a few famous French chansons in my repertoire from working in London at Gerard van de Meer's 3 venues, such as "Domino," "Mlle de Paris", "La Seine," etc.

One decade later, when I went over to Istanbul to show Frank, my husband, this beautiful and interesting city, not one hand tried to touch me up. Men, I do believe, are essentially cowards and a male escort certainly makes a difference. I was almost disappointed, and I really do believe Frank thought I was kidding. Naturally I was intent to show him the Bosphorus and the splendid view where East meets West – i.e. Europe meets Asia – and the famous bridge over the river. When we got to the "Gold Fish," famous for its wonderful fresh fish, it was closed for a special feast. A famous military General was leaving and there was a big farewell party for him. I asked if we could just have a "peep," as I wanted to show Frank the restaurant with the fine view. At that moment the General saw us and invited us to his long, large table. It was teeming with Turkish officers. I immediately thanked him and told him I had some Turkish blood way back, and that I had sung as a young girl with great success at one of Istanbul's most famous hotels – so I would be happy to sing for them and complete it with a little belly dance. This I did, choosing the famous Turkish folk song "Usku Dara". All the men clapped out the rhythm and I stood and sang and danced on the long table. I must say, for a belly dance I was dressed quite prim and properly, with long sleeves and a long black dress with little red flowers and white highlights at the neck and bust. It was a folklore dress and in the 60s very fashionable, and the men seemed to like it anyway. As guests of the General, he wanted to reciprocate and asked the band to play some belly dance music – "the real stuff," he said, whereupon two officers got up and balancing bottles on their heads, and they started the men off dancing. In no time all the men were belly dancing in lines and in no uncertain manner. Then, to my non-dancing husband's horror – the General, a really nice older man, turned to Frank and said, "Your wife has sung and danced for us – now we must dance for her."

He took Frank's arm firmly so that he had no alternative but to join the throng of belly dancing officers. Two men and the General showed Frank the technique, and I only regretted I had no camera on me to take a photo of Frank Valdor belly dancing with the General and his officer friends in Istanbul at the Bosphorus. Frank returned to me full of respect for the graceful and wonderful dancing of the Turkish men folk. He said to me and the General, "We European men dance to get a girl in our arms and with luck get much further, but the respectful Turkish men dance for the joy of dancing with no thought of a sexual thrill in their minds at all."

What with this most interesting and enjoyable interlude and my husband being everywhere with me as my male escort, I never ever needed a hat pin. I really think he didn't believe at all my hat pin story and probably put it down to his wife's vivid imagination.

CHAPTER 64

From Big Shows to Big Shock!

Back in London, after many family and friends' greetings, the girls wanted to see all my new acquisitions, above all my super accessories, only available in England for lots and lots of money, if at all. I did not show my sovereign gold bracelet; Mum had put it immediately into her safe deposit box at the bank.

The older ones were curious to hear what I had to say regarding countries where only the very few had visited. The conversation followed mainly a pattern, starting with, "Tell us about it," and ending with, "so what are you going to do now?" I was not quite sure.

George Reid, brother and manager of the famous Billy Reid, composer of "I'm Walking Behind You On Your Wedding Day", which swept the world, had gotten me some good dates previously. I met him with Jack Moss on my return home from Istanbul. He immediately jumped into the breach. He got me into a TV show as a new French face. I only had to sing one French song, my amusing version of "Le Fiacre."

As George had not enough time, I decided to take my promotions into my own hands. I asked Netty, who had made my red Duchess satin gown for my week at Selby's show restaurant & dinner dance, to make something really outstanding for my television debut. As I wanted to be a real diva she chose Turquoise satin and had it intricately beaded. It was so tight fitting it looked as if I had been poured into it. It also had a light, soft chiffon train at the back – very mod and terribly smart. I could easily have been Duke Ellington's inspiration for his "Sophisticated

Lady." Netty agreed that I could tell the press it was a creation from Jacques Fath, who had overridden Dior as the number 1 dress designer in Paris.

Only a year or two later Netty became "Neymar" and the Couturier for many Royal names, and the maker of the famous gowns of Shirley Bassey and Alma Cogan.

I went to the two main evening papers, The Star and the Evening Standard. Both newspapers even sent a photographer to photograph me in the gown at Television rehearsals. A small photo came into the papers. Truthfully, there was more written about the dress than about my song! Amazing what the right name, Jacques Fath, and the right timing can do.

I must say, I was also amazed at the reception I got at the TV station. Apart from my own dresser, I was even offered tea and biscuits. Thank you, George! It was then that the famous Noel Coward song "Don't Put Your Daughter on the Stage, Mrs. Worthington" came to mind. In any vocation you may choose, however wonderful and talented you may be – it is going to be really hard to get anywhere at all without that good old vitamin P (Protection). When I had first gone to audition for the BBC as a child, I was just part of a queue of little girls all about my age and was told "Don't phone, we'll call you if we want you," and Sally Anne Howes, film star Bobbie Howes' little daughter, got the job. Vitamin P had worked magic as usual. Such had been the same with Julie Andrews. In spite of her beautiful voice, the fact she was Bob Andrews daughter was a huge vitamin injection. Petula Clark was the little daughter of the boss of the biggest record company in England. My dad was a practical businessman in food. He thought if I should become a "restauranteur" then he could be of help, but in show business – no way!

Shortly afterwards I heard through my manager, George Reid, that the Grades were looking for a French girl, as Francois Flor, who was contracted to be the Mademoiselle de Paris for the new "Follies Bergeres" show in London at the Prince of Wales theatre, which was due to open shortly, had gone down at rehearsals with a bad attack of laryngitis and lost her voice completely.

He suggested I go to meet the agent Solly Black and, if need be, audition for him with my version of the old Mistinguett Number "Le fiacre," which I'd done in TV, which he considered to be my best for personality. If Solly needed a Ballad then I should do "Hymne a l'amour," the song that gave Edith Piaf her breakthrough. I must speak with a heavy French accent – absolutely no English. No problem for me, as in Istanbul I spoke French all the time.

The waiting room to see Mr. Black had four or five other girls all competing for the same job. They were all blondes and terribly good looking. I had a feeling I could cut their makeup with a knife. Despite their attributes, they were all typically English. I was, as usual, by far the darkest and the smallest. Finally my turn came, and as I entered I said, "Bonjour Monsieur."

Mr. Solly Black was very kind. He spoke good French and I answered every question in French, concentrating on a good nasal accent. Finally, he told me not to stand, but to come and sit down on his far more comfortable armchair. Once seated he got up suddenly, bent over me and touched a knob in the well-padded arm of the chair. Before I could think it went almost flat like a bed. Boy, that threw me!

I was in such a state of shock that I shouted out, "Bloody hell, whatever happened?" and I jumped up in seconds with my two flat feet planted firmly on the floor again. Solly stood there smiling, very amused.

"I thought that would finally throw you," he said. "I had a feeling you're a smart little girl from London and not from Paris at all, but kid you did it well. I like your guts. We are going to get you trained, talk French, think French, we'll do the rest. First thing is that long dark hair of yours will have to go. We'll get Steiner" – the most publicized hairdresser at that time – "to fix it – we have no time to waste."

Monsieur Steiner certainly did fix it, cutting it short and highlighting it with copper and platinum. He named the style "Coup de soleil" – it became the rage – for the French leading lady (me, I believe) and the new totally French show coming to London, but not before Monsieur Steiner told me my hair grew in 24 different directions.

In the following days I was kept so busy I had no time to eat and lost weight visibly.

Andrew Lloyd Weber's father Principal at the London School of Music classified my voice as capricious. If my hair decided to curl in all different directions, it seemed to fit into the picture. I was born that much different, with a deep pull towards individualism. I'm not so good in a line. Because of this a few numbers with the girls' chorus were quickly cut, I just didn't have time to learn all the steps they did, but "C'est si bon," the main number, was a hundred percent my cup of tea or should I say my glass of wine (supposedly being French). The production people sitting in the front row of the stalls clapped and seemed to dig my French style. I loved the way I had to act, right down to the black net elastic tights that made my thighs super slim. The rest of the show was from Paris and just a little "toffee-nosed," but the chorus girls and boys were just fine, and as I had a dressing room to myself with a big silver star on the door I had little time to chatter or even to think, except for the few words I had to say or to sing. The way I stood and turned my body and walked were all important, and I learnt a lot in a very short time about body language, something I had not given a thought to before.

As I was only a stand-in my name was on a leaf put in the Program, to be removed quickly when the original star booked for the show could take over. No matter, the experience was marvelous and some big agents had the opportunity of seeing me.

Pedro de Cordobes, with his outstanding Spanish footwork, was booked for a 12-day guest appearance with his ensemble at the Lido in Paris – where, apart from all the semi-nude girls, they always had one special attraction of the superlative. Solly Black was the sharpest of agents and when my six weeks were up at the "Follies," he persuaded Pedro to take me to enhance his show for all the American tourists who were flocking to Paris. With a black wig I looked the part. I could manage to dance a jotta with the girls (a Spanish folk dance) and play the castanets, both of which I had learnt when I was chosen for the Ramsgate summer season where I had to sing the two arias from "Carmen." The English language was also imperative for the tourist trade in Paris.

It was great fun, particularly as on the first night my old student friends Jacques and his sister Henriette Duteuil came to see me, reviving the memory of that happy first season by the seaside. I had learnt from them the typical French expression "Le Taxi numero onze" which meant (as none of us had any means of transport) we would be using our two legs and walking. We joked about this and Jacques, who was now delving into cancer cure research as a student doctor, asked me if I'd change to a "Deux Chevaux," as he had that little French car to get around Paris. I was kept so busy I had no time to see if Harry Janes' girlfried Didi was still behind the bar at the Adelphi. Remembering the headlines about Harry Janes, I decided to give that idea the go-by.

During all this time I still received constant mail from Nick in Israel, telling me one day he would surprise me and turn up in London or Paris – so I should be prepared. To add to all these happenings, some weeks later Nick phoned me saying he was in London staying at a hotel in Russell Square and asked if I could possibly meet him. I was really surprised – what was he doing in London? He had a wife, a home, a son, and a good business. I got quite a shock when he told me he had forfeited all these important things to come to me in London so that we could be together. He also mentioned he had never lost touch with my father. I crossed my fingers that things would not turn out as they had done with Harry Janes in Paris.

Our meeting was special. It was a bit like our first meeting at Genati Yum in Tel Aviv. Suddenly he was a lot older than I remembered him to be, and a lot whiter. In comparison to the guys in the show he seemed small, and somehow puny – where were his muscles? Then he took me into his arms and kissed me on my lips and then all over, and after we had made love I swear he looked 10 years younger and a lot more handsome. I said to myself, "Yvonne, this must be the "grand amour" of your life. You are still quite madly in love, and he is neither a super man nor even single." It was all the traps I swore I would never fall into. I guess one should never swear!

He took me to a movie – it was supposed to be the life of the famous film star Tallulah Bankhead, called "Sunset Boulevard". She ended up committing suicide and you saw her body floating down the river. It was horrible. As we came out Nick turned to me and said, "You see how your chosen profession ends?"

For a change I was completely silent, but I thought to myself, "Bloody bugger, he is not going to stop me."

CHAPTER 65

Milano

All this time Nick was hovering in the background of my life. Sometime later in a letter Nick asked me what my favourite country was, and where I would like to live. I said Italy, as the sun, the beaches and the happy way of life had impressed me. In the latest movies, which were mainly comedies or musicals, all the stories were built around Italy. Even the language was to my ears like music itself, and now I had a new film love I adored, "Rosano Brazzi".

The next letter was from Paris and Nick asked, "How would you like to live with me in Milano?" "Quick Nick," true to his name, turned up trumps again.

He sent me a return air ticket London – Milan – London and I was so taken aback, he could have knocked me down with a feather.

The most memorable part of Milano for me was the famous Dome and all the pigeons, and how you could never sleep on a Sunday morning because it seemed all the many churches in Milano rang their bells loud and musically one after the other.

It was there where I met Nick's brother Abrasha. He was a bigger man and bore very little similarity to Nick physically or as a person. The girl he called his "fiancée" was a blonde of about 20, quite nice-looking with the high cheekbones and round face, which slowly I could discern as being from some country in Eastern Europe – later I found out it was Romania.

Nick told me, "Now I must visit the clubs. I work for a big international company, and I have been given a shop. It's on a side street, off one of the main streets here. Do you need a really smart swimsuit?"

What a question – of course I did. In no time we were there at his boutique, and I chose a new elasticised one piece in white with a lavender flowered panel in front; it also had a small half skirt, which was the latest craze. I was delighted with the back zipper – sexy!

When I asked him how one could make the sort of big money he had told me he was making, by selling only expensive swimsuits, he smiled and said, "Bella already told me how innocent you are. When you went shopping together to get a belt she fancied, you bought one for yourself and paid the price the girl was asking."

"Yes," I said. I had no idea that Italy was like the Orient, where you always had to bargain. Bella walked out with me and the girl ran after us and called her back, and treated her as if she were the Right Honourable Bella, and she got what she wanted at the price she had offered.

As for me – "Dumb cluck," the shopkeeper regarded me disdainfully, "how could anyone be so dumb to pay the price asked?"

Nick laughed and laughed. He said, "Come behind the counter." There was a door I had not seen at all, which opened and there, stacked high up the wall, I could see all the most wanted cameras in the world – like Leicas. What I saw must have been worth a small fortune. He grinned and eyed me up and down with his head to one side and said, "The swimsuits are just a cover up. This group really know their business."

We went to various clubs he seemed to know, and Nick had some beautiful custom-made suits and shirts to harmonize with them. He really started to look like the successful businessman not just in Israel but also in Italy. He wanted me to stay with him, and he and Abrasha took me to an Alpha Romeo garage where they had bought a beautiful, white, new model car for Bella. Then Nick took photos of her dressed in a special designer costume in navy blue and white. I was speechless at the lifestyle they seemed to be living.

"That can be yours too my sweet black pudding, if only you would give up this mad idea of singing around the world and be my "fiancée" too. I could get a divorce and we could get married if you want to. We could work together. You do love me, don't you?" he asked in his very deep sensual voice with his heavy Russian accent. He came so close I could feel the magic between us.

I was too young and too romantic and it all sounded like a beautiful dream, but what about my career and being independent, that was number one, wasn't it? I had to fight my emotions like mad to regain all my self discipline, the tough stuff I learnt at school. I took a deep breath and whispered, "Oh, Nick, you know I do, but, but please just let me do that June engagement in Zürich, the one that new agent promised me," I stammered. "Then I'll know for sure how I feel and how I make out on the Continent. The contract is signed, so I must go." It wasn't, but I decided it sounded better.

The word "marriage" had given me a severe jolt; marrying was the one thing I never wanted to do – ever.

CHAPTER 66

Sean Connery

The phone rang at home. "This is the Grade Office," said a female voice. "Is that Yvonne Carré, one minute please, I'll put you through to Mr. Solly Black."

I held my breath and crossed my fingers. "Hello Yvonne," said a kindly voice, "Are you free tomorrow? If so, I've got an interesting blind date for you. There are two handsome young and coming up film actors on our books, looking for a couple of good blind dates. Both are very well connected in the film – movie branch and if they were on the Stock Exchange, they would be on our BUY list," he added with a chuckle.

I had not an inkling about the Stock Exchange, so this amusing remark was completely lost on me.

"I have booked Anita Arno for one guy called Maxwell Reed." (later, film star Joan Collins' first husband) "Yours is a real strong type from Scotland, Sean Connery."

I had never heard of either of them, so I asked him to spell Sean.

He said, "Well, it's Scottish, "Sean.""

"Oh," I said, "I've got it right, it sounds like "seen" to me."

"It's pronounced "Shawn" and he is coming out in a new film. The "rushes" have been seen and we all believe his type is new and he sure has a real bright future. Now listen to me Baby – play your cards right and you can jump on his bandwagon. Be tomorrow evening at 7 pm at the Cumberland Hotel – you know, where Alma is singing with the band. Wait at the entrance of the dinner dance restaurant, Anita will be there waiting for you, look good and sexy. Fate will do the rest."

I did exactly what Solly had told me and there were Anita and a refined looking young man who introduced himself as Maxwell Reed. Then came the Scots man. He had a handsome but with a harder face and his whole manner was forthright.

He took over the leadership of our little group and shepherded us to our table. We four ate and talked and grinned at each other. Maxwell was quite a good dancer and would have looked good leading the Follies Bergere Chorus line. Sean was quite another story. He knew the "rushes" of his latest film were good and he would be in high demand, however he explained to me he only danced "under pressure."

Finally, we left the other two and as we came out Sean turned to me and said in a very matter of fact voice, "Where should we "shack up" – I know a nice little hotel not far from here. Let's hop in a taxi."

I was really taken aback. So this is what Solly had meant by playing my cards right. Sean Connery may have been every girl's dream man, but I was still in love with Nick Norovski – so Frank Sinatra was definitely more my type.

"Look," I said, "I may be your blind date, but my folks taught me not to forget who I am, and that is from a good family."

"Well, you were in the "Follies" weren't you?" he asked point blank.

"Well, that was because they needed me in a hurry – it was a happy fluke," I said ruefully, "but I'm only 17 and I've promised my father I'd make it without turning into a prostitute."

He looked down on me and said, "You're a broad, ain't you? You want to get on in this business, don't you?"

"Yes," I said, "I do, but I am still stupid enough to hope that I'll get there without turning into a whore. I want to make love with someone whom I love and who hopefully loves me, and I guess you don't – after all we've only just met."

He looked down at me almost quizzically. "Well, well, Cinderella, goodbye – let's hope your good fairy turns up for you with a Crystal Coach. Later on, you may remember that I could have been your Prince Charming," he said sardonically with a grin on his handsome face.

With that he hailed a taxi and I never saw him again, except on the silver screen as 007. I went home on the tube to Hendon Central, wondering why I was so in love with love, instead of loving money and fame.

CHAPTER 67

The Backfire

Next day I got a call from Solly rebuking me quite hard for making such a blunder.

"Well, my dear," he said, "you have thrown away probably your only real chance of becoming a famous film star. My God, you had the possibility of being Sean Connery's first real star girlfriend, just the publicity alone could have been worth a small fortune!"

"I guess I've let you down badly, but I couldn't even go to bed with the King of England without being in love with him."

"How can a girl in show business be so in love with love instead of using her ambition to love fame and the money it brings?"

"I guess I'm old fashioned," I whispered, "I'm sorry."

He put the phone down.

The next days went by slowly, and then George, my manager, called and said, "You certainly loused it up with Mr. Solly Black, but he is a kindhearted guy and after a month or so has passed he'll have forgotten everything about it, but hold your hat there's good news: The Geraldo Orchestra is interested in you for a season at the best hotel in Bermuda."

"Heavens that's particularly interesting for me, Mum told me I was actually born there."

"What?" ejaculated George.

I had not told George about meeting that Continental Manager at the Barclay Hotel, but as I had not heard from his office, the idea of being with the most famous sweet music orchestras in the U.K. and a five-star trip to beautiful Bermuda was most inviting.

The very next day arrived a letter postmarked Zürich. Mr. Gardiner, the famous Swiss agent, had an opening for me at the best restaurant in Zürich. If I should be a success, then I had to sign a contract that he would be my personal manager for the next two years, as he had a line of engagements on hand.

There I was, once again at the crossroads. At 17 it suddenly seemed as if the whole world was interested in me, and I had to decide which path to take.

Dad was as usual adamant. "If you want a café or a restaurant you're my girl, but show biz, apart from the odd charity show," which were very popular at that time, "I can't help you with your chosen profession."

Bermuda for Geraldo or Zürich in Switzerland, the country I had fallen in love with seven years ago. I weighed up the "pros" and "cons." "Stick to your guns," I said to myself, "you wanted a house in Switzerland," – I chose Zürich!

CHAPTER 68

The Perfect Lady

It's May 1953, the coronation of the new Queen of England, Elizabeth II, and her husband the Duke of Edinburgh. London was at the high point of festivities. Every hotel and restaurant tried to engage the best show as cabaret, to complement their seven-course Coronation menu. The hit song from the Swiss musical "Fireworks" by Paul Burkhard, "Oh mein Papa," had swept over the German speaking part of Europe. A little later Eddie Fisher, the young protégé of US Film comedian Eddy Cantor, made "Oh my Papa" a classic for the rest of the world with his version.

The Barclay Hotel wanted to be in and with the help of her efficient manager Lys Assia, being the original Swiss recording star, was engaged for this celebration. Approximately about this time it seems everything was about to happen to me too. I received a letter from the oldest theatrical agent in Israel telling me to make "post-haste" and get to the Barclay Hotel where a famous Swiss singer named Lys Assia was appearing. She would be accompanied by her manager, a Berliner whom he knew well. He had already written to her super efficient manager telling him of my success in Israel and the Near East. Should the Berliner want to make money, he should try his luck with me and fix an engagement to decide for himself. I was too late to catch Lys Assia's show.

When I knocked on this super manager's door at the Barclay he was already packing, as he and the now famous diva were due to leave the following day. I came straight in, introduced myself and referred to the letter he had supposedly received from Tel Aviv. I was told curtly, "Now I am packing, it's too late."

Not to be outdone, I went over to the window, giving him more space to carry on packing and said, "That's ok, I'll audition for you right now."

Before he could protest, I went straight into "I Love You For Sentimental Reasons", giving one of my best renderings a capella (no musical accompaniment). I followed this up with a second song, Gershwin's "The Man I Love". The manager stopped packing and sat on his bed to listen. He was impressed – just as the moment seemed magic and I thought I had won him over, the door opened and a perfectly groomed and elegant lady entered.

"Oh – I thought you were alone and had the radio on."

It was Lys Assia!

I had no idea that later we would be often thrown together on various galas and tours. Lys had something that few pop singers have today: a dignified stage presence. Although not a lot taller than me, she was always coiffed and clothed expensively. She undoubtedly had star quality.

Some years later, she as the "Queen of Song" and me, as the up-and-coming young star, we both toured Western Europe with the famous French pianist Jacques Dieval's show "Jazz de Champs Elysées." The concerts included such celebrities as French guitarist/singer Sascha Distel, Swedish jazz singer Alice Babs, Danish violinist Svend Asmussen, and the effusive Italian chanteuse Milva, often called "La Rossa" (at that time she loved to wear bouffant pink dresses). Young and happy with her success, Milva blew kisses to everyone in the audience.

The whole cast sat at a long table to eat and drink after the show as a sort of big family. Lys had a marvelous habit of saving money – which indeed she loved. She never could make up her mind what to eat or drink, so she went around the table trying a little from everyone's plate, as "a taster." Once through she would say to the attending waiter, "Well after all that I'm not so hungry – I'll settle for a Ragou Fin or Bouche de la Reine."

Often the smallest and cheapest meal on the menu. Perhaps that was her way to keep such a slim and trim figure.

Other times, when she really was hungry and had eaten a really big meal, she would smile at me and whisper, "Let's go to the ladies' room."

Before I knew the ropes – after some time I wanted to return to the restaurant and the others. She held me back.

"No dear, don't go yet – wait til the men have paid for us, then we can go to our seats."

There was a lot to learn about how to treat men, not just from Hungarian film star Zsa Zsa Gabor, but also from Miss Lys Assia. She was not just an elegant singer with perfect diction – she was a smart lady. She knew many men used women to their own advantage and she felt pre-destined to have the power to hit back. She was clever and hard working with languages. She had the knack of catching millionaires in her net; Miss Assia really loved the power and the glory.

Later I met her at a television show in Zürich, after her second husband, the Danish multi-millionaire and owner of many hotels named Oscar Pederson, had died in a car accident in the south of France where he was also Danish General Counsel.

Many years had passed, but she seemed unchanged. Lys Assia was still the well dressed, well poised singer I knew from the 50s and 60s, and she still loved singing and enjoyed being a star and admired. Now in her 80s, the chief of her former Record Company told me at the IFPI luncheon she was at Midem in Cannes, and had actually posed in the nude for the Swiss Magazine "Annabelle" to show that even at 83 a disciplined and sensible woman can still manage to look attractive.

I take my hat off to such persistent determination. Now if that isn't ambition for you – what is?

At that time Lys Assia left the manager Mr. Gardiner and myself alone, and he said, "Look, I have no time for you now, send me photos and any material you think good and with luck you'll hear from my office."

He then opened the door for me to leave.

CHAPTER 69

Zürich

Zürich was new ground, and I started to learn German as my school German was not much more than: 1, 2, 3, die Henne legt ein Ei. Die Henne legt ein grosses Ei, 1, 2, 3. For me it was all important to have a good contact with the audience.

The orchestra under Nino Puttini was excellent in accompanying a wild card as myself, who made the audience and orchestra participate.

My opening night at the "Hungaria," the biggest and most famous restaurant on the Bahnhofstrasse in Zürich (which was the main thoroughfare for Banks, big jewellers and world famous couturiers and a MUST for visitors), was overcrowded with tourists and Swiss residents. My special success came, more or less, oddly enough through a blunder. I always started my show with an upbeat Frankie Lane number – he was the biggest number one attraction at that time. I copied his super energetic dynamic style as it suited my own personality perfectly. After the opening song I liked to talk to the public, making them feel part of the show. I told the audience „Ich bin eine Englaenderin, aber ich bin nicht kalt – nein ich bin…" I thought quickly, I can't say I'm HOT they might get the wrong idea – so I went for the middle and quickly said: "Ich bin warm," and with that the audience burst out laughing. I had no idea why and looked perplexed which made them laugh more. Then I said, "Oh dear, have I put my foot in it?"

There were huge guffaws from the Swiss and Austrian guests. They probably thought I was a comedienne. After my Gershwin potpourri to really show off my voice, and an Edith Piaf Number,

I did the popular Lucienne Boyer and Hildegaard catchy little point number "Darling, je vous aime beaucoup" which carried on with "je ne sais pas what to do, vous avez completely stolen my heart." I was cheeky enough to ask for a man to come on the stage with me. I then tried my German, mixing it with English. It sounded something like this "Liebling, ich lieb dich so sehr, won't you tell me that you care, du hast mein Herz gestohlen right from the start" (my own half German words).

Then, with all the lightfingered pickpocketing I had learnt from the Romanian artists in the revue I did with them in Israel – something came to fruition. I deftly removed his wallet without him noticing it at all. I almost surprised myself how easily it all functioned. Then I held the wallet on the back of his jacket and turned him toward me as I sang. By that time most of the audience perceived what had happened, they all started to laugh again. At the end I kissed him on the cheeks 3 times as I was told this was the Swiss custom. As he walked down the two steps from the stage onto the floor heading for his table, I called him back and said, "Oh, I think you forgot this – you may need it later when you get the bill."

He giggled and shook his head as a man a little tipsy, and the public laughed and laughed, so did he, as did everybody. They clapped and clapped and the manager of the Hungaria, Mr. Bottinelli, asked my new manager Mr. Gardiner for a return engagement in August.

Mr. Gardiner was very sly and clever. He got me to sign a minimum two-year contract and promised me verbally in no time I could double my salary, which was ok, but nothing to shout about. Like Nick had been in Israel, he was "on the ball" and knew how to get what he wanted. He was a tall, dark, hard-faced, unsmiling man and had none of the finesse of Nick, nor the soft persuasive voice. He was very fashion conscious, and I was busy saving for a house in Switzerland. He had to have me in designer clothes, and I was once again whisked off to an atelier in Zürich of the most famous Swiss designers. Mr. Gardiner wanted me in white organdy with light mimosa appliquéd on the voluminous skirt, and then another with sequined flowers in lilac and light green leaves. He did not want me to be a sexy diva; he wanted me to be light, fresh, young, and royal. This time I was not the Queen of England as in Famagusta, but Princess Margaret who, after her highly publicised separation from Peter Townsend, was said to be hiding out somewhere on the Continent.

The film "Ein Herz und eine Krone" – in English "Roman Holiday" – with Audrey Hepburn playing the part of Princess Margaret was all the rage, and the word got around this little girl could actually be me.

Engagements poured in all over Switzerland, and I had no idea they had so many towns with Casinos, sometimes called Kursaals in the German speaking parts. In any case all really big restaurants which had at least an 8-piece or 12-piece band and then a star guest artiste – generally a singer.

I didn't possess a big diamond ring, so Mr. Gardiner told me I just had to have a mink coat and to do what he said. This meant traveling first class or with taxis, never to mix with the common folk on buses. I must act like a star and be aloof.

How to do all this on my meager savings? I was well aware of the good old English proverb, "In life you have to throw a sprat to catch a mackerel." To me it seemed more like having to throw a salmon to catch a bear! Fortunately, my sister-in-law came to the rescue once again. She worked for the luxury fur boutique in Bruton Street, just off Bond Street in London, and clothed the stars and show girls. There was a coat of good ranch mink befitting little me; it cost 10,000 pounds sterling. I put down 3,000 pounds of my hard earned savings and paid up the rest in installments. Thankfully June in Zürich was often cold and rainy, so I did not look so out of place in a full-length mink coat.

The stage dresses I had custom made in Cyprus were not to my new manager's liking, for a young princess. It is an expensive business grooming a star with no mentor to pay the bills.

While in Zürich Mr. Gardiner took me to the Baur au Lac Hotel tea dancing. After we had ordered shrimp cocktails and English tea and danced a couple of dances, which he did quite well, six young girls sidled up to our table asking for an autograph from me. The waiters put the word around I was a secret big young star and had just flown in from Brazil. As I felt very cold here, I had kept my mink coat on (actually it was because Mr. Gardiner did not like my black dress; it was slinky, and he felt it made me look too old). The Press was punctually on hand to take photos of the large queue wanting autographs from me, the new star. Mr. Gardiner showed his organising ability with publicity. He was really good and did the interview. I was told beforehand to "hold my tongue and shut up."

The shrimp cocktail was less of a success; Mr. Gardiner persisted in showing me how to eat it properly. I jabbed my fork into the large black olive sitting in the middle of the cocktail, believing it to be pitted. Full of the rich, orange-coloured sauce, it flew through the air, landing on the voluptuous bodice of an older lady's new dress. She let out a piercing scream of horror. All eyes turned to her table and her dilemma. Our bill had been paid beforehand. Mr. Gardiner was absolutely disgusted with me. Needless to say, we made a hurried exit.

I was never taken tea dancing at the Baur au Lac Hotel again.

CHAPTER 70

Three Great Lifelong Swiss Friends

During this period of my life, I had almost never a free day and did many recordings with the Chief of Beromuenster Radio (Zürich), the famous conductor and composer Cedric Dumont. He was known mainly for his light music, but he was also a great jazz pianist, and whenever we could we spent happy moments, him playing on his grand piano and me singing – both riffing. It was balm for happy hearts.

A little later, Louis Rey, the Chief of the French speaking Radio Geneva, saw my show at the Geneva Moulin Rouge. He was delighted that I spoke French, which he presumed from my name. He offered a Saturday weekly radio show, and I could even put in a composition of my own. However, his clever and amusing "Dans la Marine Suisse, il n'y a pas des matelots" (in the Swiss navy there are no sailors – only admirals… it's the gold braided uniforms that count!) became so popular I had to make it a mainstay in my repertoire.

Signor Fernando Paggi came calling from the Svizzera Italiano, Lugano, and had some great jazz musicians in his orchestra. I wrote the dreamy "It Was Down In Lugano" especially for him and his radio station.

Walter Amman was the handsome and sympathetic chief of TV Light Entertainment in Zürich, and for me the number three in line. As he was born on February the 14th I always called him "my Valentine," and he enjoyed sending me romantic cards from everywhere. This he did until he passed away. We never got closer than an occasional lunch together. I was in a way his "dream girl" and remained so.

The three, Cedric Dumont, Louis Rey, and Walter Amman, remained until their passings wonderful platonic friends – an unusual phenomenon in show business, where the bed or the sofa – at least in London – seemed to be part of the deal.

At that time Bert Kaempfert and Herbert Rehbein, the violinist virtuouso, were doing marvelous things with music. Bert made a world hit with "Swinging Safari" and later "Strangers in the Night" and of course the beautiful "Spanish Eyes", which was for that friendly nice guy Tony Christie a real breakthrough, while Herbert wrote the melancholy refrain "The World We Knew". Both the latter, and "Strangers" hit the top when they were recorded by Frank Sinatra. It was for me a compliment, and heavenly to do some string recordings with such innovative minds as the two "Berts."

The more I traveled in Switzerland from engagement to engagement the more I loved my chosen profession and my chosen country, which was always at the back of my mind. The public where I sang was well dressed and refined, and it suited me and my style. As Mum (my very discerning mother) had told me:

"You are for the wine public; beer is not your brew."

Frankly I did not care for either. Apart from that, Mr. Gardiner told me I must be secretive. For an outgoing and gullible young woman like myself, this was not easy. However, traveling always by train, and being quiet, gave me real opportunities of admiring the magnificent mountain scenery, and to meditate on how fortunate I was to be blessed with three real friends.

CHAPTER 71

A Legend: Heinz Hoffmeister

The time flew by happily. A press conference started me off at the famous Hotel Atlantic in Hamburg for the Variety Stage of Haus Vaterland as the Vedette Americaine. The Hansa Stadt loved my young girlish style and Mr. Gardiner fixed a photo session with the handsome mature René Carol, at that time the most famous pop singer in Germany. He sang the song "Rote Lippen, rote Rosen, roter Wein".

Mr. Papst, the chief of Haus Vaterland, gave Mr. Gardiner a new contract for me, this time as the star. The newspapers printed photos of René Carol and me – was it a new romance? Typical ridiculous sensationalism – but it captured the curiosity of the German public – very good for business!

It was like heaven. The bosses of these big German theatres asked me when I was free to return to their cities. The only fly in the ointment was Mr. Heinz Hoffmeister. He was the greatest Summer Tournee manager, and he was planning the next with the famous beloved comedian poet Heinz Erhardt. From what I had read he was highly intelligent and had an irreproachable relationship to the German language and idioms. I made up my mind: if Mr. Gardiner could not manage to get me on to the Heinz Erhardt tour, I would try myself.

Dad was a pillar of strength in winning battles. He told me if all the managers say "No," put your foot in the door. If it closes, go through the window, and if you still cannot see whom you need to talk to, climb up on the roof. Be like Santa Claus, slide down the chimney. He was a hard teacher, and in spite of my rebellious nature I admired him.

So, it came to pass I finally got to see Mr. Heinz Hoffmeister. Unfortunately, he had more than enough singers on his books who were long in Germany, and he was loath to take another. I thought of Dad and what he had told me. As Mr. Hoffmeister asked me to leave after saying no to me at least 10 times, I said, "Mr. Hoffmeister, I am sitting on this chair and not leaving until you have signed me for the Heinz Erhardt tour and I mean it."

Actually, I was trembling inside waiting for a harsh rebuke for my super audacious attitude, but instead he smiled. "Your enthusiasm and determination amaze me," he said. "Somehow that sort of grit will get you through your show."

He gave me the contract I longed for there and then. We both signed and I breathed a sigh of relief.

That summer I had the special experience of touring Germany with a veritable legend. What a simply super artist and what a talented human being Heinz Erhardt was! After the successful tour with Heinz Erhardt, Mr. Hoffmeister was so happy he booked me for his next tour which was with the famous Swiss singer, entertainer, and film star Vico Torriani.

Vico was a showman par excellence. After the show he would tell our leader Bobby Schmidt to go on ahead to a certain restaurant. There he and his musicians would give the word Vico would be coming at such and such a time. There would then be a dozen phone calls, and in next to no time the place would be packed. Then, at the arranged hour in a light Lurex-style suit, to a fanfare from the Sextet, Vico would enter through the door, and everyone would clap and cheer and ask for autographs. They would be happy they had something special to talk about at their next club meeting or chat about with their friends. Vico was inexhaustible and always managed to shine, even after a heavy one-hour show.

All would have been fine if some of the critics in the newspapers had not written, "Vico was good, but the young jazz singer almost stole the show with her sparkling personality. We hope on the next Hoffmeister show she would be the star in the middle of the picture frame." Vico did not like that at all, and from then onward he tried to knock me down. Shame he did not have my attitude – "live and let live."

As I was new, the boys in the band started to make my life difficult with their wandering hands. Each one wanted to be the first to lay me. The blonde singer in the show was the Austrian soprano Erni Bieler – whom they all knew from before. However, Erni and I became good friends, so to keep the wolves at bay we pretended to be lesbians. We laughed all the way to our hotel rooms on a nightly basis. Funny how young men get really concerned when we girls prefer us girls to them!

My first TV show in Germany really gave me the jitters. It was to be in a cookery show, one of the first of this popular kind. I was dead nervous. I had had lessons in almost everything from languages to gardening, from hygiene to learning how to play castanets – but I had never learnt how to cook – not even how to boil potatoes.

It was to be a contest between our famous moderator Hamburger Willi Rietmeister, our big band leader Joe Wicks, and me. How I managed to get the second prize I will never know – except I had two lady professional cooks who did everything for me. I think the camera man was very kind – showing their hands and then my smiling face. I won a German Cookery Book, so should you pass my way and have a hankering for the North German cuisine, I can promise you – by this time – I can make quite professional Koenigsberger Klopse.

CHAPTER 72

A Paris Hat – A London Trapeze
Help Clinch A Deal

Paris, for generations, was regarded as that famous city on the Seine, made specially for lovers. Nick was fully aware of this well publicised idea. When I had some free time in between engagements he decided that perhaps our love story needed a refresher course from his workplace, Milan – so he invited me to spend a short romantic honeymoon in Paris. When I arrived, he whisked me off immediately to the Jean Patou Boutique. It was the most expensive of all the famous Paris couturiers. He fulfilled a dream for me. The moment I entered with Nick and saw the wonderful collections of hats – I knew exactly which one I wanted. It was a white felt pancake style with a stand-up tail at the back, the very latest Patou creation. It possessed a little half veil in front in black net. With that hat with the big Jean Patou label sewn in and my dark brown mink coat I felt I would be indeed "The Cat's whiskers" …plus its tail!

Somehow Nick enabled me always to achieve my dreams, so when he whispered in my ear after a particularly super lovemaking session that he had the possibility of starting up in business in London – all he needed was a few thousand pounds more to help him through the initial period – I was still floating somewhere on cloud nine. Then he asked me:

"Do you think your dad could help?" then he put on that little boy smile with his head to one side, to observe my reactions better.

"Oh, of course," I said spontaneously, without a moment's contemplation.

Then smilingly he added, "Naturally you and Dad would be official partners."

The idea of having the man I loved and my Mum and Dad so near at hand, was certainly an idyllic picture. I could hardly wait to get back to London to speak to Dad seriously about this new situation. Dad was, like me, completely taken by Nick's persuasive powers. Mum was not. Firstly, she felt Nick was far too old for a lively young girl like me, and somehow, he was too good to be true. I would tell Dad that I loved him more than myself and would stand bail for such a deal. That certainly would persuade Dad. I was literarily head over heels in happy dreams of driving a white Rolls Royce Corniche with Nick following in his Ferrari as we drove to our vacation home on the Italian Riviera.

I had no idea then that Nick had got much closer to Dad and had visited him a couple of times in London. He had not mentioned a word of such meetings to me. I could not wait to get home to ask Dad to help Nick.

Whenever I had free time, I invariably took the boat train from Calais to Dover and then on to London and home.

Going home was always special and at that time Betty Hutton, the "Annie Get Your Gun" film star, was returning for a re-engagement at the London Palladium. Frances, my sister, was all excited and George, her handsome and lively husband, had managed to get tickets for the much loved star's opening night on the coming Saturday. The newspaper was full of the adventurous Betty Hutton, who would not be toting a gun as in her hit musical movie but, daring as she was, she would be swinging from a trapeze with no safety net. She was so sure of her own abilities. Secretly I had since childhood always dreamed of swinging from a trapeze, so I would have given the world to have seen her show. After all, she had started her career as a singer. That night I had a terrible dream – a horrible premonition of her falling from a trapeze. It so upset me that I begged Frances and George not to go, but they thought I was crazy. I remembered Uncle Mick's passing, and I was not so sure if I was mad, or seemed to possess some uncanny sixth sense. The dreadful accident did occur. It was journalistic sensationalism at its most horrible and having witnessed it all Frances, like many others, was in a state of shock and stayed in bed on the Sunday. I was shattered and thankful that I was not born a few hundred years earlier, when I probably would have been burnt at the stake.

As my time was so short in the capital, I started to lose a lot of contacts, but I kept in touch with Jack Moss, my dear old friend, and of course Solly Black, who was for me a London stalwart. I hoped in time he would forget my mishandling of the date he had arranged for me with Sean Connery, which Jack assured me he would.

When I asked Dad about Nick's money problem, he was surprisingly positive, obviously he liked Nick. However, Dad asked me if I was really sure of him opening a business in London. I told Dad of my premonition with Betty Hutton and before with Uncle Mick and I thought I really had some God-given sixth sense. I answered, "I believe in Nick," and I said this unflinchingly.

Little did I know then that this odd nightmare and Betty Hutton's fall from the near-ceiling height trapeze, seemingly so far away from myself and my own life, was actually quite near, for I too was riding on some highflying cloud in my Rolls Royce dreams – which were due to burst far sooner than I ever realized.

CHAPTER 73

From Tipsy Nick to Literary Nietschke

Unfortunately, the meetings with Nick and our fantasy world were rare as I rushed from one engagement to another, and I never stopped learning new numbers and rehearsing. Nick also seemed over busy traveling, and his love of whisky improved under the strain, which I could not help noticing whenever we did meet.

Once he drank a little too much and confided in me that he had a companion in his company who had worked at the Mint and could print perfect, undetectable big money bills. This made me wonder why he wanted so much money from Dad. He actually showed me, with bravado, an Austrian Passport with another name with his photo – which, he said with a whisky slur in his voice and his engaging grin, was much easier for his travels than an Israeli passport at that time.

When he had shown me his expensive cameras with the cover up of smart, expensive swimsuits, I passed it off as black market. After the end of the long war, in the fifties there were still many commodities many people with money would pay small fortunes for, because they were just not available, let alone flooding the market. Anyone who had the luck of good connections could go into black market dealings – it was not unusual. I accepted this, but counterfeit money and another passport were, for a good middle-class girl like me, too much. I thought, with what sort of company was he involved? Suddenly I remembered the words of the house janitor at my first Tel Aviv apartment:

"Take care little girl, the man you believe to be your friend is from the underworld."

At that time, I was horrified that this worker could say such a thing about the man who had actually saved my life.

Dad had taught me a good name is worth a great deal and I knew now I could be a successful singer and entertainer and make good money with my own talents. I wanted no part of something that seemed not above board. I told Nick quite frankly I would not join his company – I would stick to my career and make that my goal. I decided I must warn Dad and then something terrible happened.

Mr. Botinelli reengaged me for the "Hungaria" in Zürich. On my opening night the weather was cold and windy, and suddenly during my third song – a strong ballad – a man in a shabby looking overcoat entered the restaurant without removing his old trilby hat and started shouting.

"I love that girl, she is mine. I want her, I need her, she's mine!"

I was so shocked, I forgot the words completely. After all, Nick had not phoned me for some time, and I had no idea he was here in Zürich. It was incomprehensible for me that this half-drunk bedraggled person was Nick – smart, astute Nick, the man I had loved. Alcohol had obviously won its battle – but why? Was it his new company in Milan, or could the reason be me? People shouted at him to shush and the maître d' asked him quietly to leave, and he did. I picked up the pieces of my messed-up show and tried to carry on.

The second night was a recurrence of my first night. This time director Botinelli wasted no time at all. He phoned Mr. Gardiner and said, "This man is ruining her show. Who is he?"

In the meantime, Nick waited for me outside. He reeked of whisky, but was not too drunk to say, "I believed in you, I thought I could rely on you to be my partner in life, but you my sweet black pudding let me down, as Nietschke would say "It's better an end with a shock than a shock without an end.""

The third night, Nick came again – Mr. Gardiner came too and in a hard voice he asked me, "Who is this man ruining your show? Is he mad or what?"

I tried to explain – Mr. Gardiner stopped me. "Can we have him thrown out?" he almost spat.

"Oh yes," I said, closing my eyes and heaving a huge sigh of relief.

In my third song on the third night a fully alcoholized, bedraggled Nick started to shout, "I love this girl – she is mine! She is mine!"

He got no further. Two heavy weight security guys grabbed him by the shoulders and threw him right out into the street.

As Nietschke said, it was an end with a terrible shock!

CHAPTER 74

Coca Cola Bottles

This could not happen today, and in any case my temper is much milder now. At that time, a Coca Cola bottle had a special design and was made of glass. Coke was the most popular drink. Some drank it out of the bottle, some with a straw, but in most restaurants, it was served and poured into a glass. The bottles had a small deposit on them. Whether it was in Hamburg or Duesseldorf I can't quite recall, but the name of the bandleader who accompanied the artistes including myself was Rolf Tragau. A good orchestra with a good-looking bandleader.

One night I left the Theatre Restaurant later as I had to collect some of my music for some recordings at the Radio next day. As the band packed up too, Mr. Tragau asked me if, as his digs lay in the same direction as mine, he could walk me to my residence and at the same time carry my music for me, which was not light, as my "dots" were in heavy black books with my name in big gold embossed letters made professionally in London, so I was glad of the kind offer. At my gate he asked if he could come in. I flatly refused, saying with recordings the next morning I needed all the "beauty sleep" I could get. I tried to be polite, but it didn't help. He then asked me for a kiss. I offered my cheek, but he became nasty and tried to kiss me by force and said, "If you don't let me come in, tomorrow the band will mess up your music and your act will be dead."

I was shocked at this unorthodox attitude. I managed to break loose and rush into the house shouting defiantly, "You wouldn't dare," and slammed the door.

Next evening at the Theatre, the bandleader never caught my eye as is usual for the entries of each number and seemed to concentrate entirely on his musicians. Then followed discord upon discord – I could hardly believe my ears. I could not recognise my own music and so he had kept his word – he was messing up my show. I could feel my temperature rising and finally in a fury I took off my right silver court shoe with the high stiletto heel and threw it directly at Rolf Tragau's head. It caught him on the side of his face and I, with my head held high and my eyes flaming, stalked off the stage. I ran down the stairs to the canteen, asked how much deposit 10 Coke bottles would be, promised the girl the money, and then one after another I smashed the ten bottles to smithereens. The Managing Director arrived breathlessly as I was smashing the last bottle and feeling decidedly better.

"I've spoken to the audience and to Tragau," he said. "I've arranged all Yvonne, they are still clapping. Now Tragau will play your music properly."

I ran up the stairs with my other shoe in my hand and the audience clapped like mad and the waiters shouted "Hurray!" and whistled. Tragau offered me my right shoe. I put my shoes on and the band played nicely – the show was saved. The press took note of the foul play, and the audience had lots to tell their friends and relations. I was then christened "Little Spitfire" after the English fighter planes – thank Heavens I was British and not German, or they might have preferred to call me "Little Focker!"

CHAPTER 75

The Lausanne Special

My arrival in Lausanne was funny. I had been informed by the agency where Mr. Gardiner worked that a room had been reserved for me at the Pension Bungnon in La Grande Chene.

In Germany, after my press conference as if I were residing permanently at the best five-star hotel in Hamburg, I discovered that all the big variety theatre restaurants (and there was one in every large city) had special rooms for the various artists in private homes. The big family attractions, mainly acrobatic tumblers, trapeze artists etc., often with big equipment, generally had their own motor homes or caravans in which they traveled from place to place. Single artists and doubles, such as juggling acts, dance couples, or magicians with their assistants were normally allotted rooms in private homes or small pensions. These were usually run by a nice widow, who understood her house must be quiet in the mornings when most artists needed their sleep.

Switzerland boasted plenty of Hotel Garnis. Oddly enough, I never really found out what the "Garni" was, as they were garnished with naught, and you could never get a cup of tea — let alone breakfast. I soon changed all that with a small electric stove and a mug, which I filled with water to make a nice cup of tea. As I had Sunday free, I thought I would be clever and arrive in Lausanne one night early, so as to be really fresh for rehearsals with the new band and my opening night. This was about the stupidest thing I could have done, because the big Lausanne Expo was on and there was not one free bed in the whole town.

Madame Bugnon was kind and said I could leave my cases in her kitchen, but the room for me was occupied til the following afternoon, and she had no idea where I could spend the night. I decided to try the famous, five-star Lausanne Palace, where I was due to open the following night. I went there with high hopes. It was already getting dark, and I was getting tired of asking if a room was available at every small hotel. The night porter, realising my plight, jumped into the breach. He told me there was nothing available at the Palace or its "dependence" (annex), but he had night duty till 8 a.m. the next day and if I didn't mind sleeping in his bed, at least I could sleep.

For a moment my mind went back to one hotel during the Hofmeister Heinz Erhardt tour. I can't recall the name of the town we were playing; I only remember my hotel room was large, with two beds and a large potted plant in the corner. While sound asleep in the middle of the night, I awoke to hear someone trying to push in my door. At first, I thought I must be imagining it, but when I heard my door key fall to the floor and the door started opening, I jumped out of bed and switched on my bedside cupboard light – it was the hotel night porter. I stood there in my pajamas and bare feet and said with my best schoolteacher voice:

"And what do you think you are doing entering my room at this unearthly hour?"

Trying to cover up my own fright, my voice sounded like a judge in a court room. The night porter was obviously taken completely by surprise – Heaven knows what he expected!

"Oh – mmh oh I just came in to give some water to the plant."

I wanted to say, "Well, where is your watering can?" But realized he might unbutton his fly (zips were not in yet) and take that as an invitation. So, I quickly thought better of it and just shouted, "Out, get out," pointing to the door.

He ran out fast. After he had gone, I relocked the door and barricaded it with my case, plus a chair and a table. Being dead tired, I went back to bed and fell asleep within minutes.

All these thoughts ran through my mind now in Lausanne. I quickly weighed up the pros and the cons of this offer from the Palace Hotel's night porter. After my dreadful experience with my "grand amour" Nick Norovski, and my father's hard sermon thereafter telling me never to trust a man – I had to put all these bad experiences out of my mind. He looked a kind young man, and he knew I was to be the new singing star in their nightclub. Apart from that, my feet were killing me and my head and back were starting to ache too. I took the pros.

"Oh, thank you," I said. "Monsieur est vraiment tres gentil."

In no time he took me to his little cabin in the big hotel. It was a staff cabin and completely devoid of any luxury – but it had a single bed. He closed the door behind him, assuring me he would wake me up at 8.15 a.m. with a cup of coffee. I fell asleep blessing my good fortune. Lausanne, I said to myself, was lovely!

CHAPTER 76

At The Palace

Life is funny! There was I, having spent the night in the porter's cabin, happy to have a bed to lie on, and not even 24 hours later, after my show, I was being invited to Lady Beaverbrook's table with Prince Ali Khan himself. He was long divorced from the Hollywood film superstar Rita Hayworth, my main idol among the American movie stars. He was with his beautiful friend, the famous French model Bettina.

Lady Beaverbrook had immediately ordered the best champagne, Persian caviar and a pot of the finest French paté de foie gras and a generous portion of butter and hot toast.

From then onwards, I never needed to worry about my evening meal or bother to go to one of the many tea rooms for a cheap lunch. Being British, I love toast, and having it garnished with the best caviar and paté de foie gras was good enough for me.

"I knew you were British," she gushed, "the moment you arrived in that lovely white gown with silver sequins and that silver lamé panel in front, just like our young Queen Elizabeth wore for her TV speech."

"Heavens!" I thought, "how very patriotic good old Lady Beaverbrook seems to be."

"Oh really," I said, and, to myself, "Thank God she recognised it and that Mr. Gardiner was not there on my opening night to stop me from wearing it." I wondered if I would be eating simply delicious patê de foie gras if I had worn my Mimosa, which he would have chosen.

"Did you get it from Norman Hartnell, too?" the Lady asked.

"Well," I answered and just as I was wondering whether to acquiesce, or to tell the truth about Mrs. Papadopolous at Famagusta, the waiter arrived with a new bottle of champagne and a pretty girl in a costume came by with long stemmed red roses. Immediately Prince Ali Khan bought one for each of us ladies – so the subject was changed completely, and I was most thankful.

Lord Beaverbrook was one of the most important and publicised Lords in England and here I was – not having a bed to lay on just the day before – now drinking champagne and eating caviar with his wife at the famous Lausanne Palace Hotel "in High Society" just a few hours later, with a red rose from Prince Ali Khan sitting prettily in a vase on the table.

The next night two other gentlemen joined our table. The older man was Dr. Richter – he was not loudly dressed but, like Lady Beaverbrook, flamboyant in his style – he was Hungarian and a director of the famous pharma company Sandoz. His companion, also Hungarian, was a younger man and a fine pianist.

Mick Michel, the French fantasist, had a huge success with "Ni toi ni moi" (neither you nor me can do anything – love is much stronger). It was Dr. Richter's favorite song at that time. Fortunately, it was already in my repertoire, so every time he and his friend walked down the red carpeted stairs into the club, I had to sing this especially for him. As he was a wonderful whisky drinking client, this happened often, as he generally had three or four tables of friends that he invariably sent bottles of whisky to, with his compliments.

One night was very special. We were joined by a small bespectacled man with an amazing personality. He just sat down and joined us. He was to my mind positively outstanding; it was Aristotle Onassis, and I was spellbound at the way he took over our table. He was a little man, not much taller than me, and yet no one dared to contradict him in whatever he said (I think later I understood Jacqueline Kennedy Onassis). He seemed to like me and slowly they all came every night shouted and clapped my show and became my mentors for Lausanne Palace. If such clients come once in a while, it is considered as being very fortunate, but if such clients come nightly because they really enjoy the entertainment – that's extra. The manager asked me during the first week when I expected to be free for a return engagement.

One night, after I had said good night to our table and was dressed to walk up to my room at the Pension, I heard a loud voice half singing, half shouting in English. I thought I'd take a quick peep to see who this new English singer was. I drew the heavy red velvet curtain which guarded the famous red carpeted steps to the nightclub just a fraction, and as I did I realised the song was "Rule Britannia!" and there was Lady Beaverbrook, with one of the tall artificial palms tucked under her left arm like a sceptre, singing "con multo gusto" this tribute to Britain and her Marines.

The applause from the few people left there was deafening, so it masked my burst of laughter, and I left for home humming and musing to myself how wonderfully relaxing to most people a good cognac or whisky can be – no wonder it's so pricey!

CHAPTER 77

I Miss My Big Fish –
My Second Marriage Proposal

Toward the end of my very happy and successful month in Lausanne, Lady Beaverbrook, who had in that time become a real friend, said she had something special for me, because to her mind a nice young girl from Great Britain deserved something very special. She hustled me into a chauffeur driven limousine at her disposal and we went to the other five-star hotel in Lausanne. There she explained:

"Yvonne, you just have to meet this very special person. He could be the best cognac and the best ice cream you have ever tasted in your young life – or probably ever will. He is a handsome, cultured man, and at the moment the most famous multi millionaire."

The chauffeured limousine drew up to the hotel. The porter helped us out and lead us to a table and there he was, the most talked about man at the moment: M. Le Baron Heini Thyssen, whose divorce from the famous British model Fiona Campbell had filled most newspapers in the Western world. Apart from leaving her a fortune, he bestowed on this famous beauty her own island complete with a Gepard – I presumed the Island was some where in the South American Continent, because on our side of the Equator, in East Africa, we call them Cheetahs, a beautiful, graceful animal and a great runner – perhaps the Baron had thought that about Fiona.

Lady Beaverbrook, obviously an old pal of this very special person, introduced me and drinks were ordered. I took fresh orange juice. When he stood up to shake my hand, I realised he was really a big man, and I was struck with awe. After a few sips of his dry Martini, our host eyed me up and down as if I was some prize object at a winning tombola or lottery. Then he said, with a voice almost as dry as the Martini, "Mm, yes Lady B," (as we all called her) "I think she'll do. She is younger than Fiona and also in the news a little. I must beat Fiona and get married again before her – so why not to an up-and-coming British Teenage Singer?" Then he gave a short laugh. "That will be one in the eye for Fiona. Lady B, you're a good ole girl, you always seem to know what I need."

Before I could even conceive what was happening, they discussed hurriedly the where, the when, and the how. I was aghast. I felt like a prize calf being bought by the highest bidder. How could I ever share a bed with this huge important man – who would probably forget my name, I was so unimportant to him. I felt a bit faint and asked to be excused and rushed off to the ladies' room. I did not have to contemplate for long. I made a beeline for the side exit and left. In English I would say I was in a dead funk – at 18, it is not easy to be sensible and practical.

I really didn't expect to ever see my friend Lady B again, but that night she was there early at her usual table. She beckoned to me to join her while the club was still empty. I steeled myself for a barrage of rebukes. They did not come; she took my hands and said, "You were afraid, weren't you?"

I nodded in silence.

"You silly girl," she laughed, "However do you think these models – whatever home and schools they actually come from – get the pick of the bunch of multimillionaires?"

At 18, I had never given it a thought and had absolutely no idea how to answer. I sat there dumb and a little ashamed, because here was a famous, wealthy Lady who had taken an interest and wanted the best for me, and I had slighted her and shown no fighting spirit at all and not even been honestly polite.

Of course, she did not know of my dreadful love affair with a mafia agent and my lack of belief in my own judgment of the male character.

"Look," she added, smiling. "It all goes like this – the wealthy get blind drunk at their wedding nights, if not before. You secretly go off to bed and sleep. The next morning, the wealthy magnate asks "who are you?" and you show your left hand with the wedding ring, smile sweetly, and say "your new wife" and get out of bed and go into the bathroom. If he goes into a rage – which I'm sure he would not – you can file for a divorce immediately on mental cruelty. If you feel sorry for him, you can stay at least a little while, and the longer, the more your divorce prize. Either way my dear, you are *made* and would probably get a few skyscrapers, perhaps a famous painting, in any case excellent expensive jewelry and lots more. Heini can of course afford it all, and to have him as a lifelong friend who would be a huge asset in your hand, could have been fantastic for your future."

"I think the idea is a wonderful one, but I guess I'm too young and inexperienced to become a Baroness. I'm sure ten years later I would have been ideal."

We parted ways amicably. I must admit I had a sad sorry feeling – she had indeed been a very special friend, and I had let her down completely.

CHAPTER 78

The Swedish Folkets Parks Tour

Gunnar Silfors of the Swedish Folkets Parks (where ABBA later started their career) came to see me in Switzerland. We both went together to Mont Blanc, the first famous mountain I had ever seen – a wonderful sight. He was a truly sympathetic gentleman. On his return he sent me a three-month contract with an excellent Spanish back-up group called Rafael de Moncada. It was a Latin hit and something entirely new for Sweden. I felt really at home, almost as if I was back with Edmundo Ros.

We had a most unusually hot Swedish summer season, which, after starting down south in Malmo, went right up to the North Pole and I saw the midnight sun – what a wonderful experience. The people way up north were mostly natural platinum blonds with skin so white that I stood out like a Pink Elephant. They were quiet and reserved, but what amazed me most were the schoolchildren; when we hired a boat for me to go rowing, we passed a few larger ones with kiddies on excursions. At home their screams and laughter could be heard coming round the bends, but on the edge of the Arctic circle, even the children were quiet like little white mice. We had to buy opaque black paper and tack it on to the windows so we could sleep at every place we stayed. For us southerners it was hard to sleep with the sun shining brightly down on you. For me, who loves to go on a swing, it was a new treat to come home after the show at midnight and go on a swing, at the children's playground. A special experience; I could be a kid again, and that in the still of the night. If I was childlike going on a swing at midnight, the Spanish musicians did their best to satisfy their sexual curiosity of the tall, slender, blonde Swedish girls – who were undoubtedly willing "scrubbers" at every town where we did a concert. Parks have trees and a tour has a bus, so while Rafael and I sat in the bus chatting after the show, sometimes we glanced out of the window. The boys in the band propped the girls against the trees standing up and "scrubbed" them with "quick fixes" – the bus driver grinned, and I got used to the show. Occasionally we stayed two nights in bigger towns like Linkoping and Gothenborg and the musicians told me how unusual these northern girls were. They would go to the boys and offer them a bed at their home – next morning, mother would knock on the door and bring in breakfast on a tray and would say in Swedish, "I hope you had a pleasant night."

For the southern Spanish musicians with their strict double morals, Scandinavia was nothing short of paradise, and we had their best summer in history.

The bandleader – who preferred boys anyway – kept these guys on low salaries, but had promised them three months of complete erotic freedom – he sure was not wrong! The only "fly in the ointment" was a car accident, when our little bus landed in a pothole way up north and turned over, rolling down the hillside and ending up in a field. There were minor injuries – I came out unscathed, as I had fallen asleep in the seat by the driver and had rolled into the feet area, quite oblivious to what had awakened me.

During the tour I worked with Egon Kjerman's big band at Radio Sverige (Swedish Radio), all great, competent musicians – what a pleasure!

On our last show the weather broke; it was in the Stockholm Folkets Park, 60,000 spectators, all with different colored umbrellas – really something to see, when in spite of all the rain, they joined in wholeheartedly with my audience participation of numbers like the ever-popular Spanish flamenco "Tani Tani." Later I recorded it in four languages but not in Swedish – what a shame!

CHAPTER 79

Great News – Paris. Terrible News – London

I had the next days free and made a beeline for London. I flew, as my time was limited, and when I got home there was a telegram awaiting me telling me I had been booked by Louis Rey of Radio Geneva for a big concert at the Palais de Chaillot in Paris. It was to be the premiere of Jacques Dieval's Jazz de Champs Elysées Concert Tour through Western Europe.

Vico Torriani was to be the Swiss star of the show. Sacha Distel and the Swingel Singers would represent France. Alice Babs, the famous Swedish jazz singer, and Sven Asmussen, the famous Dane, were to represent Scandinavia, and I was to do my super Cole Porter medley and the new Doris Day Number "Oo Bang Jingly Jang" representing London BBC and Radio Geneva.

The film showing the life of Cole Porter was a big success; I loved his music and words (and so did my voice). My Cole Porter medley was also a number one hit wherever I went.

This cable gave me courage to face Dad, and hope and pray I was not too late when I phoned him from Zürich to warn him not to give any money to Nick.

When I got home, Dad opened the door and wrath poured out of him on to me. In a quiet, curt voice he said, "Good, you have arrived on time. Tomorrow we have an appointment with the Chief of Interpol, and I want you to tell your story of Nick Norovski. Do you know your father nearly got shot, because his wayward daughter seems to have a talent in appealing to criminal older men? You are too young and look, and probably are, far too gullible and innocent to be traveling around the world alone."

Slowly, through my father, I began to understand the way men think. In trouble, they would "pass the buck" (put the blame on me) – so it was all my fault. Dad seemed to forget that he had met Nick often and liked him very much himself.

Mum looked at me and said, "Really Tootsie, you wanted adventure and not a protected life like your sisters and our circle – well you certainly got it!"

Mum was my "father confessor" and I told her about the arranged marriage proposal from Heini Thyssen and how afraid I was – and obviously, upon reflection, how very foolish I seemed to be.

She sighed and said, "Best of all you need a nice young man. Surely you have learnt much from these older ones."

"I tell you what," I said to Mum, "I'll marry a young virgin male with no big car and no big bank balance and show Dad I can make the grade that way. Why shouldn't I turn the tables on these virgin-loving Oriental males?"

Mum smiled. I always had a feeling she would have enjoyed being me.

CHAPTER 80

Tomorrow You Could Be Dead

The Chief of Interpol, who was sitting at his desk when Dad and I had the appointment with him, had a rather fatherly face, but intelligent and thoughtful grey eyes. He asked me for my story first.

I told him how **Nick**, who had been my boss in Tiberias and Tel Aviv, had seemingly saved my life after a bad attack of malaria followed by jaundice. Then I told him how surprised I was when he left his wife and son, home and business and suddenly was here in Europe. I left out anything I thought too incriminating, like the Leica cameras and the luxurious swimsuits, and spoke only of the club and restaurant visits. Then, finally, when Nick spoke of small files of silver powder which I was to bring as a sort of courier, as the girl I met in Milan did, to various people in Western Europe, claiming I would earn a fortune in no time, it sounded just a bit fishy to me. The future Nick had mapped out for me started to lose its appeal when he told me of his companion who printed perfect counterfeit sterling bills in large denominations and American $100 bills that were undetectable. I was nineteen and had already had three marriage proposals – I wanted to sing, and hopefully all over the world – marrying Nick was not my goal. I told Nick I would not join in this organisation as I wanted to carry on singing. He seemed shocked about my decision, and I felt after my experience of Harry Janes in Paris that I had no wish to participate in such an unethical way of life.

Then I told the Chief of Interpol what happened later on. Suddenly, Nick arrived in Zürich, and he looked 100% different to the smart, astute Nick I had known. He was half drunk, he spoiled my show twice, and he was thrown out on the third night. Why, he was suddenly so different from the Nick I had known in Israel, Paris, or Milano – I had no idea what had hapened. The big Chief enlightened me.

"Organised criminals delight in a young lady such as you, my dear. The silver powder was not powered silver at all as you had been told by Mr. Novroski, but Hashish." 50 years ago, I had never even heard the word. "In drugs the profits are immense. Even if you did get an Alfa Romeo and a good salary, it is nothing compared to the profits of the syndicate in drug dealing. The gentleman in question," he paused, "was a mafia agent. Probably he was in love with you, that is not difficult when you take into consideration you could easily have been his daughter. After all, you are a young and very attractive girl. He also saw in you a quick way of coming into a fortune and if he could net you, plus your Dad's money too, all the better!

"When you said "no" he lost out, and as a big money-spinning agent, which he wanted to be, he is lucky he is still alive. He was always a drinker and just drank more."

I did not mention the second passport, as I have my own laws. Nick had given me some happy moments and put my feet back on the ground when I had been so sick after having had malaria. His lovemaking had been outstanding and full of fun. I had no desire to see him in jail.

Then I heard Dad's story and almost changed my mind. Dad's voice almost shook as he told of the arranged meeting with his daughter's older but most charming "good friend," when it was proposed he give him an envelope with a substantial amount of cash to help him start up a business in London. However, instead of the friends simple blue Ford, a big black Limousine with darkened windows stopped at the curbside where he was to meet Nick. A window opened halfway and a revolver pointed at him, and a harsh voice said "Money here or I'll shoot." Before Dad could recover from his shock, the envelope was snatched from his trembling hand and the big limousine drove off so quickly Dad had no time to check the number plate of the car – if it had one.

The Chief of Interpol cleared his voice and addressed me, "Young lady, you chose to fall in love with a nightclub owner; they are often wheeler-dealers." I'd never even heard the word. "Next time you fall in love, please take off your rose-colored glasses."

I was in a complete state of shock and promised my father I would repay him all the money in time. Then the kind, serious face looked at both Dad and me, and put a finger to his lips; "Do not say a word to anyone about this happening. It is a very dangerous element…organised crime. My advice is to try to forget it, otherwise tomorrow you could be dead."

CHAPTER 81

All That Glitters Is Not Gold

This engagement was with the special service for the US Forces, and I was the star. The agent who believed in me came to the rescue. The show was "Paree Paree" and I incidentally met Caterina Valente who was appearing, like myself, in a show for the special service, together with her husband Eric von Aro. He had an exciting drum show, and to be different at the end he juggled with the drums, the sticks and all, a most unusual act.

Our show had excellent artistes and it was enjoyed by the officers, the NCO clubs, and the EM clubs alike. The nicest part was we played some of the loveliest places in Italy and always had time to see and enjoy them. There was Rome, where the film "3 Coins in the Fountain" was shot, and Frank Sinatra sang the theme song. In Naples we had time to visit Capri and the Blue Grotto which was wonderful. We also visited Pompeii. Although men and older women were allowed, I was too young a female to be able to view the brothel area. I was really annoyed, but the guards were adamant.

I gave Pompeii a bad note, and the agent too – as apart from small advances we never got paid. Dad put it into the hands of his lawyers, and as far as I know the strongwoman Joan Rhodes and I were the only ones who finally received our checks. Joan Rhodes became my friend; she was good looking and at least 6 foot tall. She tore up telephone directories, inviting men from the audience to do the same – none could!

My biggest fan on that tour was the tenor sax player, a nice thirty-two-year-old blond guy from Kassel. After the tour he was engaged in Ulm, and when I went to visit him in between engagements he met me at the station with his band, and as I stepped from the train they played "Three Coins in the Fountain". It was a most romantic welcome; I felt I was back in the film world, even with no 007 help.

Summer was generally at famous bathing resorts in Belgium and the Netherlands. In Schaveningen I had to change my room with the sea view at the hotel as the weather and the sea were so vicious. Thereafter I was engaged at the casino at Travemunde, the famous German resort, but that wasn't much fun – singing at 3 a.m. doing my last show – but all were interesting experiences. Then back to Zürich, this time at the "Tabaris" with the Luc Hoffmann Group. What a saxophonist he was! "Sie und Er," the biggest Swiss magazine, came to do a write up on me with photos from Comet.

I was so often in Zürich that I regarded it as my second home and I had made lots of interesting friends and acquaintances, one of which was through James Gardiner; he was the owner of the most eminent and elegant Turkish carpet store on the Bahnhofstrasse. James had tried to convince me that I was now earning as much money as a bank director or even a big mogul such as his friend Hafiz. The famous Turk liked me, knowing that somewhere along the line I had some Turkish blood. He invited James and me for a drive in his huge, brand new American Eldorado, which was fully automated. After a short drive around the town, he suggested we three go for a drink and snack at the Savoy de Ville – the sister hotel of the famous Baur au Lac. He wanted to show off, and such ideas suited James Gardiner fine. We drove up as passers by stared and a livered porter rushed to open the door for us – but not one door of the large car would open. Hafiz tried the windows – they would not go down. It was before the techno era, so nobody had a mobile on them. We were locked in our glorious cage. Thankfully the porter was intelligent enough to run inside and phone the garagist from the hotel, and finally we managed to get out of our luxurious trap. Since then, I steer clear of too much automation. All that glitters is not gold! Not even for multimillionaires in Zürich!

CHAPTER 82

Fun and Games in Showbiz

As a small girl, like many kids I had front teeth trouble from overcrowding – too big teeth in a too small mouth. After Mum agreed our family dentist removed two teeth, one on each side of my lower jaw, which left two small spaces but helped to keep my upper teeth even and so make my smile better.

Being in television, the two spaces came out as two black spots – no good at all. I asked my dentist for help. He made me a thin gold band with tiny teeth on and that seemed to go well, until in Holland I read a review of my show in a newspaper and was shocked. The review was fine, but at the end it was written "in a red satin ball gown she sang love songs. Each time she sang the word "love" she opened her mouth wide and the gold in her mouth flickered in the candlelight of the romantic table décor."

What a write up for an 18-year-old. I may have even forgotten the whole incident, but a short time later, having dinner after the show with all the other international stars in TV, I seemed to get threads of meat entwined in the gold band with the two tiny white teeth. Unobtrusively, I spat it out into the big white cloth napkin. I decided I would try to quietly put this in my handbag, but the producer started talking to me and I forgot all my good intentions and left it on the table after dinner. I wondered what the laundress would say when she found it – probably have a good laugh.

This happening made me really change the gold band, which came out at night (like the stars!), to a porcelain bridge, and who cares how I sing the world "love" now, no matter how many candles there are around.

The next funny incident was really an embarrassing one. I was wearing a short new cocktail dress. It was very new and very light. As I returned from the loo all eyes seemed to focus on me. Many artistes stopped eating their meal to stare at me – I was seated at the last table, so I had to pass them all on my way, and they were all giggling, smiling, obviously amused, even laughing at me. I did not know why, but I could feel myself blushing purple. Then one kind girl left her table and ran to me and whispered in my ear:

"Yvonne, your dress at the back is tucked up in your bum and it's trailing a long piece of toilet paper."

I stammered "Oh my God." Just at that moment I passed a long mirror and saw the mishap for myself…wow! I couldn't remove it fast enough, and then what to do with the toilet paper? Oh horror! Why can't we fall through the floor at such moments?

While I was still with EMI I was told to go up and see the production manager of Light Entertainment. I think the name suited him. He was a good-looking, famous manager called Nils Nobach – the one Angele Durand was so fond of. I knocked on the door but, getting no answer, I tried to open it. It was wide enough for me to gauge what was going on, because there was Mr. Nobach with his back to me and his trousers down, and half laying on his desk with her legs apart was a new singer. He was in the middle of fucking her and far too busy to hear my timid knock. I closed the door, quietly humming to myself "Nice work if you can get it, and you can get it if you try" (thank you Jimmy Cliff). As I walked down the stairs. I remembered with a big grin the point number that had swept Germany: "Aber der Nobach laesst uns nicht verkommen" (but Mr. Nobach never lets girls down). I wondered if the composer knew our Nobach, chief of Light Entertainment. He was a real disarming guy.

The Wild Swinging 60s

During this period, I had absolutely no time for a private life at all. I was so booked out for galas on Fridays and Saturday nights that often I did 3 shows in totally different places in one night. Teddy was great at that time – he chauffeured me from one hall to another, carried my case and dots, and often when there was little or no time to run through my show he would sit down at the piano and accompany me – directing the drummer at the same time. He has a very quiet disposition and without long discussions just gets on with the work ahead; he was indispensable, except for picking up my requisites and putting my show gowns away. He always seemed to get entangled in the trains or the petticoats. He invariably made me laugh. He could write such tiny notes of music, but was quite comical looking after a female wardrobe – a bit clumsy, or was it manly?

We worked like a team. After my first show he'd give me a sandwich and a cup of tea from a thermos and I would fall asleep immediately in the back seat. As we reached the next hall, he just had to say "Pussy" and I'd be up sucking a lozenge, fix my face in the car and be ready to do the next show. I had learned a lot about changing clothes in a car from my regular three shows in London for Gerald Van de Meer. Generally, for the first show there was plenty of time for rehearsing, for the second show it was often a rush job, and for the third show, often in some outlandish hall we had trouble in finding, sometimes in pouring rain, fog or thick snow and icy roads, there was literally no time to even run through my numbers. He would sit down quietly at the piano, direct the rhythm, and I would get on with my third show thoroughly refreshed. Like a prize boxer, I was ready for the fray.

Offers seemed to come in daily. Most of the filming was done in Berlin, which meant being up at 4 a.m. to be ready for make up at 6 a.m. – shooting generally started at 8 a.m. Mostly I had only to sing one song and a lot of waiting around was involved. Getting up at 4 a.m. is no sweat at all, but boy, if you have a nightclub engagement and don't get to bed till 2 a.m. at the earliest – show biz and making lots of money becomes a hard day's night and a hard night's day, and being young and fit is imperative.

They were called the Swinging 60s, and for those of you who are too young to remember – I feel sorry for you all. London was the swingiest city in the world at that time, Carnaby Street was famous, and everybody wanted to wear the latest fashion and dance the latest dances and, if you had plenty of money, life was a real ball!

For Teddy's birthday, I invited some London friends and the younger set of our family to the most famous nightclub and had a cake specially made for him in his favorite color, turquoise. It resembled a bed with a Pussycat and a Teddybear in it, all in his favorite sweet food, marzipan. It was the time to do crazy things – and boy, we sure did!

Moment 1 – A Sticky Situation

After returning from the Near and Middle East, I met a quiet young man with blond hair and blue eyes whom I once allowed to cuddle me in bed and stayed the night.

I feel really sorry for the younger set of today. Everything with reference to sex is so easy and open, nothing is forbidden – to my mind a huge loss of creative fun.

Years ago, things were quite different, not just in the UK but in the entire Western Hemisphere. If you were living at home with Mum and Dad and you had a guy in your bed, or even your room, and someone informed the police, then your parents could be accused of keeping a "wild" or "bawdy" house and could be asked to pay a heavy fine.

One day I smuggled Len, my blue-eyed blond, into my bedroom when both my parents were a little off colour and went to bed early. Next morning, I awoke with the dawn light, looked at my watch and saw to my horror it was already 6.30 a.m. Heavens – in a minute or two Dad would be into my room to wake me up! No time for Len to jump into the wardrobe; quickly I rolled him up in the bedclothes and he lay, trying not to breathe or laugh, at the foot of my bed as Dad walked in. Normally Dad would pull the sheet over my face and say:

"Wake up, wake up, it's morning." (As if I ever thought it was for a minute in the middle of the night!) It was a daily ritual. Today I had to get Len out of my room, and that quickly.

As Dad came in, I was sitting up in bed, and in a very lively voice, I said, "Good morning Daddy dear – I'm up already – taking after you," (compliments do help) "it is such a beautiful morning."

Dad gave me a look of positive surprise and said, "That's my girl," and left for the bathroom.

Len, at the foot of my bed, could hardly contain himself to not laugh out loud.

Once in the bathroom Dad's habit was to put on all the water taps. Apparently, his father had confided in him that he came from a country where water was precious, and Dad just loved to hear the sound of running water. What with the swishing of water and the fact that Dad heard it too, Len had the opportunity after dressing in seconds to creep down the stairs with me in front, and to get out of the house without being seen.

For the noise of the front door opening and closing I used as an alibi that it was me, and I took in the two pints of milk waiting on the doorstep from the milkman – a normal daily chore. I completed the ruse by telling Len to go into a phone booth a little later, and call us, whereupon I would of course answer the phone and then at 7.30 announce to Mum and Dad that an old friend had called to say he was in the area for an 8 o'clock meeting and I had said, "Oh, do come over and have a cup of tea or coffee and a piece of toast with us for an early breakfast."

This done, everything functioned perfectly and poor Len, still a bit in shock, could quench his thirst and hunger quiet pleasantly with us at the breakfast table. Naturally, he and I laughed our heads off quite a few hours later.

Pushing Through

Another time, much later when I was an up-and-coming star earning good money, I had a free fortnight and decided to go on holidays with my folks and pay for myself. We three were very happy, but Dad, who always seemed to manage to put his "spoke in the wheel" (mess everything up) at the last minute, would, every night when he said "Goodnight dear," close the door and lock it as if I was an adolescent, and even took the key with him. In spite of my success in my chosen profession, he still considered me in comparison with other young ladies – including my older sisters – as being a little "wild animal," and was a little afraid of the consequences this could bring.

Under such circumstances, one good-looking young waiter tried climbing up a tree that has a branch near my open window. I thought he was very brave, but the branch broke and he felt to the ground, and I just had to laugh. Thereafter I decided to change my room so that I could climb out of my window myself and go dancing with the boys – that was easy. However, getting back in was more difficult, but the boys hoisted me up, and I sort of fell into the room sometimes on all fours. It pays to be sportive!

Actually, it reminded me of one incident on the lake of Geneva. I was enjoying a leisurely swim on my back when I saw a big swan flying over me and then gliding directly towards me on the water. I made for our boat as fast as I could, and my pal tried to get me into the boat before the swan, who looked large and aggressive, got to me. My friend pulled my arms so hard I thought the boat would be capsized as it tilted on its side, but finally, with an extra wiggle and effort, I made it, breathing heavily, while

my pal took the oars and rowed like mad in the other direction,
only stopping when the bird was out of sight. We both gave a
huge sigh of relief and had a good laugh at the funny situation.

Fathers and male swans can make life difficult, but looking back
I have to admit it was all good clean fun in the 60s!

The Most Unusual Lover

Perhaps the biggest laugh of all was the crazy idea I had at school to make a list of all the different countries I hoped to visit, and then pick myself out a lover and give each country points from 1 – 20. I really imagined, at school, that the French man would get the first prize, but the Italian beat him hands down. Italians seem to have a great admiration for a woman's body and a woman altogether. Germans, Swiss, and Austrians are very ambitious lovers, always wanting to prove they are the best – and often are. Brits and Yanks are good talkers, but do not seem to have the Continental flair. However, my Spaniard from Andalusia took the first prize for being innovative and definitely different. After every love sequence, he would jump out of bed, slip into his shoes perfectly naked, raise his arms and, clapping his hands and stamping his feet "alla Cordobez," shout "Ole!" It was really unusual and gave the night an authentic Spanish Flamenco touch. He was an excellent trumpeter in the band and one night at the show I wondered what the audience was staring at and laughing. This mischievous musician had pinched my shocking pink nylon panties trimmed with lace and tied them on a pole, so that when he blew hard on the trumpet my psychedelic pink panties twirled round and round on the pole hoisted on high and got almost more applause than I did.

Being a kid should mean being ready for fun. Whether blowing a trumpet, swinging from a trapeze, or standing behind the microphone, artists have to be highly disciplined, but often behave like big kids and get a kick out of shocking others – but I guess that is just what the public wants!

CHAPTER 83

Burgundy Shoes

About that time, I had to be at "La Radio Diffusion Francaise" in Paris. Waiting there was a very thin young man with bright blue eyes and a big nose – but far more than his countenance, I noticed his shoes. They were a light lace-up brogue of burgundy suede and leather, with socks to match. This was at a time when men wore only black or brown shoes. Indeed, I had never seen another color except white in any shop windows. As I looked more at this person, I noticed his suit was not brown or navy blue but dark turquoise. I could not help but wonder who this young guy who seemed to be so willing to defy the so-called norm was. Certainly, in dress he was a man after my own heart – someone who had no intention to conform to tradition. He was then introduced to me as Mr. Dieter Klaus. I thought they said "Clouseau" and immediately my thoughts went to the French detective stories of Mr. Clouseau. I presumed with great respect he must be the son of the famous author.

Then we were both called in by two different secretaries into two different rooms, and that was that, and I never gave the burgundy shoes another thought.

After Paris with Armand Bernard, I was scheduled for a large concert in Saarbrucken with the big Radio Orchestra directed by Manfred Minnich. Manfred was a really nice guy with no frills. I walked into the Concert Hall punctually and Manfred was sitting in the semi darkness of the front row of the stalls, checking the sound. I sang a few notes and spoke a line, and the microphone check was done. With my music scores in my hand, I walked toward Manfred and noticed he was not alone.

"May I introduce you to our house arranger," said Manfred. As we shook hands, the lights came on as the technicians started to do their checks. Being small, I notice what's on the floor quickly, and to my surprise I recognized the burgundy shoes, and then the turquoise suit. The young man muttered something about Paris to the band leader and greeted me in French.

"Madame Carré je vous rappelle de la Radio diffusion francaise, je suis vraiment enchanté."

This was my third time being engaged in Saarbrucken. I knew Manfred and his wife quite well. I invited both to my Hotel Messmer for dinner after the show. Manfred then explained to me that this house arranger was an old friend whose musical scores were full of innovation and were excellent. He also pointed out that he always stayed with their family when in Saarbrucken.

"Naturally you must bring him too," I said.

About a half an hour before the arranged time, the telephone rang in my room, and I heard the receptionist say as I picked up the receiver, "No, young man, you cannot go to her room, now sit down on that chair and I will call Madame Carré to get you."

I was amused, and preened for the respect shown towards me. I came down and made sure our table for dinner was reserved for four, and I greeted "Mr. Burgundy Shoes" and lead him into the Hotel bar where there were also tables and armchairs. The French arranger looked at me with his bright blue eyes and said, in a tone full of disgust, "What a terrible hotel you're staying at! They had to cheek to call me "young man" and order me to sit on a chair and wait for you."

His whole face went long and dark, and I must confess I burst out laughing. "One day you will be delighted when someone calls you "young man," I rejoined, grinning my head off.

Then this cheeky, very thin young man quickly changed the subject. "I only have an old Volkswagen," he said, "but it does go, and I am a careful driver. Mr. Minnich told me after your sojourn here in Saarbrucken you are due for recordings at Electrola in Cologne. You are to do "Moonglow" in German for the Kim Novak movie and a gypsy song from the pen of the famous German Composer Lothar Olias. If you don't mind my *old car* and my *young company*," he said these words with a heavy tone, "I would be happy to drive you there as I am on my way to Hamburg and home. Anyway, you could save money, it won't cost you a penny."

I remembered that after the day in Cologne, I was further scheduled for a show in Hamburg with the Gunther Fuhlisch band and, heaven knows why, there were only 16 musicians in that orchestra. All my arrangements were for 24 musicians, and I was a bit apprehensive as to how my orchestrations would sound with only 16 men to play them. Here was an excellent arranger sitting on the armchair next to me.

Saving money at this time in my life was imperative. I decided to ask him if he knew the Gunther Fuehlisch Band and if he could do me an orchestration and write the whole score and then what would it cost? He widened his bright blue eyes, which now sparkled.

"For you, nothing," he answered resolutely, "it would be a pleasure."

After two years with James (money loving) Gardiner, not to speak of Nick and all that money I promised to repay Dad, I was surprised, and took a deep breath and let it out slowly with a big smile of satisfaction. Finally, here was a young person who wanted to help me – and there were no strings attached. Here was the unusual, a kind gentleman in the old sense of the word.

The dinner was a success, the music was a success, I was a success. It was all fine, but it was the end of November, and it was cold, grey, and even foggy. I had with me a heavy UHER tape recorder, which my new driver could carry. It was a good idea.

Not deterred, he drove well and tried to hold my hand a few times. I declined. I had had enough of the male sex for a lifetime.

At the hotel we had two single rooms, his was just opposite. I gave my partitur orchestrations of the Cole Porter Medley and another American Hit and went to bed. The recordings in Cologne were not great, and the voice sounded hardly like mine because the arranger, without even asking, presumed I sing in the usual female voice keys (I don't, I sing a third lower), so I had problems regaining my soprano notes. I did it, but it didn't sound like me at all.

Next morning, I knocked on the door opposite me. Burgundy Shoes stood there smiling down at me, the new arrangements in his hand. I was once again amazed; they were perfectly written for the 16 musicians.

"Whenever did you do all that?" I asked, visibly taken aback but delighted.

"Oh, I stayed up all night to write all the parts," he said nonchalantly – as if it were nothing at all.

I shook his hand and thanked him and invited him at least to breakfast in the hotel.

On the way to Hamburg, he asked me where I intended to stay. I told him I generally stay at the Hotel Europa.

"It's right near the station, so it's convenient for the porters to take your baggage into the Hotel Foyer, you don't need a taxi."

"Oh dear," he said, "I'm quite sure a pretty girl like you must often have trouble with men trying to find out your room number."

"Oh, yes, quite right," I answered, "they often try to get into the lift with you, and then get off on your floor and follow you."

Then I remembered the man in the wardrobe in Istanbul and then I added, "I sometimes think men are a bit mad – some seem to think they are irresistible – or is it perhaps "there is no harm in trying?"" I chuckled.

"Such men must be exasperating," said my new friend, smiling, looking at me out of the corner of his eye. "Why don't you stay in our house? You know already my father Rudi Klaus the accordionist. You worked together with the Alfred Hauser Tango Orchestra and the big Symphony styled Orchestra of Harry Herman both at NDR (Nord–Deutscher Rundkfunk)."

"Oh, I couldn't possibly do that after all I am a girl and not a male singing star, you can't tell your mother you're bringing home an old singing buddy," I responded.

"Well," and this was when that shrewd and determined young musician played his trump card, "Vico Torriani has stayed at our place and he was managed, from what you told me in the car, by your manager. Only last week Lys Assia did some radio recordings with Alfred Hauser – a friend of ours – she stayed at our home, too."

"You mean to say Lys Assia stayed at your home?" I questioned with surprise. "Well, if such a perfect lady can, I guess I can too. Are you quite sure your mother won't mind?"

"No, she'd be delighted," was the reply.

We drove up to a typical house in north Germany with a very long, slanting tiled roof, a large lawn with trees in front and a sitting bench at the side. It was, as all the houses in that area, standing alone and well maintained.

Just as I went to get out of the car, he put his arm round me and said, "It's time we use the familiar "du," call me Dieter."

"Not Clouseau," I said, laughing. "Shame, I thought you were connected with the famous French detective stories."

"We have to kiss on that," he said, and without a second to lose he planted on my mouth a kiss like a wet orange. Oh heavens, it was awfully wet.

As I was drying my face, the door opened and a smiling lady with similar bright blue eyes greeted us with "Do come in."

I thought it was his sister, but was enlightened to the fact that it was Burgundy Shoes' mum. The greeting from Rudi Klaus was warm and sincere and I felt almost as if I was expected.

The following day after a light lunch I told the two men I'd go and help mother dry up the dishes and went out to the kitchen to assist.

"Do you know," she said, "I am so happy my son has chosen to marry a singer who at least speaks a little German."

I was completely shocked. "What?" I ejaculated.

"Yes," answered the lady of the house, "he phoned us from Cologne to say he was bringing his future wife with him and we should give you a warm welcome."

"Oh, did he? Hmm, I have no intention of getting married and I hardly know him. In any case I want a career."

With that I left the kitchen and went into the lounge in no time, where the culprit was sitting with his brother and Dad chatting. I interrupted the conversation.

"Mr. Burgundy Shoes, could you please come with me into the kitchen?"

Once there I interrogated him. "How did you have the gall to call your Mum and tell her you're bringing home your future wife, of all people *me?* And all this rubbish about Vico and Lys Assia. Really, you've got a nerve. Anyway, I have no intention of marrying anyone yet."

By this time both mother and so-called future daughter-in-law were glaring at him. The young twister of a gentleman remained cool.

"Well, you will be my wife one day," was the simple answer.

"Now look," I said, "I want a career and not a husband."

"That's ok," he answered, and then defiantly, "I'll wait for you until eternity," and with that final remark he walked out of the kitchen.

I didn't know what to make of it, but I had to smile to myself – after all it was a compliment. Easier said than done.

I couldn't wait to get on to the phone to Mum and to tell her about this last episode. I wondered what she'd say?

She said, "I like the sound of that young man."

"Say what you like – Fate plays a lot of funny tricks in one's life, and Fate just lately seems to be having a ball with me."

Helsingor, Denmark

Every new country was a new challenge, but I guessed an agent or director who had booked me knew what he was doing.

My next interesting country was Denmark. Mr. Danoesti had seen me when he was on holiday in Travemunde, and later as the star of the big variety show at G.O. Palast Hannover. He booked me immediately to be the star of his spectacular new musical show at the "Little Mermaid Theater" in Helsingor during the whole summer season. It was one of my most enjoyable European summer engagements. The salary offered was royal and I was treated like a little princess. I had to do two shows nightly. The first was to show off my voice, with wonderful numbers from Gershwin and Cole Porter, ending with "Granada," a piéce de resistance. Mr. Danoesti chose my red satin ballgown for the first show. Before my debut, the girls dressed like hunters in red and green did their dance. There were about 16 of them. The décor was a large lit up staircase which they went up. Eight of them went up on one side and eight the other, with their stage trumpets blowing. A large fanfare heralded the star, who had to walk down this magnificent staircase as the trumpeters parted ways leaving a path for me to walk down gracefully. It was to be a big dramatic entry for the star of the show. Unfortunately, Mr. Danoesti had not noted I had two big flat feet and was sometimes called "little clumsy."

It was our opening night of the summer season. I did not lose my hoop on my underskirt as at Selbey's – no it was much worse. I don't know how, but I got my high heel caught in the frill of the petticoat, missed my step and went flying down the entire fateful staircase, landing at the bottom, right in front of the audience, on my derriére with my dress and petticoat over my head and my legs in the air. Being me, I burst out laughing. Pulling my gown straight I stood up, went to the audience, and asked the men in the front row – how did they enjoy my entry? I laughed and the theater rocked with laughter, the journalists included. The newspapers next day were full of my unusual first appearance in Denmark. The write ups were 100% positive and they drew crowds for the whole season, proving to the world you can even turn a blamange into a positive success, if you can learn to laugh at yourself.

My second show was more lively – mambos, sambas and plenty rock and rolls – *no staircase* – a piece of cake!

One day towards the end of the season something terrible happened again. After staying privately with a nice older lady called Stora Nielsen, I decided to rent a bungalow next to the theatre for the last month and asked Teddy to join me, and my parents too. There were enough extra bedrooms to keep the peace. Teddy and I slept in separate rooms, but shared a bathroom and dressing room.

Teddy had to pick my parents up in Copenhagen at the port, as their arrival time coincided with my first show. He was a little apprehensive that he may miss them and as I had no photo on me, I told him they were small in comparison to the Danes.

"Dad is Oriental, a bit brown, a bit bald with a big black moustache and a big white toothy smile, you can't miss him," I said.

As they were last and looking for him too, they found each other. Teddy was surprised Dad didn't look at all like my description. Dad explained to him why. The crossing on the ship was stormy. He went up on the deck, and having overdone his smörgåsbord he had to vomit with the swish of an extra big wave. His nice white teeth went overboard too. While shaving in the morning, the ship shuddered and lurched, and his hand unintentionally swerved. Suddenly half of his moustache was unintentionally gone – so he shaved most of the other side to match and ended up with a little black Hitler moustache like Charlie Chaplin. I had to smile, as I knew from my sister Frances that her husband George had spent quite some time in Denmark and had told Dad about the wonderful food, fish, and cheeses, and the delicious smörgåsbord – a feast for the eyes and the "Gaumen." Now, with no teeth, it would surely be a little different. But they enjoyed themselves just the same.

Everything was great; we four hit it off surprisingly well and the good weather and the nice little garden belonging to the rented bungalow all helped. After a 3-week holiday with us Mum and Dad went home and Teddy stayed for a last week with me. At long last we were alone. I was quite in love. I have no idea how it happened – I never do – but we overstepped our love making session and when we awoke, to my horror, I had missed my first show of that night. I hated to think how it looked to the public when the girls did their trumpet fanfare and no one walked down that fateful staircase. We rushed to the theatre and I was full of apologies to dear Mr. Danoesti, who was himself in his early 40s. He was wonderful! I told him the truth, as somehow, I hoped he'd understand – he did. He smiled at us both with a twinkle in his eye.

"It's ok, I was also your age not so long ago. We managed to get through the first half of the show without our star. Now go and get changed quickly for the second show."

Sometimes I think I am blessed! A few years later my recordings did well in Denmark, one of the big managers of Decca Records, Arfi Arfmann, became a good friend of mine, and here again the friendship lasted a lifetime.

Since my first unusual appearance there I have always liked the Danes – they all seemed to have a real sense of humour.

CHAPTER 84

Mambo, Falsies and Ooh Love

The end of 1956 was a great time for Brigitte Bardot. Roger Vadim, her husband and producer, turned her into a blonde with a flowing mane and the most important young French sex bombe ever.

The film "Dieu crée la femme" was a smash hit – in English it was called "And God made Woman" and finally it was due to be released in Germany as "Und immer lockt das Weib". Paul Mizraki wrote the music and the main song that ran through the movie was "Dis-moi quelque chose de gentil cheri" – in German it became "Sag doch etwas Liebes zu mir, cheri".

I was walking on air; finally, without Gardiner, I could be sexy, not having to go to any Swiss or French couturier and pay a fortune for a super evening gown. Yet my career was really moving! When in London, I asked Netty, who was now with her own company and making her name in London as *the* wedding gown designer, and above all making those outstanding dresses for the up and coming singing star Shirley Bassey, to make something simple but stunning for me. She did – it was a clinging white gown entirely draped like a Greek goddess, with a large built-in bosom in diamante and, on one shoulder, a train falling down the back. I wore this with long green gloves, and it was chosen for the photo session with the most famous Hamburg photographer, Hanno Wohlfahrt.

Finally, after a lot of engagements all over Western Europe, I hit Munich, which had the "Oktober Fest" but no large theater restaurant. I was engaged to sing at the Café Stadt Wien, which was famous for having the best bands in Europe and the best star vocalist. The mambo had reached the music scene and I had already been seen on TV singing the most popular "Mambo Italiano." This became such a success I made it my last number in my show, as it generally received so many encores that I had to return and do it all over again. My Swiss couturier evening gown did not have large built-in bosoms, and as my own bust was so negligible, I bought a pair of falsies to fill out what the good Lord had forgotten. Whereas in all Theaters and Concert Halls the audience is seated in a straight line opposite the stage, in Café Stadt Wien there were tables going in a semi circle, and a good part of the public could see the stage from the side. My beautiful mimosa dress, for example, gaped at the sides of the strapless top, and what God had bestowed on me was just not enough to fill it out – hence the falsies!

In Mambo Italiano I really threw myself in to it. Every time I got to the words "Hey Mambo," and that was often, I'd throw up both my arms in the air, wriggle, and jump. It was most effective, but at that moment my strapless top would gape and, as I brought my arms down in full swing, I noticed in a mirror my falsies rose and showed half of themselves, standing out above my strapless top.

It was opening night, when most artistes are on top form but very edgy – what a horror! The audience clapped and shouted "encore, encore," I rushed off to the back of the stage where there were placed a couple of empty tables. I took the falsies out hurriedly, put them on a table and rushed back and did the much-wanted mambo a second time, asking the public to join in and help me out. As I finally left the stage with a bouquet from the manager for my first night, I went to the back to pick up my two troubleshooters – only to see quite a flock of young people staring at something. It was my falsies! Needless to say, I left them there! Thank heavens nobody noticed me, so I was not asked to autograph them.

Perhaps it was the sexy young Brigitte Bardot, but I think the fault really lay with "La Lollo," the beautiful Italian movie star Gina Lollobrigida. Through her, busts were definitely in, and I didn't have too much to offer, so I used falsies, as bras were not yet foamed and wired. It seemed only Netty had that knack.

Sometime later my Teddybear, as I now called Burgundy Shoes, was marvelous and chauffeured me from one place to the other, and slowly the kisses got hotter and so did "the getting to know you part." Finally, one night he started rubbing my bust, getting excited and breathing heavily. As I was wearing falsies under my dress, I could feel nothing. We were together in a sort of semi darkness as he had dimmed the lights and taken off his trousers, asking me to sit on his lap. I was on my guard when he removed his long pants, but he assured it was only to make sure I did not ruin the perfectly ironed creases in them. Once again, I could see the funny side of the situation.

I put my hands down my decolleté, pulled out the falsies, put them on the table and said, "Now you can play as long as you like," and with a big grin all over my face I walked out of his room and left him to his own devices.

CHAPTER 85

The Palais de Chaillot Triumph – Yet Another Marriage Proposal

At the Palais de Chaillot, a sort of baroque Carnegie Hall, I decided to invite Mum and Dad as my guests. I chose the best hotel I could afford and Mr. Gardiner, who had now asked me to call him James, had booked us in a good hotel nearby. He and I had adjoining single rooms. Suddenly, while I was still unpacking, there was a knock at my door and James Gardiner entered in a wine-coloured dressing gown with gold cord braiding and a bright bathing towel draped around his neck.

I had a terrible desire to giggle. He resembled, although quite a bit taller and dressed to kill, a kind of George Raft, who had been the bad man in many old movies. He started immediately to recite a sermon.

"Yvonne, you can't be a virgin forever, or do you want to be a nun? Now it's the time to find out what the life is all about. If you'll marry me, we could make a million between us – that is my goal. It's time you grew up." I seemed to have heard that song before. "When you give your favours to the right people you will be surprised how quickly you make it to the top. How do you think I got such good connections? I pleased a lot of older ladies, and the men – as you know – with kickbacks. It's all a part of the game, my dear, so let's make our first night of our planned marriage now. I'll guide you to all the right Daddies in good time."

I was quite sure he meant business, as I could see something protruding under his dressing gown and it certainly was not one of those famous white handkerchiefs.

I did the only thing I could do, as suddenly I could see the funny side of the whole situation. I burst out laughing and asked him, if he fancied he was Humphrey Bogart or George Raft, dolled up as he was?

The protrusion disappeared almost as quickly as it had arrived and then I gave him my speech. After contemplating that he had asked me to buy for him for his birthday a most expensive ski outfit, which I foolishly did – and what did he buy for me for my birthday? Three covered coat hangers, the kind you pick up at church bazaars – I knew exactly what he meant by making a million between us. I would be the worker and he the dictator. Then I told him straight up as I had done with Nick: I had no intention of playing the field of life to his rules. My body was my private affair, my voice was for the public; as for marriage, which he had offered, *forget it!*

When Mum and Dad came to the show, they saw their baby get a standing ovation – so did James Gardner. I told them both of my manager's proposal, and my dad was furious, although Mum's reaction was more or less as if she had anticipated his behaviour. Mum told Dad about Heini Thyssen and Dad said I must be stark raving mad.

He looked at me and almost growled, "In a world where money and prestige mean Power and Power rules the world – you, little stupid, threw away a chance of a lifetime. Why, you could have owned a couple of skyscrapers in New York or Monte Carlo!"

Then suddenly he remembered I was his baby and I had had more success at the concert in Paris than all the other, older big names, including Vico Torriani, the much-loved Swiss film star who had been put on at the end because the organisers believed he would get the biggest applause.

Kurt Edelhagen and Jacques Dieval, both beaming, came over and congratulated me and I thanked them. From them onwards I was known as the Cole Porter Songstress. Belgium, Luxembourg, and the Netherlands were conquered after a wonderful summer in Sweden. I think I took my ability to be a success in all these different countries from my flexibility in languages and a feeling for what the public in each country prefer. My aim was to be international.

Dad, who had finished off Gardiner after a heavy duel of words, invited me and Mum for a short holiday in Madeira, which I accepted.

EMI Electrola came and asked me to sing the film music "Moonglow" from the latest Kim Novak movie. Then, as Brigitte Bardot started to be a star, they liked a photo of me in a sweater and shorts and decided to make me the German Brigitte Bardot. I had already been in a German movie and was very impressed by a young singer pianist and his group who were with me. His name was Udo Juergens. He was tall, slim, and had a pleasant voice. I was told he was another Austrian charmer like Willy Hagara, a very handsome singer who had already been in a few German films, but this guy was a good pianist and could compose too.

I knew I was to be BB's singing voice, but now that I knew that a big company as EMI wanted to groom me to be the German answer to BB, it was more than thrilling. I just had to celebrate, and as I had to do my weekly radio show on Radio Geneva, I celebrated with my dear friend Louis Rey and his lovely second wife Vera, formerly of Radio de la Svizzera Italiana. I chose a double cognac and a large portion of my favourite food, caramel ice cream. I had had enough champagne in Cyprus, Switzerland, Austria, Germany, and all the other places where there were admirers, some of whom had even drunk champagne out of my silver or gold stage shoes – it was already enough to last me all my life. No! Good cognac and really good ice cream are much more "my cup of tea" – viva la difference!

CHAPTER 86

What Love Can Do!

Without warning, Burgundy Shoes, who I now called Teddybear or Teddy, arrived in Munich, even though he had sent me many letters in French and never mentioned his intention. He took a room next to mine in the Hotel next door to the Café Stadt Wien where I was appearing. I was quite in love with him but wary. After the terrible show down with Nick Norovski I had developed shingles, and this malady was going to follow me for the rest of my life. It started at the bottom of my spine, which is an important nerve center, and to my horror spread into my vagina. I was in such pain I had to have a doctor visiting me and to stay in bed. I had to cancel all engagements. As I recovered, I lamented my fate to the understanding doctor.

"Oh," I said, "what a place to get it – now you are going to tell me I must never make love again, and I'm still so young."

The doctor smiled and said, "Of course, you will be able to enjoy lovemaking again, but whatever you do, do not overdo it and take my advice: when you do go to bed with a man, take with you a tape measure. You must never have intimate relations with a man who is too big for you. You are small and compact, so do be careful. One little girl I am treating for shingles is only 12 years old, she has it in her eye – believe me, that is much worse!"

Therefore, when Teddy – "my little bear" – started to caress me in his room next door to mine, I took out my tape measure. It was unnecessary – I took one look at him laying naked on the bed and said, "Oh sorry, we are not made for each other, you are great – too great. I'm going back to my room."

Then came the pleading, the kissing, and all his knowledge of super French love making delicacies were bestowed upon me – and I succumbed.

Next midday found us in the hotel restaurant, billing and cooing like two turtledoves as we enjoyed a real brunch, but a horrible pain in my lower tummy kept returning and I tried to put it out of my mind.

As Teddybear had only two days free from deadlines for his musical arrangements at many of the biggest bands in Europe, he left, and when my engagement in Munich was up I was scheduled to go on tour with the crème de la crème of Electrola recording artistes. There was Bibi Johns, a famous film star in many musicals, whom I was with at many galas – a lovely person, Angele Durand, a big Belgian singer, Ralf Bendix with his ever popular "Babysitter Boogie," Fred Bertelsmann with his "Laughing Vagabond," a couple of others like Barbara Kist, with her "Klein, Aber Oho!" and Wolfgang Sauer, the famous blind baritone, and me.

The pains got worse, but whenever I heard my intro, I'd put on my silver high heels to go on stage and I felt just fine – all pains had gone, and the applause convinced me that when you do something you enjoy you feel good.

I always knew my own body better than most doctors and I guessed it was my appendix. I called Dad on the phone and asked him to book me the best surgeon in London. He said ok, and a flight ticket was arranged.

Immediately, the tour ended, I flew home, and the great surgeon eliminated my appendix just as it was going to be peritonitis. Never having swallowed any stones of pips or fruits, I asked my doctor, "How did I get this trouble?"

He explained: "Something large seemed to have invaded your ovaries – they became inflamed and as you are tiny and compact inside, an inflamed ovary infected your appendix. Do be very careful with your sex life and take it easy." I was perplexed, to say the least.

Having my appendix operated on upset all the record company's plans of grooming me into a German Brigitte Bardot. BB was known to be afraid of flying and was scheduled to arrive in Stuttgart by train, where the great sounds of the now most famous modern orchestra in Germany, Erwin Lehn, would welcome her together with me. Then a big show for the premiere of "Und immer lockt das Weib," the German version of her hit film, was planned at the largest theatre, and finally Yvonne Carré would be launched as "our BB." The slogan was "BB = YC," and I was half French so we would be able to converse. Flyers were arranged, publicity in a big way was planned, and where was I? In London having an appendix operation.

BB, who had a heavy schedule, immediately cancelled her visit when she heard I would be unable to make it at the date arranged. Electrola cancelled all and me too. All my dreams and hopes were shattered with one big blow through one night of love!

When we are in love – why can't we see clearly?

CHAPTER 87

The Madeira Hat

Dad kept his promise and invited me to join Mum and himself at the Savoy Hotel in Funchal. Reid's was actually the most prestigious hotel on the island because Winston Churchill always stayed there, but it was a bit stiff and starchy and, above all, the pool was very small.

The Savoy was the second-best Hotel in Funchal and had a more relaxed and international atmosphere and, above all, a marvelous swimming pool hewn out of the cliffside and filled with real, fresh sea water. It was wonderful to be able to swim pleasantly and watch the big waves in the Atlantic ocean outside – although we swimmers were also in the open air. Apart from this, Mum and Dad always spent a good part of the English winter there and they knew the owners well. Mom had advised me to look more at boys of my own age and less at far older men, as it seemed to her had been my fate.

The beach boy was young, middle blond, with a mass of curly hair and muscles that reminded me of my first big love, the Israeli radio officer Gad Ben Ari. As I found out when he pulled up a chaise longue for me, his name was Virgilio, and he was tanned and quite edible. This was the time and the place to show off my luxury bathing suit from Nick's Milano shop. It had a zip at the back which was fairly easy to get up – but after a swim it was wet and became difficult to get down. Opportunity knocks, so I asked Virgilio to help and thought it would be fun to initiate him to the joys of erotic love – perhaps he was even a virgin!

I thought that would be fun, and so it was, but when I suggested a second helping, he said, "No, I'm only just 17 and I prefer to join the other guys and play football," and he left my little bathing cabana. Perhaps he was too young after all.

We three dressed for dinner and I wore the white organza model James had picked out as being particularly virginal; it was decorated with sequined sprigs of lilac. The maître d' came to our table and asked me if I would join the Miss Madeira competition.

Today the Misses make a fortune, but at that time Madeira had no airport and very few tourists. We had to fly in from Lisbon on a seaplane, which had no radar and needed a fairly calm ocean to land. It was a flight to remember. Firstly, our sea plane ran into a heavy thunderstorm and right into the middle of it, when the air pressure changes violently, some passengers were already vomiting into their bags. There was suddenly a terrific clap of thunder – we had no seat belts, and the plane suddenly went down at a dizzying speed, and we all fell forward over each other. I am sure we all thought it was the end and it would crash into the wild Atlantic. After a few terrible moments the little sea plane seemed to regain its balance and we drew into the port of Madeira – the other side of the island. It was like going through a nightmare and waking up in paradise. There were a couple of dozen young girls all dressed in their colourful traditional costumes with bunches of freesias in yellow, white, and light mauve to greet us. The air was sweet and fresh from their perfume. We all received posies of freesia and suddenly we forgot the awful ordeal and were ready for the drive over the mountain to the other side of the island, where Funchal and our hotels were situated, and where I knew Mum and Dad would be waiting for me anxiously.

Exhibitionism such as a Miss competition was, for young ladies in Madeira, not just new but totally unheard of for a decent young girl – so I had almost no competition and won hands down. There were also no real prizes, but I was presented with a large straw sun hat with appliquéd flowers all done in the lovely Madeira embroidery. The sun was hot, and it got plenty of use.

When Dad had that row with James Gardiner, it was a relief, but I knew I must go ahead and make further contracts by myself. I had immediately written to Solly Black in London, asking him what he could offer. He returned almost immediately with an excellent offer from the Embassy Club in Mayfair – the in place at the moment. I wasted no time in informing Solly I'd be flying in from Madeira where, against six other young ladies, I was voted Miss and I would be wearing my prize, a handmade Madeira sun hat. I hoped the press would be there to greet me. They were, and remembering I looked best with my chin up I put on my sun hat and made for the stairs of the plane and once more I missed my footing because I held my head in the air and did not look at the steps. I fell from the top to the bottom, landing on the airfield; it was hard. I had to have photos taken with the plaster on my leg which the St. Johns Ambulance people had put on when they rushed to my aid. It made the front page of all the evening papers – it read "The wind got under her Madeira hat."

My agent was delighted with the publicity and asked me if I could do such a fall again and again, then he could get me non-stop good contracts. Whatever talent I seemed to possess in the entertainment world, I seemed to have a real talent for falling over and falling for the wrong man!

CHAPTER 88

Frank Sinatra – Star Wars

The Embassy Club show was, thank Heavens, a true success, and they asked Solly Black when I could return next season. I breathed a sigh of relief – now Solly had surely forgotten my fiasco with film star Sean Connery, and we could work together comfortably.

I sat in his office discussing my future engagement, when suddenly the other two big chiefs came in hurriedly. I had already put myself on a little corner chair when they butted in as I did not want to leave, but also did not want to be in the way.

The three men huddled together discussing something I felt must be of the greatest importance. I had a feeling they were so engrossed that they hadn't noticed that I was even there. Suddenly, without any warning whatsoever, the door burst open and a raving small slim guy with blue eyes that seemed to jump out at you blew in like a hurricane. It was Frank Sinatra. I recognised him immediately, as I had only been to see him in concert at the Elephant & Castle a short while ago. I was an ardent fan and had seen him first live at the London Palladium, apart from in various movies. His singing was a musician's dream, his voice was undoubtedly warm and sexy, he could dance and act, and he had that hungry look that we females fall for – don't ask me why – could it be our motherly instincts telling us he needed a good home cooked dinner? He was furious and without further ado, he started to shout at the three men.

"I'm not going to Australia without my broad. I want her with me!" He repeated that twice.

It seemed he was in love again, or perhaps he wanted just to test their will power against his.

"We are not paying for her," was the definite answer – in unison.

"Then I'm not doing the Australian tour."

It seemed to me I was in the middle of star wars and plenty of star ego. For a second there was a dead silence and my peer seemed to glance a moment in my direction almost in flirting approval. I understood why we young females all swooned for him. Right now, he was not the nice shy guy from the movies I had seen, but more the tough guy and a real rough diamond. The bosses of the biggest agency in the U.K. repeated their ultimatum.

Our star repeated his and with that he almost shouted, "Then you can cancel the Australian deal."

The answer was a hard one. "Then we're canceling you *out*, and not just for Australia."

Sinatra left as fast he came in, slamming the door behind him.

The men huddled again together and came to a conclusion which changed the face of musicals and much of show business altogether.

"We want no more stars – they are too expensive and too much trouble. We will make sure the public will not come to see some famous name in musicals," as it was at the time, be it: Tommy Trinder or Tommy Steele or Zoe Gail or Pat Kirkword. "No – from now on no one will notice the names – they will book the show by name."

And so it is today, and later Andrew Lloyd Weber joined them.

No one remembers the names of the actors or actresses. What for? I believe it all ended with Michael Crawford in "Phantom of the Opera." As for the stars with big names, they didn't have to fill a theatre for weeks as they did before – no way. They had to fill an arena, but only for one night. After all, business is business, and there is no business like show business.

CHAPTER 89

My Shotgun Marriage

And so it came to pass that I went to London earlier to smooth the path for Dad, as Mum wanted to have Teddy in my parents' home. He came later; both of us took the boat train to London. We had Christmas parties and musical chairs and lots of tea and cakes, and Teddy looked so handsome in the new designer suit I had bought for him in Hamburg. When folk asked me who the handsome bugger was I answered, terribly sure of my Continental way of living, "Oh, the man I am living with at the moment, but I'm always on tour."

This got open mouths and lots of whispering behind hands, particularly among the ladies. One morning while we were making the old double bed we shared in my room (we couldn't use the guest room because it was choc full of old cases and junk and totally unusable – no one could even open the door) Dad walked in and told Teddy off.

"Shame on you – sleeping in the same room as my daughter and you haven't even offered her marriage."

Teddy was surprised. "Of course I want to marry her," he exclaimed, "but she doesn't want to marry me."

With that, Dad turned to me. "What you do in Hamburg is your business, but here in London it is against the law to be housing a young man with whom you are not married. People are already talking. The Police can come and condemn me for keeping a "wild" house. He can go and stay in the hotel across the street, but not here!"

"Dad," I said, "he is only a poor musician, he doesn't have the money for the Brent Bridge Hotel – after all, Mum said she wanted to meet him here."

Dad started to rant and make a scene. "You are a star, you wear a mink coat – what in the hell are you doing with such a poor musician – and a German to boot (noch schlimmer)!"

That did it. I said, "If I've got to choose between the two of you I prefer him, because I can handle him."

Teddy turned to me and in a brisk voice said, "Put on your coat and let's get to a registry office." – and we did.

I had been scared to have to cook on my first television show in Hamburg, but *marriage* – just the word put me in a blue funk, but I felt terribly sorry for Teddy and my father's behavior toward him.

Once again I seemed to be between the Devil and the deep blue sea. We went to the registry office to put up the banns for three days, and then I asked if we had to have a gold ring.

"Oh no," was the answer from the Justice of the Peace (J.P.) with a twinkle in his eye, "we are terribly modern here, we don't bother with wedding rings."

"Anyway, I swear I will never wear a wedding ring," I said, "it's daft – you either love a person and stand by that person or you don't, and a gold band does not mean a thing. I've seen too many men take them off when away from home. I for one am against marriage."

The man looked at me, perplexed. "Well, what are you getting married for? I deal with people daily and have seen hundred of couples and I bet you have already lived together."

"We want the certificates for our respective parents," we said, and left the man to wonder what sort of madcaps he was dealing with.

The night before our marriage I had a terrible nightmare. I dreamt I was making my way through a dark forest when suddenly the moon came out and lit up my path, and there before me swung a noose from a branch of a tree. Somewhere a ghostly voice said, "Step forward, little girl, into the noose, and you will lose your newly won freedom for ever."

I awoke in a cold sweat. I had to wake Teddy and tell him. His reaction was cool. "Don't worry, you are marrying me – you will never lose your freedom. That's something we both want."

With that reassurance I turned over and went to sleep, but next morning I was still in a blue funk. I didn't want to get up at all, feigning a terrible headache. Rosalind, my sister-in-law, came into the bedroom with a glass in her hand and a couple of aspirins.

"All of us are married," she said, opening the conversation, "and I am here to see that you get married too. Now drink this double whisky and take these aspirins and make up your mind. You are getting married!"

Mum came with as the second witness and Teddy had rushed out earlier and bought three red carnations for us three "girls" for our coats. Just before we arrived at the office I stopped and said in a loud clear voice, "I'm sure we'll have to put our hand on the Bible – so I want you three and God to know I am doing this to please our Mums and Dads, but I will never wear a wedding ring and I intend to carry on my life and my career as before. I believe in God but not marriage."

Many of you will think I am completely mad – but your previous experiences form your mind. I had sung at so many large, prosperous weddings, where the bride was referred to as a sort of an angelic virgin by the Master of Ceremonies. The compliments flowed, as did the champagne, and after one year she was suing for a divorce. She had not been so pure at all or devoted – she had been a calculator. Occasionally it had been on the other foot; perhaps the groom was either considerably younger and better looking or the bride came from a particularly wealthy heritage. After all these failed marriages from the upper-class families I started to believe in the old French proverb, "Le marriage est la tombe de l'amour." Jean-Paul Sartre and Simone de Beauvoir had lived and loved a lifetime without ever having been married. They were, for me, my peers.

Rosalind looked disgruntled and said dryly, "Well, we've all gone through it, now it's your turn."

Mum smiled sweetly and said, "Tootsie, do remember you belong to no one but yourself."

Teddy gave a big reassuring smile and said, "That's ok with me – I never fancied the housewife mother type anyway – I know we both put our careers first. They are for both of us number one."

We four went in. The J. P. read out loud what Teddy was asked to repeat.

"I, Dieter Klaus…"

My almost husband mistook the pronunciation and thought of the catholic deity and that it was Latin and dutifully repeated, "Ay diet er a kloos do take…" etc. etc.

I never heard the rest, I got such a fit of the giggles, like a 12-year-old schoolgirl. The ceremony had to be stopped for a few moments while I dried my eyes and did my best to pull myself together, but I did notice that Mum was having a secretive giggle to herself.

Finally, the J.P. recited, "Now the groom takes the ring and puts it on the bride's finger."

Immediately Teddy got indignant and said, "But you told us you are modern and we didn't need a ring."

This time it was the J.P's turn to chuckle to himself. "But I was only kidding," he said.

"Oh good," I said, like a badly brought up kid, and turned to Teddy. "Now we don't have to get married, thank goodness!"

Mum, who really liked Teddy a lot, saved the tricky situation and took off her wedding ring and gave it to the would-be groom – who recited, "With this ring I do thee wed," and put it on my third finger. The J.P. heaved a sigh of relief and continued his sermon.

The ring was far too big for me, and without thinking I let my left arm fall to my side and Mum's gold ring fell off and rolled away. That got us all on our hands and knees looking for it among the mothballs and chairs that filled the little hall. All the time Rosalind kept repeating, "Oh dear, that is a bad omen for a marriage."

Finally, it was found, and we were proclaimed man and wife.

Once outside there was cheek kissing, and Mum said, "I must get along and buy some fish," Dad's staple diet.

Rosalind said, "And I must get back to work," and Teddy and I went to a local cinema and saw "South Pacific" after we had given Mum the proof we were married, so that the police would not come and Dad would no longer be worried.

I returned Mum her ring and have never worn a wedding ring since. I have received over the next decades at least eight different decorative gold rings with emeralds, sapphires, rubies, amethysts, and a superb square cut diamond – but all this came years later.

Mother had predicted, "This young man will make his way in the world," and he certainly did.

When we married, he had exactly 500 DM in his savings and an old Volkswagen bug – all the attributes I had proclaimed to my father I would marry. A sort of "here's mud in your eye, Dad" attitude, as he was so keen to marry me off to some super rich and prestigious man, even if he was thirty years older. However, in spite of his sweet "milk on his lips" face, Teddy was certainly no virgin!

CHAPTER 90

Morocco Oriental Dreams – Do As I Say, But Not As I Do

Shortly after our marriage Dad informed me that in the coming February he and Mum would make a change from Madeira and be going to Morocco. Needless to say, I was intrigued, and visions of "One Thousand and One Nights" and the dance of the seven veils all seemed to flash through my mind. I told Dad I would like to take the opportunity to join them and see a new mysterious country.

Dad who was to my mind a born and bred Oriental had said, "If I was your husband, I would never allow you to go."

"What?!" I said, full of scorn, "I have repaid nearly all the money you lost with Nick Norovski. I have paid my way. I am an independent female. I need ask no one! Anyway, as I know Teddy, he would be happy for me to have opportunity of being with my parents and to be able to see new things, especially if it included visiting Spain and the Rock of Gibraltar."

They were going to Tangier for the first African Congress. Dad was to be only a spectator. I remembered that my good friend Gerard van de Meer owned a beautiful hotel there overlooking the Casbah. When he had told me about this hotel with architecture like a Moorish palace, I never dreamed that God would ever give me the opportunity of being able to see that special old hotel, a so-called symbol of Tangier. I believe it was called "Ville de France" at that time. Apparently French film star Charles Boyer was playing Pepé le Moco in a most successful movie all about the Casbah; it was called "Algiers," but it was all about the Medina of Tangier. He also co-starred with the

Viennese beauty Hedy Lamarr. Both were guests in his hotel. All these thoughts passed through my mind, and I was excited.

Dad was shocked in his old-fashioned way that my husband would allow me to go with them. I was amused.

"Dad," I said, "Get it into your head: I am a star, a professional – I have paid my dues, and after all I'm going with my parents, aren't I?" Anyway, I was over 21, thank Heavens.

We stayed at the brand new Ryf Hotel, which also housed the Congress and all the African Ministers. They all seemed to speak good English as well as French and Arabic and in no time, I got to know quite a few of the younger set. Mum and I had fun at the cafés because we were not allowed to sit with Dad. We had to go upstairs with the women (naturally, he as a man paid for us as his belongings). These women astonished me, because the moment we were among the female sex they took off their yasmaks, scarves, and veils, etc., some which were richly embroidered with sequins. Most of the young ladies wore thick make up – almost ready to go on the stage or television. I was really flabbergasted at how very good looking some of those girls were. Dad was incorrect when he had said, "Most of the women are so ugly I, for one, am happy they cover up their faces."

Some of the younger ministers asked me if they could have a small party in my room – away from the other members of the Congress. I later understood why they asked me for my room. They brought with them quite a few huge magnums of Scotch whisky, which they could drink in my room but, as good Muslims, not in theirs.

A little later another youngish man came in – he smiled when he saw me and said, "Your dad has patience to witness that Congress."

I grinned to myself; after all, Dad was definitely hard of hearing, so he as a spectator could not join in the arguing and bickering and had no option but to remain interested but passive.

The young man then sprawled himself out on my bed and asked the others, "Where is the whisky?"

"Here!" shouted the others in unison.

This man was cool – he drank heartily, then took a "pain" from the basket to remove any traces of alcohol from his breath. After some small talk with the others, who were obviously all friends, he stood up and said, "Sorry, I've got to get along again. Au revoir," and he left us.

After he left, Mahdi, the most sympathetic young minister with impeccable English, turned to me and asked, "Do you know who that was?"

"No," I said, "haven't a clue, but he seemed to have a definite thirst for good whisky."

"Ssh," was the reply as Mahdi put his finger to his lips, "that was our Crown Prince – one day he will be our King."

"Oh," I said to myself, knowing full well that in the Muslim religion drugs were ok, but alcohol forbidden.

I was told that later on, during his reign, he made the country much more Muslim and expected his people to be far more religious than previously, but when he laid on my bed drinking whisky he was no royal, just a normal, real young man! Then he turned out to be a "Do as I say, but not as I do" King – a clan to which most of the upper set belonged.

CHAPTER 91

Prisoners in Tito's Realm

It was then that I was approached by Peter Ahrweiler to play Chérie in Francois Campaux's "Chérie Noire" in German. I love a challenge. I agreed and was given the book to learn over the summer season and told to pick up a nice dark tan. However, as big a challenge as doing a whole play in German was my acceptance to do a summer season in Yugoslavia, which, unbeknown to me at that time, turned out to be a real adventure story. I was the first Western artists to venture into a communist country other than East Germany, and it was an unusual adventure story going to sing in Tito's realm.

On our way we drove over Italy and met my parents in a dream destination – Venice. Dad had procured four seats for an evening cruise on a gondola with music and song. I was in my element. Here I was, with my beloved Mum and Dad and my handsome young husband, on a gondola in Venice at night. The weather was good, the music delightful, and the soprano sang all songs we knew and liked, e.g. "Come back to Sorento" and "Isle of Capri" etc. As I went to hold my new husband's hand and tell him how romantic it all seemed to me, he pushed my hand away, saying "I need both hands to put my fingers in my ears – heavens, that woman is singing sooo flat."

Far worse, traversing the famous Bridge of Sighs, we looked from the bridge to the water below and I turned my face to Teddy, who had his arm around my shoulder, and said, "Here we are in Venice, let us both sigh together on this very bridge."

The reply was typical Teddy with his black humour; "Don't look now, there's a dead dog floating by – now that's something to sigh about."

This unromantic attitude disappointed me; it was the way he looked at things so pragmatically, so differently to me. Love's young dream starts diminishing when you wake up to the fact that boys often think quite differently to girls. Many young girls may rebuke me for this deduction, but in their subconscious they would have to agree with me…so much for my dream of romantic Venice.

Teddy had packed the car. At the back he had put his old accordion, as he felt for sure he would spend some time writing some new compositions and in all probability the private digs we would be allotted would not possess a piano. He covered it with an old blanket, in case he would have to drive over potholes in some poor roads and the accordion may fall and get damaged. I put in my Uher tape recorder, which I used constantly to record my shows to improve on myself and then practice. We also had with us a hot water heater for tea ("Tauchsieder"). Teddy chose to cross over the border at Trieste into Yugoslavia at Jesenice. It all sounded so fine to me. The customs officers in the little hut on the other side were asleep when we arrived. I had a feeling no Western person had ever gone through the customs at Jesenice. They stripped the car as if we were part of a criminal band. They confiscated our portable radio, my electric hair dryer, my most important Uher Tape Recorder, and Teddy's accordion. The fact that he had wrapped it in an old blanket was, for the ignorant customs men, a definite sign we were criminals. I showed them my contract with their government, proving that I would be appearing for the month in Bled Slavonia. I am not at all sure that either of them could read and even if they could, the contract was in English.

In Yugoslavia, under the communist rule of President Tito, everything apart from my contract was in Serbo-Kroatic. As the writing was similar to that in the USSR, I could not read a word. Finnish had been difficult, but at least I could read and manage to make myself understood more or less.

In my Serbo-Kroatic dictionary the pronunciation was put also in phonetics, so that was a great help – but not for the customs inspectors. I seem to possess an uncanny instinct to understand the gist of what people are saying to each other when they think a) I can't hear or b) I would not understand anyway.

"Oh God help us," I whispered to Teddy, "they seem to want to confiscate the lot, it would bring them in a nice prize money – and we need our equipment."

I tried to explain this miserable fact to the two men. If only other Westerners would come – but no one came to the Jesenice customs and I had a definite feeling no one except us had ever ventured over that obscure border line in that remote part of the world.

Both men regarded my contract as if it had been toilet paper. We were lost. Suddenly the clever words of an international businessman (my father) came to me, "Money speaks all languages and don't you forget it, my traveling daughter."

I waved a 100 DM Note in front of them and some thousands of Italian lira, plus a 10 pound note I had in sterling.

This seemed to change their eye work regarding us two "criminals." Then the older one spoke for the first time in halting German:

"Do you know," he said, "here in our country you can buy a house for the price of that accordion?"

Now it was Teddy's turn to look amazed. "What?" he said incredulously, "it's my father's oldest instrument – it's just for me to work on if there is no piano."

The men spoke more between themselves and then brought us to a room in a small house nearby. They told us not to try to leave as the door would be guarded, and to make sure they went out, turning the key in its lock, and they took the key with them. After all, in their eyes we were criminals and a car such as our brand new Citroen had never been seen in this part of the world. What to do? There was a window, but it was a bit small – but so was I. I opened it quietly – it was not locked – I had only one thought in mind: I must get help and that quickly. I managed to squeeze through, and Teddy threw my shoulder bag after me with all my important papers and, above all, my contract. I ran toward the little town and found the post office with a telephone and dialed the number on my contract. Fortunately, the person who answered spoke fairly good English; he was the manager, and said he would contact the customs officers to not confiscate anything – but unfortunately the best part of my monthly salary would have to be forfeited as penalty for smuggling such goods into the country. I breathed a sigh of relief.

How does a romance break? When your illusions crumble and melt away under a burning sun. I made my way as quickly as I could back to the window of the guarded room in the little house across the border in Jesenice, where we were held as "caught in the act" criminals.

I was told on the phone that all would be well, but in Yugoslavia everything took a lot of time. I was wished from the management in Bled a pleasant night and was assured that tomorrow "You will be free to come to us with all your possessions – but a rather hefty punishment fine will be on the way. However, your super salary as the first foreign artist will cover everything easily, so regard Bled as a sort of holiday."

I was relieved but awfully tired. I managed to find a foothold and clambered back into our guarded room. I wanted to tell Teddy the good news and just sleep and sleep. Teddy, just like a real bear, was already in bed and looked as if he was asleep, or at least pretending to be. When I turned the light on I saw to my horror, a large black spider hanging on a self-made thread, starting on a web –directly over my pillow.

In my romantic girlish mind, now was the time for this young man I married to jump into action and get rid this spider for me completely. After all, he was supposed to be a man and was considerably taller and more muscular than myself. I woke him up, trying very hard to get out of my mind my very first platonic boy friend, who had run out of the room when he saw a spider in our house and left me to dispose of it.

Well, my husband would not budge. I coaxed, I implored – the only reaction I got was, "Oh, I'm too tired, come to bed!"

Insects have a very strong instinct. This one was clever; it ran up on the ceiling looking down on little me. I argued, "Teddy dear, you are tall enough to reach it on a chair and to kill that damned spider, but I will have to stand on a chair and put it on the bed to do it."

My "hero" just lay there pulling the covers tightly round his face. I glared at that young lazy monster, took the only chair in the room, put it on the bed and then gingerly climbed onto it, which was no easy feat. It was a balancing act, as the bed was a soft and springy one. I killed the intruder and threw its remains out of the window. I had a feeling my husband had been watching me through half closed eyes. I put the chair back and went to bed, contemplating how odd men were! All my romantic illusions lay shattered on the ground. Fortunately, I didn't have to sweep them up.

My husband was great at music and before our marriage he had often sent me lovely bouquets of flowers. When his old Volkswagen bug had broken down, he had got out of the car at night in the pouring rain, seemingly in the middle of nowhere, without a word of rejection. He had even found help! But a little bit of primitive man he certainly was not. He was not going to be my great protector or my benevolent provider. In many ways that night was the beginning of the end – my prince had fallen from his throne on our first night in Yugoslavia, and I was too young and inexperienced to realise that not even a prince charming is perfect.

We saluted goodbye and were on our way to Bled. When we arrived at the Theatre Restaurant with stage and band, we found there were some discussions going on. The amplification was not working. I was horrified and told the smiling manager they just must get some good electrician, as I could not possibly do my entire show without a microphone and loudspeakers that functioned properly.

The reply was a special one I will never forget. The manager and the bandleader, both smiling, turned to me and said, "Don't worry Miss Carré you are no longer in Western Europe, you are here in a good communist country. You will receive your salary if you work or not. We must wait three days for the new equipment to arrive here in Bled. You surely are tired from the long journey and the trouble you have gone through with our Customs in Jesenice. Take a three-day holiday. In the house where you will be lodging during this month here are Mr. and Mrs. Zupan, lovely people who speak good German, and you will eat good Slovanian food. Our town boasts a lovely lake and a beach with boats – you will enjoy it here."

It all turned out to be true, and it sure was something else, suddenly coming from a confusing hell to a friendly and peaceful place on earth.

CHAPTER 92

President Tito

The next day found us both on the beach by the lake. Teddy was reading one of the many books he had brought with him. I was learning my part as "Chérie" in German for the play "Chérie Noire" when two young men approached us. The first, with sleek brown hair and eyes to match, introduced himself as Sava. He spoke good English and told us they were on holiday, after which he introduced his friend, saying, "This is my friend Miladin. He is the son of a big communist minister, and we are staying at their holiday home. We have a boat. Would you care to join us for a short ride on the lake?"

He pointed to the fair-sized rowing boat anchored on the shore. I pricked up my ears; I loved rowing and was quite good at it – Teddy not so much at all. The other boy, with sandy colored hair and big blue eyes, turned to me and said, "We would be happy if you would join us, it would be nice to talk to the first tourists from Germany."

Sava then butted in, "That wonderful car parked outside – that is yours is it not?"

He was genuinely excited. Teddy turned to me and said, "I'm really not so keen on boats – you go, Pussy, you like rowing."

Teddy, I discovered, was a very quiet, somewhat closed-off person who enjoyed his own company – so I agreed, and at the same time explained we were not exactly tourists, but had three days holiday because the microphone and amplification had broken down. The rowing became a regular daily sport, although it was never expected of me to do this. The boys came often to eat a meal with us and enjoyed the show, which also had a juggler, a small chorus line of local girls, and a magician apart from the good music — a local quartet.

One evening, quite unexpectedly, the waiters seemed to be excited and in a flurry. A long red carpet was put down and suddenly the band stopped and played the national anthem. Everybody stood up and in marched President Tito with entourage. He wore an interesting uniform and boots. They took seats at a large table which had obviously been prepared for them. I had just done my opening number "It's a Great Day" and was about to do "Besame Mucho", which I did as a pot pourri with "C'est Si Bon", when I was beckoned to wait from the wings. I had no idea how to greet the famous President of Yugoslavia, and it was much too late to learn something in the local language. I just said, "My next song is a pot pourri, which I dedicate to President Tito and his entourage," and explained in English, ""Besame Mucho" is in Spanish and "C'est Si Bon" in French. In Serbo-Kroatic I think it would be "Poljubime Slatka Dragi," oh, that's Dobra, Dobra, Dobra!""

These were the first words Miladin had taught me on the boat, once when Sava had his back to us and was, I believe, steering.

My explanation was greeted with chuckles and laughter and clapping — so all was well. The visit was a short one. Immediately when I finished my show Tito and his all-male company stood up, giving me a standing ovation. The President then came on to the stage, shook my hand and said, in English, "Thank you."

I said "Halla leppo," as best as I could in my bad Serbo-Kroatic. I threw the company a theatrical kiss and left the stage and they finally left the theatre. Different to many presidents, Tito was a man holding his multicultural country together with a strong hand and a remarkably strong personality.

CHAPTER 93

Journey to Dubrovnik

The boys met us every day and were not just enamoured with our two-coloured, super modern car, but also with Teddy's moustache. In their eyes this made him a real Serb. Apparently, this was very good indeed, as they both came from the capital in Yugoslavia, Belgrade. They called him Teddy, but sometimes they asked in German, "Wo ist unser Serbische Baer?"

Miladin, who was nicknamed Saban, explained to Teddy that the roads from Bled to Dubrovnik were 90% open roads and in poor condition, and certainly not well signposted for a foreigner. Then, looking at me longingly, he said, "I have just enough time free and know the roads well; it would be my pleasure to navigate you both to your destination. We must stop on the way, but I know how to find good lodgings and for very little money."

I had already told the boys of our unpleasant adventure with the Yugoslavian authorities when entering the country at Jesenice. They both laughed and Sava said, "No one ever comes over the border at Jesenice, it really is almost unknown territory. You were probably the first foreigners they had ever seen – and perhaps the last."

Teddy seemed really relieved at the thought of having a Yugoslavian pal with us, so the deal was done. I felt that a blind man could see that Saban had fallen for me, but my cool calm husband from the north seemed not to have noticed. Without Miladin we never could have made that journey; there were almost no signs, not even in the local language. The driver just had to know himself where he or she was going, and at crossroads which road to take. We drove through some shockingly poor areas, and whenever we stopped for a snack or to visit a café, when we returned our car would be surrounded by curious kids and people. It was the centre of attention. Compared to the old, half broken-down cars we did encounter on our way, our car gave the impression of having been sent from heaven. What shocked me most when we lodged at people's homes – as a guest house – was the primitive lifestyle in comparison to the super modern, neutral in the war countries like Switzerland and Sweden, where I was so often engaged. Old calendars would deck the walls – just because there was a nice picture on the front. There were no photos or framed pictures, no mirrors and no ornaments, and very little furniture at all. Getting gas (petrol) for the car was also an achievement.

Whenever Teddy left us alone to repack the car, Saban took the opportunity to whisper how beautiful I was and to kiss me passionately. For a young woman, being desirable is really important, and both Teddy and I had been so busy working we had lost this feeling somewhere along the way. The young Serb, with his tousled head of sandy colored hair and almost almond shaped big blue eyes, was an ardent admirer and it did my ego good. I started to want him almost as much as he seemed to want me. Sometimes one is surprised at oneself!

Dubrovnik lay before us, an old walled city with a big marketplace and a town square with a large clock that worked. Such old buildings and labyrinths gave you the feeling you were living in the good old days, and somehow in some sort of museum. The roads were terribly narrow and winding, made more for mule trains than cars, but our Citroen with its hydraulic equipment did those roads perfectly. The room that was designated to us in Dubrovnik had its good points. There was a small adjoining bathroom and a fair-sized balcony with two garden chairs and a table. They looked out over the winding mule path going directly to the market. Further afield was the beach and the surf.

Teddy said he would go into the bathroom first, but returned far quicker than going in.

"I can't go in there," he stammered almost with fright. "There is a horrible black animal in there."

I immediately thought of a big black sleeping dog. This made Teddy laugh. "No, it's a…" I decided not to wait till he found the word in English and went in to see for myself. It was a huge black cockroach. The "Daddy" of them all!

Having made my acquaintance with these big insects on the lake of Genesaret in Israel I came out triumphantly and said, "Don't worry dear, I've had my experience of these roaches in Tiberias. I can kill it."

I picked up one of his shoes, a heavy beige lace-up. "No, no, not my shoe," he screamed in a falsetto voice; he became quite squeamish. "I couldn't stand it being killed with my shoe – take yours!" He was in a blue funk!

I was in my early 20s and liked to look sexy; I only had three pairs of high heeled shoes with me.

Muttering to myself, "How ridiculous," I took the only closed shoe I possessed, a beige, stiletto heeled court shoe, marched into the bathroom and gave the troublemaker a fast, sharp whack.

"Practice makes perfect," Mum had told me.

"If you want a thing done – do it yourself," Dad had told me.

That night I proved both of them right!

CHAPTER 94

A Clandestine Love Affair

My contract with the government was for the only nightclub, with the strange name of "The Hole in the Wall." The weather was perfect, and it was all in a walled garden and my little platform to sing on was under a lemon tree. The old walls around the city were extremely thick, and to enter the nightclub you had to pass through an arched doorway cut out of the thick old walls – hence the name. It was all worthwhile, as the views over the old city and harbour were superb. Somehow you had the feeling that you were transplanted into another world and era. The accompanying band was adequate, and the bandleader's wife sang a few songs in the local lingo during dancing. There was also a pretty local girl dancer. Our evening meal for us was also included in my contract, and it was always the same…mincemeat, string beans and pureed potatoes.

Teddy swore if he cut himself mincemeat and green beans would come out, but I said, "Don't look a gift horse in the mouth; they are poor and it's food."

The beach was lovely with clear water, as there were mainly cliffs and rocks, but there was enough sandy beach to play ball and we bought a blow up lilo and played in the water like kids. Saban bade us farewell and flew home to Belgrade, but not before he whispered in my ear "I will come back."

A week or so later a young man called Sin came to the beach looking for us. He told us he was a pal of Saban's and his uncle "Cika Jova" (in English we would say Uncle John), and that this uncle would be coming down to meet us too. He worked with Saban's father in the ministry.

Finally, Cika Jova arrived. He was a jovial, slightly podgy man of about 45 or 50. He seemed to have a perpetual smile on his round face and his eyes often twinkled when he spoke. He spoke good German as well as English and was soon engaged in deep conversation with Teddy. This gave Sin the opportunity to get closer to me when he whispered, "Saban will arrive in three days time. He will meet you under the large clock in the town square at 1 p.m. Will you be there? I must let him know."

I took a deep breath to cover up my surprise. "Oh really," I needed time to think. "Oh – ok I'll be there," I said.

Then Cika Jova and Teddy, still in deep conversation, walked towards us and Sin adroitly changed the subject.

I sat there contemplating my situation; Teddy had ruined many of my dreams of a dashing romantic lover. On our honeymoon in Majorca, I had gazed out of the window on our first night telling him how beautiful the stars looked in a black velvet sky. I asked him to join me. His response was, "Quickly, close the window before mosquitoes come in."

I think that many young girls dream of a real clandestine love affair and, being far too romantic, I was no exception.

I glanced at my watch three days later at lunch. I pushed back my plate feigned the heat was too much and I needed to lay down in a cool room. It was no lie – I just did not say where and with whom. As the clock struck one, I was in the square. Seemingly from nowhere, Saban emerged from the shadows. Without a word he took my hand and let me to an old house in the square. We climbed stairs and stairs and finally, underneath the roof, he took out a key, turned the lock, closed the door and suddenly we were on that old iron bed, completely lost in each other. It was pure magic. When I returned to this world, I saw the only washing facilities were a jug of cold water in a bowl and a large, somewhat threadbare white towel. Looking out from the window in the roof we had a perfect view of the square, and the room had green shutters. It was all I had longed for – old world romantic and a young ardent lover. Thinking to myself, passion is, after all, not prone in the UK. Then, laying as we were, naked, looking into each other eyes, he told me his story.

On his return home to Belgrade, he immediately looked up his old chum Sin. Sin was older and had experience and he was very close to Uncle John too (Cika Jova). In no time the three of them sat in a café drinking coffee deciding how to help Saban attain his dream. Sin would go first to Dubrovnik and make the acquaintance of Teddy and his famous wife with the nickname of "Pussy." Then Cika Jova would follow and tell Saban's parents he would invite the boy down to Dubronvik for a week or so to stay with him. The sea air would do the young guy good – as he and Saban's parents had noticed he was not eating and not looking quite himself. To make everything quite in order Cika Jova and the two boys would stay together in lodgings, and our little room with the green shutters would just be our own little love nest until my engagement was finished. The idea appealed to me and every lunchtime I would feign the heat was affecting me – so we had a few hours to be together in paradise.

CHAPTER 95

I See The Light

Towards the end of my contract three couples from Hamburg arrived at "The Hole in the Wall," all friends of Teddy's. After my show we went to the only beach place with live music. As we danced by the band, Teddy said he found the lady singer attractive. She had a moustache and that showed a great temperament. I was young and at that time quite insecure. I was jealous of the singer, and I was shocked that a hairy female could be the choice of my husband, it was so contra to my Anglo-Saxon standards. We all ordered drinks upon drinks.

I, as a first class "show off," told our new friends, "Just knock them back – then you can drink and drink like me."

Suddenly, during the time they were ragging poor Saban that his country was not just poor but had no taste, one of them dropped a "Mickey Finn" in my cocktail glass – I think it must have been a triple Slibovitz. I shouted "Cheers!" to our company and knocked my drink back. The effect was immediate. I was suddenly devoid of any inhibitions, I was annoyed with the Hamburgers because they had ragged Saban endlessly, making fun of the poor lighting and the bad table decorations and just everything.

I jumped up on the table my glass in my hand and shouted, "You Germans are all arrogant; you have no real red blood in your veins, only lukewarm water. Waiter, drinks for all. Drinks for the band, and a double whisky for the lady singer with the moustache."

I then started to dance on the table and every time we got another drink, I threw my glass and everyone else's on the stone floor. The sound of smashing glass was wonderful, I was blind drunk and the centre of attention and the boss was afraid someone could start a fight with all the uninhibited glass smashing. Teddy, who could drink anyone under the table, was completely sober. Suddenly he picked me up and carried me out after telling the boss that of course I would foot the bill the next day. Everyone knew who I was – so there was no problem there.

Once home he threw me on the bed, but then I screamed, "Oh my God the walls and ceiling are caving in on me. I must go in the fresh air and sit up."

This I did on a chair on our balcony. My head was spinning badly. Then, at about 5 a.m. a whole line of mules laden with heavy bags on both sides with their respective farmers passed by our path on their way to the market. It was an unforgettable, special sight, with the moon still up and the morning sun slowly coming through. Finally, I decided I must rid myself of this ghastly drunken feeling. I made my way to the beach slowly and carefully, then threw myself into the briny. A wave came and enveloped me completely and as I threw my head back and took a deep breath, like a bolt from the blue a voice called me:

"Yvonne, Yvonne, you must leave Germany. You promised yourself a long time ago you would buy a house in Switzerland. Now it's the time."

It came so hard and so clear to me it was like coming out of a dark tunnel into a bright light, I was completely sober and very clear in my mind.

Suddenly I was swept back in time. I felt I was in Tel Aviv again, with Nick Norovski, and as we entered the club there was always a large long mirror by the cloakrooms, but on that particular night the mirror had a huge crack in it and was broken. I was devastated, but Nick was quite calm.

"It's ok dear," he had said, "I know who did it and why. He had
a row with his girlfriend and breaking the mirror made him
feel so much better. It's a sort of shock treatment. When you are
drunk it's good to get a slap like breaking glass or cold water being thrown at you. In that moment you are completely aware of
your subconscious – and you know exactly what decision to take.
Normally your so-called commonsense will prevail and your subconscious will be completely obliterated, but have a shock after
a drunken night and you will know exactly which way to go."

And so it was with me. I rushed home, Teddy was up and saw immediately that I was completely sober and spoke quite normally.

"When we get back to Hamburg, I have no time as I have rehearsals for "Chérie Noire" so I am tied down, but you are free. Take
all my savings and go to our friend Fritz Mueller in Winterthur
and ask him to recommend a good Estate Agent. I will buy a
home in Switzerland as I once planned in Lugano when I was
still a kid. Now is the time. I think I have some Swiss Francs on
my account." I had been paying Dad back in installments.

I don't think too many people can say "You know, I bought our
home in Switzerland because the night before I got blind drunk.
But when I came to, I knew what I had always intended to do –
somehow I suddenly saw the light."

CHAPTER 96

Cocktails by Yvonne in Bremen

When Bremen booked me for my own TV show, I never dreamed of the problems one can encounter. We booked a student group with a great singer, guitarist, and trumpet player (Peter Beil, "Cindy oh Cindy"). We were all more or less kids together. I had already booked a young freelance journalist at "Hoeren und Sehen" as PR man. Dieter Broer, whom we called "Big Bear" to help his prestige, and Teddy (little Bear) was booked to do the music. Dieter Broer then booked Walter Haas to write the texts.

Peter Beil once came into rehearsals white and worried. A nice older gent in a red Ferrari had offered him a lift home. He accepted, only to find it was the king of all publishers. The second time, as the gents hand strayed above his knee to his inner thigh, he got the message of the deal. The senior had offered him the best publicity in the country, but Peter was in love with his little blonde bird, he called her "Spatz." He jumped out of the car quicker than he got in. Rex Gildo followed suit and did very well until he got older.

Teddy, who wrote the musical arrangements for the shows, plus some of his own compositions, and I, who was the star, bought a "hammer" of a car, a big Citroen in cream and orange and boy, could that go fast. It also had a hydraulic movement, so it could get higher and go over fields with ease like a Land Rover. For us it was very handy indeed; in a line of traffic on a high-way, Teddy would just go off the road, drive over a field, over-taking the whole line of traffic, and then we would just butt in at the front. Fortunately, there were no police around. In those days we were both a little crazy (and like the Bellamy Brothers,

"Now we're going sane") but getting to an engagement on time was our motto. No matter what!

The drummer of our TV show group fell in love with our car and bought a similar model Citroen for himself. The same day of the purchase he drove like a madman, 220 km on a North German Highway, lost control of his new car and crashed into a beton plank and died in hospital. He had bought the car as a present to himself for his birthday. It was a terrible loss; he had just turned 21 years old.

On my TV show I mixed cocktails and sang and danced to the various ingredients. As Peter was no dancer and had problems with the steps, we got a wonderful professional dancer called John Schapar, who had been in many big shows. In our jive and rock'n'roll sequences he threw me up in the air and then under his legs – I still could dance as if I was double jointed, and what's more I thoroughly enjoyed the dance routines too. My dancing partner preferred boys and would have loved to have been me. He told me I should always be seen with a chiffon scarf fluttering from my hand. I had problems trying to keep a straight face just at the thought of it. He told our boys they were crazy and did not know what they were missing, sticking to the female sex. Ah, well, we all have our differences!

Life is odd! My first TV show in Hamburg was cooking, and at that time I did not even know how to boil an egg; now in my own TV show for N.D.R. at their Bremen Studios, the public saw me mixing cocktails, and I don't drink, except the occasional cognac when I feel cold or very tired.

Shortly after the first three shows our excellent book writer had a sudden heart attack and died. We were all heartbroken. It was a terrible shame, as the producer, the director, and the entire team including Teddy and I were all such good friends and a nice group, but without our good friend and writer Walter

Haas it was better to close. However, I managed to leave my mark there.

A few times I had said to the producer, "I firmly believe that its better to be primitive than degenerated."

In no time it caught on and on every studio wall there hung a frame with the words:

BESSER PRIMITIV ALS DEGENERIERT – Yvonne Carré

BETTER PRIMITIVE THAN DEGENERATED – Yvonne Carré. I have been told a couple of my sayings are still on some walls, so at least I left my mark there.

Chérie Noire in Hamburg

Back in Hamburg I managed to persuade Mr. Peter Ahweiler to turn Chérie Noire from a light Boulevard comedy into a light musical, and immediately suggested Teddy, as my new "prosaic" husband was beginning to be recognised, having written an excellent arrangement for the large Symphony Orchestra of Harry Herman. When Harry chose popular tunes in English, German, French and Italian such as "It's De-lovely," "Bei Dir", "Mon Coeur est un Violin" and "Arriverdeci Roma", not forgetting "Cherry Pink" in three different languages for my debut with his large symphony-style light music orchestra, Teddy wrote the arrangements. He also wrote for the Alfred Hause Orchestra – later our friendship grew, and I nicknamed him the "Tango Bear." Teddy often wrote arrangements together with my dear friend Cedric Dumont of Radio Beromunster fame (which was actually Radio Zürich). So it was not so difficult for me to fix with Peter Ahweiler that my "little Bear" should write two songs for Chérie Noire. The first was the title song. He decided on a special rhythm which he called "Cha-Cha Rock". Later Chubby Checker gave that same rhythm the name of the Twist. The beat and the dance took off and somebody made a fortune! The second song was a lovely Hawaiian-style foxtrot called "Balikou," which was the name of the island from which Chérie, the little "good luck bringer," originated.

Cedric was so pleased with the recording of this single he brought it out on the Swiss Ex Libris label with a really beautiful cover of me with my once again long hair (I let it grow to please "little bear") adorned with a large white flower. I had the photographs taken in Dubrovnik with a piece of flowered material draped around me as a sarong. The cover was an eye catcher, the music was pleasant, and as it was especially written for the show it did very well in German and English. This meant that Teddy had to be around at rehearsals, so my wish that he should go to Switzerland to find my dream home had to be put on hold.

Finding the right male star to be my hero was not that easy. I visualised some man like Paul Hubschmid but was not one bit disappointed when I was told that Lanz Eckberg (he was perhaps the Rock Hudson of German movies, a super attractive real manly man – but he wasn't!) had been signed for the role. As I was literally living out of a suitcase with all my radio and show engagements on the Continent and in Scandinavia, I did not know of Lanz Eckberg personally, but from the photos I was shown he certainly was a very handsome man about 6'2". Since I always had to be barefoot in a grass skirt, I must have looked diminutive against him. Teddy told me that as famous as Lanz Eckberg was as a male lead, he was also famous for his hunger for young boys and had only managed to avoid a prison sentence for rape of a good-looking youngster with the help of an excellent lawyer. So here was another challenge, and I was interested.

Finally, my handsome hero arrived and so did the press. He was indeed a gorgeous "hunk" and I was delighted when for the press photos he was asked to go down on bended knee before me, as I was supposed to be a sort of little jungle princess. When the photographers then shouted for a kiss, I opened my mouth to laugh with embarrassment, when suddenly strong arms enveloped me, and a male tongue was thrust into my mouth almost to my throat. Later I was told this was typical show business strategy to look like the real "He Man." Anyway, whatever the press said, I was contented with my hero, til one day at rehearsals Peter Ahweiler left Lanz and I alone to carry on our second act, where he was changing his ideas and falling in love with me. We were alone on stage when Teddy, who constantly spoke the hero's lines when testing me, decided to pop in and see how our rehearsals were progressing. The stage door was at the back to my rear. Lanz, being tall, could easily see the stage door over my head, while I had my back to it. Suddenly in the middle of his lines he started to stammer and even tremble. Remembering the terrible fits my first marriage proposal love Jack Winehouse had had, I wondered if Lanz also once suffered in childhood with rheumatic fever.

I asked him, quite disturbed, in a worried voice, "Lanz are you ok? What's wrong?"

Still stammering and quite out of himself he pointed over my head to the door. "Who, who's that? Who's just come in?" he asked.

I turned around to see who it was who had knocked this handsome guy literally off his feet. Could it be a ghost?

"Ooh, hello little bear – that's my husband," I said with a big smile, and then, "May I introduce you; this is film star Mr. Lanz Eckberg, and this is composer and arranger Teddybear Klaus – he's my other half, Lanz – the one who goes over my lines with me every night, so that you and Peter are not disappointed with me at rehearsals."

Lanz gulped. "He's your husband?" he asked incredulously and then, as an afterthought, "Excuse me, he looked so young I thought he was a kid."

"Oh, his mum looks ever so young too – it's the genes in the family – but he is not. He's a lot older than he looks."

Teddy gave both of us a sheepish grin and looked so shy that I knew why all the secretaries at the various offices we visited fell for him and said "He looks as if he still has milk on his teeth."

I had tried to tell them one should never judge a book by the cover, covers could be deceiving. When I realized that this poignant moment was just the beginning of a one-sided love affair between my stage hero and my innocent-looking husband, I decided to step into the breach and asked him not to come to rehearsals anymore – once the music side was to his liking.

I was so busy and at the same time thankful that I could wear a bra under my paper flowered lei, as at that time Hamburg was by far not as lax as Paris with Marpessa Dawn as "Chérie"… My bust had to be covered, and not only with flowers!

The Reeperbahn with their girlie shows and the Herbert Street famous for its multitude of professional prostitutes were quite apart from the business class and family public of the theatres that are in the precincts of the Alster, as ours was. "The Kleine Komodie."

I wonder if any of you can imagine, when you see two persons in a play or a movie and it all looks so romantic, what it's like being the heroine while the hero is saying out loud, "You are really wonderful and lovable too Chérie," then, in an undertone so only you can hear, "Why aren't you your good-looking husband?"

It takes a lot of self control to culminate it all with a passionate kiss.

My good fortune in such an uncomfortable situation was Helga Keck, a nice-looking willowy blonde and experienced actress who played the part of the mistress of the house and also of our hero – and actually the person who had engaged Chérie (me) as au pair. She told me on such a day when Lanz was abominable to me, he had said to her in an undertone as she sat on his knee and stroked his hair, "Get away, you smell like a woman."

She with all her theater experience was far more used to such undertone talk than myself. She hit back with a real backhander: "I use Miss Dior," she said pertly, "what do you want me to wear? Dior has not yet made a male perfume; how about Old Spice?"

Then, out loud, "My big, big love," and again in an undertone, "or would you prefer my aftershave, Hattrick?"

She and I would laugh our heads off in our dressing room that we shared. On the stage we were rivals. Off stage we became good friends.

After the opening night I asked Teddy to go to Switzerland to buy a home for us to live in as a permanent residence. My only stipulation was it had to have a view of a lake and mountains and to have a garden and be not too far from a station or airport as we both had to travel so much. The show had real positive results with the public and press, but getting a home in "my promised land" did not. Teddy informed me by letter that the Swiss Francs on my account could at the most buy a garage, but not even that in the area around Lugano – my dream location.

While Teddy was away, I got a surprise visit from Cika Jova. He came to see the show and thanked me for being so kind to his nephew and teaching him the value of true love. I tried to pretend I was above it all, but I think he knew deep down inside I had suffered at the loss of his nephew too. Politics, boundaries, and bureaucracies often keep lovers apart, leaving them alone with the memory of an unattainable duration of those perfect moments they had shared together.

Finally, Teddy wrote that with the help of a colleague of Fritz Mueller he had found something and the fact that we were in the music branch had helped enormously. He had found a house in Central Switzerland in a little village called Walchwil on the lake of Zug, and opposite the mountain that had so impressed Ernest Hemmingway that he wrote "you must see the Queen of Mountains, Mount Rigi, before you die." The location sounded full of potential, and I was happy I had given him "carte blanche" to buy. The fact it was on an open country road and was a bit lonely didn't bother me. After Israel and Yugoslavia,

I felt I could master anything. With the help of a big strong Ice Hockey player (my latest conquest) who had come to my rescue when three Italians followed me in Zürich and started to get too close for comfort, I really felt prepared for anything. I wondered if Teddy was.

CHAPTER 97

Pepito

The film company that had Lanz Eckberg under contract had lent him to us for a certain number of months, and now they had a meaty role for him and wanted him back. All the actors who were available looked puny against handsome refined Lanz Eckberg. A suitable hero could not be found.

I was scheduled to do a line of return engagements, one of which was at the Palace Hotel in Lucerne. I had no idea then how much brighter my future would look when I was singing again in one of my favorite hotels in one of my favorite cities.

When I was not rehearsing or singing and dancing, then anyone who knew me well would have known where I was. Bet your life I would be swimming in a pool, in the sea or, as it was at that time, in Lake Lucerne. Normally if one of us had to do some running then it was me. Teddy, if he was in a hurry (out of the car), would just use a determined stride. It was not in his character to run, so while I was having a leisurely swim in the lake on a glorious day at the beginning of September, I was quite surprised to see him running towards me. He beckoned to me to get out of the water, and then told me, a little out of breath, that a phone call had just come through for me from a Mr. Horst Fuchs.

My mind went back immediately to Cologne and the EMI recording studio where the tone engineer had been particularly good looking and most sympathetic. The sort of man that a girl like me could definitely fancy, but when I had heard he was already married to a large motherly type of woman and had already a couple of children with her – I had put my mad smoke dream out of my mind. Now I was myself married and some years had passed – what did he want?

Teddy made it short:

"Apparently Horst was in Hamburg and saw you as Chérie Noire and had the exclusivity to record a German version of a Cha Cha called "Pepito" which he thought could be ideal for you. Did you know it?"

When you are working nonstop and have already had your own TV shows, it is not unusual to get quite a few offers from big recording companies to record songs. It was at a time when "Schnulzen" (sob stuff) was in, and I knew I could not have success with a song I didn't feel comfortable with. Oddly enough, I had heard that Cha Cha when I was back in Sweden in the summer. I remember thinking to myself, now if I could get that number in the German language, I'd say yes. And now in Lucerne this handsome man was asking me if I could record this in Hamburg. How he had found me in Lucerne, I had no idea. My guardian angel must have been at work again, I thought to myself.

"Yes," I shouted, hardly believing it was true.

"Now look," said Little Bear, "it means you must be ready to record it on Wednesday and I should do the arrangements for a small group, and the Golgowski Quartette." (The most famous singing group in Germany at that time). "The B side," he added, "you will get first when we arrive at the Hamburg Music Hall. Fuchs said as a real pro you will master it."

I shrugged my shoulders and added to this summary, "I sure will – I can't let a guy like Horst Fuchs down."

"Do you think that the Manager will give you the Wednesday afternoon free? After all, you are under contract here." asked Teddy in his orderly way.

I grinned. "You bet," I said. "Thank heavens I had recorded that Cha Cha on my old tape recorder as soon as I heard it on the radio. That's lucky, so I can start rehearsing right now."

The manager was really kind. He smiled at my enthusiasm and agreed to let me have Wednesday afternoon off, after I'd shown him my ticket with the return flight already booked, which would get me back on stage for the evening show at 10 p.m. easily.

The whole thing was a gas! I knew all the musicians from Hamburg, except the bandleader, who was an Italian – that is why he called his own composition (my B side) "Gelati"…it was a fun song and my favorite food – loving ice cream, it came to me easily.

Because of my engagement in Lucerne my time was very limited. Teddy went over "Pepito" and "Gelati" with the band and the Golgowski quartet were, as usual, perfect. I did one take and Horst Fuchs was delighted. He asked if I wanted a second time, I did. He was the producer and engineer with Teddy. We all listened to the playbacks and decided no one could do it better. "Gelati", being unknown territory, took a little longer but not much. The two songs were in the can and Fuchs said, "That's great – like this we'll get the Christmas trade!" – never dreaming it would be a world success … outside of Germany too.

Promptly at 10 p.m. I was on stage ready for my evening show in Lucerne.Teddy had listened to me and done the music exactly as I wanted, and we both felt contented with our busy afternoon.

Compared to the Miles Davis group – who told the press it took them three months of rehearsals to get their special album – we certainly did it better!

When the people at Decca heard the recordings, they put me under contract immediately. They all felt there and then it was going to be a hit, but how big – none of us knew.

The moment it went on the air the fan mail came pouring in on all sides. Thousands and thousands went shopping and even more asked for autographed photos. Decca immediately arranged for loads of secretaries to satisfy the demand and Teddy likewise signed hundreds of autographs for me. I was so in demand as it hit the top of the charts, I just had no time for anything except trying to keep my head above water. It was like being put into a whirling machine and I had to have at least 3 different stage dresses made, one in light turquoise with pink frills, one in deep turquoise with dotted frills on a white background and one in bright red satin with red and white striped frills. In no time I had a sombrero and a black hat which remained with me till the end of my career. It became a regular feature of my show.

It was really exciting. In those days a hit really was a hit. It was played on most radio stations two or three times daily. It could even be heard on the ice rink when I was ice skating in Arosa or buying goodies at Karstadt in Hamburg. Every big store played it and people whistled the catchy earworm on the streets.

It's a funny, good feeling, but with time you get used to it. Like seeing one's name in lights – you worked and worked for such moments, and suddenly they are there!

It even got me my first two big mortgages and a loan from Credit Swiss, so I could achieve my dream of a home in Switzerland. All this because of a cute little number called "Pepito"!

Yvonne Carré

Yvonne Carré

四ケ国語で歌う
美人女性シンガー
ンヌ・カレー

Hanno
Wohlfarth
PHOTOSTUDIO
HAMBURG

CHAPTER 98

"Schwarze Perle" in Zürich

My guardian angel came as if on call, as a handsome couple arrived a week or so before our closing. It was a well-known Swiss producer and his vivacious wife. They were very impressed and told us that Francois Campaux, the author of "Chérie Noire", had got in touch with them after he had of course visited our "Chérie Noire" in Hamburg. He sang praises of me and our German version with music, and Peter's production. I was, he had told them, exactly the happy little wild beauty he had visualised when writing the play originally. For my part, I felt very at home in the role of "Chérie" and learnt a lot from this very happy but wise little character devised by Mr. Campaux. It was a deal – I was to go once again to Zürich, but this time at the most popular Bernhard Theatre. When I arrived, the whole town was full of posters with the face of a tropical maiden with a large flower in her long dark hair – me! Cedric Dumont had turned up trumps and Ex Libris was delighted, and so was I. I looked completely different from the little BBC jazz singer and entertainer who was quite white with short hair and had a definite resemblance to Princess Margaret of England, which my manager Mr. Gardiner sold so accurately.

It was in Zürich where I met my next "big love", and he really was a big professional Ice Hockey player. I was going back from rehearsing in Zürich to my room at the Muehlebach Street when three Italians started following me, chanting "bella cantante" etc. They came far too close for comfort, and it was time for me to stop and open the gate – suddenly a sharp droning voice said "Leave that girl alone," and a firm hand came and took my arm. He was a huge hunk of a young sports man with full lips and smiling brown eyes. I heaved a sigh of relief as he ordered the three small dark Southern Italians to "beat it," and they did just that quickly.

I asked the young sportsman where he had left his coat of armour. "You have been a real knight errant and saved me from these awful guys," I said.

"That's the price of being famous," he said, smiling down at me. "After all, your photo is hanging all over the city."

"Then do come in," I replied, "let me give you at least an autographed photo."

I did and wrote on it "to my knight errant who saved a damsel in distress".

It worked; he came to my opening night, as did many others, and it was a real lucky stroke. "Chérie Noire", called "Schwarze Perle" (The Black Pearl) in Switzerland, went down fine with the Zürich public and in next to no time my knight and I were a pair.

(Please note Frank was over busy in Hamburg).

James Gardiner, although out my life in most countries, returned with a vengeance in Zürich. He had, as I remembered, a very good friend, a journalist for Zürich's main daily newspaper "Neue Zurcher Zeitung" (NZZ). James, who was full of hate and envy, requested him to give a bad report of our "Schwarze Perle" and, of course, definitely of me. This gave a bad impression, but the "Tages Anzeiger" and the "Blick" were very positive about the show and me, even though my "hero" was not nearly as good looking as Lanz Eckberg and often smelt of alcohol.

This dreadful critic did not ruin the show, as James would have wished, but it certainly did not help either. When I had a big TV show with a live audience in Geneva, the TV studios received a menacing letter stating, "Do not employ Yvonne Carré in this show. If you do, I have arranged with a group of boys to throw tomatoes and bad eggs at her to cause a riot and ruin the show." Louis Rey, my good friend, wasted no time in employing a smart lawyer. Mr. Gardiner had to shut up immediately and was never to be heard of again. The jealousies and envies in show business are only a small part of the evil found in every profession and nation in the entire world. Evil behaviour can only be likened to the snake in the Garden of Eden. But fortunately, although I don't like them, unlike many women I am certainly not afraid of them – my positive attitude says "We will prevail" come what may! Now that sounds a bit like Winston Churchill.

CHAPTER 99

The Beatles and Me

When Lanz left to make a new movie in Berlin, I left to do a re-engagement at the most elegant night club in Hamburg – the Delhi Palace. It was situated in the better part of the Reeperbahn and only a few steps away from the much-publicised Star Club.

Everybody who was anybody knew that only top stars appeared at the Delhi Palace and that only top groups played at the Star Club.

After grass skirt Chérie had closed because a suitable hero could just not be found, I went very soon for my re-engagement at the Delhi Palace. Teddy told me Uwe, his younger brother, was already a great fan of the four boys from Liverpool now playing at the Star Club. The group was called "The Beatles" and they were a *must*. Of course, we went along to hear them. They were also in a re-engagement. I thought they looked really cute, all with their bobbed black hair and dressed alike – but Teddy was awed with their music and tried to explain to me that they were highly musical, using chords and some harmonies which were quite new to the popular music scene.

Next night when I finished my show, they were all standing there in the foyer of the Delhi Palace waiting for me to give them 4 autographed photographs. I thought they were most congenial guys, full of fun, and I told them how much I enjoyed their music, never dreaming then that this group would sweep the world and in a comparatively short time millions of fans would be asking for their autographs.

They say that necessity is the mother of invention and when I went on a tour of the English provinces much later, I had a week's engagement in Liverpool. It was one of the dreariest provincial towns you could imagine. Even at the best available hotel, on a Saturday afternoon they switched off the heating, as at that time who would visit Liverpool? Only businesspeople, who went home at the weekend. That determination of The Beatles to get ahead and be innovative comes a great deal from real necessity, and those boys sure showed terrific energy and will to be the best. They were hard workers, and they all had a real sense of humor. If Frank was impressed with their music, I was certainly impressed with Paul McCartney – what a pleasant voice – and oh boy! was he handsome!

After the Beatles had finished their engagement in Hamburg, Uwe, Teddy's younger brother, asked me to ask Mum to send me the first record they had on the market. This was made in London and had not reached the German scene yet and he was not sure if it ever would be issued on the German market. Mum was a good sport and obliged and sent the disc for Uwe. She wrote a covering letter:

"Herewith the record of the British group who were playing almost next door to you and asked for autographs. They may be good in your eyes, but what a horrible name! With a name like The Beatles – how can they ever hope to be a success?!"

The Beatles were the beginning of a new era in music. The big bands were still popular but were slowly being taken over by small groups. Some were absolutely excellent, after all, four men who play and sing and fill the house are a lot cheaper than a big band of over 24 musicians excluding a singer or two. How times do change!

CHAPTER 100

Japan and Pepito

One night while appearing at the Delhi Palace, one of the waiters put a visiting card into my hand as I left the stage. I glanced quickly at it, and saw it was from an agent in London, so after changing I went over to his table.

Being from London I felt at home with him immediately and he probably with me. After I had ordered a hot lemon tea and a strawberry ice cream, he said, "Look, I'll make it short, I have been sent here to see you from our biggest recording company in Tokyo, King Records. They are together with Decca, your record company in Germany. They also have an agency. Your version of "Pepito" is hitting the charts over there and it's different. Spanish and French have had their successes – you may remember "Les Lavandieres de Portugal" from Yvette Giraud. This was in French, a new language for Japan. She did well over there. We know you are photogenic from your many TV shows. My people want to have you in Japan for a 3-4-month tour of the entire country. There would be many TV shows and longer engagements in Japanese night clubs, which are not like those in Western Europe but cater for thousands.

"You would be the first German singing artist in Japan and the fact that English is your mother tongue would be a great advantage, as all the radio and TV stations there and the entire nation in general speak English – it's their second language. What do you say? Are you interested?"

Was I interested? Dinah Washington, Dakota Staton and Eydie Gormé may have been my peers, but Marco Polo had been since schooldays my hero. He really had traveled the world. Apart from that, Japan was becoming the fastest moving country around the globe and people were clamoring for their technical goods. Everything and anything made in Japan was in and the fact that my cute little cha cha was in their music charts was a very good reason for me to accept that offer. King Records were big, and with such an offer there was the chance to be a little bit of a tourist and to see the most important and interesting places in that country, which I had only read about in books. It was like bait for me. The opportunity to appear for so long in the land of the Rising Sun opened up a whole new world for me, at a time when only a very few could afford to visit such a far afield destination. Here was a real chance to be the first German singing star over there. I had upstaged my eldest sister when that rich Italian industrialist who Dad had thought would be a perfect match for her had instead chosen me when I was only 14. Now, some ten years later, I was being asked to upstage Germany's number one pop singer Caterina Valente – also a world artist.

I will be quite honest; I was also afraid. I had never met a Japanese man in my life, and I had a few nightmares about small yellowish men with slitty eyes running after me. How wrong I was! The men I had to deal with were serious gentlemen. I took with me in my hand baggage my yellow Teddybear, given me by my ice hockey player – my "knight errant" – to protect me on the long journey. Frank decided to christen him "Kunibart". The Teddybear had always his face outside my shoulder bag and soon became quite a TV star as I carried him just everywhere, mostly grinning at the world from my rucksack.

Flying over the North Pole was a new route to Japan and an adventure in itself. The sky was quite clear, and I could see miles of white snow and ice below us. Being the only girl among the passengers and knowing whom I was, the pilot invited me to his cabin. The assistant pilot explained to me many interesting features. As I had to rush to get the plane, I still had my makeup

on from a TV show in Germany. We had a stopover in Alaska –
such a cold place with such warmhearted people, but I didn't
manage to meet a polar bear. Later, when food was served, lad-
en with chocolates and souvenirs from the pilots I returned to
my seat by the window and fell asleep. When I awoke we were
landing in Tokyo.

CHAPTER 101

Complications in Japan

Perfectly organized, two real Japanese ladies in traditional kimono and obi were there to greet me with two lovely bouquets of flowers and many photographers. The journey to my hotel with the limousine was not far short of amazing. I had never even heard of Sumo wrestlers and was surprised to see two huge men (for Asian standards) walking in the street almost naked, with only a thong to cover their buttocks (I only saw them from behind). I was quite shocked til the ladies informed me they were traditional Japanese sportsmen. Then we passed several men peeing on the street side, and several ladies in full evening dress standing by. Finally, there was further along a kimono clad lady obviously doing likewise under a tree.

"Other countries, other traditions," I said to myself. I knew I was going to be in for a most interesting time.

The first day I was due to meet one of the chiefs of King Records, I walked down the huge staircase at the hotel to the large foyer below, which was obviously a meeting place for the very many guests. There you could also drink green tea and choose dim sum, a variety of delicious Japanese snacks.

To me all the men looked alike. They all wore dark suits with white shirts and non-descript ties. The thing that shocked me most was the huge number of people just everywhere. Suddenly I caught the eye of one man who seemed to smile at me, so I edged toward his table and he bowed and asked me in English to be seated. He immediately ordered for me a green tea, which fortunately I liked, and two small dumplings from the dim sum trolley. However, when I asked him about my schedule, I found I was at the wrong table – he was not from the record company at all. I asked if he did not have a photo of me, and he replied that he was there to meet a lady from Spain, and for a Japanese it was so difficult because in his eyes we European women all looked the same. When I stood up to leave, amused at our double mistake, he bowed and another Japanese gentleman stood up at another table and beckoned to me. He then produced his credentials – I was indeed finally with the right man from the record company and the agency, but to my eyes all Japanese of about 40 or more looked like brothers. Oh dear, I thought, this is going to be fun and games.

I was then introduced to an older gentleman edging towards our table. He was the chief of the agency, the A&R (artists and relations) manager. He scrutinized me from top to toe and then gave a contented sigh with a smile.

"From your photos we knew you had a pretty face," he said, "but I was worried you may be of plumper body, which fortunately is not the case, as during the entire first week you will only be on television a) with "Pepito" and your own dress, but b) showing off the latest styles in Japanese fashion, starting with bathing costumes."

I was just 48 kilos and slim, and although considered "petite" back home, here in Japan I was told I was mannequin size. I really felt I was going to enjoy my time there.

Posing in swimsuits and dresses was no problem, but at my first TV show of "Pepito", after the first chorus I was expected to dance with four male dancers who finally lifted me up and walked off with me. I had to have my arms raised and after waving to the public I had to be singing all the time. Today all this is easy, as playbacks are the order of the day – but at that time in the 60s, everything was live and I knew well from my own TV shows for

NDR that even when you were pleased with yourself, one of the camera men may not have been happy with all his "takes" and we had to do the whole thing again. Oh yes, that first show of "Pepito" with the four men was a lot of hard work, and I realised then that a lot more was expected of me than the comparatively simple expectations of a song or maybe some text and a few dance steps, as it had been on the TV shows in the Western Europe.

The Japanese were a hard-working nation, with hard, long hours, they were self effacing and seemed to be happy with very little remuneration and even less food.

I was a bit embarrassed by the diminutive size of a plate or dish, and when I went to eat at the cafeteria in the hotel, I was still hungry and like Charles Dickens' "Oliver Twist" I just had to get a second portion. It took a few weeks for me to get used to the way of eating less.

Kamakura – Japan

I don't mind admitting that when I am in a new part of the world, seeing all the places of interest is a must (quite different to most artistes who stay in bed till midday).

Kamakura, apart from sounding romantic, also housed the largest sleeping Buddha in the world, and even better, was a seaside place with a nice long beach. I was given for the trip a secretary from the agency and after visiting the long lying Buddha, she had letters to write, and I left our hotel for the beach, which was quite near. Everything and everywhere was written in Japanese so as I walked on to the sandy beach. I removed my sandals and made a photographic note in my memory: "The road to my hotel has a bicycle shop directly on the corner, so you can't miss it."

I strolled and paddled deep in thought and even enjoyed a swim. Coming back, I decided now I must look for the road with the bicycle shop on the corner. To my surprise, there were quite a few roads like the one leading to our hotel, all with bicycle shops on the corner. How come? I had no idea.

As dusk was falling, I chose the road most likely and was really happy with myself when I saw our hotel with lights on. Going inside there was a middle-aged lady at the reception, which seemed a bit different to the hotel lobby, but when I asked for the key to my room she looked at me quizzically and asked "Are you new here? What number has your room?" Thank heavens I remembered it. Then she said, "Sorry, we have no number like that. This is a hotel primarily for *men* to rent a room by the hour or rent a girl too. I think you're looking for the hotel on the next parallel street."

"Oh dear," I said. We both grinned and with a sigh of relief I found my way home and did not have to spend the night by the beach like the statue of the sleeping Lord Buddha.

While in the Resort of Kamakura, the secretary from the agency said she would be happy to get me some lunch. As I could never make out what all the pictures various dishes on the menu represented, I mostly stuck to the same, which was Beef Curry Rice. She returned with two small dishes of food, and just as I thought to myself, "Heavens, only three small cubes of meat," she looked at the food smiling happily and said:

"Oh the curry is good – so much meat!"

Most people, I noticed, in Asia and later in Africa were quite content with a staple diet of rice, beans or maize (depending on the region where they lived) and some sort of sauce, or maybe some vegetables – even a small fish or three tiny cubes of meat was, for them, like a feast – a luxury. Slowly I contented myself with only one dish, and I wondered how much slimmer I would be after the Japanese tour, thoroughly delighted.

The first week was just one TV show after another, mainly with "Pepito" or "Gelati", but often with interviews. The funniest was, when the MC asked me where was home, and I answered, "Zug, in Switzerland."

He looked at me and said, "Oh, that's in Oklahoma isn't it?"

I was really amused and said, "No, Walchwil is in Zug in Switzerland."

"Oh, yes, Sweden," was the reply, looking at me discerningly – "the land of tall blonde women and naughty sex films," but his eyes said, "Where do you fit in there?"

We both laughed. Maybe I should have given him a stem of edelweiss to jog his memory.

The biggest disappointment for me was I was sure I would arrive at the height of the cherry blossom season, but a strong wind blowing in from an oncoming typhoon took all the blossoms off the trees and there was far more to be seen of flowering cherry trees back home in Walchwil.

After sporting totally different sorts of swimwear, from sporty suits to two-piece bikinis and lots of dresses and tailor-mades, I opened at the "Copacabana", which seemed to me to be more like the Westfallen Halle in Germany from the size, or almost like Zürich arena, except there were at least 700 hostesses. This was not so surprising, because in those days men went out alone or with other men. Wives were not taken out to nightclubs. The hostesses, I was assured, were well versed in world affairs, from politics to economy, so they could converse with the clients on any subjects they may choose.

As "Pepito" became a hit, I changed my signature tune from "Sweet and Lovely" to the introduction in cha cha rhythm of "Pepito", as it had 16 bars. It was a good move because before I came on stage the audience started clapping and whistling, which I had not expected from such a disciplined nation. At every show I gave one stem of edelweiss to a lady when I did a medley from the popular movie and show "The Sound of Music". When not singing in the modern idiom, my voice was almost identical with that of Julie Andrews. The edelweiss was from my own garden. This special flower from the Alps and the change in my voice was, for Japan, a real sensation. As the ladies in the audience were all hostesses, the edelweiss was then returned to my dressing room, so I could present this specialty for quite a long time.

When I went to see the boss of my Japanese Recording Company, he told me they had taken over another record from Germany, the Spanish flamenco "Tani" in cha cha rhythm, but did I think I could master two recordings in Japanese, in which case he would ask his wife to be my tutor and I could meet their biggest pop stars. They were Cemi Eri, a lively little person who helped me with the phrasing, and Kyo Sakamuto, who was also a famous pop composer. In Japan I could never really judge how old or how young people were, they all looked like kids to me.

I then set about learning at least the words of my Japanese songs, which were to be recorded in English and Japanese. My tutor was kind and patient and I practiced Japanese vocals and intonation almost daily in the afternoons. For a Westerner it is a difficult language, but also amusing because they cannot pronounce our "R" and instead use our letter "L". This creates a lot of fun, asking for some more Rice when you have to call it "Lice"! For us English speaking folk, this was invariably a cause for a good giggle, behind hands of course! Another very popular Japanese word is "moshi moshi", "hello" in English, but all the German speaking businessmen, engineers, monteurs etc. got a kick when they picked up the phone to make a call, and a sweet feminine voice said "moshi moshi, can I help you sir?" One male friend told me "It was a bit confusing, for a moment I thought I had got a crossed line and was connected with a brothel." He was not alone, most German men had a good laugh, just by picking up their hotel phone.

Once I just had to visit the bathroom while practicing my new Japanese song at the studios of our record company. An older gentleman was to conduct me to where this was, as it was a large building. When we arrived, he apologized profusely that there was no special ladies room and that I must pass through the men's "pissoir". I assured him I was married but it was unfortunately imperative that I go through. When we opened the door there was a gentleman standing in the middle of a comfortable pee.

Without a moment of hesitation, he went up to the man and said, "Mr. Suzuki, may I introduce you to our guest from Switzerland, the singing star Yvonne Carré-san." San actually meant Mister at that time, but as I was visiting without my husband I was always regarded with respect and that meant I had to be called Mister. Carré. A woman in the 60s was of a lower category. Mr. Suzuki stopped his pee, dried his hand on his dark trousers and immediately gave me his hand – which he had learnt was how one greets politely a Westerner, that is to say, those with the round eyes and high noses, as the Far Easterners called us. I would have almost preferred the Japanese bow! After a while I realized the differences in our culture. In Japan bathrooms and nakedness were normal in public, but eating in a good restaurant with one's family was a strictly private affair and it would be a big insult to disturb any group who were eating. Often French "paravents" flowered screens were put up to give complete privacy. The record company invited me to many lovely restaurants, mainly outside in beautiful Japanese gardens where we were guests of honor. As the tables were low, the kimono-clad girls cooked the suki yaki and tempura and served us almost on their knees in a crouch position, as in accordance with Japanese etiquette, our heads must be higher than theirs. I decided there and then that these Asian women must have very good joints, since they spend so much of their time on their knees – mine would be killing me. Apart from Cemi Eri, the Japanese women seemed to me to be far more submissive than their Western counterparts. Obviously, the saying "East is East and West is West" was quite correct, and what a difference there was…just try picking up a green pea in your soup with only chopsticks in your right hand! I was given that as a test and not allowed to leave the table until I accomplished this feat. It was time for a good laugh at our differences.

CHAPTER 102

Unforgettable Kyoto

Kyoto was unforgettable for me, firstly for its beauty and places of interest, and secondly because on the radio we were told a typhoon was heading for Kyoto and should hit us sometime at night. I was so frightened I may not survive, I wrote my last Will and Testament and hoped some living thing may find it. Suddenly there was a terrible silence, nothing moved – not one tree. It was eerie; all the dogs started howling simultaneously. It was about 2 a.m. and the lights of the town were still on, but not a soul on the streets. I fell asleep wondering if I would ever see daylight again. Fortunately, the typhoon changed its route and Kyoto and I were spared. "What a Trojan folk," I thought; those Japanese were to be able to face earthquakes and typhoons and all those natural disasters with pure fatalism.

One day, while having a snack and green tea, I noticed the two men sitting at the next table looked strikingly familiar. Then I remembered I had read in the English newspaper that Yul Brinner and Richard Burton (Elizabeth Taylor's husband) were working on a movie partly shot in Kyoto. When Yul Brinner glanced in my direction, I gave him one of my wide smiles, which he returned. He then said something to his partner Richard Burton, stood up and asked me if I would like to join them for a few minutes. I was annoyed with myself, as I had no camera, but of course I agreed. The two men were entirely different; Yul Brinner was a refined gentleman, while Richard Burton, who had an almost pock marked heavy complexion, could easily have been a truck driver with his rugged good looks. Then, wonder of wonders, Elizabeth Taylor – hailed as "The Most Beautiful Woman in the World" by the international press – appeared. I was happy to note that she was definitely not six feet tall and possessed natural womanly curves. She did not resemble one of those skinny, miserable looking models that my husband classified as "bohnen stengeln", bean stalks. Her make up was perfect. She came to our table and sat down next to me and her husband; no introduction was necessary. Her profile was fine and feminine. Being rather close, I noticed her arms were covered with fine dark hairs and her famous violet blue eyes were enhanced by two pairs of dark eyelashes and really stood out. Richard Burton reacted to her presence and perfume like instant coffee in hot water – his hard core melted, and he became appreciably amiable.

The minutes passed like seconds, then Yul Brinner stood up and said, "We have to get going."

The famous couple left with a hasty "Bye."

Richard Burton went through the door in front of me, almost pushing me aside as the Japanese men were prone to do in lifts and public places, while Yul Brinner held the door open for me and said, "After you, Madame," an action I couldn't forget when I later saw him as the tyrannic "Emperor of Siam" in the movie "The King and I".

CHAPTER 103

Wild Water Geisha Me!

I had, in a really adventurous moment, signed up to go Wild Water Rafting – "only for the good swimmers and the true adventurous" was written underneath in red. I had never seen this in the UK, and certainly not in flat Hamburg. It was one of my few free days. When I and other tourists of the same genre came to see this sport in motion, we heard the screams and I realised it was a bit like a diluted rollercoaster, in rushing water over large round stones and sometimes steep inclines in the riverbed. As one might expect, I was with four other persons and the captain. There were three or four other rafts in front of us, all of which mastered with ease the most perpendicular bend in that wild water river. Our raft, which was last of the bunch, hit a particularly large, boulder-like stone, capsized and turned on its side. We all had to get out in the water and help the captain to get the raft back to normality. As the water was fairly shallow – it came just about to my knees – it wasn't really a big deal. But the others were more mature than me, and seemed to be old Brits; I grinned to myself, while others complained bitterly, I was secretly thanking God for making me richer with yet an other unusual experience in that Far Eastern country, but I never went Wild Water Rafting again. Once was enough!

I had been taken to kabuki, the Japanese cultural theater where the men dress up as women and the ghost comes into the audience to get the female spectators screaming in fright. I had been to huge shopping centers under the roads on three or more floors with lots of colored lampions, but I had never been in a private home. Finally, it was arranged, I was invited to go with the secretary (a lady who spoke good English who was often my guide), and the promotions manager, plus the man who would conduct the music for my forthcoming Japanese record, and have a light Japanese meal at the home of a higher member of the staff of King Records. This, in Japan, was a special treat because normally all entertaining was done in nightclubs or restaurants, and not in private homes.

A very tidy and beautifully arranged little garden greeted us and after removing our shoes, as we entered, tatami (the matted Bamboo flooring) was everywhere; there was very little furniture. The living room displayed a long sideboard with a large Japanese vase and three giant-sized chrysanthemums arranged in the ikebana style. After admiring the simple beauty and the large window with the view of the little garden, we were shown into the dining room, where we were invited to partake of some rice with chicken, all lightly spiced and slightly sweet. The agency's secretary, the A&R man, the conductor musician, the host and myself, made up a party of five. It was a tiny room like a pullman with two benches and a table in between them. I was happy we were all small and slim, it was more like a cubicle at an eatery in the USA.

The host, an older representative of the company, was really proud when the secretary remarked to him, "My word, what a roomy dining room you do possess."

How lucky we were, compared to so many other nations, hit me again when I was taken to a Japanese park in Tokyo, I saw people literally standing in a disciplined queue to take photos of a particularly beautiful rose. I thought of all the lovely roses in my own garden back home. Similarly, on a tourist trip all the Japanese were amazed at one scenic point where there was a waterfall coming down the mountainside, which they photographed from left to right. We had one similar on the road where I lived in Switzerland. However, the trains from Tokyo to Osaka were super modern and fast, and everybody took off their shoes. The bamboo boxes full of Japanese goodies to eat which were sold at the kabuki theatre, where the show could have lasted at least four hours, were also being sold on the trains. Sandwiches were not yet en vogue.

For six weeks I experienced a Japanese monsoon; just everywhere was wet. Apart from the main roads, all side turnings were not yet cemented, and wet feet were inevitable. Although in Tokyo my schedule was mainly one show and plenty of TV spots, in Hokkaido and Kyushu, for example, it was three shows sometime in different places. Just as I was getting undressed and going to bed feeling really tired, two men from the agency arrived and told me to hurry as we had to catch the overnight flight back to Tokyo for another TV show, again choreographed with dancers. In Japan, the money was good, but I was literally worked to the bone and it was not always so glamorous.

Once I had to spend two nights in an artiste pension from the agency when my usual hotel was overbooked. I switched on the light to go to bed, only to find the room and bed were crowded with small beige cockroaches. I was happy I had brought plenty of DDT with me from Hamburg. What a marvelous powder that was; I got rid of the intruders in no time. Japan was spotless – except when it wasn't!

I was required by the record promotions department to have a real Japanese day, starting with their wellness. Firstly, I was put in a Japanese private sauna machine, for a photo, then to view their baths etc. After we went shopping for a kimono and obi and the typical Japanese thong white socks to be worn with the thong sandals. My hair was dressed and bejeweled like a geisha, and of course I was given a fan. I refused the thick white make-up the real geisha wore. The obi was excellent and made sitting on cushion on the floor not so bad, as the support they gave was almost like a back rest. A visit to a sushi restaurant was something else. The noodles swam in soup and in it was a whole fish, including head and tail. Trying to eat all that delicately with chopsticks while kneeling on a cushion on the floor and being photographed was no easy task. One was expected to suck and slurp and make a row smacking one's lips, but this was the order of the day and everyone in the restaurant was making such a noise you had no worry about conversation with your company – you wouldn't have been able to hear one word anyway; sometimes this could be an asset.

CHAPTER 104

Sayonara Nippon – Goodbye Japan

Finally, with all the rain and weeping walls everywhere, I lost my voice completely and hot sake and lemon drinks did not help. I had to see a specialist if I wanted to record my Japanese songs, which I had learnt so diligently. One was an amusing cha cha taken from an old Japanese Folk song "The Kompira Song" – all about Japanese indoor games. As these were generally with the hostesses in games rooms behind the nightclubs – little was left to the imagination. I flavoured the ditty with some amusing English words. The A side was a tune written by Frank for my TV shows, but it was so melancholy in a minor key that it fit the beautiful words "Sayonara Nippon" (Goodbye Japan). A choto, a long Japanese instrument a little like a large antique lyre, was played by a lady exponent, and it was a lovely ballad to which I also wrote the English words. But how to sing when I had no voice, not even to talk? The company took me to the best specialist in Tokyo – he had studied and got his diploma in Bale (Switzerland).

He asked me a few questions, the trickiest being, "After all these months in Japan, surely there was one admirer whom you liked and who was fond of you? I want him to be a good and experienced lover, because you are all tensed up what with all the work and TV shows and no real sex life to relieve and relax you, what you need is one good orgasm, and your voice *will* return."

I must admit, I was really taken aback, but I tried to cover this up by smiling slyly and saying, "What, only one?"

My Cultural Minister from Argentina, who had often invited me for lunches when we had time in our hotel, had obviously been wanting to get closer to me and had waited for all that time. He was delighted with the good news. He was a real Latin macho man – tall, dark, and handsome, perhaps about 40/45 years old. A man who really knew how to treat a woman. I was still in love with my young Swiss Ice Hockey "hunk" – but this Cultural Minister really knew his onions and his cabbages too, and they were cultured! The fact he was father of seven children (the seventh was born the day we met, and he had invited me to celebrate this happy happening with him) and that he had a girlfriend flying in the next day did not deter either of us. We had a beautiful night and it *worked!* My voice came back, I could record the song, and Kyo Sakumuto had me as a guest star on his TV show, so I could air the song almost immediately. He then thanked me and wished me a good flight back to Europe and put a small manuscript in my hands.

"Its my latest composition," he said, "perhaps you could record it in Germany."

Sometime after, while on tour, Sakomoto's plane crashed and, unfortunately, he died with all the other passengers; so he could never hear my German version of his composition written for me, called "Sukiyaki". That was the end of my time in Japan and of 28 quite hectic TV shows!

I flew home the Eastern route with a new Canon film camera and a million interesting memories of Japan in the 60s. Finally, "Pepito" hit the number 1 in world music charts. There was a lot to be learned in Japan, in the way they organized their business promotions. They are a nation of high IQs.

I returned in the 80s, only to find it was just like USA or Western Europe, all fully automized. The women wore pants and were self-assured. Gone were the kimono on the streets; they were kept for the tourist attractions like the tea ceremony. So, I savored my memories of a past epoch – gone forever!

CHAPTER 105

Frank's Cutting Edge – Walchwil

NO FOREIGNERS THANK YOU.

At the beginning Frank was a skinny obliging kid whom I happened to fall in love with, but before I went flying off to Japan he showed his teeth (apart from being so good looking, I thought his teeth were false – I was wrong, they were natural). This was a time when foreigners in Central Switzerland were definitely not on the Swiss shopping list. Frank finally found a home for me to buy in Walchwil (Switzerland).

Mr. Schaeppi, the Estate Agent, whom my friends in Winterthur had recommended, said beforehand, "It's going to be a difficult job buying something in the canton of Zug, where foreigners are definitely not welcome," but determination won through. How times change!

Teddy, who wanted to be called Frank because he was a Sinatra fan, was surprisingly smart. He noticed, when taken to the home of the landowner of the two single houses on which the architect and builders were working, that a large red ribbon was tied round a Tuba which stood where one entered the hall, plus a congratulatory plaque to Mr. Kaspar Huerlimann – the most famous surname in Walchwil. Frank immediately turned the conversation to music. He mentioned casually that his wife was the voice blaring out of various radio stations in the catchy little tune "Pepito". To add to these laurels, he presented himself as a composer and arranger, a sort of Mr. Music. To clinch the deal on the house, which as a foreigner in the 60s was extremely difficult, Frank promised to write a composition for the Walchwil Music Society.

The builder and architect said, "Ok, but I have a little summer cabin on the lake called "Ali Baba". The new composition must have that name."

Frank agreed and the deal was done over a homemade nut liqueur, and then a large kirsch (cherry schnapps). With Frank, and most men, a little alcohol always helps a deal.

On a free afternoon (as I was appearing nightly in "Chérie Noire", the "Schwarze Perle", at the then famous Bernhard Theater on the Lake of Zürich), Frank drove me over the unnamed open road to our new home. It was a split-level house on the side of the mountain, on, for London standards, a large plot of land. It possessed a really beautiful view of Lake Zug and had Mt. Rigi as a sort of protector against winds. The whole land was picture perfect, full of cherry trees and huge boulders going down the mountainside to the little pink post office and station just above the main road by the lake. It spelt, for me, peace and harmony, and after my last few hectic years, mostly working in large towns, it was pure perfection.

In and around Hamburg, in the north of Germany, I needed no manager; the offers flowed in — that was the good side, but the fans were crazy. When I was in a TV show with a live audience, it was not unusual for some girls armed with scissors to cut off pieces of a frill from my dress or even my hair, shouting, "I got a super souvenir, a piece of her "Pepito" dress," or "a curl of her hair."

The winds from the North Sea in the winter cut through my clothes, making me feel I was naked, and so I was blessed with one cold after another and terrible coughs that really ruin one's singing voice completely.

Walchwil and "harmony" were sold to us as being the Riviera of the German part of Switzerland, and that it hardly ever snowed there. This turned out to be pure fantasy. The first winter was the worst ever – it snowed relentlessly. I had no car and no husband. Frank had taken the car to Hamburg, where he had more work. I always had something like eight pieces of baggage. In Zug there were no taxis at the station at night, only the occasional train. Without my Ice Hockey friend, I never would have been able to climb up the mountain side to our little home, which also had its drawbacks – definitely in winter!

In no time I had Franz Huerlimann, a farmer, as my gardener and guide – a little man full of humor, who made sure I was going to be real Swiss and immediately planted edelweiss and enzian in my garden. I was delighted, as when I left for Tokyo I had a bunch of freshly-picked edelweiss with me. Apart from the fact that the movie "The Sound of Music" was one of the most successful films of that period, it featured a song called "Edelweiss". That was a brand new idea for Japan, and at every show I gave one stem to some lucky lady.

We had only one neighbor in Walchwil, who lived in an old chalet three minutes down the street: they were the family Liniger. Mr. Liniger ran the post office together with his wife, and when I came in to post a letter he said, "Was bringt ein Star wie Sie dazu, in so einem kaff wie hier in Walchwil zu wohnen, wo die füchse gute nacht sagen?" – "What in the hell brings a star like you to a tiny little village like Walchwil, where the foxes say goodnight?" I wondered if I should tell him that the prices of homes in the Ticino (Tessin) were way out of my reach. I decided there and then that his odd question needed no answer. I was Yvonne Carré and not Peter Kraus or Catarina Valente.

Returning from Japan, television was almost everywhere on my list, and I was so impressed with geisha and the Twist which was constantly on the silver screen that I composed a song called "Geisha Twist". It was quite a riot in the German language and also in English.

Of course, the kimono and all the geisha gear bought on my "Japanese Day" came into really good use as I twisted my way from TV in Holland to TV in Germany and then Scandinavia.

The sad thing about returning to Europe was that I was informed by the agency that my dear old colleague and agent Solly Black had passed away with a sudden heart attack in my absence, so I was left to deal with agents and managers myself. My dear friend at Radio Geneva suggested his wife, Vera. I had already received offers of managements from various sources, including two famous French ladies – but when I noticed that I was their "cup of tea" for other duties too I declined on the advice of Dad. I must say there was a lot to be said for keeping one's head above water and one's flat feet firmly on the ground.

Blowing the Trumpet for Walchwil in Switzerland.

During a television interview in Germany, I was asked – as a famous traveler – which place was the loveliest in our world. I said with no hesitation, "Walchwil on the Lake of Zug."

Some enterprising travel agents latched on to the affirmative and in no time bus loads of tourists came to see the "loveliest village" and to look at our house "Harmony" and at least the top part of the garden, as it was split level built on the mountain side. Pension Aesch became Hotel Aesch in next to no time, and both guest houses, Sternen and Engel, threw off their old musty garb and spruced up – also with their prices. It was the beginning of a prosperous era for our village Walchwil in the Canton of Zug.

The best happening was when I went to see the chief of the income taxes in Zug. I was greeted pleasantly and told, "Don't worry my dear, you are no longer in North Germany – you are now in Switzerland among people with hearts."

Fortunately, he had seen "Die Schwarze Perle" and his children had all bought my records, which I had autographed for them with a photo. To add to this, his youngest baby daughter had her birthday on the same day as mine. In no time, he and I became lifelong friends.

The other side of the picture was I was special – a celebrity in a small village. The man from whom Frank had bought the land was best friends with another gentleman from the Council, and of course the Music Committee. Suddenly, when Frank was away and I had company, and had just invited them to supper, there was a ring at the door and those two gentlemen were standing on the threshold with a bottle of Sandiman's Port Wine. They wasted no time in telling me their mission.

Thrusting the wine bottle in my hands they said, "We bought this for you. We thought it would be nice if you would undress and stand on a table naked while we sit there and admire your golden-brown body."

Thank heavens my reaction was quick and generally positive. I kept the bottle of Port and told the gentlemen I was sorry I could not oblige as a) I had company and was just serving supper and b) I was a singing star not a table dancing stripper.

I guess some older villagers cannot differentiate the difference – after all, I had been dancing about the stage barefoot in a little grass skirt, but the South Sea Island costume I wore as "Chérie Noire" did have a top, and was in propriety for even the highest society; and after all, Walchwil in Central Switzerland was far removed from the fantasy island of "Balikou".

Furthermore, I became the first in the whole village to have a spin dryer. I found this was a "must" when my black chiffon night dress with the white lace trimmings disappeared from the clothes line in the garden. Later I got a phone call from a road worker with a heavy Yugoslavian accent, telling me he had taken it and was enjoying sex with my see through nightie. Unfortunately, not even the telephone company "Swisscom" could ascertain who the culprit was, as the call had come to my line from a telephone booth. I guess that is the b-side of the glamour of being a celebrity.

Frank Becomes a Good Angel & Gets a Blessing Too.

The fact that we had a car on the mountain side when no one else did in our area (perhaps an odd tractor), except for the local Zugersee garage, which was down in the village by the lake, was a help when Frank was there alone. He offered a sort of gratis taxi service to those few who, like us, lived on the lonely mountain side, and needed to visit a family member in hospital. Fate was also good to Frank who, with the records "Pepito" and "Geisha Twist" firmly tucked under his arm, landed a contract with the then largest record company in Switzerland to make a series of LP albums of famous American classics for the new jukeboxes in the States (USA), which were being manufactured to take the Long Players. My memory for good American songs was a bit like an encyclopaedia. I didn't just know the titles, I could sing hundreds in perfect tune with all the words. At a school of at least 800 girls, I was always chosen to recite Shakespeare or Hillair Bellock's Cautionary Tales, even when they had 24 verses. My memory had been a big plus to Frank, and he and the company were most successful. Frank loved doing orchestration for big bands and conducting, and I felt happy being able to help him get a real foot in the door in the recording business in the USA.

My First Home Goes Red

When I returned to Hamburg, Teddy had already found a lovely flat in a brand new block in Garstedt – just north of Hamburg. He was very clever and knew exactly that our balcony, which overlooked a green field, would get sun because it was facing south. I'm afraid I'd never given it a thought.

I moved in with him without being married because a) with all the work in the area it was the most practical thing to do, and b) the thought of living with a guy and having no marriage certificate proved I had no wish to conform to society. I was modern – and still very young. In any case, for the best part of the time I was in some other town singing.

After appearing with Barnabas von Geczy in Kalastaija Torpa in Helsinki, the Finns took me into their hearts, and I did many recordings with Erkki Ertama and the Rock specialist Eric Lindstrom.

Wherever I was, I was on the phone to Mum, and the German Press said I had "telefonitis". On my first phone call from our Hamburger home, I asked her what to do, as I was shocked with Teddy's behavior.

"Teddy tried to pick me up and throw me out of the window, and we are on the third floor," I complained.

"He must have had good reason," said Mum, "what actually happened?"

"Well," I said, "you know I have absolutely no idea about cooking and I thought spaghetti with a good tomato sauce would be simple, but there was a typing error in the cookery book of the ingredients and they wrote tbl (tablespoon) instead of tsp (teaspoon) of salt, and after all my trouble the sauce was far too salty. Mum, I got so mad that when he came into the kitchen, I took the whole saucepan of oversalted tomato sauce and threw it half at the ceiling and half at him. We have to get a decorator to redo the kitchen; it is in such a mess."

"Well," said Mum, "I can quite understand him. To live with you he needs to have very good nerves indeed!"

Sometimes it's good to see somebody else's point of view.

CHAPTER 106

Goodbye Mum

Once installed in Walchwil with Mrs. Staub (I liked her name because in English it meant "Mrs. Dust") as a housekeeper to keep our place on the lower floor clean (upstairs were the renters in a considerably larger apartment – a very nice young Dutch couple), and not to forget Franz Huerlimann, the farmer, as our gardener, I invited Mum and Dad to come and see our home for themselves, as Dad had lent me 10,000 Swiss Francs to help the meager money I had to put down to get two mortgages.

Fortunately, the weather was good, but Mum made me promise to not renew the rental contract, but to move upstairs ourselves as soon as we could afford to. She was going to be seventy, and this seemed to me to be so awfully old. I asked Mum how she felt about soon becoming "three score and ten years old".

She was a wise little woman and said to me, "Every age has something good about it – you must sometimes just look a little harder to find the good side of life. I am now looking forward to leaving this world. Thank God you are now settled, so I can go to see my Mum and Dad and my brother Mick again."

I was horrified. "Mum, how can you speak like that? They have passed away."

"Because I could not stand another year of having to live with your father."

I was shocked. Dad was no easy person to live with, but that Mum felt so strongly about him I had no idea – how she must have felt for ages having to live and serve a man she did not really care for, purely out of a sense of duty. What a ghastly way to have to live one's life – and yet so many women of that era had had no choice, and still this applies in many countries today.

It was becoming my way of life. I had to leave my parents because I had to be in Germany, Holland, Luxembourg, and then up to Scandinavia. This was my young girl's dream come true and in no time, I would be able to repay all my debts. Above all I was wanted everywhere, but I had no time for a private life, not even for my own mother – even though I had made her part-owner of the house on all legal papers, should she ever need a refuge.

Even today I can visualize myself leaning out of the train window, waving and blowing kisses to Mum as she ran after my train waving to me.

The constant tours made a mark on me, and I had to go for therapy to help the terrible headache and neck aches I was experiencing, particularly when I belted out high tones really hard. At the therapy I was told to lay down on a wooden bench, which was then covered with sacks of camellias and hay…then I was covered with a blanket and told to relax and close my eyes. The light perfume of camellias and hay pervaded my nostrils. I fell asleep into a traumatic dream.

Three black angels came to take me away, just like that awful stone angel of death Dad had in the dining room. My head and neck were aching so violently, I stretched out my hand and implored them, "Take me, please take me," I said. "I cannot bear this pain anymore and no one will miss me I'm sure. Please take me."

The answer came almost like a low moan: "No, we are not here to take you; we will take you when your time has come. We are here to take the closest and dearest person to you in your family."

Suddenly the dream had gone, and a voice was saying, "Come on, wake up, your time is up."

I just said, "Oh, I had a most fearful dream."

When I got home, Teddy opened the door. His face was white and strained; he opened his mouth to speak and said, "Your brother Raymond phoned."

"I know," I answered, "Mummy has gone – the angels visited me and told me so."

Frank gave a sigh, almost of relief. "I knew it, somehow I've married a witch." He paused. "I know Mummy was your best and dearest friend," he added, "please, Tootsie, when the wound starts to heal – can I try to take the place you had in your heart for Mum?"

I had such a huge lump in my throat, it took time to answer. "Only if sometimes I can call you Mummy," I whispered, and then ran into the bathroom and locked the door to have a good cry.

How cruel was fate – I would have given all the fame and fortune that seem to be falling into my lap at that time, only to have my dearest and closest friend back again in this life: my mother.

CHAPTER 107

Australia – The Land of Oz

In spite of our lovely home, my first year in Walchwil was definitely sparse. I only managed to spend eight days in our new home, and almost everything was left to Frank – house, garden, renters and all. I just had to see the big bills were paid, which was all for the best as "Pepito" had hit the Far East and finally reached the so-called "Land of Oz" – Australia.

The flight there was once again unforgettable, as I missed the first plane to Rome connecting my original reservation, owing to a mix up of times. Frank said, "Be ready by 8.15," and I heard "8.50" and was late. We parted ways with one of our proverbial quarrels – by the time I was in Sydney it was all more or less forgotten.

As my plane for Sydney had left, I had to be put on a special plane for young emigrant mothers from Italy, and all with tiny babies – a ritual nest! The babies, swathed in blankets, were cradled in nets hung from the luggage racks, where they laid and screamed for the best part of the flight. It took me at least a half an hour with the W.C. mirror and my own, to make up my tired eyes, slam on thick lipstick, and plonk a sombrero on my matted hair to look like a star for the photographers. It's not always that easy to be glamorous for the press when one arrives in a new town or country.

Going to Australia was also Mum's wish. Her sister and her sister's husband and two daughters had left Johannesburg in South Africa when Apartheid came through, and immigrated further to Sydney, Australia.

Apart from my shows, I was on Channel 8 weekly in Sydney, and the record company took over our version of "Besame mucho", which we entitled "Kiss me while we dance Bossa Nova" (Kuess mich beim Bossa Nova) – the newest Latin rhythm catching on everywhere.

Of course, it was nice seeing Aunty and my cousins again, particularly Edith, who was a real beauty and already divorced, working as a supervisor in a restaurant, as her husband had taken off to somewhere unknown and left her to fend for herself and her baby son too.

Apart from the so-called "Blue Mountains", which the Swiss would have called hills, I was not at that time terribly impressed with that new, large country. They called me a "Pommy", meaning a Brit, but Australia to my mind was very much like Britain, particularly Melbourne, so was not all that different except in size and vegetation – and animals of course. My favorite town at that time was Adelaide because it was very pretty, and the people seemed to be more laid back and loved my refined style and lots of Latin rhythms, like the cha cha and Bossa Nova. The big difference between the UK and Oz was the men.

When a fellow wanted to compliment you on the way you kiss, he would say, "Blimey! That kiss was bloody beaut."

I had to go to the zoo to be photographed with a koala bear. They chose a giant one for me and he became so nervous in my arms that he immediately did it all down my dress – an expensive model, but as an artist I kept on smiling. Of course, there were also kangaroos and wallabies – they were something else, and so was the manager of the Hilton Hotel in Melbourne, where I was contracted after Sydney. I realise now I was not a "tart" but a sexy girl, and my life was often flavored by over-virile men – including the young manager at the hotel. When I arrived with backache, he immediately offered his services, smiling, as a professional masseur. I'll admit it did me good – but then it seemed he thought I should do him good, too. Once, when visiting his office, he had a male visitor whom he introduced casually and then, staring at my presumably provocative red sweater, he made a grab at my bust and said to his visitor, "Isn't she lovely?"

I am by nature a spontaneous person and my reactions are swift – sometimes not for the better! I immediately made a grab at his privates in his pants and said, with my schoolteacher voice, "No way with me, sir, what's good for the gander is good for the goose!" and walked out of the room without further ado.

There were also some other funny moments in Aussie Land. Having a natural love of the coast, I had looked forward to swimming in the sea almost everywhere I was contracted to sing. I forgot that, around the Pacific coastline of Australia, sharks swim too. On every beach there were strapping muscular young men with strong blast whistles sitting aloft lookout posts for those hungry intruders. This, of course, gave the swimmers a sense of extra security, apart from the heavy netting strung across one point of Bondi beach. This meant that the actual swimming facilities, with so many people, were limited. The waves were big too, which meant my pants would be pulled down often and my bra knocked up – so us bikini girls were kept busy trying to appear proper. One day there was a huge lifesaving show of all the lifeguards from around the entire country, a huge array of different coloured swim costumes on not such handsome faces, but marvellous muscular bodies. Whistles were blown, men rushed to the boats, and the crowd felt safe and excited.

Then there was a loud gong and an announcement: "Now we are going to launch our newest acquisition, a fibreglass life saving boat – being far lighter, they can go much faster to the person or persons in distress."

This special attraction started: six men pushed the glossy new lifesaving boat into the briny before they jumped in for the display and took to the sea. Along came an extra huge wave and in seconds, despite the weight of the six men, the wave turned the boat right over. I left the beach trying vainly to hide my wide grin, because once again, nature had shown men who was king.

Later, revisiting Australia in the 80s, there was definitely a change for the better. I no longer had to live on milkshakes because the meat was like shoe leather, and the food oldfashioned British even in a five-star hotel. The influx of Continentals and Asians immigrating to that big new continent had made a marked change. The Italians brought pizza, the Indians curry, and the ever-industrious Chinese had already made their imprint with a "Chinatown" and umpteen Chinese restaurants and takeaways. Then the new Darling promenade was certainly worth an outing, and the unforgettable famous architecture of the Opera House overlooking the beautiful Sydney harbour all made Australia the in place for enterprising tourists; not to overlook the striking impact Ayers Rock and the outback had on the younger generation, stimulated by the outstanding "Crocodile Dundee" movie. This made Australia impress the entire world, well before film star Nicole Kidman arrived on the scene.

It became a destination for students from many countries like Switzerland or Germany, who all wanted to see Judy Garland's ever famous movie "The Wizard of Oz" and follow the Yellow Brick Road, made even more famous by Sir Elton John.

CHAPTER 108

South Africa

Frank Buble, my Australian agent (I have no idea if he was connected with "heart throb" singer Michael Bublé), did well by putting me with Trevor Boswell, Eve Boswell's husband.

In England, Eve Boswell had a big recording success with her version of the folk song "Zucker Bussi" (in English it was called "Sugar Bush"), while her husband Trevor was running South Africa's biggest theatrical agency in Johannesburg with his father-in-law Hugo Keletti. Both men were excellent at their job and the nicest of people. They arranged together with Telefunken (the sister company of Decca) to bring out an LP album of my recorded successes in Germany in English and German.

They had already written to me to be careful with apartheid, for example, "If your legs get too suntanned, please wear white stockings. Whatever you do, don't sunbathe." Unfortunately, at that time I had no blonde wig, so I used a light make up. My arrival went well, but I noticed that owing to my name and my start at the Folies Bergere, I was expected to be once again French. No problem, except for when my brother-in-law's sister living in Jo'burg read in the newspapers about me and called me on the phone. Of course, speaking with my French accent, she became confused and I had to tell her to meet me in my room at the hotel so that the secret could be kept, at least for the time being. The owner of Ciro's, where I was engaged, was also an excellent musician and in no time, we were composing together.

Do As We Say – But Not As We Do! Even in Jo'burg…

One night a large table of Japanese were in the audience. They were delighted with my smattering of their language and my Japanese song, especially directed to them. I asked the boss how come, in apartheid, they had no problems.

"Oh," I was told, "the Japanese are all big businesspeople, we welcome them whole heartily, for us they are white."

Sundays were free, and I was invited along with the band and singer Maureen to the Boss' home up country. A beautiful place set on well over an acre of land, with many servants – they abounded everywhere in Africa.

Dinner was announced with a large gong and everyone trooped into the big dining hall. The French windows going on to the garden were open – it was a lovely balmy summer evening, and I got a mad desire to play "La Paloma and Santa Lucia" on the polished black grand piano, both of which I could play by heart and accompany myself singing. I did this in a soft voice with half-closed eyes, feeling really happy and romantic in the dimmed lights and the moon light. Suddenly instinct told me I was not alone. I opened my eyes wide and saw a huge tarantula standing on the grand piano. Remembering evacuation, when I saw its counterpart on a long table in England, I left the room in a flash and was more than delighted to join the rest of the party in the dining room, which had no open windows, only large ceiling fans. I was annoyed with myself for being so afraid, but I breathed a sigh of relief when I was safe and sound back in my own bed at the President Hotel.

My First Safari In South Africa

Hugo Keleti was really nice and booked me into the Kruger National Park for two nights for my very first safari. I slept in a little round African-style house with a high, pointed thatched roof, as did all the other tourists. It was indeed an experience. I

went with the other English-speaking tourists on the "pirsch"…
as they called it. Early morning and at dusk – apparently most
animals seemed to sleep during the day. The first day there was
not too much to be seen, but the second day we were in luck's
way. Our guide took us to a low-lying glade with really green
grass and shade trees. It was choc full of "Thompon's gazelles"; a
more peaceful scene you could not wish for, and above there was
a huge, I thought stuffed, lioness – or was it a statue? Whispering,
I asked our guide if this was put there to enhance the picture.

"Oh no," she assured me, "it is a lioness biding her time to pounce.
They always choose by nature the weakest animal, and she is
"playing dead" while searching for the exact prey!"

The next seconds were amazing. My statue lioness came to life
and jumped from her high-up perch right on to the weakest
gazelle in the herd, and within the blink of an eye the whole
herd fled, and the peaceful green leafy glade was again completely solitary.

Later our Land Rover came across that lioness again, with a
bloody side of a Gazelle in her teeth, trotting on her way to feed
her hungry cubs.

Next stop was Durban, which I thoroughly enjoyed because of
the lovely beaches and the predominantly wealthy Indian public.
They were mainly schooled in the UK or USA and were absolutely fluent in the English language, so I could crack a joke or
two and come out with some of my rather caustic remarks and
get the audience laughing in no time. The papers even called me
"an eye catcher and really spicy," and remarked on my sharp wit
that brought everyone into the fun.

Cape Town was beautiful, but no bathing in those high waves,
and then I returned to Jo'burg to record "Tell Me Why" and
"Heartless". To the first I wrote the words, to the second the

whole composition. It was a real rock! And then I was on my way to Rhodesia, now called Zimbabwe.

Looking back at my life, I think one of my most amazing and beautiful gifts from God was a day trip to the Victoria Falls in neighboring Zimbabwe, as a thank you gift for my success in their country. Both Hugo Keleti & Trevor Boswell, my managers, were great guys!

I have been fortunate enough to see the falls in Rheinfelden in Switzerland and of course Niagara, but none can compare with the Mosi-Oa-Tunya ("The Smoke that Thunders") in Zimbabwe. The water coming down from the Zambezi River is tumultuous and the falls seem to abound all around you, and the spray covers your face in the part where you are able to walk with a guide. It is, in my opinion, an absolute "knock out" of nature, not just for the eyes but also for the ears – the water literally thunders down. The magnitude is unbeatable – but the whole atmosphere that surrounds the world-famous falls makes them an a superb memory that cannot be erased for a life time.

CHAPTER 109

Rhodesia – Zimbabwe

The audience was nearly all English expats, the club large and just fine. On the first Sunday my boss took me to the races. I bought a large sun hat and dressed up as if I was being taken to Ascot. My boss knew everything about the horses and had with him a book giving the names of the various competitors, and then their family tree and when a particular horse's father had won the Derby etc. My boss gave me the equivalent of about 30 pounds sterling and told me to bet on whom I fancied – he, of course, was well read in horse breeding and knowledge of races.

I had not a clue, having only known the old grey mare I rode on when staying on the farm with the Johnsons as a tiny tot. I decided to take a look at the riders and their shirts, as I appreciated young men and racy looking shirts far more than I did horses. There is the expression "beginner's luck" and I was lucky, because I put my money on the riders and shirts which I personally fancied. I managed to turn the 30 pounds lent me into 75, and so could solace my very equine knowledgeable boss, who had lost his 30 pounds entirely and was feeling a little disgusted with that Sunday at the races. I gave him back his 30 pounds and we split the winnings.

Salisbury, the capital, had a beautiful wide main street and fortunately, when I was there, it looked superb. There were royal palms and deep blue blossoming jacaranda trees all along the way. It was by far the best main street I had ever seen. To add to this joy, there was the largest, most famous cactus garden in the world and to my surprise, some of those special cacti only blossomed once every hundred years and that year was it – and they did. What an outstanding sight that was!

My brother in law's sister came over from Johannesburg to see me and this phenomenon for a short holiday, and as I was on a diet once again and never partook of the wonderful lunch buffet served at our hotel, she could have my lunch ticket and was delighted. She was quite a plump lady!

The boys in the band were very friendly and full of good humor and asked me to join them in a séance with the most famous lady, who had actually cured the manager of our club. I had never been to a séance but had read about one in a book by Agatha Christie, and I was curious. The boys were very amusing. We all, about 15 of us, trooped into the room where the séance took place. We all had to put a piece of jewellery on a plate and then sit at the séance table, in somewhat dim lighting. We were then told in a special priestess voice to open our legs so the voices of the people in the next world would be able to really come into us through the spirit.

This idea really was appreciated by our boys in the band, and they whispered in my ear, "Very good idea, Yvonne, don't forget to open your legs so the spirit from the next world can enter."

We all, like kids, went into suppressed laughter. I was really surprised at how much this woman seemed to know about me, as I had only recently lost my mother – my dearest friend and inspiration. She told me the tears would now be over because very soon I should be meeting my really big love.

I was surprised again and said out loud, "How come, that's not possible, I am already married," and was secretly amused, because being a normal person and not a nonconformist like myself, she had probably noticed I did not wear a wedding ring.

Her answer came quick and firm: "It makes no difference if you are married or not, you are going to meet a big love who will become a special person in your life, whether near or far."

My next stop was to be Nairobi in Kenya.

CHAPTER 110

Nairobi – Surprises

The plane from Salisbury in Rhodesia to Nairobi arrived in the evening and I was delighted when two handsome young men rushed towards me to welcome me to Kenya and relieve me of my hand baggage – mainly cameras, hats for the show and my music notes, all in heavy covers, as without that I would be lost.

The taller man was apparently the Manager of the Equator Club where I was to appear and definitely, from the way he spoke, an American. The other had clipped accents in his English, but when I had time to scrutinize his face, I thought he was of Greek origin. He said with much aplomb, "We have reserved a room for you at our best hotel "The Stanley". Of course, when one is interested in explorers and in geography, we all know the words of the famous British explorer Stanley, Mr. Livingstone I presume."

I felt as if I was living in history and was quite excited at having a room booked for me at that famous old Hotel, but when I saw the tiny room and single bed with no view, my excitement turned to disgust, and I said quite adamantly, "No way! I have far too much baggage for such a tiny room surely designated for a servant," and I thrust my chin up to show my defiance. I turned to the American as I said this, but then he seemed to address the other young man, who I then decided was probably of Indian origin as I had met quite a few in Durban. The smiling swarthy face emitted a sigh and "atta", and it was not a sneeze. I then explained to this guy, who introduced himself as Amir, I must have a larger room. He said he would arrange this if I didn't mind just sleeping there the one night as it was so late.

The American said, "Miss Carré, just call me Hal."

I said, "Call me Yvonne."

"Tomorrow I will come for your rehearsal, which is set for 3 p.m. So sleep long and well. The hotel will remove all your belongings to your new room – we do want you to be comfortable here in Nairobi."

I was so tired, I agreed.

The next day I was given a double with a pleasant view, and I unpacked happily. Then Hal picked me up and for the first time I saw the famous club "The Equator". It was more African than Africa itself. The décor was real zebra skins, from the long bar to all the seating, etc. There were pictures of safaris and handsome men in khaki shorts and long white socks and safari shirts, and some dead trophies on the wall behind the bar. For the first time all my musicians set to accompany me were black. I knew, just like in Japan, I would have to get used to them before I got the names right. Once more, to my untrained eye, they all looked like brothers. I gave each one my notes and counted in 1, 2, 3, 4 and there was a horrible din from the sextet. When I went to see what had happened, I saw half of them had my notes upside down on their music stands. No wonder, not one of them was able to read music.

In a state of absolute horror I turned to Hal and said, "Take me to the boss, I'm leaving. I have no intention of doing the show with non professionals."

The same young fellow in shorts from the airport was there again smiling at me like a large Cheshire cat, it was such a forced grin down from the mouth but not the eyes. I became angry. I had had enough. I said, "I want to see your father, I'm leaving. I cannot do my act without a proper musical accompaniment. Take me to your father!"

Then came that Cheshire cat smile again. "I'd love to take you to my father, but unfortunately he is dead."

With those last words the smile I did not care for faded. His voice became softer and his eyes clouded over for a few moments.

"When Mr. Kenyatta declared Kenya a republic and no longer a British protectorate, the owners of this famous British club to which you have been engaged left hurriedly for their homeland, and everything fell into the hands of the administrators. My friends and myself, all educated at London University, were their lawyers, so we took over the Equator Club until it would be finally sold and the money sent to the rightful owners. Each one of us takes turns of being Director for 3 or 4 weeks until all the legalities are sewn up. Now it is my turn, and I actually engaged you after reading all your excellent critics in the newspapers sent to me by your agency in Johannesburg. I like the fact they all called you "spicy"." He grinned. "We need to get this club back on its feet again now that so many British have left this beautiful country – I thought with your help," and with those words he looked at me straight in the eyes, and I saw that his were almost black in the electric lights of the club, but they shone with an inner warmth I had never noticed before – all the cold air of that impassive face departed as if blown away by some warm wind, and I wished I didn't, but suddenly I felt sorry for him. Young as he was, perhaps in his very early twenties – he was allotted to be my boss.

"Look," I said, "I am not asking for the moon, I am a real entertainer, so I could still bring in the crowd," remembering some gigs in "God forsaken" places where we arrived so late that Teddy had to accompany solo on the piano, and I still managed to twist the crowd around my little finger and make them happy.

"Listen," I said, "he or she must be a real professional pianist, who can also direct the drummer to help back me up."

Suddenly my new boss' face was all big smiles. "Why yes," he said, "our Chief of Television and Radio is from London; he lives here with his wife and son who takes marvelous photos of wildlife. Mr. Masters is a great musician, whatever his price I will get him for you, I promise."

I crossed my fingers and my legs, I took a deep breath. "You understand if he's no good, I must leave."

"Don't worry," was the answer, and he left us.

Hal, who had been standing by, was 100% positive. "Amir is a good guy and a smart businessman. You're gonna be pleased Miss Carré, oh, I mean Yvonne."

An hour passed and then the door opened, and Amir returned with a small wizened older man. I could not believe my eyes til I recognised the voice.

"Yvonne, my God, what a wonderful surprise being with you again after all these years. Remember Bournemouth? I believe your very first gala engagement as a solo entertainer, when I had to get permission from your Mum and Dad?"

I was so relieved I could not say one word. We fell into each other's arms full of real warmth and serenity. I had to pinch myself to believe that once again God was on my side, and this was real life and not a beautiful dream.

Hal had left after I had asked him to call me Yvonne, and Amir was all real warmth and genuine smiles. He said, "Great that you two know each other. Oh, thank God for good fortune."

He stayed for the rehearsals, helping us with our choices. We all drank good English tea with milk and Reg Masters had a small flask with cognac, so we three took a sip, and our world seemed saved once again. My arrival on the scene brought in a lot of expats who had remained in Kenya and lots of higher-class Africans and Ministers – later on including Mr. Kenyatta himself. Reg Masters and I were a huge success. The newspapers printed our story and we and Amir breathed huge sighs of relief. Our hopes had been fulfilled.

As my contracts til now always included meals (I had my eye on paying up my second mortgage) and after the upheaval in Kenya there was no restaurant at the club, Amir apologized for this error and asked if he could take me to lunch or dinner or both. Owing to the confusion of that horrible little room at the Stanley, I had left my fold up baggage with most of my clothes at the club, so after my first show, when Amir asked if he could carry my paraphonalia for me to the hotel nearby, I agreed readily. Reg had gone home, and I was elated. Once up in my room Amir spoke of safaris which he would like to do with me, being born in this area. It all sounded really exciting, and I told him of my previous experiences in South Africa and the Falls, and above all Kruger National Park and the lioness. I thought it had been some sort of statue who came to life in a split second. Amir was a good raconteur and a good listener, but when we both paused for breath – he looked at me his dark eyes all aglow and asked me outright if he could stay. He assured he could really make me very happy. I thought it over for a few minutes, but his attitude seemed so warm and kind and I had been now for so long with no time for love, I began to think it could be a good idea. His bright smile showing very white teeth and his hand holding mine seemed re-assuring.

Once snugly tucked in bed, both of us feeling happy, the phone rang loud and clear, jogging our reveries back to reality.

I picked up the receiver, a voice said, "This is the reception. Madam we think there is a man in your room, and this is unlawful and not allowed in Nairobi."

"Oh," I said, "really? Then I will look under the bed – sorry there is no man there."

I put down the receiver with a devilish grin and we both burst into fits of laughter.

We carried on "getting matey" as they would say in Aussie Land, when the phone rang again. I picked up the receiver and once more the receptionist said, "Ma'am, no gentleman came down, is he still in your room?"

Feeling really amused I answered, "Maybe, he jumped out of the window," and put down the receiver.

My young boss at the club started to look really miserable, as all his wonderful illusions seemed to be going up in smoke.

"Don't worry," I said, "I'll fix it in no time."

Dad taught me ages ago, "money talks all languages." This time, I called down to the reception. "Look," I said with a chuckle, "just charge for two persons and that for my whole engagement."

"Oh, thank you Ma'am," said a relieved voice the other side of the line, and I settled down to a lesson in Kama-Sutra, and he to a lesson of the simple word "spicy."

CHAPTER 111

A Little Wonder

I began to feel really at home in Nairobi, a wonderful town with crisp dry air, where I felt more alive with four hours sleep than back home with eight.

Reg's wife invited me often for delicious meals and desserts – not always ice cream, but often banana and cream with slices of crystallized ginger. I believed this would surely keep my "spice" really "spicy" and it tasted so good.

Then Reg's son Martin asked if he could take me to Nairobi National Park, and there we had a super experience of Mother Nature. Martin was an expert wildlife photographer who possessed great patience. He knew of many waterholes unknown to others in Nairobi National Park. In the 60s the tourist trade was almost non-existent and certainly not in the mass production of tourism as it is today. If you possessed a car and knew how to say "Rifiki," meaning "comrade" in Swahili and "Simba," meaning "Lions" and raise your voice in a question mark, the park guide would give you directions how to find the lions in Swahili and broken English, and there were so many lions at that time, you would surely go back to your hotel not being disappointed at all.

Martin pulled up at a smallish waterhole and we saw a family of little warthogs (a delicatessen for patient lions) pass by, without leaving our car. Then, just as I looked at my wristwatch thinking it was time for me to go, a large giraffe passed us further down and went into the water. She opened her legs wide and to our astonishment gave birth to a baby giraffe – a real little wonder to see. Its little legs were really spindly and mother giraffe had to pick up her little one by the back of its neck a few times because the fine little legs collapsed underneath him. Finally, it could stand properly, and without further ado, afraid of lions waiting in the thicket of the African bush, she went quickly into the surrounding jungle with the new baby by her side. What a wonder of nature I had just witnessed, it was so special, and how lucky I was to be able to sing live in the best hotel, and also have such an unusual experience in the afternoon. I began to love safaris in Africa.

CHAPTER 112

Mombasa – Why I Recorded "Malaika"

After leaving Nairobi I flew to Mombasa. More unknown territory! I was booked for "The Oceanic", a small exclusive club for the rich Kenyans and anyone who wished to be included in that class. It was owned by wealthy Indians and Amir assured me the audience would love my "joie de vivre" and my wit would be appreciated, but the good news was that he was coming too, as he had a small apartment on the beach. His mother would be there, and he would like me to meet her. Also, he wanted to see his cousins who owned the Club. Slowly I understood that he was part of the Aga Khan family, although not terribly close.

The flat was ideal, small, and practical. However, I was shocked that although his mother was a woman of character and sari clad as most Indian ladies of her class, with gold bracelets almost up to her elbows showing her wealth, she had light bulbs hanging naked from cables. The bits of furniture were somehow haphazard. Yet this very same person had sent her son to London University to get his law degree and her eldest daughter to the Sorbonne in Paris. It seemed to me that for the better class Indians an excellent education was number one. Her cooking was marvelous and her curries unbeatable. We did not have much time for each other, but a swim in the warm Indian Ocean was a must. We were the only ones on the beach – it was gorgeous, and in the water, which was glass clear, "skinny dipping" was no problem; the only ones who could see us were the little monkeys who inhabited the beaches around Mombasa, which we called the "beach kittens."

The time came so quickly for me to leave, as I had already agreed to carry on my African tour and to go on to Sudan. For me all these places had been only names on the map, but my album "Yvonne Carré" could be purchased at any record shop in Nairobi and all over Kenya. When I had recorded some extra numbers for "Continental Records" at the studio in Jo'burg, I had the pleasure in meeting the original composer of the Swahili world success "Malaika". He was a simple man who had composed the haunting little melody with the sad words of unrequited love, because he had not enough money to pay the parents of his lovely young "Malaika" (little star) for her hand in marriage. One would think that after having composed a song that is sung around the entire world, he would have had more than enough – but as he explained to me this was not the case, as he was so poor and needed the money offered him by the record company. Without knowing it, he had sold all his rights together with the small sum of money offered. His education was too humble for him to comprehend the legal wording of the contract. These things happen all the time, but at that time no one knew the simple little melody would be such a success. However, I promised him I would record his "Malaika", which I did on my album titled (in the USA and English speaking countries) "Folk Songs around the World", after which it received International acclaim and became a standard in many repertoires.

Amir tried to persuade me to stay, but I still had a contract to fulfill from my management company in Johannesburg for Khartoum in the Sahara Desert, so I flew to Sudan. My adventurous spirit had prevailed.

CHAPTER 113

Khartoum – in the Sahara Desert

I had been warned about the Sahara Desert's sandflies, so I wore tights under my jeans – but when I arrived at the airport it was dusk, and the sandflies were the most aggressive I had ever experienced. They actually stung through my well-covered feet and had a nasty habit; when you swatted at them, they would fall on the floor like thin pieces of wood, only to pick themselves up and fly away to sting the next unfortunate foreigner. My hotel, as was always the case in Africa, was the best – it was smallish but beautifully located in the middle of the old town. I was happy to see my room possessed a balcony which overlooked a main road with passers by, all in Arab or Muslim garb, reminding me a little of Morocco in the 60s.

The balcony had contained a little table and two chairs. So, I asked the servant to clean it up and announced, "Tomorrow I would like to have my breakfast served there outside."

The manager who had met me at the airport gave me beforehand a few words of warning. "There are, here in the Sahara, Three Step Scorpions." Until then I had never seen a scorpion in my life – I only knew they were black and could sting. "We call them this because after being stung you can take three steps only before you fall down dead – so much poison they can inject into your blood stream. In the hotel I do not think you will manage to meet one, but to be sure, when putting on shoes, shake them upside down should one be hiding inside. We put little bowls of water under the legs of our beds to stop scorpions attacking us at night – they don't go near water."

He did not mention the blue-black blister beetles, which when walking over your feet left a line of blisters. These I met later, but fortunately no snakes. Naturally, I began to have quite a few misgivings about this club, and my dreams were mixed with nightmares.

Many of you must be wondering by this time why, when I loved East Africa and would be leaving with re-engagements in my pocket, did I ever bother to include Khartoum in my African Tour? Perhaps it was the romantic of Lawrence of Arabia, but it was more the persuasive charm of Hugo Keleti who assured me I would be working as the star of a big variety show at a beautiful, large open-air garden theatre; the musicians would be Italian and professionals; There would be just one show nightly; and to crown it all, the boss was an English man from Purley in Sussex England (where our family dentist came from).

It all sounded so reassuring, and then when I was still not sure if I would sign the contract or not, he added, "It is The Place in the Sudan; why, they even have a revolving stage like they one at the Lido in Paris." Then he reeled off a short list of famous English singers who had appeared there. That did it; I signed.

The next morning my breakfast arrived and half asleep I said, "Put it out on the balcony, I'll eat it outside."

When I went out, I saw that my idea was first class stupid. The balcony chairs and table were covered with sand, and I had to save my little breakfast plate before that too was covered. Khartoum is bang in the middle of the Sahara Desert.

The boss himself introduced me to the band, and the pianist was the bandleader and also did many vocals. His name was Marcello Oleari, at that time well known in the Italian music world. He had discovered Milva when she was working at a candy factory. In the daytime the Theatre Restaurant looked a bit deadly, but the band of eight was good and the pianist bandleader absolutely "simpatico." At night the whole place turned into a wonderland, with pretty lights on every table; the stage was down below and the tables all arranged in tiers above in a large semicircle. With some Yuka trees, and stars above, it honestly looked like a trip to fairyland.

I was waiting to see the revolving stage. The waiters were all dressed in Sudanese Muslim style, in white sheet like garments and a sort of turban headgear. About six or seven waiters started from the side to push the round stage and slowly it turned around – indeed, Hugo had told the truth, but as it turned some disturbed creatures like rats, mice, and chickens, clucking as loud as they could, ran out – all felt annoyed by that untimely disturbance. That alone was a spectacle and I felt myself having a good laugh at it all.

The club filled up nightly and the boss from Purley in England must have been making a fortune, because all the Embassies and such were invariably in the audience. The spotlight was good and one night, while I was singing "Tani Tani" to end my show, some ghastly looking huge spider like insect wanted to share the limelight with me. Everywhere was dark the little electric lights on the tables all were dimmed and the whole audience stared at me and this huge, I can only presume bird-eating-spider-like insect walked nearer and nearer to me, sharing my song in the spotlight. Of course, I saw it too, and while I was singing at the stand microphone, I was contemplating what to do. It came very near just as I was singing the last words and with a huge swinging of my arms I took one step toward it – the audience sat with bated breath – and then I jumped, landing with my two feet directly over the head of this outrageous intruder. Fortunately, thick platform shoes with wedged heels were the fashion, and they were heavy. At the same time, I shouted "Ole!" The audience stood up and cheered in appreciation and the bandleader left his bandstand and congratulated me. I felt like some prize fighter returning from battle and was proud of myself. It is amazing what one can do when necessity calls.

However, I am not always so courageous. One night, I was coming back form the show with Marcello, who had now become quite a pal and told me lurid stories of the Ha-Boob, the terrible desert storms that brought clouds of dust into every nook and cranny, which he hoped I would not have to experience during my engagement there. As we got to my room there was a black scorpion on the white door. I knew they could jump, and I wasn't taking any chances. There was no one in the reception or about at all – I had a key to get in, as my show of one hour was at midnight, so I was the only hotel guest to return at such a late hour.

I turned to Marcello and said, "I'm not taking any chances, let's spend the night at the airport."

I still had 3 nights to spend at the "Castle Hotel" and so I rolled up my dressing gown and put it in the slit of air between the door and the floor. I slept hoping my "guardian angel" would make sure that the 3-step scorpion would not want to revisit me, and I could end my engagement in peace.

The boss wanted me to stay on, pointing out the British Club had my LP-albums and I was very popular, but I was happy to leave that part of the desert. Marcello, who perceived the boss would try to make me stay on, had fortunately fixed for me a new contract in Addis Ababa in neighboring Abyssinia (Ethiopia), which he assured me I would really enjoy, as there would be many Italian and French people there. Apparently, he had been there with his band for six months. He had already rehearsed with me four new Italian songs for my repertoire. So, off I flew to Addis in Abyssinia, which had a much better climate.

CHAPTER 114

In Ethiopia – the Lawyer, the Emperor, & Italian Star – Me!

Marcello talked me into it. While I was in the area, I simply had to go do Addis Ababa where he had played at the best club for 6 months. He told me they would love me there and I would not regret including that country in my African tour. Apart from that, if I had a signed contract then not even the Khartoum King, as they called the English boss, could hold me and I just had to leave.

I arrived with the manager of the club and the steward just as there was a big feast in Addis Ababa. When I got into the Main Square, with the two gentlemen bringing my baggage, the band played a loud fanfare and the crowd cheered. First came soldiers colourfully dressed for the occasion. Then came an entourage, all carrying oriental style umbrellas with gold tassels, then a bejeweled elephant and finally Hail Selassi himself. He was a little man, even smaller than myself, but he called himself their Emperor. In any case, he was very popular in the UK newspapers. It was pure pageantry and the cheering crowd loved it.

There were also placards almost everywhere saying "The Great Italian Singing Star Yvonne Carré of "Pepito" Fame", would be coming to Addis (as everyone called it).

I decided I must brush up on my Italian immediately and was quite relieved that Marcello had made me learn "Luna Rossa", a lovely melody, "Tintarella di Luna", which was lively and very popular, Dean Martin's "That's Amore", a definite for audience participation, and of course "Pepito", which was also my signature tune, so I entered dancing a little cha cha. This was often requested as a second encore too.

At this point I must say Amir and I had phoned each other when the phone lines allowed, and Frank never ceased to send me interesting letters with little drawings of his own busy life back home. When I had arrived at the Airport in Addis Ababa, I was surprised to see everywhere the Lion and the Star of David, and then I met my next mentor (big fan) in Abyssinia (as Ethiopia was called at that time). Like Doctor Richter in Lausanne, he was a wealthy man of high prestige, a doctor of law; he immediately invited me and some other tables to champagne to celebrate my opening night. Obviously a big spender, he seemed to be famous as "The Lawyer-Advocate", and was greatly respected. Oddly enough, he was Greek, but seemed to be the most famous man in Addis Ababa. He drove me to all the places of interest. We visited the UNESCO building, a veritable landmark on Main Street, but we could not use the elevator provided. The lift in the Palace had broken down and the Emperor had had the one and only other lift in Addis Ababa, at the UNESCO building, removed and reinstalled in the Palace. The meeting with that intelligent older person was positive because he could explain the emblem of the Abyssinian flag. Apparently, the Queen of Sheba (Abyssinia) was so impressed with the wisdom of King Solomon that she decided to make the long journey to Jerusalem to visit the King of Israel. During her visit, King Solomon went down with some incurable fever and she, staying at the Palace, ordered pitcher upon pitcher of water which she drank and urinated so much that she could dab it all over the King's face and body – and it being an excellent disinfectant, as was known also later by the preachers of Ajuveda, she cured him! King Solomon was so delighted with this beautiful queen from such distant shores, that he offered her gems for which he was famous. She asked, however, for some Israeli men who could father babies, with the hope that some may one day be as wise as the king himself. So, even in those days, genes were found to be most important. Hence the Israeli Star of David with the Lion of Judah on the flag, and emblems were everywhere.

Later the same interesting Greek gentleman took me to the famous natural sulphur swimming pool situated in the rich verdant landscape of the hills. We walked above looking down on the river dotted with little islands. The lawyer looked and said, "Oh what a pity, there is not even one crocodile and I did so want to show you one from here."

I looked down at the little river below and on the islands. I could have sworn the long pieces of wood had eyes and there were actually quite a few smaller crocs. "We have a bet," I said, "they're crocs."

He said, "You're crazy, they're long pieces of wood dropped from lumberjacks."

We both threw down stones and all the "pieces of wood" jumped into the water. I won, and proved once again to myself the importance of natural instinct.

Such large cars as that driven by my famous lawyer were almost as rare as himself. Whenever we left to drive off from a place, he would give me a fist full of coins to throw out of the window to the ragged beggar children, much as if I was taking part in a Charlotte Bronte or Jane Austin novel.

Before leaving Khartoum, I had to spend some local money, so on advice from the British boss I purchased a python skin coat.

Flying back to Zürich from Addis Ababa there were astounded stares from many women at Zürich Airport; no one had ever seen a real python snakeskin coat. In one of the skins at the back there was a real bullet hole. Although not one live python had crossed my path in the Sudan, when people stared at my coat – some even pointed – I held my head up high, thrust up my chin, and felt like a real big game hunter.

Just before leaving Addis Ababa, the manager told me that the Emperor had heard so much about me, he would be present with his entourage to see my show that night. This he did after telling me how much he had enjoyed Great Britain and also his visit to Switzerland, both of which he had done with so much pomp and glory that he had become the darling of the press. He then presented me with an 18-karat gold brooch or pendant, which he explained was the Star of Africa as his ancestor, the original Queen of Sheba, had designated. Sometimes having an adventurous nature makes life really worthwhile. At a party in Switzerland it disappeared; C'est la vie!

CHAPTER 115

My Private Life in Hamburg – The Girls!

My private life revolved mainly around Frank and Hamburg, where he had procured an apartment at the Hotel Stadt Altona in the famous Reeperbahn, which was number 1 for all tourists and just full of life – similar to Montmartre in Paris.

Above us Shmuel Rodenski (undoubtedly the best European Tevje in the huge musical success "Fiddler on the Roof") resided. He practised his songs daily and was a real example of "hard work will get you there."

We were also in walking distance of the notorious Herbert Street. We received show biz visitors almost non-stop. They were all men, all interested in a visit to that special street, and this included my old boss and friend Gerard v. d. Meer. We went there as a group. Frank went with our promotions Manager Dieter Broer and his wife Berbel, and Gerard and I brought up the rear. As we came to the first open window there were two obvious older prostitutes of the commoner sort, but the third was a very young little blonde with an innocent look of a Virgin Madonna. The blue-eyed little girl looked more like a country bumpkin than Maria Schell or Liselotte Pulver ever did in their "Heimat" movies.

Dieter was quite taken with her, and he cried, "Oh, look at that poor little mite she doesn't look a day over 14 – whatever is she doing here?"

"Du blöde Affe," screamed the husky voice of the "country maid" at poor, totally shocked Promotions Manager Dieter. "What d'ye think them girls here are me mothers? I'm here to fuck you, ye old bloody bastard, put ye doe down here."

Both he and his naïve wife looked so shocked, I just had to burst out laughing. I had learnt a lot of the way of the world in the meantime and had lost many of my innocent illusions.

We all hurried on to the next windows, til quite a nice look-ing, heavily made-up shady lady told Gerard, "Mensch, du bist mein Bier, komme herein,"with a saucy grin, showing some very white thigh.

"No – not at the moment – thank you," I said quickly, stepping into the breach, "he's with me."

"No problem, lady," shouted the whore, "I'll take on the both of you."

The five of us looked at each other, grinning our heads off as we left the famous street behind us. It had been a funny expe-rience. Today we of the fairer sex are not allowed to enter this street. "For Men Only" – no more funny experiences for us poor girls. Tut! Tut!

Slowly I had gotten used to the fact that you don't leave a good looking, successful young man in his late twenties or early thir-ties alone for very long. In spite of his sparkling blue eyes and so called "milk on his lips" expression on his face, he was actually a reincarnation of the Devil in disguise. Every time I returned from a gig, a TV or a longer engagement, a pretty girl would come out of the bathroom or bedroom and say, "Oh! You're Yvonne," a little taken aback, apparently, that I should turn up in the small apartment when she was there. Often I would find other women's clothes and undies in the closet, but I was not taken aback, as it became a sort of a habit. After some years the girls became darker and darker; I got used to that too! Generally, we would become pals – that is if they stayed. Very often they went! I guess there was never a dull moment in my life with Frank Valdor in the 70s and 80s, when he was selling millions of albums around the world, and his record company had asked me to manage him to put on a show, as fans wanted to see him live. I had to engage 2 part time secretaries, one for English and one for German, to fly around Europe as his manager and even find him a good girl singer from the States. At the same time, I had to fulfil all my own singing engagements. Thank Heavens life is a lot more peaceful now.

CHAPTER 116

Roberto Blanco – The Black Bomber

The first time I ever met the now famous "Black Bomber" was at a TV Show in Frankfurt. Those of us who had a short interview and a song to sing sat in the first row at the studio. The second was reserved for those with no music, only an interview. Frank Valdor, my husband, was on one of his rare occasions with me on my right; the other chair on my left was at first empty. Sometime later in an agitated hurry, a good-looking young black guy sat down on the empty chair. He seemed a little lost, so I asked him if he had to sing, as if not he had taken a seat in the wrong row. He answered he was there to promote his first recording and he was very nervous. I calmed him down, as he had to be the first guest on the show.

"Well, he is certainly not like Kenneth Spencer," Frank commented to me.

Ken had been killed in a plane accident, but had been much loved by almost everybody in Germany and myself. His voice was a rich operatic baritone. He was tall, slim, and cultured, and was the only black guy in Germany who had had such a big success. Now German TV stations were looking for someone to take his place.

Behind me sat a young girl who was also nervous and doing an interview for the first time – her name was Iris Berben, and she told Frank and me that she had only recently arrived from Israel. That brought back lots of unusual memories for me – in no time we chatted together and when I left the studio, I wished her lot of luck. Little did she know that after some time she would become a very popular German film and TV actress.

Also, this young coloured singer, who told the "moderator" he was from Cuba and whose voice could not compare with Kenneth Spencer, later became a most successful entertainer – known as "the Black Bomber". His personality was electric, and he danced as only a Latin can. He was obviously a natural talent. He, like Iris Berben, had no idea he would develop to be a 24k gold Entertainer in Germany and Spain.

After that first TV show we were often thrown together in various shows, but I really got to know him when we did a Hoffmeister Tour, and I was told I was to drive with him in his now famous big white Mercedes. I am sure lots of German girls would have paid to have my seat!

Most of us in show biz were always delighted when we hit Wiesbaden, because we could generally count on the fact that we would be staying at the luxurious Park Hotel. I loved that place; it was pure romantic luxury, none of that businesslike décor mostly offered by Hilton and Intercontinental hotel chains. You could tell a woman owned it and the feminine love of detail and romantic was just everywhere – from the flowers arranged in a beautiful vase, to the lace frills around the pretty scalloped pink night lamps on the table stands. To add to this there was always one act, generally well-known, appearing in cabaret at the ball-room. In no time the owner Edith and I became colleagues. She told me that Roberto had been left to her to look after as a young boy, as his father wanted him to have a proper education and not go from town to town and country to country as was the way of the world for true artists. Dancers were often called "gypsies". She had arranged for him a good musical background with singing lessons. Moving on stage, he didn't need to study – it came naturally.

In time she regarded Roberto more or less as an adopted son, and later he became her intimate friend. She in turn made sure he had the smartest custom-made suits and shirts and a special changing room with long mirrors to admire himself. Every year he was given a brand new white Mercedes to harmonise with his black coloring. Traveling with Roberto in his beautiful white Mercedes was considered a huge asset. The others went on tour in a small VW bus. On tour all the girls were jealous of me, as we were always allotted hotel rooms next door to each other. Lots of people thought we had a more intimate relationship. How wrong they were!

a) Being of gold coloring myself, I preferred blond or light brown haired men with blue eyes.
b) I was at that time quite in love with my young Swiss Ice Hockey player who had played knight errant for me in Zürich. Being already married, short visits while on tour from this big 6'2" sportsman naturally did bring certain complications.

However, Roberto's complications were far worse. He was hopelessly in love with his father's mistress. What odd situations an artist's life can bring!

If I had luck with most males, Roberto had million-fold more luck with most females.

We had rooms next door each other on this tour and every night he had swooners (musicians call them "scrubbers") – so he obviously had the pick of the bunch. He seemed to be a tireless lover as, night after night, when he ejaculated, he let out a roar which would have done justice to a lion in the wilds. This also invariably woke me up and meant my nights were not quite as peaceful as they should have been.

To add to this, after the show he would come to me most amicably and say, "Edith is sure to phone you and ask if I am with you and behaving myself. Yvonne, don't forget to answer "but of course" and calm her down."

After all, Edith had been a wonderful mentor to him. In show business many a mentor may be years older than the protégé – this is a "norm." From Maria Callas with Meneghini and later Onassis, to French actor and chansonier Maurice Chevalier, who needed the rage of Paris Mistinguette, or Gilbert Bécaud with the fantastic Edith Piaf.

I remembered well the advice of George Scott Wood, when as a kid singer on my way to Glasgow for my first engagement at Greens Playhouse he had warned me, "With the boys, Yvonne, be like the three wise monkeys: See no evil, hear no evil and speak no evil!"

I told Roberto he could rely on me, and we became buddies. This became my regular after-show telephone call. I liked Edith enormously, as did Roberto himself, and we both did not wish to hurt her. It was obvious she did not trust his youthful male hormones and had not learnt of the three wise monkeys and my own motto of "live and let live."

However, next morning my help to Roberto became far more complicated. Regularly at a certain time the phone would ring, and a worried whispering voice would say:

"Yvonne, you must take this girl off my back. I must get rid of her. I've given her money to go to the hotel beauty parlor and have her hair or face done." And then a pleading note, "Please take her! We'll meet down at the parking lot in, say, half an hour, ok?"

If it was or was not, I had to acquiesce – I guess I am one of the few women who really understood him on that tour.

After a few more minutes there would be a knock on my door and Roberto and a very young blonde would be standing there. In an apologetic voice he would say, "Yvonne, we must be on our way, or we'll be late for rehearsals at our next destination. Please be so good and bring this sweet young lady to the Hotel hairdresser, she wants to have her hair fixed."

Before I could answer "yes or no" he had gone and left "the one-night stand" with me. I had little alternative but to bring the girl to the Hotel hairdresser and quickly disappear to the hotel parking lot and the big white Mercedes. The porter would already be waiting with my baggage to put in the boot.

Roberto, for his part, would be sitting in the driver's seat reading a large newspaper trying to make him self as inconspicuous as possible.

Once on our way he would give a big sigh of relief and tell me all about Mireille, the girl he loved, and the sticky situation he was in with his father and even with Edith. Generally, he phoned the latter to console her. This he did and regularly assured her of no misdemeanors on his behalf, but oddly enough he always called her "coño," apparently a bad Spanish word – perhaps more like the Yiddish word "shmuck," which means the same but is also used as an expression of endearment. In English "little dummy" or "little stinker"!

Mireille I had never met, although Roberto assured me I would. I only knew she was French Swiss and at a certain point on our tour I would have the pleasure of meeting her.

Roberto seemed to be very serious about his intentions with her. He definitely intended to play his father out and marry the girl. Knowing him I knew he would. I only hoped on this tour, with unaccountable one night stands, he would have sown all his wild oats, however plentiful they seemed to be. I wondered if he could settle down to being a good family father, apart from being a great entertainer.

Finally I was introduced to Mireille, a really nice, not blonde, French speaking young lady who was in his father's show. She was certainly different to all the others, and I wished with all my heart he would make her happy.

I had no qualms regarding her relationship with Roberto's father. He was the boss of their show. I only had to remember my own life previously and how in love I had been with Nick Norovski, a married man easily old enough to be my father, but also my boss at that time.

Very often an older person can help us to grow up and master the crossroads that can befall us in later life. I could not help but wonder how this very delicate situation would fare. I decided to just sit back and cross my fingers for them both, as I also did for myself.

CHAPTER 117

The Letter – Amir –
the Total African Safari Vacation

There it was, with a Kenyan postmark; instinctively I knew it must be from Amir, and it could not have come at a more appropriate time, as I had just three weeks free. I swear I have a guardian angel in Heaven!

It read:

"Dear Yvonne
The time with you was unforgettable almost like taking part in a movie. Therefore, may I ask you to meet me in Bombay at the famous old hotel – The Taj Mahal – and let me show you at least part of the interesting country of my ancestors – India.
Should this idea not be to your liking then let us spend some weeks touring my homeland Kenya and beautiful Tanzania on Safaris. Unfortunately, when you were singing here, both you and I had so little time. Please Yvonne, let us make up for it now. The decision is yours. Please do not disappoint me.
Amir."

The letter was so eloquently worded I almost expected it to be signed "your faithful servant, Amir."

India and "The Taj Mahal" sounded terribly romantic and exciting, but I was young enough and inexperienced enough to still be afraid of some countries and India was definitely one of them. It was still too mysterious for me, whereas Kenya and Tanzania and real time to live at lodges in the midst of wild animals, and yet knowing somehow I was safe and secure with Amir in a huge national park, was a comforting thought. My love of animals was so great, as a kid I had been keen on working in a zoo – I didn't have to make up my mind. After calling Zürich Airport I sent a telegram immediately:

"Arriving Nairobi Thursday week. African Airlines 115. Cable me, if ok" – it was!

Frank had been great and said surely it was the opportunity of a lifetime and I should definitely go. My Ice Hockey love was not so kind and asked me whatever made me want to return to such a black Continent. I said, "An excellent engagement being on tour in two beautiful countries," and flew off, not knowing what really would await me, but surely this was going to be the honeymoon of a lifetime – the sort of thing I had dreamed about as a small kid digging sand castles in Llandudno.

Alone in Elephant Country and Tsavo Area

I have no idea what was brighter – the welcoming African sun, the washed and polished new Citroen (so similar to ours), the multi coloured bougainvilleas all along the roadsides, or the large warm welcoming smile as Amir saw me and hustled me and my baggage into his new car. Now it was my turn to have to pinch myself to make sure I was not just taking part in a movie.

We left the bustle of the big town immediately and drove into the lovely countryside and stopped at a pretty Agip Motel, small and neat with a thatched roof half covered with flowering honeysuckle and bougainvillea bushes everywhere. There seemed to be very few guests. I never noticed any – we were so wrapped up in each other. After two years of absence there was so much to catch up on and so many kisses to re-capture; I really felt like some new bride as Amir went through all his plans for our safari with great pride. He knew and loved those two East African countries, Kenya and Tanzania.

Our first stop was at the famous Tsavo-Lodge in the heart of elephant country, and there we had some odd experiences. The tourist trade was negligible and was only arranged from a few of the larger hotels, and there were posters everywhere "Beware of the African Elephants – if a large elephant blocks your way, back up and choose another route immediately, otherwise your car and the occupants may look like this" – and there was a drawing of a car completely squashed.

We had a similar experience when two female elephants crossed the road in front of us with no problem, and I could put my

Japanese Canon Ciné Camera to good use, but they were followed by a huge male who obviously wanted to show off his masculine superiority. He stood in the middle of the road, blocking our way, and just would not budge. I think both of us got visions of that "Beware" poster. Amir put the gear into reverse and our car backed away gingerly, hoping the huge king of the bush would not follow us. I was happy Amir was on the wheel and not myself, as backing up was never my forté.

Another time we met a huge male on a hill, but fairly near the roadside and our car. I thought this must be the picture of a lifetime and I started to film when Amir stopped the car. I wound down the window to get a clearer view, only to notice in my exuberance that I still had the black cap on, covering the lens. I was so annoyed with myself I shouted out "Bloody Hell, I've still got the cap on!"

Unfortunately, this display of bad manners displeased this Elephant King and he let out such a loud trumpet I thought my ears would fall off, dropping my camera to the floor. I rushed to wind the window up before his trunk came through to us. Amir quickly started up the car, with his foot on the accelerator just in time.

"Look back," he said sharply. We both saw a large heard of elephants trumpeting and rushing down the hillside toward their leader. "Whew," said Amir, "that was a near shave – we and the car could have been trampled to death."

We moved on to a safer haven, the beautiful beaches of Dar es Salaam in Tanzania, with the loveliest natural harbour I had ever seen in my life and a walkway promenade of shading cashew nut trees, silver sands, palm trees and the clearest aquamarine sea. Dar es Salaam lived up to its name of "Peaceful place" – it was still really dreamy in the 60s.

Ngorongoro Crater and the Kilimanjaro

To see the Kilimanjaro in Tanzania for the first time was like looking at a huge chocolate pudding with white icing on top. To me it was like a Salzburger Noggel and seemed to possess a terrific radiance of peace.

It was 100% photogenic and when I saw it again more recently all the icing had disappeared; the warming of the world's climate had done its job. However, years before, the odd elephant or giraffe with the Kilimanjaro as a backdrop made a marvellous picture. It was "sans tourists" and it seemed as if the animals were living in paradise – it was so peaceful.

Ngorongoro Crater is about the perfect area to meet almost every animal in a quiet atmosphere.

One of the nicest and the most romantic part of this lodge was, after an early evening in the crater and a short swim in the icy pool above, nothing was more welcoming than a lovely open fire burning in our room to welcome us after a light dinner.

I was so enchanted with this romantic open fire that the following year I returned on holiday with Frank. Although the knock on the door and the servant entering with "early morning tea and biscuits" was as before, the warming coals of the open fire were gone, replaced by a gas fire. There were also some tourists – we were not alone in the wilderness anymore, and yet another Paradise was lost – or slowly disappearing.

In the early morning one could see every animal doing its daily toilet routine. Two male lions passed us by, possibly exchanging the latest news. They walked by our Land Rover completely unconcerned (in the crater you could only go with a qualified guide), and perhaps the lions had not noticed us at all. The climate in the crater itself was hot. At the hotel way above the huge hole, it was almost European. The pool was freezing, dahlias and chrysanthemums were growing everywhere, and the management was English.

On our way we saw every animal conceivable, even a lioness patiently waiting while she smelt and heard a nest of warthogs underneath, just as our domestic cats can smell a nest of mice, and show great patience till the first one comes out for air. Then "wham!" She got it!

We had an unusual experience before reaching the crater; we found a rivulet with large steppingstones to the other side. A large king lion arrived and stood on the middle stone, and then as if he was being paid homage from his clan (maybe it was his birthday) one by one came the lionesses followed by younger ones and then cubs, seemingly to greet him. Animals are far more related to our species than we dare to think. I filmed the whole ceremony with my zoom as we sat as spectators in the car. After returning to Mombasa to meet Amir's sister (whom I liked immediately) and her doctor husband, we went for the last two days to the Whispering Palms Hotel in Mombasa with its crystal-clear waters. At that time, I could go into the kitchen myself and return to Amir (who was idly sitting on a swing) with a tray of goodies and a large pot of good English style tea. As the waters were clear and having the beach to ourselves, we could leave our swimsuits on the sand and go "skinny dipping." We slept under mosquito nets; it was primitive but romantic. Those were the days!

"Hatari" – Danger – Hardy Krüger's Momella

John Wayne was probably the most sought after male film star at that time. He was invariably the sheriff in cowboy land or the boss of the camp in an adventure movie. About this time, "Hatari", filmed in East Africa, was the most talked about film of the day. Italian film star Elsa Martinelli was the heroine, whom Wayne hated at the beginning, as he regarded her as being in the way – being a female on male territory – in the Wild African bush.

Along with the Italian actress were a young French actor and a young German actor – namely Hardy Krüger. After the film was a huge box office success, we all read about Hardy Krüger having fallen in love with Tanzania – he had bought land there and had built a small lodge for himself and a few guests. It could be seen in the movie. It had a nice size swimming pool and the usual thatched roof, African style, an eating area outside and a bar of course, and a kitchen and a big sensible dog, apart from guards for the night. It was not in lion country and Amir, having met Hardy Krüger, knew it was one of the only places safe enough to go out exploring on foot. Apparently, there were no bison to trouble us either. The place was called "Momella", meaning "Giraffes" in Swahili. As big as they are these animals are quite timid and peaceful. We were the only guests and Hardy was not there to chaperone us, as he was away filming. The second day Amir suggested we take the dog and go to the waterhole, where surely we should see one or two animals coming for a drink, if only gazelles or giraffes.

We made our way down though the thicket, keeping to the little trodden path till we saw the water, and there in the middle, with large jaws open, was a hippopotamus. We had seen flocks of ostriches running, herds of zebras grazing, monkeys squabbling galore and little babies hanging on Mother Monkey's belly, even a rhino from a distance, but never a hippo. I could hardly contain my excitement, as my Canon had a zoom, so it could stay where it was and I could film happily. Suddenly our dog started to bark, and I had a feeling the hippo was coming nearer and nearer, and yet my camera was no longer on zoom, as I'd switched that off. I found out then that as curious as we are to scrutinize wild African animals, they – not having seen anything like us before in such an outlandish place – are just as curious as we are. This hippo was ready to get out of the water to get a closer look and, perhaps worse, a feed.

Amir shouted, "Run for it!" and that we did for our lives! Our dog in front barking, lest we lost our way, and the huge hippo on our tracks behind; I could even hear its heavy breathing. I said a little prayer to myself asking God not to let me fall over some of the huge stones on the small path. Never have I been so relieved to see our Momella Lodge with the guards with their truncheons ready to shout and beat the huge animal away. We rushed to our room panting with relief.

After laying quietly on our loungers by the pool, I turned mine around and sat up so the warm sun could touch my back. Suddenly I saw something dotted moving like a tail, followed by another and another. I roused Amir, who had fallen asleep. There was only a small hedge dividing our pool from the heavy green jungle outside.

"Oh," said Amir, "seems like cheetahs, they won't attack us, but let's move to the other side of the pool," where there was a stone path and the lodge walls for protection.

Later in the middle of the night I heard some huge "plops". We heard guards shouting and rushed to the windows to see what was going on downstairs.

The pool was lit up and there were our three guards, all armed with truncheons, trying to get "our" hippo out of the pool. Obviously it had followed us and was delighted to find another waterhole. Finally, the native guards won the battle and sent the large grey black apparition on his way, back to the waterhole he knew and called his home.

When I recounted the story to Frank later on, he said that was an ideal name. "Let's call our own record company "Hippo"."

The Statue in Kampala

I don't mind admitting I fell quite madly in love with this handsome young Indian.

After our hair-raising escapade with the Hippopotamus in Momella, Amir was determined I see Uganda, where he was born. He even fixed me a Gala in Kampala, the capital, where I sang for one night with just a good pianist as I was on holiday and had no music with me.

Kampala reminded me more of London even than Melbourne had. Of course, it was a lot smaller, but the houses and just everything, buildings, shops etc. were just like the areas where Dad was still living in London. Very similar to the homes built in the UK between the 50s and 60s. There was a great square in the middle of the town with a big statue paying tribute to a hero. When I looked at the name engraved, it was indeed the maiden name of Amir's mother.

I knew that he was related to the Aga Khan's family and his mother came from a prestigious wealthy family – but that Amir's own grandfather was there as a statue in the capital's main square was something I had never dreamed of, or experienced. I wondered what it must be like having Lord Nelson as my own ancestor. Mum had always encouraged me, when I was disgusted at not growing a centimetre after I was 11 and being just 5 ft, by speaking of Nelson, whose statue adorned Trafalgar Square on a high pillar. She told me he was a great hero but only about 5 ft tall. Amir was of course very proud of his grandfather, and I was so impressed. I for once was speechless! Whenever I am in love I never see clearly. I believe many of us fall for the impossible – after all the grass seems so much greener on the other side.

I had a plane to reach, but at that point my guardian angel disappeared. I have no idea what happened, but the open wild road must have had something like an oil spill. Our car skidded off track and went smack into a tree. Fortunately, owing to Amir's careful driving, we were just shocked but not injured. We were in the middle of the African Bush.

Amir said quickly, "I'll go to get help," and left me with a half-wrecked car alone in the wilds. I walked up and down and waited. A few natives passed by. I just stood motionless and looked in the other direction in case they thought I'd make a nice "Apéro". A huge snake slithered by me, but once more I remained motionless, trying hard not to breathe, and fortunately it passed me by. I decided to wait should the snake have an entourage following, but it was alone. Then rejoice, I could here the noise of an approaching motor. It was a truck driver, who was kind, saw my plight as I motioned him to stop and he brought me to our camp, where Amir had fixed everything and I could fly home, after some of the most marvellous safari experiences to make all my wild dreams come true.

The last picture in my mind I had of Amir after our amazing African "honeymoon" was him waving goodbye to me at the airport, his shorts standing out like a flag hoisted on high by his Kama Sutra penis that just refused to go down. Such an eternal erection I had never seen in my life and never would again. I'm afraid I laughed and laughed at that funny situation, and boarded the plane still grinning to myself and thinking how much easier it is to be a woman. He told me on the phone he had to go immediately to a sex specialist, who told him he had been overdoing things but managed to put him and his "best part" back to normality. 40 years later there was again a difficult situation, but this time it was comical – it needed a lot of help to stand up at all! Time sure does take its toll, but in this day and age there seems to be a remedy for everything … Viagra!

CHAPTER 118

A Dream Home in Africa – Africa & Us.

The black continent either gets a strong hold on you, or you never want to return again. It got a hold on Frank, and I was already sold – for me it spelt pure adventure. Today it's pure tourism.

During my engagement in Nairobi at the Equator Club, a Mr. Branson owner of a big, well patronized hotel had approached me with a wonderful offer, most enticing in the cold and grey winter months in North and Central Europe. I flew again to Nairobi, to Amir's great delight, and the Nairobi public made me their darling and Mr. Branson won his bet – I filled the hall and the media and Ron Masters made sure the radio and TV gave me plenty of coverage.

Frank had to get a taste of the safaris, but this time we went with two other European couples to Ngorongoro Crater and a large part of Tanzania. Around this period anybody who was anyone had seen the film "Hatari", where John Wayne had the difficult job of netting rhinoceroses for American and European zoos, and probably knew that word meant danger in Swahili. Our guide driver was determined to give us some real thrills and drove straight at a large rhino mother grazing with her small offspring, then swerved quickly in the other direction, giving the big rhino such a shock that it charged violently at the side of our Land Rover. Maybe rhinos, like bulls, get excited from the colour red – I was wearing a red T-shirt. The big, shocked animal charged straight at our Jeep, whacking it on my side just where I was sitting. We all screamed – me most of all, but the clever routined driver had turned off the motor and as our Jeep came to a standstill so did the Rhino with a snort. We were not moving and the big horned animal lost interest immediately and returned to her place by the infant rhino. After a second round, all camera shots were taken and the driver assured me that the Land Rover was used to those big bashing rhinos – I assured him I was not!

As the Frank Valdor Orchestra was now selling albums almost quicker than he could record them, and as I earned a lot of Kenyan Shillings, which I could not take out of the country, and properties were so madly cheap in comparison to our part of the world, we decided to buy a beach property in Mombasa. Gulie, Amir's sister, and her husband were alerted, as Amir was away in Uganda on business. We were immediately invited to their home where they introduced us to a huge man who was apparently a big shot in real estate and law. We four looked at various suitable properties and Frank and I fell in love with a large house with grounds stretching down to the beach. The owner was in mosaics from Italy and was also the Italian Consul in Mombasa. He was delighted to sell the lot to us for 8,000 Kenyan Pounds, as he wanted to return to his homeland. It was arranged the Italian Embassy in Nairobi would then rent the lovely Italian style home from us for the next Consul. We planned to build a little holiday home in front, where we could run barefoot into the ocean. There were many palm trees and plenty of small monkeys with their families. Not knowing what thieves they were, and in our complete innocence, we thought this future home could be heaven on earth.

When we left to fly back to Switzerland, all had been done legally and we were the proud owners of a lovely property on the most expensive resort in Kenya – Nyali Beach.

Little did we know then, that we would be the dreamers.

My Folk Album
Goes Around the World and So Do I

Frank's first album, "Tropic Beat", with Peter Beil and me doing a few vocals to help him out, had done fairly well and soon after an enterprising American businessman, who had already heard some of Frank's musical arrangements on his Juke Box LP albums, asked Frank to do an album for his record company called "Dance Party by Frankie". It was in strict dance tempos, and I wrote four songs and did the vocals in English to help the marketing along. I wrote a Foxtrot and an English Waltz and included my first composition from when I was still a kid; I called it "I Wake up Dreaming" as at that time the whole family called me "Joseph the Dreamer" because I spent a lot of my time daydreaming about my future. For my birthday they wrote on the card, "Sorry we could not find a "coat of many colours" so we hope you like this scarf of multi coloured tulips." This birthday present and the song I had written were both for me very special, because I wanted to prove to the world daydreams are important and with great determination, like Joseph in the Bible, you can make those dreams become reality. After all it is up to you to make your dreams come true – in your life.

With "Dance Party by Frankie", Dave Miller made an excellent start in Germany and indeed all over. Frank made one huge success after another and was later called "The King of Dynamic Party Sound". Dave was sold on my voice and when we got together, I told them now was the time for Folksongs of the entire world. In the USA the album was called a "Back Pack of International Folk-Songs" with all the Hippies and young people who longed to travel later on in mind.

The album became a bestseller internationally because it was not always in the same idiom as, for example, Joan Baez or John Denver. Every song was not just in another language but was entirely different.

Frank Elsner, at that time Chief of Radio Luxembourg – German Programmes, played the entire album for his listeners, because it was musically and vocally so different.

The album was sold just everywhere, and one gentleman came to my door in Walchwil and asked me to autograph it, telling me he had purchased it in the Far East (and yet another man in Singapore). He said that while working on a project in Singapore, he never dreamed that the streamlined Glamour Girl on the record cover could be almost a neighbour. When years later I had a respite, and I was asked by the International Woman's Club in Zug to put on a show for them at the casino in Zug, I discovered that quite a few ladies had this album in their record libraries. Often their husbands had purchased it in unusual places while on business in Hong Kong, Tokyo, or New York. It was truly international, which was something I had always wished for — bringing people together from all over the world with my songs.

The Dacca Deal / Bangladesh

Adventure was always written big in my life, so when Mr. Branson in Nairobi told me he had a good friend form Switzerland who was general manager in a new International Company in Dacca, I thought he meant Dakar in Senegal, North Africa and I said I'd go. When I got my air ticket on Pan Am, I thought they'd got the spelling wrong. Pakistan was not so much in the news as today, and I only knew that Decca was my record company. It was my first engagement on the sub-continent and I had the good fortune of having an American sitting next to me on the plane who knew Dacca was the Capital of East Pakistan and had already stayed at the Intercontinental there while on business. So, when I saw everywhere was under water, he put my fears at rest and said that happened every year about that time, but not to worry; the Intercontinental was on a hill, resplendent as a Palace of the Orient. He also warned me that the beggars at the gates of the grounds belonging to the hotel would be lepers and not to be shocked, and preferably to look at him and pretend not see them in case I faint. He was right; to see leprosy is frightening, and I was really shocked at what I had let myself come into. Little did I know then that some of the men I would meet in this outlandish leper country would turn into lifelong friends.

The first came at rehearsals with the good Italian band at the beautiful Chamberley Room where I was to appear. Suddenly a voice with an intonation as Yorkshire as the pudding said, "Hallo Duck, heard you are a good old Londoner – would you like a cup of real English Tea?"

It was, with all that strangeness, as if this young man was the incarnation of an angel from Heaven – his name was John Wareing.

Little did I know then that John would remain a lifelong friend. After the tea and a piece of toast and a good rehearsal with a good Italian band who could read music, I was taken by John, who was the Food & Beverage Manager, to the general manager, Mr. Max Herr – as Swiss as his name, with a lovely American wife, Marion. After the first night with an excellent English-speaking audience who seemed to appreciate my sense of humour, I settled down to a really pleasant engagement, where the patisseur & confiseur Rolf Huglin was from nearby Freiburg, just over the border in Germany, and Toni Lopacher, the young sous chef, was from Aegeri in our Canton Zug; he was the second in command to the executive chef, German Manfred Kessel, who was there with his wife Doris. Altogether we embodied a bit of home in a distant area of the sub-continent now called (as it was well before) Bengal.

Apart from being an innovative confiseur and pastry cook, Rolf was also a good organizer and a good friend. He even helped "sous-chef" Toni remove maggots from the bails of rice which were damaged in the floods. Sometimes to keep their humour up, I would help Rolf and Toni by singing the old soldier song "There was lice, lice mixed up in the rice in the Quarter Master's Stores". It was not that easy to get new supplies in an unusual country that had been under water.

Rolf arranged a boat trip and a picnic for all of us Europeans. It was amazing to me. In deep, wooded and green places, suddenly a hundred little faces would appear through the foliage, waiting for us to leave some food which they would quickly grab when we threw a half-used picnic box to them. Then they would fall upon it like a pack of hungry wolves. Another thing that amused me, which later I was to find all over Pakistan and India, was the love of white skin. There was a lesbian singer called Maria in the band who was plain and white, but with a truly lovely voice; after all, a golden tan like mine was great for Scandinavia but not really to the taste of the sub-continent. There were even large advertisements in the newspapers – "How to whiten your skin", "How to have the beloved white skinned limbs and face of the Westerners or at least the people of Kashmir". One episode I shall never forget with Maria came through our general manager Mr. Herr. He too was taken with the singer's pleasant voice, but was sure I could improve her general appearance. I was given money to go with her and our two young male bodyguards to the nearby market and buy some lovely materials to make some suitable evening dresses for her to sing in with the band, as she only seemed to possess one grey frock which did nothing to enhance her plain appearance. Off we four went to the big market for materials. Just as Maria had a particularly beautiful length of mauve and gold patterned brocade in her hand, over her shoulder I saw the most horribly eaten leper's face I had ever seen, and if she should turn, she would be face to face with this live apparition of ghastly ugliness.

Thank Heavens one of our bodyguards had seen this as well. I said in a low voice, "Maria, *non bouge* – don't move, stay as you are, we will buy that material for you, but don't turn around until our guards have removed something dangerous behind you."

We saved her and the lovely kaftan style dress my dressmaker had made for her – otherwise that phantom could have easily given her a traumatic shock.

Maria was delighted with her two new dresses – she confided to me her dreams and secret hopes she could be my lover, with a feathered hat, riding to me on six white horses.

"Sorry," I said, "I am not fond of white horses and I shall not be coming round the mountains to you at any time."

One day, stepping out of the hotel, I thought I'd try the jogging track. There before my eyes an Aston Martin drew up. The porter immediately opened the door for a dark, handsome young gentleman, while another helped out a gorgeous girl, stylishly dressed with long, full, curly red hair. I asked who they were.

"Oh, I'm the Crown Prince of Bhutan and this is my bride. We are starting our honeymoon here and then probably on to the Far East and maybe Europe and America," he said off handly with a pleasing grin. "When we get back – you must come to Bhutan as our guest."

I told him the Princess of Nepal wanted me to come to the famous Soaltee in Kathmandu.

"Oh, Birendra," he said, still smiling; "he is the King, you know, a great guy, maybe we'll see each other there."

I left them shaking my head; I had never seen such utter poverty and such overpowering wealth all so near to each other as here on the subcontinent during my Dacca Deal.

Nepal – The King and I

I think most of us had heard of Kathmandu from hippies and the new popular trend toward folksongs. As for Nepal, I believe most of us knew the tallest Mountain in the world was in the Himalayas, and they were in Nepal.

Max Herr was, through his work for Intercontinental Hotels, acquainted with the King of Nepal – Birendra, whose sister ran the biggest and most exclusive Theatre Club in Nepal. The Princess had heard of me and as Nepal was in the area, so to speak, she had asked him to persuade me to come to Kathmandu to sing. Once more my mad desire for a new adventure invaded me and I agreed.

Just flying to Kathmandu was quite special. As they had no radar, we had to be grounded twice up Patna and then fly back to Dacca, as the weather in that mountainous country of Nepal was often foggy with such poor vision it would have been extremely dangerous trying to land there.

One inexperienced English man who was with us in the transit room at Patna rolled up his light trenchcoat (Macintosh) and put it on the window sill above his head. As I declined the Coca Cola offered (the bottles were open and looked a bit unhygienic to my discerning eyes), I had time to notice the window above the man's head was slowly opened and a pole with a large hook was thrust high, and the trenchcoat disappeared, never to be seen again.

Aunty Esther, Mum's younger sister in Johannesburg, had written Mum about this stealing technique used often by African servants on rich people, but to see it actually occur before ones very eyes was different. It was a job done in seconds, and before I could alert the ignorant Englishman – it was gone.

I, for my part, was quite happy to return to Dacca and my friends there at the hotel. We swam together, we ate together and really, we were all buddies.

I was quite apprehensive and asked Mr. Herr what happens in Nepal when, owing to poor weather conditions, I, as the much-heralded singing star, could not arrive on time. The intelligent general manager smiled and said, "There will be a large advertisement in the local papers about the poor weather and your predicament and it would make the people even more interested to see you as soon as possible."

Kathmandu was different. The main square also housed the child Virgin and the priests of the Hindu religion. If one waited long enough, one might see the face of that little girl pressed against the window. She was considered to be as sacred as a swan, and there were carvings depicting this part of the Nepalese Hindu religion. The weather was mostly rainy and cows, often quite dirty and muddy, roamed the streets, because here they were sacred. I was happy free laundry service was included in my contract, as cows would pass by without saying "excuse me" and, more often than not, their hides were full of mud as they touched or pushed you in passing. Under religion as practised in Nepal, steaks were of water buffalo, and so was the milk. Both took some time getting used to. Houses were small and to go in, even little me had to bend her head. Nepalese people were small in general, although the King was definitely not, and some of the younger generation were more of medium height.

In spite of being two weeks in Nepal, I only managed to see the peak of Mount Everest for about 2 minutes, before it got swallowed up again under heavy cloud. There were some hippies, but only a few, and nothing like what we had read in the media back home. For me the best part of my engagement there was that the young King Birendra came to see my show twice and both times invited me to sit at his table. His English education was excellent, and he assured me that once he was married he wanted a family and above all to try to modernise his country and bring it up to date with the world outside, in a democratic fashion. He was a visionist with humour and not a bit arrogant, as so many Pakistanis and Indians I would meet later on, when I returned to sing in that part of the world. Rolf, our patisseur at Dacca, confirmed my very positive opinion of King Birendra. He had been sent by our general manager Max Herr to stay at the Palace to organise the wedding party with our Executive Chef Manfred, and of course to make the many tiered wedding cake.

While he was all alone in the large Palace kitchen, a young man peeped his head around the door to see what was going on with this famous cake – he seemed quite inquisitive. Rolf noticed him immediately, and being alone, he shouted in true practical German style, "Don't stand there, come over here and help me, I need a strong hand to stir all that mixture."

Without further ado, he gave the willing young man a large wooden spoon, which he stirred and stirred as if he had been a seasoned cake maker himself.

Sometime later, after the royal wedding ceremony and the main meal, the Master of Ceremonies bade everyone be seated for the grand entry of the many tiered royal cake. The musicians played an accord and Rolf entered with the huge cake, ready to give the knife to the happy couple for the first cut, all under loud applause.

"Yvonne," said Rolf breathlessly, "I nearly dropped the wedding cake and the knife too when I saw it was the King himself who had taken the wooden spoon and stirred the mixture for his own cake. He just smiled and gave me a quick wink. What a great guy that King was."

Horrifically, years later King B's uncle did not share his views of modern ideas on democracy, so he started a bloodbath at the palace and had the King and Queen and the entire family brutally murdered while sleeping in their beds. It is amazing what people do for power! And it is often the nicest people who are sacrificed.

Noblesse Oblige – West Pakistan

My favourite town in West Pakistan was Lahore, and I would joke about that name in my show, to the obvious delight of the audience, comparing it to the English word "La Whore". One early evening I was taken to the biggest and best brothel in Lahore.

I was sorry I did not have my camera with me. The girls stood on balconies with pretty colourful saris blowing lightly in the breeze, wearing thick make up, with flowers or jewellery adorning their lovely long dark tresses. They were a sight for sore eyes. Men, mostly younger ones, arrived all in open horse driven coaches. As they came nearer, they waved to the smiling girls, who threw down roses or carnations to their would-be lovers. It was a very gay and happy atmosphere, nothing sordid about it at all – it gave me the impression of a picturesque student feast. Perhaps that was why they took me to that particular "House".

Once, out shopping with the daughters of the President and two bodyguards, we saw an old man put outside a house like garbage in the street, where he lay groaning. I became immediately distressed that the girls and men stepped over him as if he was rubbish and, being spontaneous, I shouted, "Oh, we can't leave the old man like that!" and then I heard the cry of a baby coming from inside the house.

"Can't you hear the baby crying?" asked the older girl. "The old man is very old. On the street with no food or water, he will pass on much quicker to the path of golden Paradise and there will be enough food to feed the baby. Children are the future in this world and much more important. His life is over."

"Oh," I said to myself, "like the Eskimos!"

After shopping and leaving the President's daughters and body-guards at the Palace, the limousine drove me to the hotel, and as I went in laden with some lovely glitter material in a shopping bag, the Big Boss now, John Wareing, came rushing over to me in the foyer – ordering a valet to relieve me of the bag and take it to my suite.

"Really, Yvonne, you are our star, you my dear cannot arrive in our foyer with a shopping bag. You are not an ordinary guest. "Noblesse oblige" – the chauffeur had to bring that in for you."

"Oh dear," I said apologetically, "even being a full-fledged VIP takes learning!"

I guess the French were right – "Noblesse oblige."

My dear friend John gave me a special "bonus" in Pakistan – a VIP visit to the famous Shalimar Gardens at dusk. It was absolutely memorable! I was met by the boss of the famous gardens, who ushered me through the gates. Then, as darkness fell, all alone as I was in that wonderland, within a minute all the lights and fountains came on simultaneously – just for me. It was breathtaking and I felt like Queen Elizabeth and Cleopatra in one person. That was how Pakistan ended for me, after the bustle and noise of the then business centre Karachi – home of beautiful emeralds.

CHAPTER 120

My First Far East Tour

I must admit, I found the sub-continent intriguing, and after my successful Volkslieder album and many concerts of folk music I received an offer to work for the American Special Service all over Thailand and beyond, sometimes with famous old American film stars like Bob Hope and James Cagney etc. Was I interested? – Yes I was! The agent was a woman and her letterhead had some very long, almost unpronounceable address – but then in brackets: (just by Bangkok Towers Hotel).

I received the plane ticket with the contract and a letter assuring me that she would be at the airport to pick me up. I arrived after 10 p.m.; everywhere passengers were being picked up, and taxis and private cars drove off until there I was at 11 p.m., in Bangkok for the first time in my life, and no one came to take me.

I never flew to any engagement with money, because to my mind every new country was a challenge. I had to come to make money, not to spend it, and whatever happened I always went to the office and took an advance. Now, for some odd reason, I was on my own with plenty of baggage and no pickup. However, I did have an AmEx credit card and above all the will to win. I took a taxi to the Bangkok Towers Hotel and asked them to pay the taxi driver and put it on my bill and went to sleep on a good bed with the idea to find out where this unreadable address of my agent was.

Next morning, I saw there had been flooding in that area, and the address was pointed out to me by the reception. It happened to be an older house that just stood alone in a field, but like the whole area in that vicinity it now stood in at least 8" of water. Not to be deterred, I waded through the flooded field and knocked sharply on the door. Finally, it was opened by a Thai servant. In clear English, I asked for my agent and the servant seemed enough to understand and said her name and the word "visa" and then the name of a neighbouring island, and I had to presume my agent was there to get the visa to return. I was in Bangkok – what to do?

Years before in Tel-Aviv, my agent friend who had made the connection with Mr. Gardiner in Zürich for me had given me a visiting card from a famous young Israeli guitarist who had gone to work at the biggest nightclub in Bangkok, and apparently had been "raking it in" (making a fortune, as we would say) ever since. Years had gone by, and Bangkok was prospering with the American Forces there on R&R (Rest and Recreation). Could it be this guitarist virtuoso was still around? I had no alternative but to try to find out. Somehow, I needed to get to the "Café de Paris" and see, but as a young girl alone – in those days I would never be allowed in.

Not having eaten for quite some time, I decided I looked slim and trim in my white Bikini, with a small frill round the bras and the briefs. I went to the hotel pool and lay on my towel by the side, looking as enticing as I could. Nearby two young American officers were chatting and contemplating what to do that very evening. Sitting up with a warm smile I asked if I could suggest the best place in town was the "Café de Paris". It was a bet like throwing two lots of sixes when playing dice. The men brightened up and said they would be delighted if I could accompany them.

The club was big, exclusive and beautiful, with an excellent eight piece band lead by a good looking guitarist, and I thanked my lucky stars and my guardian angel that on the large blow up placard of the band and obviously famous bandleader was the same name as that on my visiting card.

In the pause, I excused myself and rushed off to see the bandleader. He gave just one look at me and asked if I'd like to be the star of the show doing 99% American numbers, starting tomorrow. The money he offered me was $600 a week. My contract with the female agent who left me standing at the airport alone was for a lot less.

"Yes, Yes," I said without contemplation, "I'll do it."

Next night I wowed the primarily American and English-speaking audience, and I was in.

From Heaven to Hell… Thailand, Laos & Vietnam

After a couple of really good weeks at the best place in town, one night a big blonde woman introduced herself as "my agent." I told her what I thought of her and her lousy set up, and I was doing just fine without her agency. After a thousand apologies from the big German blonde, I started on the special services tour. Anyone who has ever worked for the services knows the huge difference from a concert for the officers or even the NCOs and then a show for an E.M (Enlisted Men's Club). The closer you get to the frontline, the worse it becomes.

One night at an E.M. Club, some white-faced artists came back into our only dressing room frightened to death. It was a couple (girl and boy) with a good dance and acrobatic routine, who were booked to go on before me. They were nice people. The guy stammered, "Yvonne, I warn you don't go out there on that stage – those guys out there are dangerous. They're throwing beer bottles at each other, one landed on stage we had to duck, and then get off quickly."

I had always regarded going out on stage to a difficult public a little like a prize boxer going out to win at a boxing fight. I was, as usual, the closing act of our little show. I said to myself "Let's see who wins, it's got to be me," and with my shoulders squared, my head held high, and a firm belief in my guardian angel being around, I went on stage to face the wild herd.

There was a loud catcall chorus of "Take it off, we wanna see a striptease," and just at that moment a huge American made a loud belching noise and yawned and started taking off his jacket, and that was right in front of the stage, in the very first row. I latched on to it immediately:

"Hey guys," I shouted, "I got competition, look at him, c'mon baby – take it off."

"Take it off," others chanted.

I shouted, "Let's have your shirt and see your hairy chest, maybe he's even got boobs."

The huge man sat down feeling like the uncouth idiot he was, and the guys started laughing and clapping and after a couple of short bawdy jokes, I could do my show and do no wrong. Our show scored top marks, and there was no more beer bottle throwing. In show business quick reactions are imperative.

In one of the officers clubs I met a really cultured and intelligent major or colonel from an island in the Caribbean. When he heard I intended to go right to the front line, he bought me a pillow and gave me a happi coat. He asked me to use these as bed linen, as he had a feeling both would come very much in handy. He was right. The last port of call was some godforsaken hole in Laos, and the Captain excused himself that the only hotel where they could give me a room was "not so nice."

Hm! Hm! Not so nice? It was ghastly! No bed linen on the filthy mattress full of stains. I was really relieved to have my own pillow and happi coat, which I spread out as a sheet. I realised from the smells and the noises the hotel had been a hotel but was now doing its duty for men on the front – it was an glorified brothel. I took out my tin of DDT and made a fence of the powder around my impromptu bed linen.

In the night I awoke to a sort of crunching noise. Switching on the light, I saw a hoard of black bed bugs all around but perfectly stopped by the "kill all" power of DDT.

Even though I was disgusted at the sight, which I can never erase from my memory, I was so tired but I felt as if God was with me and fell fast asleep again.

Next morning after a good American breakfast in the officers' mess, I was taken to the biggest Army Chief who asked me if I would not be afraid to fly over the so called "Green Hell" (wild jungle) in a tiny plane sitting next to the pilot to do a show in my simple African Katanga for the thousands of boys directly at the front. He said he was loathing asking me, but I seemed to be such a "game young lady," as he put it, and he knew the boys would just love me. I would be bringing so much happiness with me.

I said a silent prayer and jumped in the little propeller plane next to the pilot in the cockpit. It was all a marvellous experience, and helped to obliterate the crowd of bed bugs and the night at that horrible whore house. The welcome and cheers of ten thousand men made the whole deal worthwhile. Flying back, looking at all that thick green wild foliage, I knew why it was called "The Green Hell". If anything happened, no one could be saved in such a jungle. I remembered telling Mum as a young girl I wanted to taste the good and the bad of everything our world had to offer, and somehow, I knew that my guardian angel was for sure in the vicinity. Shortly afterwards, safe and sound in Bangkok, I heard I was the last female to be allowed to fly to the front. The Green Hell was finally considered too dangerous for any female artist. Perhaps it was because no other female singer was considered "a game young lady."

These were the most negative sides of my contract with that big blonde agent. The positive side was that I danced with James "Jimmy" Cagney. He was still light as a feather on his feet, but his eyesight was not so good. I guess it was my long dark red wig which looked great and saved lots of time for me, because at first he said:

"Well would you believe it, if it isn't Gypsy Rose Lee."

I was quite amused and enlightened him. I could not believe it either! Bob Hope was a regular with the forces and great at making the boys laugh with his quick responses. He was as bad as Cagney, and announced me as "that famous film star Yvonne de Carlo." This happened a few times also with guys in the audience.

When I quipped at Bob, "The name is Carré," He quickly responded, "Well guys doesn't she look great — I guess she was poured into that gown." So everyone laughed and clapped and forgot his mistake. In a way he was right. I had the figure, even if the bust was helped along with a pair of socks, but I always had to have a helping hand to zip me up at the back. Tight clinging evening dresses were the fashion en vogue and curves had to be in the right places. The other positive side was that along with the Special Service tour was a three-week guest appearance at the Djakarta InterContinental Hotel in Indonesia. It would be my first visit to that country and, as usual, I was curious.

Djakarta – and a Pretty Girl

After my first shock at Dacca with the extent of the poverty and leprosy – which I had til then only associated with biblical days – looking back, I realised I had really enjoyed working for that five star hotel and I hoped Indonesia would be as pleasant. It certainly was! Good Italian bands seemed to be everywhere and that was, for me, an important factor, and secondly the general manager of the hotel was Swiss.

One day two young female students from the local University came to ask me for autographed photos and then offered to go with me to the market where I could buy some real original Balinese wood carvings. The three of us went in a tiny tricycle rickshaw, which as a means of transport was very popular there, but which I had never tried. As we went over a pothole in the road the rickshaw driver lost his balance and we three all fell out. It's funny how an accident shared can bring people closer together. I purchased with their haggling in the local lingo a lovely tray, which I thought could be more useful than a wooden carved Balinese lady. I invited them next day to our coffee shop, where they had their first ice cream sundae and milk shake. They were excited like little kiddies – it was fun to watch them.

I was invited to both of the girls' homes. One had a real bed to sleep on, but again no bed linen; but she was very proud of her bed mattress. The other girl slept with her two sisters in a tiny room in the shack they called home and slept in hammocks which they hooked up when not in use. We sat in the little garden by a canal or river under a big shade tree, and when a large mango fell down, mother announced, full of pride, "Oh good, now we can all have something." No wonder they were all so slim.

Later I invited the two girls to my first show and asked an American business friend to chaperone them. When I got back to my room after the second show, I found him waiting for me sitting on my bed with tears in his eyes. He was crying. It seemed that he, like me, particularly liked the darker young girl, and said, "Oh Yvonne, we must help – such a lovely young girl, having to live under such conditions." I realised then that although he was by far my senior, I had already seen a lot more of the third world than he had. There were no lepers in Djakarta.

"Well," I said, "please don't cry, I will at least try to help the sweeter girl. The other is in her little world a snob, and most probably will stay here, and remain one."

When I left Djakarta, they both gave me a little gift. The brunette, called Lana, made a pretty flower brooch, sewing it on to a safety pin. She confided in me her dream was to live in Switzerland.

"If I were you," I said, "I'd concentrate on improving your English and German, and get a job as a guide to British, German or Swiss tourists as the travel fever is taking hold of many Europeans. Look for a single man and Number 1 let him pay your air ticket. Once installed in any of those three countries, I will do my best to help."

It did not take long before I received a card from that sweet little person.

"God has blessed me, as a guide (as you suggested) here in Bali, I have met a young German, who wants to marry me and take me back to his hotel which is on an island in the North Sea – it is the German Bali."

With all my fantasies and imagination, I could not picture for the life of me any German island that resembled Bali.

The German Bali did not exist, I replied. Later she wrote the lovely island was called Helgoland!

SINGAPORE

After Bangladesh and Nepal, Singapore seemed really Western, and as the general manager of the Park Hotel on Orchard Road was Swiss, I was soon initiated into his family. 90% of the audience were English-speaking, I could joke a little, and Singapore with its flowering bushes and very clean, well-maintained streets and good fun-loving audiences became a favourite for me in the Far East, and thankfully I became a favourite with them and my Folk Songs album did well.

MALAYSIA

Kuala Lumpur in Malaysia followed the Intercontinental Hotel in Djakarta and was the first hotel that had not yet a pool, despite belonging to the Merlin luxury hotels. It was the 60s and not at all ready for the tourist influx as today.

Apart from the lack of a swimming pool, the worst part of Kuala Lumpur at that time was to my mind the lack of control.

My rehearsal with the band was arranged for 1 p.m., but the first musician did not arrive till 2.30 p.m., just as I was "blowing my top" with all the English swear words I could muster.

Finally, at about 3.15 p.m., the whole band was ready to rehearse. When I complained about this terribly lackadaisical art of time keeping, the bandleader looked at me, raising his eyebrows, and said, "Really, Madame Star, we are not in Switzerland where everything from trains to watches go exactly on time, we here are in Malaysia and have to wait often for buses and trains that run one or two hours late. It is a way of life in the East, you have to get used to it."

This K.L has to be put with all the other parts of Kuala Lumpur.

CHAPTER 121

Seeing Stars

It was a time of songs of the sea. Freddy will always be remembered for "Junge Komme Bald Wieder" ("Young Man Hurry Home to Your Mother Who Waits"), and Lolita of "Seemann Lass Das Träumen" ("Sailor Leave Your Dreaming And Come Back To Me") was a simple German girl married to a truck driver. She netted a No. 1 in the German Hit parade – like myself, well before the "Beatles" with their complete change of style. She was a down to earth, simple woman who seemed surprised at her popularity, but she did possess a pleasant deep voice.

After managing to get a hole in one playing golf, it is about as remote a chance as hitting No. 1 again in the Pop charts. My producer came up with a sort of second Mexican Hat Dance called "Gaspar". Seconds are never like firsts, and I certainly felt the Hat Dance era was over, but the 60s was a period where Record Companies sent huge bouquets to their recording artists whenever they appeared in concert halls and top hotels were paid for. We also received good royalties on records sold, but with all this spoiling we had to sing what we were given. The B side to "Gaspar" was "C'est Si Bon", which I personally preferred.

Frank was working on a new label for Polydor (Deutsche Gramophone) called Heliodor. He was trying out all new voices. He was totally enamoured with Heidi Brühl and a real charmeur from Austria called Udo Jürgens, whom Peter Meisel the Berlin Music Publisher had brought for recording and with whom I had been filming in Berlin and who later hit the Jackpot for Ariola with "Merci Cherie".

Frank became a freelance producer and we recorded "Besame Mucho" as a "Bossa Nova", which was the latest South American beat. We called it "Kiss Me While We Dance Bossa Nova" and coupled this with my own composition "Geisha Twist", which made the charts in Europe but not the top 10. However, it did well when I toured Australia after being regularly on TV. I'd brought all the gear from Japan, so it was very visual, although "twisting" in a kimono was not so simple.

Back in Germany I was asked to record all my German hits in English and Spanish.

I was put in one TV show after another, often with Vico Torriani (who would not even pay for my cup of coffee), lots with Siw Malmkwist of "Schwarze Kater Stanislaus", which was invariably fun, and often with film star Bibi Johns, who was also petite like me, but blonde, and her bust was decidedly bigger – she didn't need to use foam! She was a kind person and particular in taking care of the famous blind singer Wolfgang Sauer. A really nice sensible person, who was always gowned in beautifully beaded cocktail dresses, and managed by her husband, was soprano Anneliese Rothenberger. We were very often together in Hamburg. Then there was Lou v. Burgh, a fatherly affable guy from Holland, and Chris Howland "Mr Pumpernickel" who was Mr. British Humour in person. All of these artists were so often together with me and I with them, that and it was a homey good feeling and we greeted each other on big TV and Radio shows like good old friends.

Once on a German TV extravaganza, I walked into the overcrowded dressing room of a load of stars, and Nana Gualdi ("Junge Leute Brauchen Liebe"), who was then the ex-wife of Frank's (studio in Maschen) partner Joe Menke and was together with the Phillips record producer Benny de Weil, was sitting on the only washbasin having a casual pee. When she saw me, she announced with a voice full of awe:

"Freddy is in the other room, he is so arrogant he will not speak to anyone."

That did it; I left the others after greeting Nana and went into the room where Freddy was alone. He looked thoroughly fed up. I greeted him smilingly and said, "Well, well Freddy, "Ohayo go-zaimasu."" ("Good morning" in Japanese). He turned to me with a big smile, as if waking from a bad dream. We both settled down to our Japanese experiences and apart from being a great artist (at that time No. 1 in Germany) he was simply an interesting guy.

Daliah Lavi, whom I worked with some years later, was a special case. Like Lys Assia, she was perfectly rehearsed and never made a slip. Her music was always perfect. She was tall and slim and sported a full-length silver fox coat. She could have easily been a top model. Her voice and intonation reminded me of the equally popular Adamo. Many of the German Producers and Directors at TV seemed to know her intimately as each greeted her with a passionate kiss on the lips and not just on the cheek, which was the norm at that time.

Gitte Haenning was just the opposite, small and with lots of temperament. Frank told me her music was generally a disaster to read, but she had such a definite jazz feeling and was great on stage, so you could forgive her for any lack of perfection.

Rex Gildo was a young gentleman, perfectly groomed and handsome, but always a little nervous, but a very likeable person.

Rene Kollo, on his way down south to his parent's home, would pass by our Swiss home. He played the piano and sang with a natural jazz feeling, but as nobody bothered to get him a really good song, he decided after we had had a long heart to heart talk to cross over the stream and go into Operetta and real classic Opera, in which his father had excellent connections. He really made a big success, and the decision was definitely a good one.

While on the subject of really good classical music, a funny incident happened to me. Dieter Broer had arranged for photographers to meet my train, coming from Frankfurt Airport as I had been such a long time away from Europe. The journalist asked me if I had met anyone interesting on the train journey. I said that I shared the compartment with a very nice man who told me he was also in the music branch, but classical. He was a conductor on his way to Vienna. We exchanged names, and he mentioned his was Herbert von Karajan, but I had been away so long I had never heard of him. I told him I was Yvonne Carré and as I was a pop star would he like a signed autographed photo? The fact that I had no idea that this pleasant personality was the star conductor of the year in the classical world amused everyone in Germany. That funny little incident went around the world press, proving to all I had been away a, long long time.

CHAPTER 122

Hot Spot Beirut

My girlfriend from Swiss Air had already told me about El Hambra, the very chic main street in Beirut that had so impressed one of the chief pilots she knew that he chose to take his bride there for a four-day honeymoon, before both had to get back to work at the Airport in Zürich. His new, young and pretty blonde wife went window shopping one evening together with him. Then fate stepped in, unfortunately; she saw a Versace boutique over the other side of the street, and that got her really excited. Pointing to it, she said, "I'm popping just for a minute or two over the other side, to get a better view."

With that she ran across the road and her new groom became engrossed in a shop with the latest electrical equipment. When he turned around, his bride was nowhere to be seen, and was never to be seen again. Beirut at that time housed many super rich Sheikhs from neighbouring countries, my friend told me. All these men had wads of money in the Lebanese banks, and all owned harems. These wealthy machos, like the Pakistanis and black Africans, adored pretty young blonde women, and the wealthier often hired a large black Cadillac Limousine with tinted windows. The driver had to drive slowly near the curbside and the two men on the back seat were there on the lookout for the right "spoils": a young blonde alone. In seconds the backdoor of the car would open, a black sheet would be thrown over the unknowing captive, and with a gag and quick shot from a syringe, that blonde would be the new prize for a super rich Sheikh.

The story was true, said my friend, and yet I could hardly believe it, so when I had an offer to be the new show star at the Beirut

Intercontinental Hotel from the general manager who was not just Swiss, but from Canton Zug, like myself, I wanted to see this fascinating city. I wanted to find out for myself if it really was such a "hot spot", as she had described it.

The hotel, a super modern high-rise building with 600 bedrooms, was large, bustling and extremely popular, in the middle of everything, and yet on the promenade by the Mediterranean Sea.

After unpacking, a bell boy came to take me to the general manager who turned out to be the nicest of men, the sympathetic fatherly type. After giving me my usual advance, he asked me to make a firm promise to not accept an invitation from a Sheikh from a Muslim country, because he explained these Sheikhs have other ethics when it comes to the female sex.

He then told me that if a girl accepts an expensive gift from such a man, then she is his property, because he regards this act as having purchased her.

"Just recently," he added, "in our best and most luxurious night club by the world famous "Casino de Liban", there was a line of dancing girls from Austria as part of the show. One blonde dancer was asked out to a party by a Sheikh, and accepted also a heavy gold bracelet as a present from her admirer. After enjoying the party which was in a large suite in the Penthouse of a skyscraper she asked the gentleman to take her back to the small hotel which housed all the girls in the show. The Sheikh did not agree, or even allow her to call a taxi.

"He just explained that in his country if a woman accepts such an expensive bracelet as the one she was now wearing, she belonged to that Sheikh, as his possession. When the girl argued and tried to scream two large turbaned bodyguards were motioned to come. The girl was just thrown out of the window. Of course, the police came, and the club was closed for some time, and then money was passed into waiting hands and that was that. These men have no scruples regarding women, who also have no rights in their own laws. Stay with the excellent personnel in the hotel who are all Christians. The wives will be happy to show you around."

I took a deep breath and started to appreciate my friend's words, and that it was not just a figment of her imagination.

Nowhere did I find more warmhearted and welcoming women than in Beirut. All the sweetmeats and the nutty delights I had to try were very sweet but delicious. Sometime later on, I was invited to a party in the home of the Assistant Manager and his very kind blonde wife. I remarked that the Lebanese seemed to still go in for larger families than their counterparts in Britain or in Switzerland.

She replied, "The Arabs are coming into our country from all sides, when we have five children, they have ten, and one day they will overrun us. They have the money and the power. We all at this hotel have Green Cards, so when our death knell sounds, we will all be off on a plane to the States. We love our country but in not so many years, there will be more of them than us. We are true Phoenicians – they are not!" There was bitter defiance in her voice.

Until that moment I had been really enjoying myself, but then I felt a deep sense of sadness and hoped the change would not come too soon.

Already arriving at customs at Beirut Airport I felt my guardian angel was on my side. A tall dark and handsome young officer inspected my baggage. Seeing my passport, he said in French:

"Bonjour Madame Carré grande vedette mondiale de la Suisse – soyez la bienvenue dans notre pays de Phéniciens. When you have time it would be my pleasure as a University graduate, doing this job temporarily, to show you with great pride our beautiful country." This he did with great aplomb – from Balzac, with the wonderful view all around, and the dancers all in their national costumes, doing the traditional dances of the old Lebanon, to the large garden restaurant called "The Arab Table" – where we were smothered with 42 different tiny dishes of Arab specialities. There we could see many Sheikhs arriving with some of their families, followed by some favourite ladies walking behind. It was not a bit like Morocco, where Mum and I had to sit upstairs in the ladies' area, and Dad downstairs with the men. It really hit me then, how good it is to be born in the Western Hemisphere, and not where they still have Harems.

During the shows at the hotel, I shared a dressing room with Nadia Gamal, who was the star belly dancer of Lebanon. She spoke excellent English, as well as French, and she appealed very much to the large American public because, apart from being an excellent dancer, she was slim and aesthetic with no fat wobbling flesh. She was not underage, as sexy little Nana had been in Cyprus, but a woman well in her 30s but with a supple body and graceful movements of a star ballerina.

Owing to the huge influx of Sheikhs we were not allowed to go into the Supper Club ballroom at all, so Nadia taught me a traditional folk song in Arabic, and also to really belly dance properly. I tried to teach her to sing "When I Fall in Love", which was her favourite song. We did all this in between our two shows nightly. Our general manager was really delighted with us both and said, "No programme could be more perfect."

The only drawback was the Coiffeur Salon at the hotel, which was so famous; they refused to give me a special price, so I went daily to a hairdresser down the street, wearing flat shoes and long pants, my trench coat loose with no belt, and a scarf tied round my head. I would avoid the curb particularly when I saw a big

Cadillac with dark windows. I walked as an old maid and did my best to be as unattractive as possible. Finally, the star hairdresser asked if I would pose as a model for a new fantasy hairstyle. I agreed if he would fix my hair for the rest of my engagement. So, I didn't have to do that alien walk anymore, for which I was truly thankful.

When Frank wrote me that he was saving up to buy a new Cadillac, I was understandably not in favour.

I was so enamoured with Beirut, I wanted him to see it and managed to fix a contract at the super large Holiday Inn Hotel for a smaller part of his orchestra and his new "Brazil Tropicado" stage show. Just before he left Europe with the band and stage show, war broke out in the Lebanon and the first bomb that struck a building in Beirut was the Holiday Inn. My God, it had happened far quicker than anyone had thought. I thanked my guardian angel that Frank and his company had not yet left for that unfortunate hotel.

Only now, years later, could I make it up to Frank, and we walked along El Hambra street, admiring some really beautiful evening gowns and cocktail dresses. There must still be some very elegant ladies in Beirut today. It was a real eye opener to all us "casual dressing" women of the Western world.

CHAPTER 123

A Wild Dream Comes True

From the Big Top to the Top Cruise & Top Star BB's Advice.

I seemed to be wanted everywhere and by so many different five-star hotels — but I tried to keep the tropics for our winter and to enjoy the summers in Norway, Sweden, Denmark, and Finland. The latter was the "Linnenmäki" Circus Theatre with top acts. I was generally engaged for the closing month of August, when at the very last show every act tried to do another act they never had done before. Ever since I was a kid I was mad about the Bertram Mills Circus which Dad took Roxane and I to, and which we enjoyed so much every year. I must admit I dreamed of the "Daring young men on the flying trapeze" and wondered what it must feel like. So, when we could choose I said immediately: "let me live a dream — not to fly through the air, but I have strong muscular legs, let me climb to the top." (I love climbing and have no fear of heights.) "I can hang from my knees on a trapeze, and to be different if you can fix a mic up there I'll sing "C'est Magnifique"."

This unusual display of fearlessness and even singing brought the house down and I thoroughly enjoyed it, swinging and seeing the audience from a different angle. Only climbing down those thin little metal sticks, as steps, was the worst part of all, and I and the CEO Mme. Chicki Ekelund breathed a sigh of relief when I felt my feet finally touching "terra firma."

She said, "God help me for allowing you to do that feat — I really thought I may have to visit my star in hospital," and we both laughed, and clinked glasses over a good cognac, not to forget a little ice cream too.

In the meantime, my London agents asked me to be the star attraction on the Cunard Flagship "the Queen Elizabeth" – all first-class treatment, visiting NY and Montreal for the World Fair, and going up the St. Lawrence River at a time when all the Maple Trees were crimson red. It was such a peaceful trip and such an exquisite sight. I thanked Mum, who I was sure was up there helping my guardian angel to get the best for me. Roxane and Herman were living with their two boys in Montreal, so I could visit and stay with them. As Frank had a respite he came on the "Queen" too, and we had time for the World Fair, an experience to remember. It fitted in great, and we saw all the latest shows on Broadway in New York. I also kept a menu just to remind me of how first-class passengers were really spoiled in the 60s. I was back to my days at Lausanne Palace. Persian Caviar was always available and Paté de Foie Gras – and that already at breakfast! My word! As for my accommodation, although balconies were still unknown, each first-class cabin was different to the next. Mine had padded silk or satin walls, in a light rose pattern, a large bathroom, lots of mirrors, a dressing room and a large double bed with a canopy and a pink satin eiderdown. It was beautiful.

Back in Zürich at the in place, "The Tabaris", I was accompanied by the Georgie Auld of Switzerland – Saxophonist Luc Hoffmann and his group. It was where the young set could listen and dance to the best jazz available, and it was great working with Luc and such an appreciative audience.

The most widely read magazine in Switzerland at that time was "Sie und Er", and a photographer from Comet and a journalist were sent to get a story on me. The journalist was out for sensations and had read that apart from ice skating and swimming, I loved rowing. As it was summer, he suggested we hire a rowing boat and I showed him my prowess on the lake of Zürich. Suddenly during the pleasant half hour, he leaned forward and made a wild grab at my hair, which I had left long and open, not elegantly high on my head as was the fashion and the way I wore it on stage. He pulled so hard; I screamed and asked him if he had gone mad.

"Oh no," the journalist answered. "I did just that last week when Brigitte Bardot came to Zürich to help launch her latest film. I knew in her very first movie before she was the Great B.B. she had had short dark hair, so I wondered if that long blonde mane was a wig – and it was! So I couldn't help but wonder if your long dark hair was a wig too."

Later when in Paris, Louis Rey of Radio & TV Genève, who was good friends with BB's private secretary, arranged for me a meeting with the much-loved blonde film actress. When we met, her secretary had briefed her on me. She told me immediately how sorry she was I had to get appendicitis. She was at the time a bit afraid at visiting Germany and almost relieved at the cancellation. I mentioned in an offhand manner the meeting with that Zürich journalist and the rowing boat affair.

BB was just great. She laughed and laughed and turned to me and said, "You know Yvonne it doesn't really matter how you do it – it's the end effect that counts."

A clever after thought, I never ever forgot!

CHAPTER 124

Big Troubles – Mombasa – Helgoland and Hamburg too!

It was a tearful phone call of "Help." Apparently, the nice gentleman in the hotel of "the German Bali" went sour. He expected his new "fiancée" to clean – also in other hotels – and to wear her traditional national dress in the evening behind the bar and later on to be nice to his better clients. My orders came fast and furious: "Get this hotel man to buy warm clothes for you, you'll need boots and a coat for the coming winter, that done, stop cooking or cleaning for him. Then ask for a ticket to Hamburg, where old friends want to see you."

It would have been fine, if I had only some time, but as usual my life was full of happenings and a half normal private life was out of the question.

My big problem now was Mr. Kenyatta, who suddenly decided no "foreigner" could own beach property at Mombasa's best beach, namely Nyali. It was to be reserved only for Kenyans. I got this news in a letter from that huge Punjabi Lawyer and real estate man – he had wrapped up the situation by saying "Don't worry Ms. Carré – I shall sell this lovely property for you immediately." Although a colleague of Amir's sister Gulie, there was something about that hulking personality I did not feel comfortable with. His eyes were too shifty for a start. I knew that Ron and his family were now qualified Kenyans and he was a "big wig" on Radio and TV in Nairobi. Amir was now out of the question as he and his family were Ugandans, and he was fearing the rise of Idi Amin as President there, whom he knew hated the prosperity of the smart and hardworking Indians in his country and indeed in East Africa.

I called Ron, who immediately promised he would buy the property for me under his name (same way how I originally procured Walchwil in Switzerland), when foreigners were on the Not Wanted list. The idea was good, but the sinister lawyer got in quicker. He sold our property without our agreement and confiscated the money. Later I heard from Ron how the lawyer was hated, but had many friends in politics and could somehow do no wrong.

"Right," I said, "they say "you've got to be a thief to catch a thief – surely you know with all your connections one other Indian lawyer who hates this man. He shall get the money paid, from him, and put it in the famous old bank where your wife works – at Grindlays."

When all this was done, I was already back in Nairobi singing at my dear pal Branson's Hotel, then back in Dar at the Kilimanjaro with the Levi family, and then back again to Nairobi, which slowly was becoming a sort of second home – I loved that city with its fresh clean air, that worked like oxygen in the springtime because of its situation and heights.

In the meantime, poor Frank was left alone with Lana and after a couple of nights on our only sofa, he had to be off with his orchestra on various big galas. He had to ask his father, who was rather old fashioned, if he could put up Lana til I returned from Africa and had found something suitable for her.

To get out of this difficult situation he roped in his friend and associate Joe Menke – later also known for his "Truck Stop" group. I had introduced Frank to Joe, as he was often with his "Starlets" singing group together with me and he was a very amusing individualist and particularly diplomatic, and was the owner of Studio Maschen. Frank knew if he asked his father to take in Lana, the answer would be "No way – Mama is away in Thüringen – what would all the neighbours say – me with a young Oriental girl? You must be mad."

Joe clever as he was, with his diplomatic and sympathetic voice, nearly brought Vati to tears over the young girl's plight, and Frank had to work hard not to laugh. Joe was a born actor and comic, and so the strange situation was solved, and thankfully I could get back to Hamburg in time to explain all to Mutti – as woman to woman, and finally I was able to take the young girl back with me to Switzerland, where I was sure I could get her a job as an Au Pair girl with our Gemeinde President, a close and very dear friend of mine ever since our first meeting in his office.

East Goes West

Back home in Walchwil, I was happy to note that our little befriended Indonesian girl was slowly learning our way of life, from making beds to putting on "Strumpfhosen" (tights).

I had to see an old acquaintance in Zürich, who was staying at a good three or four star hotel on the river. He had phoned to ask me to a lunch to discuss business, and if I had a girlfriend it would be good, as he had a man friend staying with him. I took Lana with me. After lunch my business pal and I discussed business, and when I looked for my little Indonesian girlfriend she was lying on the friend's bed, being undressed by this young man whom she didn't know and neither did I. I was shocked.

In abrupt hard tones I said, "Lana, get up, put your clothes on, we're going."

The culprit grinned apologetically and said, "I'm sorry but she offered no rejection to my suggestion."

We left the hotel, but not before Lana got a really hard lesson from me.

"What in the hell did you think you were doing?" I asked brusquely.

"So so so sorry," stammered the young Indonesian "in my country we have to do what a man says."

"Now look," I said sharply, "you are here in the West where women have equal rights with men. You are in Switzerland, and you want to be Swiss – so behave like a good Western girl. Have respect for yourself and your body. Here you can learn to say "No way – thank you.""

In no time, those tired passive feelings had gone. I managed to place her as an au pair in the big chalet belonging to our Gemeinde President (Governer of our village, Walchwil). She went to school to learn the language and more about Swiss cooking and tastes and when she left, she already had her next job at one of the most exclusive restaurants in our canton.

In time she had learnt some superb recipes, which she passed on to me, and I could welcome many business associates from all over the world and surprise them and get them asking for second helpings. In spite of her diploma from the best hospital in Djakarta, only an English or German diploma was recognised, and I encouraged the pretty Indonesian to go to London. Number 1, go to the YWCA and then to do everything to get her English diploma. Number 2, in her free time I advised her to get a part time job near by the (for us) famous Edelweiss Club, where all the Swiss students hung out after English classes to meet their buddies (pals) and get all the information they needed, after which a beer or two at the pub across the road, was considered as the final meeting place, where a pretty exotic barmaid could be an added attraction. There was the best opportunity to meet lots of young Swiss men. The poor ones she should forget – the wealthy ones from a large town should be the target, with her eye on the future and to become Swiss with a British diploma.

My good advice was heard, and after perhaps a year or so Mr "Right" (for that period of her life) came along. I gave her future mother-in-law a splendid picture of Lana's home and family – "gilding the lily" to a degree, and finally she was married to a handsome young blond Swiss from a prestigious family, and I, and probably she too, breathed a sigh of relief.

If you can help people along life's way to find their niche and be happy, this can give those that assist a lot of pleasure. I was delighted with this progress – that at least one Eastern girl could find a good life and fulfil her dream of Switzerland.

The Kenya Battle

Then the letter arrived from Ron saying his Indian Lawyer pal who loathed the big man from Mombasa had been really smart – he actually got the money which Frank and I had paid for the lovely home on Nyali Beach. I was elated and flew into Nairobi because I was told the money was in an Indian Bank under the name of the Indian Lawyer from Nairobi, but not in my name!

"Clever sod," I said to myself – "but don't play your dirty Asian games with me. My Dad was born an Asian too."

I made an appointment with the Manager of Grindlays Bank, and he was a good and forthright man and said, "All the sale of the home you purchased was perfectly above board legally, so bring me here that money your husband sent from Switzerland, and it will be back in your account at the Swiss Bank at the end of this week if not earlier."

I asked if Ron's wife could come with me as a witness, and with great determination we went hand in hand to see Rastan the Nairobi lawyer. He was a canny man and made every excuse under

the sun not to give me the money for the Manager at Grindlays
to transfer back again to our Swiss account. Finally, he said, "Ok,
I'll bring all the money from my Indian Bank to you. Come tomorrow morning at 10 a.m. here to my office and it's yours."

Suddenly I remembered how I got my first Hofmeister Tournée
by telling Mr. Hoffmeister I would not leave his office until he
signed a contract with me. I looked the lawyer straight in the eyes
and said, "Oh no, you may fall off your horse trying to get here
on time. Go and get our money right now or I'll call the police
and have you arrested, because you know as well as I do and the
Manager of Grindlays that what you have done is in truth ille-
gal. Now do as I say – Go now!"

I said all this in my schoolteacher voice and felt a bit like I was de-
livering Portia's speech from Shakespeare's "Merchant of Venice".
Ron's wife was witness. Rastan got up and went – he had no alternative, and within two days the money was back in Frank's
account. Whew, was I relieved.

I proved to myself that once again the early bird catches the
worm. Having cleared up that messy business I had to see about
Dad. He had been thoroughly dependent on Mum to look after him and even needed help to make a cup of tea since Mum
had passed away.

I had cancelled contracts to go to London and look after him and
had sung in London again at the BBC and various clubs; now,
after meeting various ladies in his age group, he had decided to
re-marry our Aunty Maud, who was the widow of a younger
brother, Uncle Sam. All was left to me to sell up the house and
contents as Aunt Maud laid down her part of the deal, from a
brand new big diamond ring, to a mink jacket, to a modern apartment in a new block in the area she wanted. Although I did not
live in London, and apart from Roxie & Herman in Montreal,
all the rest of the family lived fairly near by in London and the

women did not work anymore, everything was left to me, under the motto "Do not Despair, Yvonne is there." I even surprised myself with how quickly I managed to sell up and do just everything myself with only the aid of my sister-in-law, who had been so helpful when I was just starting my career. Now she offered to drive me around as I had no car. I began to feel like some worn out battle axe, going from one battle to another. Summer was on the way, and Scandinavia was calling. I was needed to make some records with Erkki Ertama (the sweet stuff) and Erik Lindstrom (the Rock & Roll stuff, which was becoming very popular). There really was never a dull moment in my life. Thank Heavens I was born a workaholic!

CHAPTER 125

Dar es Salaam

"Dar Es Salaam" means "place of peace," and after I had recuperated with Amir on that "African Honeymoon" after that scathing experience with Elephants in Kenya, I remembered it well. So when I was asked to open Tanzania's first large 5 star Hotel "The Kilimanjaro", and as I was once again singing in Nairobi at Mr. Branson's famous hotel, I was comparatively near at hand and agreed.

The manager and his wife and main staff were Israeli, all from a luxury hotel management company in Israel.

They were a young and innovative team contracted by the Tanzanian government to put the Hotel on its feet for a certain amount of years, teaching the natives how to run and maintain five-star hotels.

Sundays were free and we all went as a family to the general manager's vacation home on a postcard-picture beach. The perfect silver sands, the natural palm trees and little huts with thatched roofs to change swimsuits, picnic or whatever you fancied, the crystal-clear water, which got us diving for sponges and pumice stones among multicoloured fish; it was indeed a paradise.

However, in the Garden of Eden we all know lurks somewhere a snake, although I had never given it a thought.

Coming back to town one late afternoon I decided to look at the general manager's garden, as they had purchased the beach house with a lovely tropical garden themselves. Their little daughter of about three, toddled and ran in front of me. Suddenly, something that looked in the twilight like a branch that was entwined round the trunk of a large shade tree was hanging down by our path.

Suddenly it fell down in front of us and to my horror it was a huge snake. The little girl ran towards it in curiosity. Thank heavens I had a quick reaction; I grabbed the child and made a beeline for the open glass door of the house. Mrs. Levi immediately called the Snake Brigade and in no time, they arrived at the garden and netted the huge reptile to return it to its natural habitat.

Turning to me and Mrs. Levi they said, "You saved the child from a Black Mamba."

Now that was worth a glass of cognac and an ice cream, too.

I returned to The Kilimanjaro three years running. On the last Sunday at the paradise beach, we opened the local English newspaper and were shocked at the headlines: "All Beach Property To Be Confiscated From Foreigners" (The Communists were on the move – a real shock for our Italian band and the Israeli group, and also for myself). It was the end of a very pleasant engagement that had even taken me to Zanzibar, but I guess that Black Mamba was some sort of forewarning of what the future held. However, my time in the beautiful harbour town of Dar es Salaam was not to end on such a melancholy note. The young son of one of the biggest entrepreneurs, with the largest factory producing toiletries and cosmetics, fell in love with me as young and old do often…madly!

Finally, he asked me if he could make love to me, and in next to no time was gyrating up and down next to me in bed, then he muttered in exasperation, "You know the funny thing is I can't feel anything." A terrific feeling of victory ran through my veins – so here it was at last, Dad had preached for years to us girls how important it was to be a virgin. I had asked most men I knew at that time if they wanted a virgin and not one had answered "Yes." After all, I was in London and not in Saudi Arabia! Dad had cut me out of his will when he learnt from that red hot love letter from the headstrong Radio Officer on that Israeli ship that his youngest daughter was no longer a virgin. This had led to one hell of an argument and Dad had even cut me out of his will.

Finally, I told Dad in my usual forthright manner, "I'll live my life as you machos do and I will have a male virgin."

But till Dar, I had never met one. Now here was a really nice naïve guy doing his best to have sex with a pillow and not feeling a thing. I burst out laughing and decided it was time I played teacher to get this really nice young man on the right side of the tracks. He learnt his lesson well and I had my virgin. Oh, I would have loved to see my father face when he read that letter about my male virgin!

Years later I received a letter from the same man, telling me he had taken over the factory and got married. He wrote, "Thanks to you and your lessons I could make my new bride truly happy. No more frustrating sex with a pillow!" A great big smile of satisfaction spread over my face. It's a good feeling making others happy.

My Indian Bonus

Taj Mahal

It's amazing how small our world is in Show Business, but this is also the case in the top jobs in big International Hotels.

I kept contact with Rolf the Patisseur and John the Food & Beverage Manager from Intercontinental Hotel in Dacca.

Rolf, the pastry cook & confiseur, was doing well. The big entrepreneur Mr. Oberoi was so delighted with his sweet meats at his famous hotel, "The Mermaids" in Calcutta, that he asked Rolf to stay in India, and to open the new Oberoi InterContinental in New Delhi. Chatting together, Rolf mentioned me, and Mr. Oberoi asked him immediately for my address. He lost no time in writing and asked me if I would be interested to open his new hotel in New Delhi.

I had never been to India, and the offer was a fabulous one.

John, however, was not too happy in Colombo, Sri Lanka, although the salary was excellent. It seemed he was worried about the political situation and the rising up of the Tamils. He felt he had not come to that part of the world to get involved in wars.

I liked New Delhi immensely; it was very colonial, clean, and very British. Having tea in one of the big old hotels was for me pure delight. Where I worked and entertained, I only mixed with the Indian and British gentry and some well feathered tourists. Ice cream (my favourite food) with fresh mangos was served with a generous coating of pure 22 karat gold! At first, I thought it was a shocking shame to eat pure gold, but I was assured it was terribly good for the bloodstream and the throat, and as I was invariably invited to that delicious and super expensive dessert, I said to myself, "Relax and enjoy it!"

The third delight was that my compatriot Toni, who hailed from Aegeri in Canton Zug, Switzerland, had been promoted to Chief Executive Chef and was so well in with the Swiss Embassy that we were given a Mercedes Benz with a chauffeur – enabling us to visit the world-famous Taj Mahal. Just saying the words "Taj Mahal" brought back memories of my terrible fear of India. Funny how one's fears disintegrate once you are really working in the country you feared. The male sex in the sub-continent and Far East were, at least to me, far more respectful than their Western counterparts.

The journey to Aggra was unforgettable. Firstly we touched Jaipur – a marvellous place where Monkeys are respected and are everywhere. When one jumps on the bonnet of your car with a "plop" and looks at you directly through your windscreen, it's a funny feeling, when you are driving through heavy traffic. As we neared Aggra the land was so barren it seemed to be merely dust. It was hard to imagine that in the 15th Century – the time of the great Maharajahs – Aggra was the great city, the hub of the world. The only thing to stop depression at such vast dreary wasteland – once again God stepped in, and among small bent trees almost too dry for bearing leaves were many peacocks of every hue, brightening up the miserable landscape. Then, suddenly as if from some magic wand, there was the Taj Mahal, shining white marble, glistening in the afternoon sun.

The long straight path and well-kept lawn leading up to that wonder of the world was so exactly as photos and on TV that you had the feeling you had been there before and you had to pinch yourself – it seemed almost unreal. What really impressed me was a part of Samuel Pepys' diary was on display, where he wrote in the 15th century as one of the most travelled Englishmen of that age:

"It is hard to imagine any town in the world richer and more prosperous than Aggra where even the Elephants wear richly bejewelled coats. London in comparison with its poor roads, rickety bridges and smelly river – just cannot compete with so much wealth."

The beauty and perfection of the Taj Mahal in the middle of nothing made us ask ourselves what had happened. Tony had to get back with the Mercedes, so we watched the moonshine on the domes of the master and his mistress and left the answer to the following week, when Rolf and I flew with a small group to Kajarou.

Kajarou

I think I had one of my best lessons not just on India, but on the entire world in Kajarou.

Of course, we had seen some pictures of stone carvings, but as sexy as they may be, nothing could beat Kajarou depicting life at that time among the Jains. There were, on wall carvings, the oversexed Jains, who obviously over ate and drank and fell into such a state of obesity that they had young strong servants who lifted up these obese males, as they could no longer go through the motions of intimate sex. There were displayed in every sexual position giving sexual gratification that Kama Sutra ever thought of – to me really only for acrobats! Our guide stubbed out his cigarette in a rather forward niche of a female pelvis, to express the Jains' disregard for women. There were orgies on walls and also with small horses. It was really something else. The thing that brings down each great civilisation is *excess*. Too much food, too much drink, too much sex and too many drugs – til man loses the will to work and becomes obese and lazy, and the greatness that once was that nation disintegrates to nothing. It has not changed since the days of the great Egyptian culture and the Pharaohs. Since Solomon's wisdom and his hundreds of wives, til Alexander the Great and the Greeks, the Turks with the Sultan's harems, and the Courts of France and Louis the 14th, and the Austro-Hungarian Empire, right through to the huge British Empire. My own father told me it is not so difficult to get ahead in the UK, because this wonderful, enterprising nation has become lazy. It is a real shame, but Western civilisation is falling apart because people want more and more and are willing to give less and less.

Leaving Kajarou was more difficult than we anticipated, and our group were told:

"Your plane to get you back to Delhi has been taken over by Calcutta businessmen. They paid more money than we could afford. You will leave tomorrow morning and spend the night in your room already allotted to you, you may eat at the buffet restaurant."

Later I learnt that if I wanted a place on a plane or train, then I had to have ready a box of cigarettes with a certain money note half showing. This would be taken unobtrusively by the overseer in uniform who would suddenly say, "Oh, yes, yes Sir, your name is here on the list, Madame. Your seat is reserved; please go through to the plane."

Rolf was dismayed that without our knowledge we would be leaving first on the morning plane – he had to be up at 4 am in the hotel to bake breads, croissants, and Danish pastries for the breakfast. Finally, he and I were put on an ordinary night train to New Delhi. What an experience! We shared a sleeper with an Indian businessman who, as was normal, brought along a faithful servant. The businessman took the lowest bunk, Rolf the one in the middle, and I was, as usual, on the top, which I preferred. There was a pretty filthy washbasin and toilet, but with a door. The train, probably from the Victorian days, was a good old steam train fed with coal.

As our bunks were purchased for us by the travel company at the last minute, our sleeping car was fairly in front and when we looked out of the window, which we had to open for air, we were very soon covered in soot.

It seemed to me that half the tickets were paid for and the other half not, as they were only servants and they had to wait till the train started slowly to chug and move away. At this point their masters would help them to jump in by opening the doors of each compartment. Some other non-paying passengers climbed on to the roof and the slimmer, smaller ones were pulled through the open windows. Once on the train they had to set about the luggage and making the beds for their masters. They had to sleep in the dirty latrines on the floor.

Arriving in Delhi, it was once again pandemonium as many climbed down from the roof of the train to pack up the used bed linen and then jump off the slowing down train balancing the cases on their heads. After that feat, they had to take their masters to their waiting chauffeur driven limousines, where they then sat in front with driver feeling most important. We arrived blacker than white – but a couple of lessons of the way of the world wiser.

Ravi Shankar

Bankers, when the stock market does well, plump for bonuses. After the wonderful experiences of monkey-loving Jaipur, and of course the colourful peacocks around barren Aggra and the unforgettable Taj Mahal, and the unusual Kajarao, when Mr. Oberoi was delighted with my shows and asked if I preferred money or something really special, I chose the latter.

Of course, the sacred town of Venares was on my list, with the Ganges and the most beautiful saris in the world.

On the way, quite unexpectedly, at a sacred place I was asked to walk up a hill where a beautifully bejewelled elephant was awaiting me, plus perhaps the most famous Indian musician in the world, Ravi Shankar, the world-renowned sitar player. I was helped up to my seat on the elephant's back, and as the bejewelled giant moved slowly down the hill the great Ravi Shankar accompanied us on foot, strumming some melancholy Indian melodies.

Later Mr. Shankar emigrated to Canada and Amir, once settled in Vancouver, wrote to me full of pride; he was taking lessons on the sitar from none other than the great star sitar player... Ravi Shankar. After some time, the great Indian musician went on to the USA, and for those who are too young to appreciate the soft mystical sounds of the Indian Sitar – you are sure to know the soft wailing sounds of his crooning, piano playing daughter, Norah Jones.

Udaipur

The next special treatment was Udaipur, years before the British actress Elizabeth Hurley, Hugh Grant's pal, wanted to have her spectacular wedding with Indian millionaire Ayun Nayar on that lakeside paradise. At that time there was only the historical old Palace, no tourists – it was a sanctuary for the miniature green parrots, who seemed to have taken over the island for themselves. The palace stood alone on a lake and was beautiful.

At dusk multitudes of the pretty green birds would return, and it was indeed a sight to see.

The room allotted to me was huge. Apart from the large, canopied bed and a neverending number of closets, there was, in the middle of the room, hanging from the ceiling, a big swing, and the ropes were entwined with flowers. I wondered vaguely what Maharajah had enjoyed a swing so much, as to have one fixed in his bedroom. He must have been someone like me.

Delhi

This all occurred on my second re-engagement in Delhi for the Oberoi InterContinental. Of course, New Delhi had that British Colonial touch, beautifully planned and relatively clean. I longed to see old Delhi and finally I did. It was like rolling back 100 years – tiny narrow streets, throngs of colourful natives, and only horses and carts to get from one place to the other. It was worth the courage! One should never let such opportunities go by, but it was nice to know that I certainly did not have to spend that night there.

CHAPTER 127

Vacation in East Africa

Soon Sheraton Hotels had joined InterContinental Hotels in asking for my show; Lord Moyniham was in the House of Lords in London, but loved show business, so he used his royal connections to get his foot in and actually wrote me how he would love to place my show in various five-star hotels – but first I really needed a rest.

I decided to go back to Africa with Frank, this time not building our little "Pad" at Nyali Beach, but as guests at the Mombasa Beach Hotel, the newest top location in that area.

Things had become worse in Uganda, and all the Indians in that land became refugees, and many in Kenya were worried with the new Kenyatta laws that things could become similar. The Aga Khan was wonderful in that difficult situation and did very much to help his sect of Ismailis. Many Indians found refuge in Canada – mainly Vancouver, where the winters were milder, as did Amir and co. (in the meantime he had married and had fathered a baby girl).

He and I had had two short "long weekends" behind us, namely in Paris and London, but now he felt he and his family must flee for their lives. He explained to me how difficult life can be, being an Indian, and he would never dream of bringing me down with him. Although I never heard another word from him, I kept in contact with his sister Gulie, who left for Mauritius with her doctor husband having sent both their children to universities (colleges) in the UK. Idi Amin, as Dictator of Uganda, brought a huge upheaval into the pleasant lives of all folks with Indian ancestry.

However, we had Serengeti on our list, a very dry game park where the pack of lionesses we saw looked very hungry indeed, then the Ambroseli Tent Camp, and finally visiting the Massai in their region.

Ambroseli National Park – Visiting card

While Frank and I were on safari under canvas at Ambroseli National Park, at night we all sat round the campfire, a group of about 20. In no time I got them singing and snapping their fingers and clapping their hands to the popular Hava Nagilah from my Folk Album. A senior man came to me full of admiration. He congratulated me on my little show, which I had ended with "Under The Spreading Chestnut Tree", making everyone join in.

He said with an all-American twang, "That was great and very professional, you are quite a little Miss Show Business. Should you ever be in the Far East, my son is the general manager at the newest and most beautiful Hotel there, "The Siam Intercontinental" in Bangkok. He sure would love to have you as his floor show star." He then gave me his card.

Remembering how sensible I had been to keep the Visiting Card to Nino at the Café de Paris in Bangkok – a wonderful town – I decided this meeting round a campfire at Ambroseli National Park may have been arranged somehow by my guardian angel, and I decided to sit back and wait and see.

Dacca had given me lifelong friends and they were all enterprising. John Wareing, my Yorkshire buddy, had taken on an offer to open a brand new hotel in Colombo, Sri Lanka for Fortes, the brothers who had made a fortune bringing something new to London – milkshakes! – and had never looked back. Now they were branching out into the hotel business in a big way.

My German pal Rolf, after bidding farewell to Dacca, had gone on to "The Mermaids" in Calcutta, and was now on his way to New Delhi once again for the Oberoi chain.

I kept in touch with both by letter. There's a big difference between sleeping under canvas or enjoying the amenities of a National Park Lodge. Each tent had a little table with two chairs outside. an aluminium bowl, and a jug of cold water with a bar of soap if we wanted to wash our hands. As it was only for one night, "to get a feel of a night in the bush as Robinson Crusoe or Tarzan" – that was it.

We were told specifically not to leave any personal belongings on that table, as there were plenty of monkeys around. Til now we had not seen one.

Suddenly we heard shouting and when we went to see what the commotion was about, we saw our crowd looking up at the top of a tent, beseeching a large monkey not to drop or throw the owner's expensive Leica camera, but return it to the little table in front of the tent, where the owner had stupidly left it. The leader monkey was now the star of the show. He looked down at us, baring his big teeth, and literally laughed as he swung the camera (which was encased with a strap) over his head and threw it with all his strength into the thicket around us. As a star of the show, I was perhaps not such a sensation as that big male monkey (it could have been a baboon for all I know), but I believe our little group preferred my show at night around the campfire. One of the gentlemen even offered me a cognac.

A Massai Marriage Proposal

The Massai men looked as I had expected, tall, slim, and handsome in their dark red robes, barefoot with long spears in their hands; they were really very photogenic. The women not at all, carrying their heavy loads of twigs and branches and drying cow dung to fix the roofs of the huts they lived in, and the babies – lots of them, their little faces covered with flies.

Frank and I discovered a tree with wild figs and smothered in monkeys, but suddenly we were not alone and 2 young handsome Massai "warriors" (as they call themselves) spoke to us in English. Years before the film "I was a Massai Bride", I could easily have been one. The older man introduced the younger one to us as "the son of the big Chief here in Massai country," his name was Meidiki. We met and spoke with these two young men. They told us of their lives, and we told them a little of ours. On the third day Meidiki confessed to Frank he had fallen in love with me and wanted to have me as his wife. He even offered Frank 24 first class cows for my hand in marriage, but Frank, with diplomatic aplomb, refused the fine offer, pointing out that he could not accept as he would not be able to get the two dozen African cows through Swiss customs. At the same time, he whispered in my ear he didn't know I was worth that much. As poor Meidiki looked so dejected, he looked down at Frank's beautiful Italian shoes with the pointed toes, which was all the fashion back home and said how he would love such a marvellous modern pair of shoes. Immediately Frank took them off and asked our handsome new friend to try them on. They fit! So, the deal was done; Meidiki did not get me as his bride, but a wonderful pair of Italian leather shoes, and as I had my Cine Camera with me, one of my best shots was Meidiki with his spear in hand and his blanket draped over one shoulder, walking away in his new pointed toe, almost Cuban heeled shoes, into the African bush before disappearing out of sight. Later he sent me two letters to Walchwil in surprisingly good English, which I kept in a file with my African souvenirs.

CHAPTER 128

Hong Kong Adventures

"Stop or I'll Shoot"

Hong Kong is a place most of us who enjoy travelling this world want to visit, and I was no exception. My album of International Folk Songs was available and the general manager of the Hilton on the island had purchased my album and was interested in engaging me for his renowned supper club at the top of the tower called "The Eagle's Nest".

When some famous "Lion" from the International Lions Club in Delhi wanted me for a weekend Gala at the "Mandarin", and the air ticket was paid, besides my fee, I had the time, and began to really enjoy my life in the East. Compared to Europe it was easy. The bands in the Far East, I discovered, were not Italian, as was the case in Africa or Pakistan, but all Philippino and were really good. They enjoyed giving me a background chorus and above all, for me, spoke really good English. Shows in Asia were pure pleasure. When the general manager heard from me at the then voted "best hotel in the world", the "Mandarin", he immediately gave me an irresistible offer for his "Eagle's Nest" at the Hilton. He was also awaiting a large ship from the States, full of ex-servicemen who wanted to show their wives Hong Kong and the famous hill or mountain at the top, where much-loved Hollywood movies like "Love is a Many Splendoured Thing" and "But the Wind Cannot Read" were shot.

After the "Mandarin" I was taken to a "Food Palace On The Waters" – where happy pairs were put on thrones and crowned "King and Queen" – at least for the photographer.

Being back on the Hilton Circuit was also great, as that time there was no InterContinental Hotel Company in Hong Kong. For my show I used just a spotlight for the intro of a song, often getting more lights later on, particularly if I wanted audience participation. I had been asked to sing "Hava Nagilah" by a party of 20 businessmen from England and the USA, who had come to Hong Kong because the exorbitant salaries the Trade Unions were asking for workers in the clothing industry were killing their businesses. They planned to give the new designs etc to various factories in Hong Kong, so that was the beginning of the Chinese era.

It was towards the end of my show and I only had the spotlight on me, and the supper club was in its usual subdued lighting. I started snapping my fingers and in a low voice started with the intro. I'm sure I had only sung 8 bars of the very popular Israeli folk song "Hava Nagilah" when a big man in a dark shirt stood up with a gun pointed at me and shouted, "Stop it, stop It or I'll shoot!"

I realised in one wild moment I was in a direct line with the killer. I don't mind admitting it, I froze! Before I could think twice, the lighting man did it for me; in a second the room was plunged into complete darkness and someone grabbed me and pulled me behind the curtains at the back. In seconds all the lights went on again and there was a buzz of excited people talking. Two of the security men had gone to the killer's table and I was told hurriedly it was the Ambassador of Egypt, who regarded an Israeli song as a personal affront.

I went on stage again after telling the Food and Beverage Manager I wanted to meet this gentleman from Egypt after my show. I told the audience and the 20 men who made the request that "As an artiste I have no interest in politics. The song I wanted to sing may be from Israel, although it is a Hora and that dance originates from Hungary and possibly the Romani. The words are absolutely non–political and mean "Come on comrades, let us dance together and be happy". It is a folk song which has caught on all over the world and without any biases. I do hope you will all join with me now and snap your fingers and clap your hands to the music. As for the gentleman who wanted to stop me, I shall be happy to join his table amicably after the show, but I hope right now he will join in too, with us. If he would like me to sing a happy Folk Song in Arabic, I shall do this with pleasure after I have had a proper rehearsal with the band."

Everybody clapped and shouted, and after the show I met the Ambassador of Egypt, who was so ecstatic with my offer that he reserved right away a table for 22 Arabic friends to see my show two days later. The management was delighted – they had not reckoned that a British singer could sing Arabic and do a belly dance too.

Needless to say, I had to engage the band for a rehearsal the following day and they were impressed. My ambassador was so delighted with me that within the week he made me a proposal of marriage. He promised me a Mercedes Benz with a chauffeur always at my disposal, a big house with servants in a fine suburb outside Cairo and an olive tree in the garden, which naturally secures the fertility of the mistress of the house so I would be blessed with many healthy children. Ye gods!

It would have been pointless to tell the willing bridegroom I was already married and had no desire to practise bigamy. Apart from that, I was not fond of olives or what they apparently stood for. I had chosen freedom! I left the table and asked the restaurant manager to tell the VIP I unfortunately had another engagement elsewhere and I had to be on my way, but I wished him well even though I could not accept his kind offer. My contracts would not allow this. I thought it sounded better than to say my husband would be flying in to Hong Kong the following day and would hardly approve of me accepting another marriage proposal; plus, pistol-packing men, like olives, never were my cup of tea!

Cherry and Boys Nite Out

The journalists in Hong Kong were great. Some knew me from Australia; they were a real cool bunch, and we were buddies, particularly when I informed them I liked Hong Kong so much my husband would be flying in direct from the recording studios in Hamburg.

"Well, he must have a night out with the boys," they said in chorus, and were probably a bit surprised when I was all for it.

"Of course, I'm working in the evenings," I said, "so I think that's a splendid idea and a real fair deal – as long as he lets me know how everything went off," I added with a big grin and a wink.

Next day he told me he had chosen the pick of the bunch; she was called Cherry and she was doing that remunerative job because it was the best paying and she had to see her brother had a really good college education. Later on, he could then get a good job to be able to support a family and perhaps his parents in old age, too.

"What about you?" Frank had asked.

"Oh, I am a woman," she said, as if Frank had thought for a moment otherwise. "For us, it's not so important in Eastern laws – the son or sons must look after the aged parents. The daughters lose their family name on marriage and live in the town and house where the husband wants to be. We are not like the Western women who have rights."

"Oh my God," said Frank "isn't that awful?"

"No," Cherry smiled "you get used to it and it's much better than working in the rice paddies day in, day out and having to do non-stop what you are told and to please the planters, too."

"Oh," said Frank vaguely, "I never thought of that".

Funnily enough, just to prove how small the world was, when we went for a walk, we decided to go out for a snack and not go back to the hotel to eat. He hailed a taxi, a pretty girl got out and smiled at Frank, and we got in.

"She was nice," I said, "Had you seen her before?"

"Yes," said Frank, "that's why I said good evening – that was Cherry."

"Oh, good for you," I said. "You'll be wanting to go out with the boys again. Boy, you've sure got a good taste."

Frank left for Hamburg and the studios and so did I, quicker than expected – the cruiser ship bringing all those happy American servicemen and their wives or families hit an old war mine and the ship sank. The hotel had emptied out, being booked for them. There were only a few rich Chinese left, who at that time only had an ear for their own Asiatic style music. I immediately got in touch with the general manager at the brand new Siam InterContinental Hotel in Bangkok, whose Dad I had spoken with while on Safari at Ambroseli Tent Camp. Once again, I had kept the visiting card. The answer was positive:

"Do come – I've heard so much about you." My departure from Hong Kong was positive too – I was paid in full until the end of my contracted engagement. I had done some promotions for my Folk album and some TV, and Frank and I had had a great time – what more could I want?

Best of all, I finally persuaded Frank to fly back, with a really beautiful painting of Hong Kong depicting the sunset with red skies, red water and sampans, and all the electric lighting on the many high-rise Buildings. Admittedly it was with a very heavy frame.

OK, Frank had baulked at the idea – but after such a good holiday and such good nights out with the boys, how could he resist?

Bangkok I'm On My Way

If there were lots of millionaires in Hong Kong, where shopping had been a paradise and every café and restaurant had its own Philippine band – there were still a few millionaires from Germany, USA and the UK left over in Bangkok.

Perhaps my biggest trophy at the Siam InterContinental Hotel was that during a conversation with the American general manager – son of that nice senior man who had given me his visiting card while we all sat round the camp fire at Ambroseli – we spoke of John Wareing, who had won a scholarship to Cornell University and was considered an outstanding student with diplomas.

"I could really do with a super guy like John to help me here. Do you think he'd consider coming back to the InterContinental chain?"

"I do think he would be happy to return if you used the right diplomacy," I said, smiling.

John came to Bangkok and from that day on he never looked back. In a short time he was made the CEO for all the hotels in Pakistan, and later the Far East and even Polynesia. Finally, he came to Australia Southern Cross in Sydney, and then was chief for that entire area. John and I remained friends for life. His homes in the Surfer's Paradise area were works of art. It's funny how little me singing round a campfire in Africa could change other people's lives so much.

The Siam Intercontinental Hotel was the prettiest hotel imaginable, with a lovely garden, a pond, a boat and an arched bridge; the

hotel was all in typical Thai style. There was also a small zoo –
it was very special and not like any other hotel I had ever seen.
The hotel was not planned architecturally for shows, so I did a
floor show to the international public, some tourists, and many
wealthy businessmen. During my engagement there, a wealthy
German businessman invited me on a private boat, to glide down
peaceful canals to far off parts where no tourists had ever been.
Somehow, I fit into the scenery, and many Thais thought I was
one of them.

After my engagement in Bangkok, I stayed in Germany and
Switzerland just long enough to promote my "Jet Set Album".

CHAPTER 129

The Price of Fame – The Chancellor, the President, and the Rapist!

Helmuth Schmidt (who was the much loved and admired chancellor of Germany at that time) chose me to sing for the opening of the European Congress in Hamburg. There were 7 European countries involved and I was asked to sing a favorite song for each of those countries. After my show, a picture was taken of Chancellor Schmidt thanking me. The fact that we looked into each others eyes swept Germany and made the front page in every popular newspaper. They forgot to mention that his equally loved and admired wife, Loki, was standing nearby and smiling. The journalists fabricated a new flirtation for the Chancellor and "show star" me and the newspaper sold better than ever.

Similarly, a year or so later, our village of Walchwil got into the news once again because the new Swiss President, Hans Hurlimann, hailed from that pretty area guarded by Mount Rigi on the lake of Zug. A big celebration was arranged to celebrate Walchwil's 700th Birthday. I gave him my Jet Set Album, and he gave me a "thank you" kiss on the cheek. There again the press forgot to mention I was sitting next to him and his wife as guests of honor, but a kiss or an admiring stare always seem to get journalist's imagination going in the direction of sensationalism. Whatever it was not – it was positive! Such news is good news and agents and managers wanted me all over.

I returned from a Far East tour, when I even found a couple of free days for Cambodia and to be able to visit Angkor Wat, only to find my garden so overgrown that it resembled a poor relation to that temple. I immediately put an advert in our local "Amtsblatt" for a strong man gardener who could help.

A man arrived with two small children, one on each hand. He told me he lived on our road, which was extremely long. He explained he was a neighbour and family father and needed the job. He started down the thicket, which seemed intent to cover my home immediately. As I am a born optimist, I planted myself some flowers and told him to weed as much as possible as I had to be on the road again and in the air. When I returned full of hope, the family man "from down the road" had pulled out my new plants and left the weeds, which were really doing well.

In exasperation I told the would-be gardener to go and never come back again.

That very evening, I got a call from a friend of my dear television cooking pal Holger Hofmann whom I had met at a cocktail party, saying he had to stop over the weekend and asking if he could invite me to the Swiss Chalet Restaurant in Lucerne by the Lion Monument. I had never been there and managing Frank's Orchestra and show and my own had kept me too busy to even find help. Frank was topping charts for big band music on albums and neither of us had any time at all.

After my host had finished our excellent meal at that famous Lucerne restaurant, my big Hamburg businessman, who was obviously a good friend of the owner, was asked if we would care to have a look at the kitchen. I was delighted, so with an extra glass of Chateau Neuf du Pape we finally left the Swiss Chalet much later.

As we arrived to Walchwil's little "Harmony" there was discord. I was surprised to see no welcoming lights turned on, so I jumped out of the car and into the garage where I could switch them on to see if they were working. The lights went on. Dieter Jansen, the big Hamburger, gave a shout of exclamation.

"Look, the grating going down to the floor below is up! Oh, my dear it seems to me as if your home has been broken into.

You have a look upstairs to see what is missing and I will have a look downstairs."

All seemed exactly as I had left it, and my mink coat and stole were still on the next floor in the wardrobe. Suddenly I heard Dieter say, "Come out, come out, whoever you are."

I was so shocked at the thought that some robber could point a gun at my host, I rushed downstairs hoping to stop any violence. Then to my horror apparently from behind the armchair in my bedroom came my bedraggled would-be gardener, so highly drunk the stench of the alcohol nearly knocked me out. Dieter had seen a half of a man's foot protruding from the armchair.

Taking over the situation like a police officer of the highest order, Jansen said, "What are you doing here in Madame Carré's bedroom hiding?"

The little man stuttered, "Please don't call the Police, I didn't steal anything."

"What did you want?" asked Dieter.

Then came a horrible laugh form the culprit, and pointing a shaking finger at me he said, "I only wanted her."

That was enough to send shivers down my spine. "Oh, my God," I whispered; all this horror in lovely peaceful Walchwil.

"Please don't tell the police," stammered the man.

"Get out," shouted Jansen.

The intruder did, but not through the grating.

I begged Mr. Jansen to stay in my guest room and the next day our President of Walchwil immediately got in touch with the police; as he told us, the whole family was bad and the oldest brother was in jail on manslaughter, and he would breathe a sigh of relief to rid our village of such garbage.

The police, as usual, went on the side of that would-be rapist, asking me if I would not like to take back my claim; after all he was a family father. As he had stolen nothing, it was only "Hausfriedensbruch" – someone who broke in stirring the peace of our home.

I was shocked when they said "It's very disturbing for us that a famous and beautiful young woman like yourself should be here alone. Can't you have a good police dog?"

"What, with all the flying I have to do?" I commented scornfully.

"How about a bodyguard, if you don't want a gun?"

I decided on a Tear Gas Spray.

When I phoned Dad, he was very shocked and annoyed. "My girl, when your husband is so busy he has no time to protect you, then get a bodyguard," he almost spat. It was a command.

I could hear Aunty Maud in the background saying, "Traveling in the world alone – it really is a dangerous thing – she must get help."

I looked up at the trees and the sky and said, "Guardian angel, thank you for sending me this invitation from such a stalwart friend as Dieter Jansen."

As that little man got such a mild penalty for breaking the peace, I took the sticky situation into my own hands. I fixed all the gratings and locks and went to the biggest, most widely read newspaper in Switzerland, the "Blick" (similar to the German "Bild"). I told them Frank was coming to Switzerland with his famous Orchestra and Brazil Show, and then I said emphatically, "and I am looking for a bodyguard." So, Whitney Houston was not the first singer who needed protection. The editor asked me for photos and the next day the news broke that Frank Valdor was coming to Wollishofen, plus a few descriptive lines, but there was a big sexy photo of me with my red wig on and showing an awful lot of thigh in a costume I'd purchased at Carnaby Street in London and had never worn after that photo session, because I had found it too daring and not quite the thing for an international singing star. However, it *was* the thing to cause a sensation and get that would-be rapist out of our village. The heading was "Who Wants To Be Her Bodyguard?"

I got the warning "Get out before you are bombarded by men and boys." I took refuge in the Tessin till the sparks had died down. My neighbours told me there were Rockers, Harley Davidsons, but the most hilarious was a big cat dompteur, Rene Strickler, who later had his own wildlife park in Switzerland. Finally Frank Valdor took time off and we chose the 6 most likely entrants, and the winner was a handsome, well-dressed guy whom Frank felt was most suitable. He drove me to meetings etc. and soon decided that show business was the hardest business in the whole world – and then he turned out to be the son of a famous Swiss millionaire, and he only went into the competition to be my bodyguard because he had a bet with his girlfriend that he would win, and he did!

My next bodyguard was the light director of the biggest and most popular "Moulin Rouge" in Vienna. He was 1.94 metres tall and had been a Green Beret, which apparently means a very daring and sportive young man. He was clever and musical and, after taking a course in business management, also a smart manager. So finally, I had for the next three years a man who could not fight "big cats" and who was not a multimillionaire, but really was a damned good bodyguard.

CHAPTER 130

"Good Lord!" – Lords Tour

Lord Madison from the British House of Lords was another Lord with a weakness for show business who put his good connections to use. He wrote me that he had heard of my success over the world and asked if I would like to work with him for Tel-Aviv and some West African luxury hotels. I said why not? Israel had changed violently since I first arrived to sing there, and even in May the weather was not anywhere near as hot as it had been a decade ago in March. The tree planting had made a huge difference, and when I flew in from Switzerland it was hotter in the Alps than in Israel.

Fortunately, various TV directors were present at my show at the "Magic Carpet" at the Sheraton Hotel in Tel Aviv, so that on my return home, there were several interesting offers. The general manager at the hotel was a Canadian called Glenn Brewer, who had formerly been a "Song and Dance Man" himself. As usual for me, I asked for an advance on my salary on arrival. However, against all odds it was Friday night and already the Sabbath.

The man sitting at the desk in a perfectly tailored light blue suit was the spit image of famous British film star David Niven, and his blue eyes had that same quizzical look that Niven had in the much talked about movie "Around the World In 80 Days".

"Come along young lady," said a warm and cultured voice, as he stood up to greet me. I realised he was quite a lot taller than his famous counterpart, and the voice did have a slight North American twang.

"Oh my goodness," I said, "I really thought for a moment I was confronted with David Niven."

The general manager smiled pleasantly and in no time, I was given an advance on my salary and he told me he had spent about 20 minutes at my rehearsal – and he was impressed.

If you can judge a man by his wife, then this man had my respect. On my opening night the general manager's wife seemed to float into the "Magic Carpet", tall and slim with shoulder-length blonde hair, wearing a white flowing evening dress – I was impressed – she could have easily been a famous model. Her name was Paula and I later found out she had been the boss' secretary and was originally from Saskatchewan, from where my first pen friend hailed. The main town there was Regina. The fact that I knew quite a bit about her hometown, which most people had never even heard of, gave me a flying start to our friendship, which was also mainly through letter writing and has lasted til today.

The Sheraton engagement in Tel-Aviv was a rip-roaring success. The public there seemed to enjoy my "Let's have party and some fun" attitude and they even all got up and followed me and the band into the parking lot at my matinee show on a sunny Wednesday afternoon. We did a conga line. I had learnt a lot about promotions and had phoned a few newspapers, knowing they generally liked something a little different. The idea did well, and Lord Madison sent me tickets and contracts for five-star hotels in Lagos, Nigeria and Accra in Ghana.

In Nigeria many women wore the burkha, which I thought was awful until I had the opportunity to talk to some ladies who spoke English. It was for me an "eye opener." I found the idea of being imprisoned in a black burkha absolutely ghastly, but to those Muslim women, not at all.

"No one needs to know the figure in the burkha is you," they explained. "A new pair of shoes on your feet, and you can meet your lover, and no one is any the wiser."

Television and movies have changed many women's ideas about their lives. Falling in love was primarily thought to be the stuff to build ones dreams on for books and cinemas, so when the husband your father chose for you had to go away for a few days on business, what fun you could have, away from all the prying eyes and malicious twittering tongues, under the cover of a big black burkha.

From Muslim Nigeria to Christian Ghana

Moving on to Accra, I did many concerts all over Ghana – lovely people, and a lovely country. I also learnt bodysurfing in the big Atlantic waves and was quite surprised at my aptitude. If West Africa seemed to be devoid of wild animals, there was certainly no dearth of mosquitoes and cockroaches. The audiences were just fine and the general managers, mainly from Great Britain, knew how to treat a star. Large ballrooms and good electrical equipment were also part of the deal. They do say "travel broadens the mind" – after all those tours, mine must be very broad indeed!

CHAPTER 131

German TV / Sex Bomb – Me

Once back on home ground, Frank set about making a new album for me and I was asked to join a TV show called "VIPS of Song", which turned out to be a lesson in sex. Germany was showing its clout, and famous stars from Hollywood were becoming more and more popular on German TV. Our show had the predominant blonde actress trying to oust Marilyn Monroe, and I think everyone knew, with all the publicity, that she slept in a rose-pink bed shaped like a heart. The actress from Hollywood was Jayne Mansfield.

It was not a bit unusual at the end of the marathon show that we walked downstairs one after another and took extra applause for the finale, and then we all stood in a line and there was a fade out and the names of producers, directors etc. were shown. I was allotted the step just above Jayne Mansfield, and from there I had a bird's eye view of the décolleté of her evening gown. I took my usual photograph in my mind at what I saw. I must point out that busts were "en vogue" as "La Lollo" – Gina Lollobrigida – had such publicity, that worldwide, busts were *in*. What I saw was a boned bodice with thick foam at the sides and a large platform of foam underneath. Although Jayne Mansfield was at least a good half a foot taller than me or more, her bust was just as small as my own. They rested happily on the built-up foam, giving the small grapefruits the impression of being melons! From that day on, all my new stage gowns were made a little differently – I too became a sex-bomb!

Flying High for Frank Valdor,
Myself And A Few Others

As I flew home with a bundle of contracts for the biggest hotels in the world, Frank said it was time I hired my own jet so I could take on all my engagements. My album was called "Music for the Jet Set" and it never ceased to amaze me how many there were in that "Jet Set." I posed for the cover in a tight red sweater, black hotpants and white boots by a Commodore Jet at the Limess Business and Private Jet Center at Zürich Airport. At that time, I did a lot of private jetting, until one day a Swedish guy promised me he would get me to my next engagement quicker if I would fly with him in his plane, a two seater.

We ran into heavy fog, and I couldn't stop thinking about how the Onassis' son had crashed in such a small plane. Fortunately, we made it, but I promised myself that that was the last time I wanted to fly in such a small private plane, in spite of my adventurous spirit.

"Pepito" was not just a big boost internationally for me, but also for Frank. The boss of the biggest record company in Zürich asked him to do the orchestrations of a series of famous American Evergreens to be played in Jukeboxes, especially for albums – a very new idea which caught on like wildfire all over the United States. Those albums were strictly instrumental, but I would sing to him the exact melody as my own repertoire of evergreens ran into thousands; having started at age four was indeed a great help. As is usual with great ideas, other record companies followed suit, and Frank returned to Hamburg, where the German market was really taking off. Dave Miller, a smart American businessman, knew of Frank's excellent music in the USA and asked him to join forces with his partners. The Album "Dance Party with Frankie" (on which I did 4 vocals, wrote the words and some of the music) became a best seller, and Dave established a new label exclusively for Frank called "Somerset". The promotions were great, he was named "The King of Dynamic Party Sound," his lively happy music set a trend for parties and his long-playing records were sold and played at every mega store on the continent and in Scandinavia. T-shirts, blow up cushions, and table mats with his bearded smiling face printed on them were all part of the promotions drive, and he sold more records at that time than his Hamburg compatriots Bert Kampfert and James Last, both of whom I had worked with previously – great guys! Oddly enough, Hamburg composers all seem to be very quiet individuals.

Fact was, the record company wanted Frank Valdor to appear on television and on stage. They roped me in to help. Frank could write groovy big band arrangements and compositions seemingly overnight, but he was shy, not a dancer or a showman. I had to find a solution.

His girlfriend choices seemed to be getting darker and darker. The present one was truly black and had been a good-looking Tassel Dancer. I suggested it could be good for her figure to dance again, and if she could bring in her earlier show partner Bene, who ran a Brazilian dance school in Brussels, perhaps he could arrange some other Brazilian dancers who were willing to travel and rehearse.

Frank and I flew to Las Vegas for first class stage materials and requisites. Rehearsals started, and in no time I was made the manager, had 2 secretaries, and apart from my own show was directing his tropical show too. I was flying around the continent making contacts and contracts. Frank's big breakthrough was a huge TV spectacular, "Brazil Tropical". He engaged his good friends "Los Paraguayas", who were also extremely popular, and added 4 girl singers as a backup group – no blondes for his show, but dazzling costumes, tropical music and the beautiful black girl dancers was something new. His Tropicado shows took off with a bang. Even the musicians wore South American style clothes for the show. It was trendy, it was different, it was a big success, filmed at the huge Market Hall in Hamburg. It was shown all over the world. When we arrived in Israel at Lydda Airport (now named Ben Gurion Airport), the stewards and air hostesses stood in line to get Frank's autograph, as his show had been on TV just the night before. Many remembered "Geisha Twist" and my version of "Sukiyaki" too, in spite of my new blonde hair. Israel, similar to Italy, had seen us both on TV so that meant "no rest for the wicked," and slowly we went further afield where no one knew us.

My sister phoned me from Montreal to say that all the big stores in Quebec were playing my version of "Pepito" and even announcing my name, probably because it was French. At the same time, it seemed Frank Valdor's version of "Una Paloma Blanca" was getting a lot of air play and both of us were wanted for radio and TV interviews. We had to cut that short, as Frank had to be in New York and I had already booked a short holiday in Barbados for us, which Signor Rima, the boss of the Kuoni Travel office in Zug, had suggested. I worked a lot with Signor Rima – Marco Rima's dad – who arranged all the flights, not just for me and my pianist or guitarist, but also for all the musicians and dancers coming from various countries for Frank Valdor, slowly, with 42 persons and technology. One day Sgnr. Rima confided in me his son Marco wanted to give up his job as a teacher and to try his hand at being not just a semi pro with his partner but a professional comedian, and what did I think?

I said, "He is still young – let him try at least for a couple of years."

"But a teacher is a good job and there is security – but on the stage there is none," argued Mr Rima with a shrug.

"But a teacher can never become a big star and make people laugh like a good comedian, its wonderful if you can make people so happy, I've heard he is really good – let him try to become a mega star." …And he did! Our "Zuger" Marco Rima.

Frank and I relaxed in Barbados and then returned to Miami, and that started off another interesting part of my life.

His TV show was shown in many countries. He was asked to do a special album for Scandinavia which really scored, the more-so I guess as on the cover there was a smiling happy Frank Valdor, and why shouldn't he be − on either side was a pretty blonde naked to the hips. Very sexy, but the songs were not at all sexy, mainly Scandinavian folk songs.

Back home as a Jet Setter

Apart from the Beatles and Lady Beaverbrook, I think the 60s and 70s were a 100% Jet Set epoch. Gunter Sachs was for sure the playboy of the day and seemed to be almost everywhere. He engaged us in big galas. The Badrutts in St. Moritz were lovely people, and while it was in family hands they had some marvellous gala nights. One of the most memorable was a Snow Bail Night. The whole area was lit up with flaming torches; many arrived on Skis or horse driven coaches. It was fun to sing at such galas. Others were with big shows and, being befriended by the family, a year later I booked in Frank's new orchestra and did a spot myself, along with my wonderful Japanese guitarist. Tropical music and costumes made a stunning contrast with the snow and mountains as a background.

It was well before the mass tourism which so affected Africa and the Far East but also the mundane St. Moritz.

CHAPTER 132

Amsterdam

Holland was one of my favorite countries. It was definitely mutual. I liked those friendly, warmhearted people, and they seemed to like me. I appeared there often, many times in re-engagements and much on radio and television, at that time VARA and AVRO, the former in a starlight specialty show just for me. The musicians were great, even though the weather was often windy, cold, and wet. In Scheveningen, I had to change my room because of the stormy weather, and that at the height of the summer in August.

One of the last nightclub dancehalls with a show was the famous "Blue Note" and my placard was all over Amsterdam on the "What's On" towers. The tourist audience was good, and everything was fine; the only drawback was my last show was at 3 a.m. and I am more of a "morning person" for breakfast, not to sing.

Frank came to visit, and as I was still young and slim, he would buy some wonderful creamy marzipan pastries and the morning paper from Hamburg to greet me for breakfast at about midday. To keep myself awake at night I made it a habit to drink strong double mocha cups of coffee at the bar, where the crowds were finally thinning out at 2 a.m. There I had a regular rendezvous with three very well-dressed Dutch gentlemen. We got on like a house on fire and I was always curious to see what smart new rings or suits one of them had on, and they would admire my sapphire jewellery from Bangkok or my emerald and diamond ring from Karachi, or my dress, if I was wearing an evening dress they hadn't seen before. We became "Bar Buddies" and their English-style sense of humour was good.

One morning, having our large cream pastry breakfast with coffee, Frank let out a "Well would you believe it, and we were in the same class at school."

"What's that?" I asked.

"Oh, the King of all Pimps," he said with a chuckle. "Apparently he made a fortune dealing in women and has grand homes in Spain and Monte Carlo. Not bad going, eh?"

Full of curiosity I asked, "How do you know, if you meet a plausibly pleasant man, if he is a pimp or not?!"

"Well," answered Frank knowledgeably, "they are generally middle height and very shrewd when it comes to knowing what women like and how to please them. They are smart and ruthless businessmen and love to be well dressed. Normally they wear big "klonkers" on at least two or three fingers."

"Aha," I said, "that's interesting."

That evening everyone at the club seemed to be agog with the frontpage story on most newspapers about the "Super Pimp." I spoke to my three bar pals about that story and I added in my naïve way, "Frank said you can tell a pimp because they are all well dressed and like to sport big rings."

With that, six hands suddenly disappeared under the bar, and I felt like a complete naïve idiot. After that I drank my double mochas in my dressing room and never at the bar.

Once, earlier on in the evening at that famous bar, I noticed one particular lady with a slight slant to her face of the Far East. She was obviously a regular and was always quietly dressed. She seemed to prefer quality to the bright fashionable trends. After some time we got talking, and she told me how much she enjoyed my show, so I asked her what her job or profession was.

She looked at me and smiled and said, "Why, the oldest profession in the world. We all have a room for this at the hotel across the road. It's a very practical job and brings in the "lolly.""

With intense interest I asked her, "How did it all begin?"

"Oh," she said, having heard my story of my Indonesian experiences. "Over there, as you know yourself, there was no future for a woman if you are not from the top ten thousand. You had no choice and no way to make enough money. I had one friend who had already landed in Amsterdam and was doing well. At first, I had to drink some whisky and be a bit tipsy to be able to slip into that profession, but in time I got used to it and learnt a lot. Now, after many years, I could tell my husband to throw in his factory job. I had enough for us both. We moved to an uptown area in our own house. I now have a baby son and a nurse for him, and no one knows just how I bring home the bacon," she said laughing.

At that moment a really handsome ship's captain in his outstanding white uniform came over to us and offered us both a drink. Of course, she chose the best champagne, and I had to leave them for my next show after wishing them a pleasant evening.

After my show I was surprised to see my new Indonesian acquaintance once more alone at the bar, looking quite disgruntled.

"Whatever happened?" I asked, "That Captain looked the goods to me."

"Oh," she said, "can you imagine, he wanted to invite me to dinner."

"Well, that's nice, isn't it?" I asked.

"Are you crazy?" she retorted. "What a waste of time, I could have had three clients in that time. I'm here to make money and not to mess around hearing faked life stories and eating dinners."

I was a little taken aback at her hard tone. "But how did you manage to do all that so quickly?"

I guessed in her eyes I was a real dumb cluck who only went with a man when she really fancied him and then for free.

"Well," she said, "number 1 no kissing, number 2 no undressing. I only remove my panties and roll a French letter on my client. In no time you learn the right moves and then it's "Wham Bam Thank You Ma'am." He gets what he wants and I get what I want, so we are both winners. Not everyone has your talent, you know."

"And not everyone has yours," I answered.

CHAPTER 133

The Miami Kick, Manager Me, & the final Spanish Kick

"Pepito" had been successful in Montreal, and Roxie, my sister living there, told me they always announced my name (probably thinking I was French) and that made my folks there proud. Now it was Frank's turn with "Una Paloma Blanca". He could not accept a TV spot, as I wanted to say hi to my folks in Toronto, and Frank had to be in New York for RCA, after which we had just a few days left for Miami Florida.

Glenn Brewer, who had also been the general manager at the Sheraton in Tel Aviv, Israel, and some time later at the Sheraton-Oberoi in Bombay, was so pleased with my success wherever he seemed to be that he decided to offer me something special. Paula, his wife who became my letter writing friend, had sent me a newspaper cutting saying that he had been chosen as Vice President for the Holiday Inn chain and was working in downtown Miami, where he had to look after the whole of Florida plus the entire Caribbean. She was happy to be back in the States for a change. Glenn had penned in the letter:

"Anytime you young people hit Miami, you'll get a Penthouse Suite with all the red carpet trimmings," and I was determined to take him up on this deal.

We had left Canada in thick snow, and it was *freezing*…so arriving to warm weather and palm trees at the airport made the Miami welcome especially nice, and the Airport was managed mainly by Latinos, which gave us that holiday feeling.

At the hotel all was fine, particularly for Frank, who appreciated the bottle of whisky in the fruit basket. A few days later Glenn and Paula arrived from Jamaica and, to Frank's delight, took us for a ride in their super motor home (for us both a new experience). For Frank, who had never been in a vehicle where you could drive and still sit back comfortably and drink, it was Heaven!

Then something very unusual happened; we had never seen a mobile home park, and this one was where Paula and Glenn called home. It was situated just before Key Largo, off the main road US 1, and only a couple of miles on the other side of the road was the multimillionaire's playground, the Ocean Reef Resort. Paula showed us their home – a doll's house to my eyes. She explained to me that as they always had a suite at the hotel where her husband had to be inspecting, the cute little mobile home was sufficient and the maintenance negligible, particularly when they had their lovely big motor home, which besides the sleeping accommodation also possessed all facilities, such as a compact kitchen and a bathroom with a shower.

"But let me show you the Exhibition Home, you are going to love it," Paula said emphatically, almost as if she was an estate agent herself.

We all left and walked over to a manmade lake of quite some size. The home was what one called a double wide, which meant it was twice the size of a normal single wide home, such as the mobile home of the Brewers. The colours inside were apple green, lemon, and turquoise, with splashings of orange, and it was perfectly arranged and very tropical… Frank fell in love with it on the spot. All the furnishings and fittings were perfect, plus the mega sized refrigerator and freezer. Frank always seemed to feel hot and loved iced drinks.

In no time Glenn had told the manager of the park to come over. We all sat down, Paula supplied the sodas, and Frank asked the

Manager how much such a perfect little home would cost. The drapes and bed linen all matched the wallpaper perfectly. It was the prettiest little home imaginable, with two bedrooms and two bathrooms en suite, a kitchen and dining area and a lounge, all in a very tropical design. The view was through large sliding glass doors, showing a manicured lawn with a flowering tree dipping down to the lakeside. It was all postcard-picture perfect. When Frank heard the price, he couldn't believe his ears.

"Is that including that mega sized refrigerator?" he asked.

"Oh yes," said Paula, "it certainly is, with your German Marks it's a giving-away price, it's almost peanuts, why don't you buy it for Yvonne?"

With that she gave me a quick kick under the table, as she saw me opening my mouth and probably guessed I would say, "Key Largo is not exactly around the corner, and what are we doing with three homes and no time to live in any of them?"

Frank saved the situation. "My goodness," he said, "I spent more than that just on our sauna and bathroom in Hamburg."

Paula whispered in my ear, "If he pays that much for his girl-friend – you certainly deserve something better."

"How about buying it?" said Paula again, and Glenn added, "Go on Frank – be a sport."

I suddenly remembered as a kid when we wrote down our dreams for the future I had always said, "I'd like a home in Switzerland and a vacation home in Florida."

So, I just said:

"Mmm, it sure is beautiful."

Then Frank really decided to be smart and feeling a bit cornered, he said, "It's great, but I have no money on me, and I leave tomorrow morning for Germany and recording."

And with that he pulled out his empty pockets, showing the lining (a trick he had learnt from Dad when we had been with my folks in the market at Marrakesh on holiday). Suddenly, to our astonishment and above all to his, a $100 bill fell out.

Bob, the manager, picked it up immediately. "No sweat," he said. "This $100 bill will be your down payment. Sign on the dotted line and this lovely Exhibition Home is yours."

Frank was flabbergasted and so was I.

"You're friends of Paula and Glenn – that's good enough for me." he added.

I have a feeling Frank flew back to Hamburg not really knowing what had hit him.

I thought the idea was wonderful but a bit unreal. Frank had to get back to Hamburg the next day and I had just one week's respite before I had to fly back to London and then on to West Africa.

And so we became owners of our first mobile home near the Florida Keys, situated on a little lake at the bottom of our garden where I could swim with the wild ducks and anhingas. There were also large, shy turtles all coming in from the Everglades. I would swim across the little manmade lake to an Austrian lady who always had a pot of coffee ready and chat a little, then I'd swim back with all those ducks and anhingas following me. Glenn took a photo of Frank carrying me over the threshold and so we added that to our collection. It was country and dreamy and I loved it in the winter when I had time to enjoy it. 1 Sometime later, when Frank came down with some friends, he wrote me that he had started feeding a baby Alligator, and that made him feel he was really in the Everglades.

In the meantime, Paula proved to be a very smart lady and purchased another home in the park for me, the smaller sort. At home you couldn't even buy a car for that price. She rented it out and was most business like. I never dreamed that apart from singing around the world, I'd end up having two secretaries back home in Switzerland. I'd be flying around Europe for Frank Valdor's Orchestra and Tropicado Show and even be a "landlady" down in Florida.

In no time I had visitors from Roxane's family in Canada and my cousins Edith and Tom in Australia, so a couple more mobile homes followed suit. We all fell in love with southern Florida and after many years, my family became Floridians.

A Casita in Andalusia

Once I had an office at home in Switzerland, various big agents wanted to work with me, and big houses and halls too. In no time I was booking first-class specialty acts from The Lido in Paris to Scandinavia.

Today I have no idea just how I managed it all, but I was about four inches slimmer then than I am today and my pants were literally falling off me, as time to eat a meal was a luxury. After proving to myself and Frank that I could get him to the Palladium in London within a year, I told Frank to get a good secretary, as my own goal had been reached in that sphere and all the work involved was becoming too much. He didn't care for a skinny overworked wife, even though I wanted to prove to myself I could do it, but being a manager and a star singer fulfilling engagements around the world was just too much. Other stars had asked me to manage them too, but I only took on real specialty acts and even brought over a magician with an unusual personality from the USA, who later appeared on the Circus Krone New Years Show with "Gold Finger" Gerd Frobe on a TV Special. It was fun at the beginning, but later on it all became too strenuous. I became very sick, as I always seem to do when I overwork completely.

As a thank you present for all the work I had done for him (like some good musicians, and a great girl singer, and not forgetting, of course, the Palladium in London) Frank bought me a typical Spanish "casita" home in Andalusia, a dream in bougainvilleas with a pool and stables. I loved horseback riding on the Sierra Nevada with Frank and our trainer, til one day a new horse came and was naturally overexcited. When our trainer asked who would like to ride on him, I with my usual optimistic spontaneity said I would. Suddenly, the new horse reared up and I, taken unawares, sprang over the saddle and the horse bolted. I hung on to its leg with all my might, my hair trailing on the ground, praying I would not be trampled on, till the trainer finally called the horse to a halt. I never went horse riding again. The shock was too great! Later the famous "Truck Stop" guys came down to Andalusia and took over many homes in the little resort, and the German television guy who ran the barrio and had designed it left, and so did we. Like many other artistes, including the Kessler Twins, we had lots of problems with homes and corrupt people, but in Spain RCA, Frank's Record Company, gave us great support with excellent lawyers and we finally won our case in Spain. I decided to stick to our mobile home in the Everglades and my lovely "Harmony" in Walchwil in beautiful Switzerland. Often what one reads in glossy magazines sounds wonderful, but if you are not around to really keep an eye on gardens and homes, you are better off without them – experience is the best teacher for sure. Finally, dream homes were no longer on my menu.

CHAPTER 134

Post Script India

Oberoi Hotels are now famous for service and luxury over the whole of the Eastern Hemisphere, but the Sheraton Oberoi which opened its doors in 1979 in Bombay (now Mumbai) was really something else – it truly was the pick of the bunch. The carpets were rich purple with leaf green touches, and you really sank into them. All the furnishings and décor were exquisite and beautifully planned, and my friend Glenn Brewer from the Sheraton in Tel Aviv was chosen as the general manager. Good looking and super smart and trendy, he did an excellent opening campaign.

For the first week he and Biki Oberoi, the younger son of the founder of the Oberoi Hotel chain, turned to Hollywood and invited the most famous old stars from film and television to a wonderful festive week at the inauguration of the hotel. Among the stars were Elizabeth Taylor's second husband from the UK, film star Michael Wilding, who had played the part of Ashley, with whom Scarlett O'Hara (Vivienne Leigh) was so in love in "Gone with the Wind", and of course his world famous compatriot and one time husband of Vivienne Leigh, Laurence Olivier; Joan Fontaine, one of the foremost actresses at that time, and her sister Olivia de Haveland; Audrey Hepburn; Cary Grant; and as Danny Kaye was sick, he sent his wife with daughter Dinah. There were also some famous American TV personalities.

For starters, Glenn arranged that Biki Oberoi himself should pick me up at the airport in a large vintage Rolls Royce Corniche. The word got around and people lined the streets to wave and throw streamers at us and I never got tired of smiling and waving and sometimes holding hands (wearing my white gloves). Biki was an excellent organizer.

The show was the best of Indian talent, the awakening of "Bollywood", and I was the guest star of the show – a huge success. The Hollywoodians and I received big fruit bowls, garlands of flowers, mostly jasmine, and of course a large bottle of good Scotch Whisky every day in our suites. As the Anglo-Indian band leader seemed to be in need, looking after his mother and new wife with an even newer baby, I gave him my whisky regularly, as he could sell it easily at the market and could well manage to make ends meet, which was not so easy in India at that time.

One day we were all flown to New Delhi to be guests at the home of Goodie, who was Biki's wife. She was not only young and good looking, but a very modern lady. Her home was super mod, with decor mainly in red and black and quite wild lighting. It was like a huge disco – before the disco rage. The garden, although not on the side of a mountain, was tiered like mine in Switzerland, and the music and the champagne flowed. What interested me most was the fact that all the stars, just like Joan Fontaine, danced til the very last strains of "Goodnight Sweetheart" at the super ball arranged for them, but showed no signs of fatigue when they got a wake up call at 5 a.m. to be ready for an early breakfast at 6 o'clock. They were all bright and breezy, proving once again that in show business "the show must go on."

Film stars are special people; the same could be said for the following week, when Glenn's wife Paula asked her friend, the Afghan Princess Zarin, to make an invitation list of the royals in the area: the Emirs and Kings from the oil region of the Middle East, the most famous princes and princesses of Thailand, some of the younger set of the Japanese royal family, and just a few of the wealthier Maharajahs of India. It was amazing how the oldest and most Royal Princess of Thailand walked up a rickety mountainous path to see the wonderful cave carvings of Antique India.

Her back was straight, her head held high, and holding a daintily decorated parasol above her. The will of them all was the same; to always set an example of leadership to perfection, in that heat, amazed me. During this week I was as before introduced to many of the royals; one was the delightful princess of Kuwait, who was looking for a governess for her two young daughters.

"Do you happen to know of any nice middle-aged lady who may be suitable?" she asked. I immediately spoke to the bandleader, who assured me that he had no room at his home for his mother and such a job would be a gift from heaven for her. The lady visited me next day and looked typically English: tall with carroty hair and a fair-sized high nose – no one would believe her mother was Indian, only her intonation of certain English words gave her away. We discussed what she should wear and how she should behave when I introduced her to the Princess. Heaven was with us, or was it my guardian angel? Anyway, she got the job. We kept in contact for years, mainly through letters, and occasionally meeting in London til the girls grew up. The princess was so happy with the choice, she gave me a much-beaded top in the colors of the flag of Kuwait. It was as the song I opened my show with, "Well It's A Good Day", which I also sang on German TV quite a few times. Things seemed to be going well in India.

Only one person was highly agitated on this auspicious royal week: the Punjabi Master of Ceremonies. Just before the Grand Ball premiere, the general manager Brewer, the food & beverage manager, the Afghan Princess Zarin, the general manager's wife and I were all sitting together in the Grand Hall, trying to organize the events of the evening, when the poor MC, who was head and shoulders taller than anyone else, said in a trembling voice:

"Good God, here we are discussing the running of this eventful evening and two rows behind us is sitting King Birendra of Nepal. This is a terrible slight, we must never have our backs to a live monarch. However can we excuse ourselves for this dreadful faux pas? We must all go up one by one and bow and whisper our sincere apologies for this awful occurrence."

I said, "It's ok, I'll put things right. I know his Majesty from my engagement at the Princess' place, the "Soalthee" in Kathmandu." And with that I got up and ran over to the King, greeting him in my usual spontaneous way, "Hello, dear Majesty."

He looked at me and smiled. "Yvonne, are you going to sing for us tonight?"

"Yes, I am," I answered. "I do hope you will forgive us for having our backs to you, but honestly we had no idea you would already be going to sit on your designated area so soon."

He looked at me and grinned and shook his head and said, "Oh, dear, they will all come now one by one, bowing and scraping and asking my forgiveness."

I took his hand and said reassuringly, "King Birendra, you are such a good person. I know you want modern democracy for your country Nepal, as you have told me yourself. I'm sure you will understand our predicament."

And so a sticky situation was saved and a contented middle-aged lady got an excellent job with one of the nicest princesses you could ever wish to meet.

The following week was reserved for all American travel agents, not a patch on the stars or the royals. They were aghast at the 5 a.m. wake up call, left the big ball by 10 p.m. and were all tired and annoyed at the idea of a 6 a.m. breakfast. As I had already been to the festivities in New Delhi I did not have to go to perform or even go to breakfast at 6 a.m. I just turned over in bed with a big fat grin on my face; life was serene.

CHAPTER 135

Ladies of Song

There are two "Ladies of Song" whom I have met and thoroughly enjoyed, but have not mentioned til now: Judy Garland and Mireille Matthieu. I think we all loved Judy Garland after the film "The Wizard of Oz"; she was so hard-working and sincere, a real pal, and nicest of all she was only a fraction taller than me.

Mireille Mathieu had an amazing similarity in her voice to Edith Piaf and we were on a show together, sharing a dressing room. I forgot my handkerchief and went back to get it and found her sitting there all alone. I asked her if she would not come with the other artists and musicians to dinner.

She looked at me with large sad eyes and with a low voice she said, "Oh no, I am never allowed to mix with any of the other artists. Johnny wouldn't let me do that ever."

"Why ever not?" sprung to my mind, but than I realised why and just nodded my head and muttered, "I do understand."

Johnny Stark was a strong man and lived up to his name. He had whipped up a fairytale around his protégé and as long as she was under contract to him as her manager, he was intent to keep that wonderful tale intact – with good reason. The whole world and her fans wanted it that way, and all she had to do was to agree.

I never met Tina Turner personally, but followed her career with real interest after seeing her at the Congress Hall in Zürich, when she was still with Ike Turner. Thank heavens for Roger Davis, who believed in her and put her back where she belonged, and for Erwin Bach, who I found not to be just a smart businessman (he was the Chief of her record company, EMI, in Switzerland), but also a gentleman. Both men were most supportive for Tina, and really got her back in the spotlight. Many times in London and Switzerland, and even in Florida, I have been mistaken for this great star and have signed many autographs in the hopes she wouldn't mind, not wanting to disappoint quite a few young people. I have done enough of my own, but for somebody else it certainly was amusing.

Then there was Norwegian Wenke Myhre, a pretty girl with whom I shared a dressing room on a German TV show. We chatted a lot. She told me her father, who was a policeman, had managed her since she was a kid and done very well too, but her second man, after the dentist and father of her two children, really showed her his abilities on a TV special – that was TV producer Michael Pfleghar. Many other stars, including myself, were on a TV show with him, including Udo Jurgens – who at that time even showed us all his prowess as a good dancer.

In London my eldest brother Ray took me to a restaurant and at the next table a producer and two very famous film stars were discussing the coming movie "Autumn Crocus". Ray knew the producer vaguely, and I knew immediately it was 007 Roger Moore and he looked just great.

Ray asked me quietly, "Have you any idea who the lady is?"

"Well," I said, "she looked like – but she couldn't be Ingrid Bergman's mother, could she? There's a definite resemblance."

Ray smiled and said, "No, no, that's her. You are in show business long enough, you should know what good lighting and make up can do."

"But she is speaking real American, why, Meryl Streep had more of a Swedish accent in her film "Out of Africa"."

My eldest brother gave a short little laugh. "The show must go on," he whispered, "most of us live on illusions."

CHAPTER 136

Philippines

When you are an international star singer and are travelling the world alone with no manager to smooth the path before your arrival, then it certainly is an asset to have a good sense of humour.

When I arrived at the Manila Intercontinental, right in front as I entered the lobby was a huge blow up of the sexiest blonde I had seen for a long time, á la Marilyn Monroe but with a sophisticated superior smile, showing a beautiful décolleté with a bosom like two ripe melons. I presumed that this sex bomb with the superior smile was playing at the supper club at present and little me with my foam and socks bust had to follow her show. "Oh Hell."

I read the name – it said: "Yvonne Carré of the Latin mood."

For travelling I found dark red a better color than blonde, as I had had that surprising stop over in Bombay at night and knew that men with black hair and dark skins seem to think blonde girls are "easy pickings." I quickly put on my jacket so that the man at the reception could not ascertain the size of my bust, which had at least improved to 34 inches from 32 as a teenager (today it is more than 40 – how times change!). I decided there and then no one was going to see me outside my private room, other than as that sexy blonde. Easier said than done!

This meant that even the waiter bringing my breakfast had to see me as a ravishing, sophisticated blonde with big eyes and long curling eye lashes. As John Wareing taught me in Karachi, "Noblesse does oblige"!

My opening show went really well, and I was told that both President Marcus and his illustrious wife Imelda were there to see me, but if they were this was done with no pomp or glory, as did the famous last Emperor Haile Selassie or even Tito of Yugoslavia.

As I came off stage to go to the room allotted to me for my dressing room, a Philippino gentleman came up to me, full of compliments for the show. He took my hand to kiss it in a true chivalrous fashion and carried on kissing my arm until my shoulder. I was not quite sure if it was from true admiration or to get his eyes nearer to my white chiffon décolleté to make sure that what he had seen on my huge blow up in the lobby and around the hotel was indeed real. In any case, he became my best conquest, as later I was to find out he was the richest and most powerful man in the country and the biggest supporter for the President.

My guardian angel was definitely by my side in Manila, as Braulio (that was his name) only wanted to look at me and have my company occasionally. As a devout Catholic, he felt God was with him but only when he adhered to the rules, and that meant "no sex please, I am a true husband to my wife and family."

As Braulio was so admired with great Christian awe, many of the ministers came to visit me to talk and drink coffee, each one bringing a bouquet of flowers. That meant that even when I could not remember the gentleman's name, I had to remember which flowers he had brought me, so that when he entered my suite the right bouquet would be there. As I had a fair-sized dressing room attached to my suite it was not so difficult, and I had a lot of fun telling my steward to put away the white orchids from the last suitor, and put out the bright red tropical flowers (looking almost unreal) from the next visitor, who would be arriving in approximately 25 minutes. No one dared to touch me or even give me a French kiss as I was considered Braulio's girl, and therefore if they did not wish to fall into terrible disgrace and lose their own amount of power – I was untouchable!

I found the whole situation amusing and extremely to my benefit, and I enjoyed their conversations and learnt much before Bill Gates and computers gave the world the Internet and Google.

My best friend was Senor Roderiguez, Braulio's friend and right hand. I found him most congenial and when I had the time I liked to listen and observe. Braulio was a great advisor and on my first night he said kindly to me, "Beauty needs beauty sleep – don't accept any invitations to go down to the nightclub. I will be here tomorrow at 11 a.m. to show you around our great city Manila."

Later I heard from the English newspaper outside my door and the main receptionist in the lobby that there had been a "shoot up" in the nightclub downstairs, and this was not so unusual. From then onwards I decided to wear everyday my girdle, which was designed to give me the right figure in a tight-fitting evening dress – but this time for protection from any stray bullets which happened to be flying in my direction. My fears were not as stupid as it seemed. Apart from the really nice American general manager and assistant manager, I was mostly in the company of VIPs who were also extremely wealthy. Braulio would drive me in his huge limousine with the smoked glass windows to show me some of his pineapple plantations, which seemed to stretch as far as the eye could see. The first time, as he was driving and I was sitting next to him, I heard a sound from the backseat and was horrified to see a young man laying on that seat with a huge gun. Braulio pacified me immediately:

"Don't worry Karri." (He always used my surname, as he explained in "Tagalog", the Philippino language, Karri is something most delicious to eat, so he felt it suited me perfectly.) Above all the young man laying on the back seat with munitions was Braulio's bodyguard and indispensable in such a special country, where at that time many men lived by the gun. If Braulio was delighted to show me his plantations and tell me about his 6 children, then Rodriguez was likewise, but he showed me the homes he had made for his four different wives. All were large and in different areas just outside Manila. He assured me he was loved by them all, so each wife had a family of three or four children. He looked after all his siblings too and with his excellent connections got them into really good schools and jobs. For me it was an "eye opener" when I thought of my father, always complaining how a father like himself could keep a family of five but not one kid could keep a solitary father. I think Rodriguez never had those problems and he thoroughly enjoyed being a sort of "Father Christmas" to three or four different families. He was a wonderful, warmhearted and interesting personality and I reveled in his companionship, as did dear, very important Braulio.

Life in the Philippines was like a fairytale until I really put my foot in the soup.

My other friends were "show business" people, the most famous moderator on television and author at the time, the intelligent and amusing José Aquirino, and the most famous lady singer in the Philippines, the lovely Pelita Corales.

It was Valentine's Day and there was a big concert, and I had been asked to sing "My Funny Valentine". Apart from some other requests, Braulio had sent me a dozen red plastic roses and I was horrified and furious as I felt then his feelings could be just as synthetic (later the florist in the hotel told me they were far more expensive than the real thing). I had not seen Rodriguez, let alone Braulio, and I was MAD. In my show I stopped the music and asked if President Marcos was there, and the waiters shouted, "No."

"Oh," I said ironically, "surely he is on his way to Switzerland or the Cayman Islands to check out his number accounts…"

I was rewarded with titters and laughter, and some even clapped their hands, but not for long. When I returned to the hotel, there was the Chief of Police to greet me. I was told curtly, "Pack your hand baggage, you have insulted our President, you are to be deported."

What to do? I called dear Rodriguez, as Braulio was not available. What a friend he was. He told me not to worry and just pass the phone to the Chief of Police, who immediately apologised, saying certain people had complained and he had no idea who I actually was. Then dear Rody told me a suite was now reserved for me at the Peninsular Hotel in Hong Kong, and that the following day I would be interviewed on television, when I would be asked to sing "Pepito" and my special version of "Careless Love". The following day I would fly back to Manila with all the "bells and whistles", as they say in the States.

Apart from the weather in Hong Kong, which was rainy, windy and cold, it was actually like a four-leafed clover, and the return to Manila Airport with the red long mat as a welcome and all the inspectors with big smiles to greet me was a marvelous feeling.

At the very end of my engagement, Braulio knocked on my door to tell me that if only I would stay a little longer he had reserved perfect accommodation at the newest hotel in Manila, and with that he asked if only once I would show him my now famous bust, but not to touch, just look. He quite understood that I would not remove my bra. Then the funniest thing happened. I put on a pair of long light pants in the bathroom and came out with a bikini bra, well-stuffed. He gave just one look, and his pants became so wet it made a big wet patch on his evening trousers. He couldn't possibly leave like that, so I washed his underpants and sprayed his trousers and put them by the air conditioning after using a dry towel. It was then I saw my first Asian penis. Well, at that time Oriental men were decidedly smaller than their Western counterparts – and so was everything else!

Later a friend of Braulios and the owner of the domestic airlines in the Philippines gave me a book of free passes and said, "Fly to Zamboanga as my guest, it is the last island belonging to the Phillippines before Borneo." Borneo was the place my mother was always telling me to go to when I was a child, and she was really fed up with me. There again I saw the other side of the coin in Asia.

The boat people, with only a raft-like boat to call their own, perfectly naked, were happy to dive for coins in the glass clear waters of the sea. Children peering at us through the windows of the best restaurant, waiting for us to stop eating and rushing to our table with little handmade pieces of cardboard as plates, scooping up the food that we had left and rushing away to eat. How far removed from my life in the Far East. I flew home with very mixed feelings, but a very handsome and friendly nation remained in my memory. Lovely people, the Phillippinos.

CHAPTER 137

The Intruders in Florida's Everglades

Intruder No.1

After leaving for West Africa and the "Good Lord's" contracts, Paula set about showing her business acumen and purchased another mobile home on our behalf, but this time a single wide, and rented this out for me so that, should I return earlier than I had anticipated, she would have some company and I would have some spending money. Times change and jobs too, and Glenn was sent to New York and Paula, as the dutiful wife, had to accompany him.

Mobile Homes look really super, but they are just tied down with large stone slabs and have no foundations at all. They normally have big wheels, and that's why they are called "mobile homes." Once, when I had a new wall to wall carpet put down in the living area, when they pulled up the old one, I could literally see the grass growing underneath the rafters of the floor. However, our home was very roomy and looked really lovely. Above all it cost to our Swiss German and British minds (as Paula had contended) "peanuts."

Without Paula, I had to put someone in charge and engaged a Mr. Ebel, a good man and like his name, he was very able. Then one day I got a call from the manager.

"Miss Carré, you better get down here as soon as you can – I had to call the Sheriff. There has been a shoot up in your rented home."

At such moments you notice that "The Keys" are just around the corner, and life there is not just swimming and making "Hush Puppies." Perhaps Malaysia was not the only country with gun-happy jealous husbands. Apparently the husband, a truck driver, returned home earlier than expected and his wife was with her afternoon lover and did not open the door. There were bullet holes all over the doors, and I learnt pretty quickly that the hardware store had excellent fill-in pastes for all types of holes in walls or doors, so I guess they were used to them.

However, there were lovely moments in the Everglades, like finding a tiny baby turtle in the garden grass and putting her back in the lake, which housed quite a few giant turtles. Another time, driving down to our beach at American Outdoors on the side of the Gulf of Mexico, I saw a large flock of bright Red Spoon Bills – much rarer than the deep pink Flamingos.

I enjoyed the early mornings, when you could see baby barracudas in the calm, clear waters. One day I saw a crowd staring at something in our roped off swimming area in the sea. As no one had the courage to see exactly what they were staring at – curiosity killed the cat – I went into to investigate. It was a sort of round fish that did a kind of jumping butterfly stroke, and which immediately swam in the other direction when I got closer. Next morning, I could not believe my ears, and soon after my eyes; it was the special deep voice of a large whale that seemed to be calling. As I stared at the ocean on the horizon, I thought I must be hallucinating – there before my very eyes was a Loch Ness Monster. It was the biggest living thing I had ever seen in my life, which seemed to come up for air and then disappeared again under the ocean. I quickly called Frank, who thought I'd gone crazy, and then I realised that it was a mother crying for her baby, and then, far away already, we saw the end of the phenomena – it was a huge fan tail of the largest giant whale, and sure enough baby was back with mum and our roped off swimming pool in the sea was no longer with an intruder.

Later the local papers were full of the story, and I felt very privileged to have witnessed such an unusual happening.

Intruder No. 2

Once, when Frank came down with a party of musician pals from Hamburg, he wrote to me that every morning he was feeding a baby Alligator, making Frank feel we really had a little "pad" in the Everglades.

Every evening he and his gang, and many others, took their chairs and sat and watched the most beautiful sunsets imaginable – often deep purple, famous in that area by Key Largo.

A year or so later I received a letter from the manager of the park, telling me it was absolutely forbidden to swim in the lake as an alligator had been seen there. Of course, I was not overjoyed at that news, and having a mad daring characteristic I probably would even have jumped in the water if I had not seen on the lawn two homes away a full-grown alligator, lying there peacefully in the early morning sun. Maybe he wanted a tan? I rushed inside to get my camera, but when I returned it had already slithered back into the lake again. I wrote to Frank and chided him for giving food to that little reptile, and told him his baby alligator had now grown into a real "whopper."

Intruder No. 3

One day, coming back from a little food shopping at the local supermarket, I saw my cleaning lady throwing a duster at something. As I got closer, I saw she had obviously opened the furthermost door to my large L-shaped built-up patio and, for some unknown reason, a huge black snake with some yellow spots had found its way inside and was rearing up its ugly head and putting its poisonous tongue out at me. I decided to be fair. I opened the other door of our patio and said, "Mr. or Mrs. Snake, both doors are open – get out and be sensible or

I'll have to kill you." The way she looked at me, I'm sure my cleaner thought I'd gone crazy.

Perhaps the huge reptile had forgotten its hearing aid, because instead of being logical it started climbing up the glass doors to my living room. "Ye Gods, that's all I need, a large, probably poisonous snake inside my home."

I did the only thing I could think of, I took the garden hoe, and every time it reared up its head, I hit it on the back of its neck like a matador goes for a bull at the bull fight. My cleaner stood far away, trembling. Finally, the reptile looked so tired I could tell her to come and hold the hoe down on the snake's neck. I ran into the kitchen and took the bread knife. "Sure is sure," I said to myself, "never do things by halves," and with that I cut off its head. It really is amazing what the will to survive can make you do. Sometimes I have even been surprised at myself, and I sure was on that day, and still managed at night to sing to an audience about that special word, "love."

Later on, I decided life could be more congenial with a really good bodyguard, and no intruders.

CHAPTER 138

The Night The War Broke Out (Masai Mara)

Many of us kid ourselves that we are tough. I suppose I belong to that type of "afraid of nothing" person.

When I had a spare week or two from my new show with the girls in "Little Las Vegas," I flew to visit my old girlfriend, Amir's sister Gulie. She told me all about the newest game park "Masai Mara", an experience I must not miss, and so I flew in a very small plane to the camp alone. It was a special experience. As we were landing it seemed that all the different animals were there on the runway of the airfield. One almost expected them to wave. There were loads of baboons, elephants and buffalo or wildebeests with horns all looking up at our plane coming down. When I wandered off to explore my whereabouts, in no time a ranger came to collect me back to the fold, saying, "Wildebeests are dangerous, they kill on sight."

At night we were all given a guide and I noticed I was the only one who was alone. My guide unfortunately forgot to put the flaming light on the table in front of my canvas tent, which wards off animals at night.

During that night, I had a nightmare that there was a war going on, and we were being bombarded. The noise was deafening. I awoke and realised my tent was the only one in darkness with no flaming torch outside; it was also at the end of the row and the next tent was uninhabited – oh horror! Perhaps for that reason, two huge male African Elephants were fighting each other outside my tent, and when they shriek, boy do they shriek! To add to this something kept hitting me in bed through the canvas wall of my tent. I didn't know then that a baboon got stuck in the middle of this giant fight and was whining and trying to come into me to get away from the elephants.

I got up, cursing myself for being so foolhardy as to come alone on a safari. I took the huge torch the guide had left for me and with all my might I hit at whatever was pushing against my canvas wall, and with that I moved to the empty bed the other side of my tent and thought how nice it could be to be not alone but with some tough lover man to protect me… is there such a thing?

I sighed and reached for my earplugs and fell into a troubled sleep.

Next morning at breakfast the rest of our little group told me how they had watched the elephant fight by my tent. They guessed they had chosen that part of the camp because it was the darkest spot being there at the end. They also saw that the poor baboon was stuck in the middle of that fight and was whining in fear, obviously wanting protection in my tent.

I looked at the six young men in our group scornfully and said in true English cool, "Oh really! I thought the war had broken out and the rescue brigade had gone to have a drink. *Have you never heard about the damsel in distress?*"

With my nose in the air, I squared my shoulders, stood up to my full height of five foot, and left the breakfast table, leaving that line of masculine inadequacy with their mouths open wide, foolishly gaping.

CHAPTER 139

The Killer Waves

It was a hot, damp, sultry late afternoon, more or less typical for the Caribbean Islands' weather during the month of April. The air pressure was so low it felt heavy as lead upon our shoulders. The bus journey to the Time Share properties was included in our package deal and we had gone, like most of the others, more out of curiosity than real purchasing interest. The bus had absolutely no air conditioning and now, on the return trip to our hotel, the air was stifling. Most occupants were perspiring, and their shirts clung to their bodies like drooping leaves, limp, devoid of life and color. It was oppressive. I, who just cannot sweat, was ready to explode.

Like a few others, Frank and I made a beeline for the beach. We both dreamt of cooling off in the briny. However, the dream remained a dream, as we saw a very rough sea, no native boys surfing, and the beach dotted with red flags for danger. I immediately ran to the hotel pool, but that had no water in it; it was being cleaned as the hotel came to an end of the high season, which in the Caribbean area means the winter months.

Frank pulled up two chaise-longues to the water's edge – then decided at least to paddle. Although the water only covered his ankles, a large wave came, hitting the shore with such a vengeance it knocked him over completely, trying to drag him back into the waves – thankfully with no success. He scrambled out and said to me, "Don't you dare go into that sea – it's treacherous!" And with those famous last words he stretched out on his chaise-longue, and in no time he fell asleep.

I sat there, legs crossed, and would have been annoyed but for the sea breeze and a native woman nearby, also at the water's edge, kneeling on a striped blanket and playing contentedly with a small chocolate-coloured baby. Just as I had decided to go to our suite and take a cold shower, the heavy waves subsided, and a really big American man went into the sea, getting over the now quieter and smaller waves with a strong back crawl. Perhaps it was the fact that it was the 15th of April, which would have been Dad's birthday if he had not passed away many years before, but somehow, I could hear Dad's voice echoing in my ears:

"Remember Pussy, the sea is your bed – never be afraid!"

I didn't think twice, I jumped into the water and with my own strong back crawl got over the small waves and was soon on par with the big American, who had noticed me and slowed down his pace.

In no time we got talking, mostly about the hotel and the ocean, and apart from the super heavy swell we did not notice we were being carried out further and further from the shore. It was late afternoon, and the sun was already on the wane, when suddenly my swim partner turned to me and said, "I'm getting cold – I'm going back."

It was there and then I made a big mistake. I looked out in the distance and saw the huge white tops were on the advance toward us. Of course, from my experience of oceans I realised not only that we were far too far from the beach, but white tops can be very dangerous when they break near to the sands, worse still on a rock somewhere under the crest of the ocean. I said, "Those big white tops are coming, I'm not sure I can make it til they arrive."

"Sorry", he said "I'm going."

And with that he started for the shore. I realised I could not wait in the sea alone til a calm spell may arrive, and dusk was falling rapidly.

"OK, I'm coming," I cried and swam as hard as I could after the big man. We both remembered to swim diagonally, as we both knew that is the only way to get out of a rip which is pulling you further and further out to sea. It was hard going, but as we finally could swim more freely the killer waves with their huge white-topped crests were already coming up right behind us. The wind was coming up strongly. The American called to me, "Can you body surf?"

"Yeah, I learnt it in Ghana, West Africa," I answered.

"OK, let's go," he shouted.

The first huge wave came. He yelled, "Now!" We both body surfed simultaneously. For me it was a piece of cake, and it was a good feeling riding on the crest of such a high wave and coming down seemingly nearer to the shore. Then the next wave came – it was gigantic. I felt as if I was once again on a catamaran in Hawaii, when the huge surf carried us so close to the sand that we could all jump out and run to the beach. Unfortunately, the stupid but pleasant thought made me lose control of my present situation. The horrible realisation that I was now in the deep wild waters of the Caribbean took up precious seconds. I lost a minute trying to put my foot down and it went into nothing but water. Suddenly, before I could decide if I should body surf or dive underneath the oncoming wave, a horrible noise invaded my ears and a huge black wall of water hit the back of my neck – and I knew no more!

My Guardian Angel

Miraculously I came to. Everything around me was jet black and I was not at all sure if I had died and this was hell, til my brain functioned, and I heard all gurgling black waters swirling above me. Yet, like a feat from God, my mouth was closed. How come? I had no idea. I did what I had learnt at school to get my bronze medal in life saving – I kicked with all my strength my legs and feet and I tried to cut the waves above me with my arms and hands, pointing straight upwards above my head. Like this, according to all the good books, I should surface and so fill my lungs with oxygen and be able to carry on fighting the cruel waves. It was then I came to the horrible realisation that my right arm and hand remained limp – they were paralyzed!

The next huge white top came, giving me no respite. This one rolled and rolled me again as if I was a piece of cork, knocking my head against a hidden piece of cliff in that wild ocean. Fight as I knew I had to for my life, I could feel myself and my hope slipping away; I was getting weaker and weaker. I called on God to help me in this terrible hopeless dilemma. I told God I must live, to carry on making others happy, and I promised I would fulfill my mothers wish to write a book to make people smile and give them comfort and courage. The answer came in a flash, my guardian angel would be sent to help me. This wonderful friend from above, who had already seen me through some terrible situations, was somehow still there for me.

Almost at the same moment a voice shouted from somewhere in the waves on my left side, where I still could sense and feel things: "My God, you're bleeding, can I help?"

With my last breath I called as loud as I could, "Yes, please help me."

In a moment, so it seemed, a strong muscular arm was around me. I wasn't quite sure if it was God or my guardian angel – but then I heard the deep voice of the American guy asking me if I could still swim a little. I whispered, "Yes, but only with my legs and left arm. My right arm seems to be paralyzed."

And so together – he pushing me – we made for the shore and "terra firma". Frank was there waiting, his face as white as a ghost. He told my saviour, "I saw her red swim cap floating on the top of waves and no head – I thought the worst."

To me he just said, "I thought I must fly home with a coffin."

I never saw my saviour again, but I knew God had sent him a) to test my courage and b) to save me to do good and try to make others happy.

Once out of the water I realized I was not just bleeding all over, but I felt as if I was being burnt at the stake like Joan of Arc or Jesus on the cross. Vivid pictures of Jesus burning came to me and gave me immense courage. If he could stand all this, so could I. The way to the main building of the hotel and our suite was not exactly short, and as the burning pains were unbearable, I told Frank (my little bear) I would sing out loud and that would stop me screaming, and so help to alleviate the ghastly pain I was go-ing through. Just as I had sung the "Blue Danube" when once at midnight I had to go through an operation with no anaesthetic, I now sang out loud "The Indian Love Call".

"When I'm calling you, oo-oo-oo-oo-oo-oo

Will you answer too, oo-oo-oo-oo-oo-oo"

I pretended I was in the bush in Africa again, with only my-self to help. With my left hand I took my right arm and hand, alternately shaking them firmly and exercising them as if they were still alive. The pain was excessive, but I wanted to get my blood circulating again. I was determined to win. Once in our bathroom I showered as best as I could under the cold spray and Frank took me to the hotel doctor, but I saw only his assistant, as the doctor had the day free. He gave me a load of heavy pain-killers and told me to come the next day when the proper hotel doctor would be available. At the same time, he mentioned to me that I was lucky, as a native lady had lost her baby when that wave came and swept the blanket away.

The following day the real hotel doctor tended me and put my arm in a sling, and the hole in my left temple was covered with medication. Afterwards I covered this with a silver star; it made me look like a hippie.

The hotel doctor told me also the story of the lost baby and said the beach was dangerous, but as the hotel owner was also in the government and tourism was so important, it was kept a secret.

I believe movement helps to keep us and our parts alive and slowly I won. My fingers, my hand and my right arm started coming back to life. I knew inside me that everything was going to be O.K. somehow – at least I thought so.

CHAPTER 140

Back Home in Switzerland

Frank told me, as he had an accident insurance for me, I should go to a reliable Swiss doctor with my X-ray photo to make quite sure all was really well. I had not wanted to spoil his holiday and took painkillers in the bathroom secretly and motivated myself psychologically, so he did not notice my impediment.

Doctor Eggli in Zug was considered with his great experience as being the best, so I took the X-ray photo to him. He glanced at it and said, "My word, down in St. Martin they must have the very first X-ray machine ever made. It is pure fog! I will X-ray you myself."

His smile faded when he looked at his new X-ray photos. He stared at me as if I had just come in from space and then he said bluntly – after X-raying me a second and a third time – "My God – you should be dead!"

"Well, I'm not," I said dryly.

"We must get you tomorrow to the American Clinic in Zürich. They have the best Scan-machine in the country, I want to know what they make of you. According to my X-rays, even if you are still living today, tomorrow you could be dead. I will arrange everything for you."

The next day dawned, and I spent the whole day being put through the "tube," other professors came in, and again the clong clong as I went through the tomography machine. Finally they called me in and stood there staring at me with the same curiously amazed look as Doctor Eggli had done when I thought he felt I had arrived from another world.

"You are a miracle," I was told.

"We finally discovered you do have a tiny membrane of 2 millimeters of bone keeping you as you are, and not completely paralyzed from the neck down, as it would be normally under these conditions. If this terrible accident you have been subjected to had happened here in Switzerland, you would have been put on a stretcher, rushed by ambulance to hospital, then put entirely from your neck down in plaster of Paris and not allowed to move for eight months."

"Not able to move for eight months? That would have been the death of me! Thank God I did not break my neck here."

They explained to me that the terrific crash of that killer wave had broken most of the bones in my neck, fractured my spine and knocked a big dent in my ribs on my left side and hip. My bones were devoid of marrow and my joints of gristle. Just on that account my whole skeleton could be cast as of that of a woman thirty years older. The good side was the terrific crash closed my mouth, saving me from drowning immediately. Any operation to better my condition was completely out of the question, as there was a 90% chance I would die. Then I was told "you are special, God wants you to live!"

I was given a list of therapists and advised to go to the Schultheiss Clinic in Zürich for nerves, as my whole nervous system was completely messed up and that had given me the terrible sensation of being burnt. They all said again, "At this stage, tomorrow you could be dead."

The next weeks were spent at therapists and, as always, after their therapies I started to faint in the streets, in stores, just everywhere and anywhere – I really started to behave like all the heroines in the old movies when they fainted, only to find they were – not to their knowledge – expecting a baby. The hero would be then told the good news. He would be overjoyed, and return to his pining sweetheart. The wedding is arranged, and the tragic love story ends happily.

However, as I was no film heroine longing for my prince charming, I decided to take the matter into my own hands. Once again, I made a decision. Logically thinking that if you have had a bad car accident as I had had several times, the best remedy is to get back into the driver's seat before you become too afraid to drive again, I cancelled the famous nerve clinic appointment and all the others too. I called my girlfriend in Mombasa, Kenya. Amir's sister and I had always kept in contact. I really liked her, and asked if I could possibly stay a while with her at her home til I had found suitable accommodation, as it was winter and all the usual Mombasa tourist hotels were completely booked with various groups and tours, including safaris. I was determined to go back into an ocean and start to try to swim again.

I flew in as an invalid in a wheelchair. My room at the house did have a bathroom attached with a full bath, just as my friend had assured me on the phone. The fact that it only trickled cold water did not matter. My bed did have a large mosquito net hanging from the high ceiling, and the fact that it also had a large holes in it did not matter; what mattered was I had a real friend in a distant land with a heart of gold. My friend went to work every day, as did her husband, and I went to work on myself at the beach.

The Indian Ocean was warm and calm, and my first attempt at swimming with a gammy left leg and a once-paralyzed right arm was nothing to write home about. I managed exactly three breast strokes. However, time was on my side, and so was the wonderful sunny weather and warm ocean water. The pleasant summer climate was like a natural tonic and balm to my wounds.

After some time I managed to walk much better, but with the sea water making me buoyant I felt swimming a lot easier! Finally, when I had to fly home, I could swim a couple of yards breast-stroke and a little on my back, and I knew in my heart I was winning, and at least this time I had done the right thing.

CHAPTER 141

Life Hits Back

Accident No. 1 "Panic"

Most of us, at sometime or other, have experienced a moment of sheer panic, when fear grips us completely, but with all the adventures I had gone through I never dreamed that such a thing could happen to me. On a peaceful summer Saturday morning when I felt fit enough after my monster wave escapade, I decided to mow the lawn. Suddenly the shorter cable the new gardener had put in between the long cable to the electric plug and the new lawn mover came unstuck and I, naïve as a babe, was mowing the grass that was wet from the morning dew in my bare feet. In a second the cable, which was meant only for indoors, instead of allowing me to return it into the plug for the lawn mower, jumped like a wild cat into my right hand, giving me such a shock that it threw me quite far onto the damp grass, and to my horror, carried on electrocuting me, burning holes in my hand.

I tried with all my might to get it out of my hand, as the electric shocks were making my body vibrate like crazy, and for a horrible moment of panic I remembered that only a week earlier a young girl in our village was found dead, electrocuted by her own lawnmower, and I could feel the shocks going through my whole body. I shouted for help but to no avail, everyone was shopping on a Saturday morning. I remembered in the old movie "Orfeo Negro" how Marpessa Dawn was electrocuted by holding on to a live wire and I knew I just had to get it out. My guardian angel came to me; I stopped panicking and remembered my big, flat but strong feet and muscular legs. I put the cable under my two feet together and pushed with all my might and finally got the cable out of my right hand, which was now pouring with blood.

I shouted again "Help! Help!" My guardian angel must have remained on the pipeline, because my neighbor from across the road was suddenly there and saw my still vibrating body lying bleeding on the grass. Thank Heavens my brain was still working and fast. I told him to take the cable out of the plug. He took the cable out of the plug, and I told him to get a teacloth and ice from the refrigerator and tied this to my hand, and slowly the terrible vibrations stopped. He came with me to the hospital in the ambulance he had immediately called.

I was told there on the operating table that the electricity had passed my left shoulder and was only a few centimeters away from my heart.

"But the fast reaction of your brain to use your feet and legs instead of just your left hand was the saving element. Do you know tomorrow you could have been dead? It seems God, for some reason, wanted you to live. You certainly do have a guardian angel."

"Yes, I know," I whispered.

"However, your hand will be scarred for life, so take care with the electric lawnmowers."

His words only went into the recesses of my mind in a file marked souvenirs. But as the anaesthetic started working, I fell asleep.

Accident No. 2 "Back in Australia"

On holiday in Australia, this time with my Bavarian girlfriend and a friend of hers, my cousin had a lovely house in Sydney and she invited all of us to stay at her home.

The day they were leaving to fly back to Munich in Germany, pandemonium reigned and Max, her friend, called, "My hair is a mess, does someone have a hairbrush?"

Forgetting my house-proud cousin's warning us the stairs were pure terracotta and slippery, wanting to help, I ran with a brush in my hand and fell down a flight of stairs, landing on my "derrière," hearing bones cracking. I said not one word until Inge and her friend had left us at the airport. Then I turned to my cousin and her husband Tom and said, "Please get me to the nearest hospital. Just before leaving I fell down your famous terracotta stairs and heard some cracking noises."

Once there I was put under the "scan," the electric tunnel that tells all. Then a professor was called in from the Prince of Wales Hospital, as the 3 doctors attending me could not believe their eyes. I was then told I must stay now in hospital:

"Do you know there is only 2 millimeters of membrane saving you from being paralyzed from the neck down?"

It seemed as if I was reliving this adventure one more time.

"You must stay here in our hospital," I was told.

"No, no, I'm here for a holiday and not to spend my time in a hospital," I answered.

"Do you know tomorrow you could be dead?" said the professor earnestly.

Suddenly I rolled back time, as I heard exactly the same words in London at Interpol and again in Zürich at the American Hospital. I looked at the Doctors and Professors and replied, "Couldn't we all? I am signing myself out. I will take the responsibility if I am dead, but right now I am going to a party because I have promised I would." – and I did!

My guardian angel kindly smiled. My cousin's husband Tom was witness to this happening and then he was – bless him – my chauffeur, and we both went for a short while to that party.

Over 20 years later I'm writing this memory – believe me, I'm writing this to you all because having faith in your guardian angel and yourself as a team is a winner!

Accident No. 3 "Souvenirs Souvenirs"

I'm sure many of us thoroughly enjoyed running down the escalators in the subways as kids. Kings Cross tube station had two really long, steep "moving staircases," as we called them. It was fun having to change lines at Kings Cross and almost fly down the escalator, shouting "excuse me, excuse me" to anyone who dared to stand in the middle of a step instead of on the right side. I guess my fantasy got me to the Olympic Games.

How time changes everything! Coming back from Punta Cana in the Dominican Republic, I found myself standing at Frankfurt Airport on an escalator step with both my hands full of hand baggage, behind a gentleman with an overfull trolley. When I got to the top of the escalator and wanted to exit I could not, because he didn't seem to budge – I shouted, "Please get off, get off I can't move your trolley is in the way!"

It didn't help I went smack into his trolley laden with everything except the kitchen sink; it knocked me completely off balance and I fell backwards, knocking my head so violently that I felt blood pouring down my face and then I lost consciousness completely.

I came to in the airport doctor's practice and the cracks in my skull were sewn up and my wounds treated, and I was given a tetanus shot. My mouth had some heavy wounds which my doctor told me later on would remain on my face for life, so I have a souvenir from that gentleman forever.

The other souvenir came unexpectedly. My boyfriend at that time decided I was a "smart cookie" and such a smart lady had to have a smart driving wheel. So, he changed the driving wheel in my car to a Formula 1 style one; it was a small, white leather wheel with gold studs and a bright gold circle in the middle, very sporty – very chic.

My pianist pal Marcello, whom I had brought to Switzerland after his contracts in Africa had expired, was now a full-fledged, much-wanted Swiss Italian pianist and singer. On a special round birthday, he invited me to a lunch at a friend's restaurant on the lake of Lucerne. The boss had secured two big fresh soles direct from the Atlantic Ocean. They were delicious, and to my amazement, and probably to Marcello's too, I ate the whole thing. Eating a lot invariably makes me terribly tired, and as my doctor had told me I must never drink coffee, I refused the espresso offered. Driving home along the lake of Zug I started falling asleep and tried making the radio louder – it did not help. I dreamt I hit a big lorry and half woke up to hear someone asking if I had insurance. I could not speak, something hot and wet, my own blood, was pouring down over me. Then I lost consciousness, and I ended up in hospital.

The next day I was told I would be scarred, probably for life. The Formula 1 Driving Wheel with the gold studs became embedded in my forehead during the accident and had to be removed. Years later, the scar is still there. It really is amazing how many souvenirs one can pick up while persuing the rickety road of a colourful life.

Accident No. 4 "Hurricane Andrew"

Apart from seeing Judy Garland in the "Wizard of Oz", I had no idea what a hurricane can do. Singing most evenings in my newest show "Little Las Vegas" with two girl dancers from the UK, one blonde and one black, I hardly had time to watch Television, but I knew hurricanes were disastrous.

Travelling the world, observing people and nature, fulfilling ones dreams and singing and swimming, one can become, to a good degree, a philosopher.

A killer wave nearly killed me; it was monstrously high, and it came after a wonderfully long period of success and calm. Life is much like the sea at its kindest, and its cruelest, and fate strikes suddenly.

Inge and I had enjoyed Venice and the beautiful Opera at Verona, where you sit outside in the old Roman theater to enjoy the stimulating music from the great French Composer Bizet and the opera "Carmen". After two days we returned for supper to the Lake of Zug and the wonderful tranquility that area can instill in you, with the help of simple good food from a family restaurant.

As I unlocked the front door of my home the phone was ringing. It was my sister Roxane from Montreal. She is, like me, quite direct.

"Hurricane Andrew has hit the Florida Keys and we saw your lovely home hit directly, and immediately in the torrential rain which followed there came a multitude of looters from the fields around. You can say goodbye to everything you had there – those sort of people take the lot."

To see with your own eyes what nature can do is incredible!

Shortly afterwards the Manager of the Park called me. "If you want to save anything at all from your shattered homes, fly in as quickly as you can as the bulldozers are coming to flatten everything."

That experience I could never forget. I arrived to a dismal Miami Airport, picked up my small rental car, and drove south to the place I used to call home Florida City. Besides the huge craters in the road there were no lights and no signposts. It was as if some huge carving knife had cut through all the lamp posts and only left two thirds of empty posts. I knew the road to our place was just following the road straight to Key Largo, but I and many others got lost on the ride down. Everywhere was devastation and absolutely no traffic lights or signposts. Many of us motorists got together, trying to help each other to get to our chosen destinations.

It was not cold but windy and rainy, and it looked so pitiful seeing the homes left standing by the roadside – all with no roofs, only tarpaulins blowing in the treacherous wind. It was like heaven to get a hotel room and get to bed in Key Largo, which, oddly enough, was not struck down as badly as South Miami, and above all the area we had called home. The next day in daylight I still had problems finding our park and where our home once had been. I knew it was on a corner on a little lake, and there I discovered our built-up patio of good cement and my bougainvilleas which I had planted myself in our garden. Someone had left a few bottles of cleaning stuff on the patio and, as I was near to tears, my old friend, a half a bottle of cognac. I could really do with a drink from my old friend, but I knew from our manager and other people who had lived there that this was impossible, because when a hurricane hits mobile homes, which are primarily made of plastic, poisonous dust is in the air and no food or drink may be consumed.

I had lost everything – my clothes, my homes, my stage gear, my half-written book, my typewriter, television, radios – the lot!

I could have sung "I Who Have Nothing", but the bulldozer men were a friendly bunch and wanted to pose with me in my hotpants for photos. My poor car with the bashed-in roof I sold for $1000 to a worker.

I told the buyer from some small town in North Carolina that it had a habit of stopping at traffic lights, and he laughed. "That's ok," he said, bashing the roof with his heavy fist, making it look quite normal again, "it's a present for my wife. We have no traffic lights where we live."

I flew back to Switzerland with nothing but memories, which I have now shared with you. No matter! After all, memories are the stalwart of life! And, as they say in Swiss, "Gopfverdammi, auch dieses Mal werde ich nicht sterben!" (You may think I should be dead, but by heck I won't lie down!)

You may think, with all these pitfalls, my guardian angel had left me high and dry – no way! The pipeline was working again. It was the last Sunday in September 2012; I'd just finished writing this book and said to myself, "Now I can pack my bags and fly to London," where my brother-in-law was dying in hospital. I wanted to give him a final kiss on his forehead. The phone rang – it was a girlfriend who rarely phones if I do not call her first. She asked if I was fine, and I said, "Sure, but I seem to have a mouth full of black ulcers and they are bleeding."

Her voice changed; what was her reply? "I won't put my phone down until you swear to me you'll go to the Emergency at our new hospital in Baar."

I called Frank, and he suggested I ask our new neighbour, who had children "so surely she would know."

In next to no time my next door neighbor was at my door, as I hadn't the vaguest idea where our hospital was and my nose had started bleeding. When my turn came at the hospital the doctor asked my neighbor to pick up some personal stuff for me as I must spend the night there. Then the Chief of the Hospital, a professor, came to me, took me aside, and said, "Of all the patients here, you are in the most dangerous condition."

I thought he must be joking and said, "Oh, I'm sure a good mouthwash will clear it all up, and if I lie down with ice on the back of my neck my nose will stop bleeding – I hope! I must fly to London, my brother-in-law is dying, and I want to see him before he leaves this world."

"If you try to leave this hospital, before you board the plane *you will no longer be in this world.*" His eyes were earnest, his voice serious. "You are bleeding all over internally, even in your head. You have Thrombopenni. To be able to live, a normal human being needs 150,000 plakets in their blood stream – you have only 2,500! Normal people are dead at that point."

"Thank God I am abnormal," I whispered.

"Do you realise *tomorrow you could be dead?*" Those old familiar words echoed in my head.

In seconds, pictures went through my mind of the Chief of Interpol in London with Dad, the American Hospital in Zürich, the hospital in Zug and the hospital in Sydney, then again in Zug where the oncoming Mercedes sportscar driver seemed to sense I'd fallen asleep and I was heading straight for the lake with no barriers, and with his car he stopped me. Somehow, I knew my guardian angel was there with me, and a curious smile lit up my face. The professor must have thought I was crazy.

"Together we will win," I said with quiet determination, and this time I did not leave the hospital. I stayed and was rolled into intensive care.

The new blood infused in me was eaten up entirely by the bad elements by the morning. No one was more disappointed than me. We all seemed to be treading on new ground. I was not just the first case of such an unusual blood disease in the hospital, but also in the whole region. Then the specialist asked me to make a decision. I said, "Yes, no matter how – let's kill those bad boys!"

"But what we have to inject into you is an overdose of poison and cortisone, and that could kill you too. I'm sorry, but I have to tell you there is no other alternative; either way you die."

I said, "Kill all that bad lot, I will survive, I know I will," and my guardian angel smiled down at me and I smiled too, as I felt the power coming into my very soul.

"Where there's a will, there's a way," I said – and I felt elated, as I knew my best friend God was with me, even as that Great Spirit had been with me under the wild black waters deep down in the Caribbean Sea of the island of St. Martin.

THE END

NB: As I finally left the hospital, the specialist took my hand and said, "We are all very proud and happy – then, with you, it was actually a matter of touch and go."
"Yes, I know," I said, "but I wanted to prove to you all that God helps he who helps himself."

CHAPTER 145

The Amazing Big Deal: Sometimes in Showbiz, The Most Amazing Situations Happen

The phone rang. At this time I already had enough terrible accidents behind me, to make me close my office with the two very capable secretaries, and to make me stop flying around the world fixing contracts for acts I considered to be outstanding. This included the Frank Valdor Orchestra and his Tropicado Brazilian spectacular show (approximately 42 people in all). To carry on living, the specialists advised me to just concentrate on my own life, and the occasional gala that required me to be just the star songstress, singing a few songs and no more. Many of the challenges of life were gone, and I settled down to a quieter time.

"Hello, can I speak personally to Mme. Yvonne Carré?"

The voice on the phone was a man's voice, suave and articulate, but it had a silken quality and a slight Italian accent, which immediately got me dreaming of all those elegant, pure silk ties with the inevitable label "Made in Italy." These were definitely en vogue for the smart European businessman. I answered:

"You *are* speaking to Yvonne Carré personally," I mimicked, then I said in a jocular fashion, "may I ask to whom am I talking?"

"Oh! Va bene Grazie Dio," not one of those "efficient" German-speaking secretaries.

"No sir, I have given up my office some time ago, my health was not on my side. I'm afraid I had too many bad accidents."

"Oh alas," the voice fairly purred. "You are talking to the great designer for the smart man's clothes Sgnr. Trussardi personally. I have heard so much about you," he continued, "and I feel you would be ideal for my special party, for 40 or 50 of my very best friends. That is to say – an intimate affair. I have a simply marvellous pianist. Could you possibly do, say a half hour show with only a pianist?" And then, as an afterthought, "Of course I will have excellent amplification and lighting, but as it should be intimate – just you with your charisma and the best pianist in Italy. There will be a dinner of the finest from one of our most famous gourmet chefs. As the clientele will be international but mainly German, it will be in a small hall in Frankfurt, with a proper stage and curtains and lots of tropical flower arrangements."

It sounded really interesting, so I gave my price after being assured I could have a full-scale rehearsal with his famous pianist.

The suave voice came over the line again with positive assurance and then said, "'I must add, we will all be members of an exclusive nudist club. Would you have anything against singing for a small select company in their birthday suits?" he said with a chuckle.

"Well," I said slowly, contemplating this new situation, "your wish is somewhat unusual, Sgnr. Trussardi, but as long as I am not required to entertain you in my birthday suit too, I guess that will be OK."

"Mme. I would be quite willing to pay you four times your usual salary, but I must ask you to be as we all will be – in our birthday suits."

That did it! My sweet voice changed to disgust. "Signor Trussardi," I said vehemently, "I'm sorry, you have the wrong number. Good day – Bon giorno," and I put the phone down on the velvet voice. "Amazing, these multimillionaires," I said to myself, shaking my head. "They honestly think they can buy anyone!" And with that the whole crazy offer sank into oblivion.

A month or so later I had a gig, or should I say first class gala, with Germany's most famous show band the Jochim Brauer Combo, who accompanied me perfectly. After the show and drinks, the band had a long pause during speeches, and backstage Jochim and I got talking, and during the interesting conversation he mentioned to me, "You know, Yvonne, it is amazing what incredible tricks these big tycoons get up to to win. Take for instance Trussardi, the world-famous designer for men."

That name rang a bell in my mind. "Oh," I thought, "the gentleman with the suave voice."

The bandleader continued. "Recently we did the craziest gala I've ever heard of in history. I got a call from this Mega designer asking our price for a short show, and some dinner music, followed possibly by an hour at the most of dance music. Lots of pauses, superb food and drink. At the most 2 hours work. All this for about 20 or 30 business friends and their ladies. Our price was considered as being fine and I was told the champagne and caviar etc. would be ad lib. There would be Tornedos Rossini, carp for fish lovers and vegetables galore from the best gourmet chefs Italy had to offer.

"Just one question," he added. "We are all members of a world-famous select nudist colony. Would it bother you or your musicians if your intimate audience were all in their birthday suits?" In our business, Yvonne, one expeiences so much, but I must admit I was taken a bit by surprise, so I said "No, as long as we don't have to be in our birthday suits too – I guess it will be OK."

"The reply came like a bullet; obviously it had been well rehearsed. "Look," the famous man said, "I will be willing to pay 4 times your usual salary, but we are a club and it would look a little funny if we are all naked and you are on stage fully clothed."

"What?" I said incredulously, "you expect us to be naked too? No way!" I retorted.

"Look," the voice on the phone fairly purred, "Mr. Brauer, I will get my lawyer to prepare the contracts. Before you say no, ask your boys what they think. I'm sure they will change your mind. Of course, for your special stage show you can wear what you like – that we do understand, but the dinner music must be in your birthday suits, to respect our club's tradition. I'll call you back on Wednesday for your band's final decision." If I hadn't spoken to your husband Frank Valdor and he hadn't told me he knew a couple of nicely married, decent friends who seemed to enjoy being members of a nudist club, I think I still wouldn't have agreed, but for the boys, four times their salaries, plus all those goodies offered and the thought that some of the ladies might have very ample boobs – they surrendered.

"Then came the night. There was, as promised, a good-sized stage, flower arrangements galore, superb food and champagne. We were all in our best moods as we got undressed, ready to go on stage. We were told to wait for the sign to give a loud crescendo, when the red velvet curtain would go up, the stewards would be clapping and shouting, and the audience would give a big applause. So it was – a loud crescendo from us, the curtain went up and then the loudest shrieks of laughter I had ever heard in my life. The guests were all dolled up in their designer formal evening attire. No big boobs from overweight older ladies at all. We were the laughing-stock of the party, and that to serious semi-classical dinner music. I swear I thought the laughter would never end. I was, as you can imagine, furious with Trussardi and told him I would sue for damages and bring it to the international press. He was sympathetic and a real gentleman, and suggested immediately we do a deal to hush it all up. He then took me aside and explained to me the whole evening was a multi-millionaires *bet...* which he had now won!

a) It would be the best gourmet food, wines and champagne they
   had ever had, and the most elegant – *it was.*

b) The music and the show should be the finest – *it was.*

c) They would have the biggest laugh they had ever had at a party,
   and they *did!*

"All the guests had bet a cool million that Trussardi could never
WIN a, b, and c, but he did.

The evening party was called the Impossible Bet and there were
48 guests all swearing he had to lose because it would be impossible for him to win…but he did! So the hush hush deal was
done, and Heavens were we all happy. It really is amazing what
those super rich guys come up with for a good hearty laugh and
to win a worthwhile bet.

"That Mr. Trussardi was not just clever at designing men's clothes –
that man sure did have smart ideas, and to really win you've got
to be truly innovative. So let's get to the betting shop and start."

I did not say a word – we both laughed!

The author

Born in Bermuda in 1934, Yvonne Carré has had an illustrious career as an international singer/entertainer, comedienne, dancer, and film actress, having recorded songs in 20 languages and travelled the world to perform them. Carré, the widow of famous composer and bandleader Frank Valdor, has now retired and resides in Switzerland.